A2 Geography

Cameron Dunn • Kim Adams • David Holmes • Bob Hordern Dulcie Knifton • Simon Oakes • Andy Palmer • Sue Warn Michael Witherick • Nigel Yates

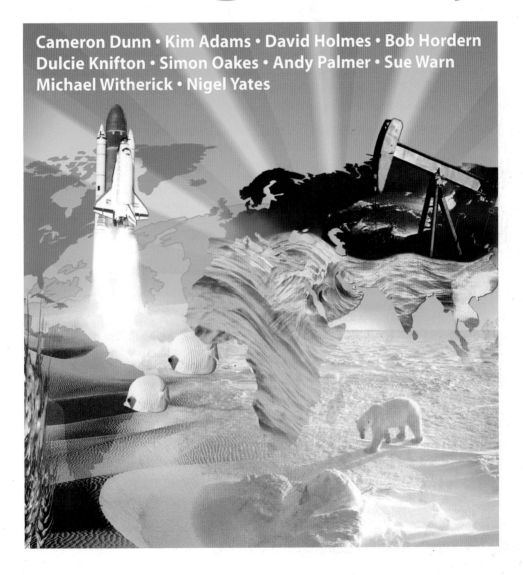

Philip Allan Updates, an imprint of Hodder Education, an Hachette UK company, Market Place, Deddington, Oxfordshire OX15 0SE

Orders

Bookpoint Ltd, 130 Milton Park, Abingdon, Oxfordshire OX14 4SB
tel: 01235 827720
fax: 01235 400454
e-mail: uk.orders@bookpoint.co.uk

Lines are open 9.00 a.m.–5.00 p.m., Monday to Saturday, with a 24-hour message answering service. You can also order through the Philip Allan Updates website: www.philipallan.co.uk

© Philip Allan Updates 2009

ISBN 978-0-340-94954-2

Impression number   5 4 3
Year   2013 2012 2011 2010

This material has been endorsed by Edexcel and offers high quality support for the delivery of Edexcel qualifications.

Edexcel endorsement does not mean that this material is essential to achieve any Edexcel qualification, nor does it mean that this is the only suitable material available to support any Edexcel qualification. No endorsed material will be used verbatim in setting any Edexcel examination and any resource lists produced by Edexcel shall include this and other appropriate texts. While this material has been through an Edexcel quality assurance process, all responsibility for the content remains with the publisher.

Copies of official specifications for all Edexcel qualifications may be found on the Edexcel website — www.edexcel.com.

All Office for National Statistics material is Crown copyright, reproduced under the terms of PSI Licence Number C200700185.

Printed in Italy.

Hachette UK's policy is to use papers that are natural, renewable and recyclable products and made from wood grown in sustainable forests. The logging and manufacturing processes are expected to conform to the environmental regulations of the country of origin.

P01365

Contents

Unit 4 Geographical research

Introduction

This book has been written for students of Edexcel A2 Geography by a team of senior examiners.

It is organised to reflect the structure of the A2 specification. Each chapter covers one topic and is broken down into subsections based on subtopics. Each specification enquiry question is addressed, and the areas of student learning indicated by the specification are fully covered.

Other useful features include:

➤ **emboldened** key words and a glossary at the back of the book, to help you get to grips with geographical terminology
➤ text that explains key concepts highlighted in pink
➤ case studies that allow you to explore issues and ideas in greater depth
➤ a range of photographs, maps and graphs to develop your analytical skills
➤ information on useful websites to help your research
➤ self-testing review questions at the end of each chapter to develop your understanding of ideas and provide extension activities

Essential exam advice and sample questions for Units 3 and 4 are provided online: go to www.hodderplus.co.uk/philipallan. The questions are in the same style as real examination questions. Answers, mark schemes and examiners' tips for success are provided to help you improve your exam performance.

Edexcel A2 Geography

The A2 specification has two units.

Unit 3 Contested planet consists of six compulsory topics:

➤ **Energy security** examines the distribution and use of energy resources around the world and raises important questions about the future and security of energy supplies.
➤ **Water conflicts** investigates water supply, scarcity and stress and examines why securing supply often leads to conflict.
➤ **Biodiversity under threat** explores the degradation of biomes and ecosystems and investigates the spectrum of management options that might secure the future of biodiversity.
➤ **Superpower geographies** examines patterns of power across the planet, identifies the emerging powers and considers the influence superpowers have on development and the environment.
➤ **Bridging the development gap** investigates the pattern of, and reason for, differences in development levels, and examines a range of ways to bridge the gap.
➤ **The technological fix?** explores the role of technology in development and environmental sustainability.

The unit focuses on the distribution and use of resources – energy, water and biodiversity. It considers the range of threats these resources face as humans continue to deplete them. The unit allows for a detailed consideration of how humans might manage these resources to ensure their future survival on the contested planet. The unit also contrasts the power and wealth of the superpowers with the state of the poor and hungry on the other side of the development gap. Lastly, the unit considers the role of technology in addressing geographical challenges.

Unit 4 Geographical research provides an opportunity to study one topic that interests you in depth. Topics range across the physical, environmental and human geography spectrum. The focus of Unit 4 is on research and investigating in depth. There are six options to choose from:

➤ **Tectonic activity and hazards** focuses on the patterns and processes of earthquakes and volcanic hazards and how they are managed.
➤ **Cold environments: landscapes and change** investigates the distribution and formation of glacial and periglacial environments and how they are managed today.
➤ **Life on the margins: the food supply problem** explores food insecurity and malnutrition, as well as environmental issues such as desertification and land degradation.
➤ **The world of cultural diversity** investigates the meaning of culture and the changing geography of local and global cultures.
➤ **Pollution and human health at risk** explores key threats to human health, ranging from industrial pollution to global disease pandemics.
➤ **Consuming the rural landscape: leisure and tourism** investigates the evolution of tourism and the threats and challenges it presents to rural and wilderness areas.

Assessment Objectives

In common with all other geography specifications, there are three Assessment Objectives in Edexcel A2 Geography. Candidates should be able to:
1 demonstrate knowledge and understanding of the content, concepts and processes
2 analyse, interpret and evaluate geographical information, issues and viewpoints and apply understanding in unfamiliar contexts
3 select and use a variety of methods, skills and techniques (including the use of new technologies) to investigate questions and issues, reach conclusions and communicate findings (Unit 4 emphasises this Assessment Objective)

Scheme of Assessment

The advice at www.hodderplus.co.uk/philipallan provides additional details about assessment.

	Assessment weighting for A-level (A2)	Examination pre-release materials	Examination format	Marks	Time
Unit 3 Contested planet	30% (60%)	Four working weeks prior to the exam a synoptic resource booklet will be given to you	Written paper in two sections. Section A Two resource-based longer essay-style questions from a choice of five. Section B A synoptic issues analysis taking the form of three essay-style questions	90 marks	$2\frac{1}{2}$ hours
Unit 4 Geographical research	20% (40%)	Four working weeks prior to the exam a research focus will be given to you	One essay question on each option. Answers should be in the form of a report-style essay	70 marks	$1\frac{1}{2}$ hours

Unit 3 Contested planet

You might think that given the small and finite nature of our planet, people would be falling over themselves to get along with each other. Modern humans have been around for some 200,000 years but so far have failed to learn how to live in peace with each other or in harmony with the planet.

In fact, as this book was being written in 2008 the world was reeling from the shock of huge increases in food and energy prices, followed by a global financial crisis and worldwide recession. There were natural disasters, for example Cyclone Nargis in Myanmar (Burma), and conflicts in Iraq and Afghanistan and between Russia and Georgia. Same old world.

The 6.7 billion of us inhabiting an increasingly crowded planet all make demands on the same basic resources. To survive we need food, water, energy and shelter. Figure 1 shows the enormous imbalance in resource use between the most and least intensive resource users.

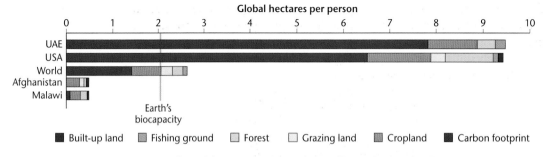

Figure 1 Ecological footprints compared: WWF living planet index, 2005

According to the WWF's living planet index, the ability of the Earth's resources to provide for us sustainably (Earth's biocapacity) has been exceeded every year since 1985.

The **Contested planet** unit invites you to explore who the winners and losers are in the battle for Earth's resources. What processes have led to the distribution of resources in Figure 1? Perhaps even more importantly, what, if anything, can be done to make resource distribution more equitable?

Environmental sustainability and sustainable development

You should recognise from Figure 1 that the average residents of the USA and the UAE are not living in an environmentally sustainable way. The size of their ecological footprint hints at high fossil fuel use, pollution and land degradation. Unfortunately the very low ecological footprints of Malawi and Afghanistan are not sustainable either. The average Afghan and Malawian may seem environmentally sustainable, but their basic needs for survival are barely met (Table 1). The least developed countries desperately need development and resources to improve this situation.

Table 1 Socioeconomic data for Malawi and Afghanistan

2008 (*2006 estimate)	Human development index	GDP per capita (US$)	Life expectancy	% of the population malnourished
Malawi	0.40	$266	43	45%
Afghanistan	0.45	$350	44*	40%*

The world faces two huge challenges simultaneously:
➤ How to create a more environmentally sustainable world.
➤ How to ensure all people have the resources they need for a decent quality of life.

On the one hand we need more resources for development, but on the other we need to use fewer resources (or switch to renewable/sustainable resources) to become more environmentally sustainable.

Contested planet is as much about solutions as it is about problems and challenges. Managing our contested planet means making some key choices and decisions about our future. As you study this unit you should consider the following issues:
➤ The views of different **players** (Figure 2) and their role both in creating problems and in managing solutions.

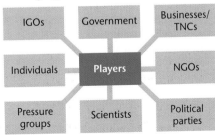

Figure 2 Players with a role in the contested planet

➤ The range of **actions** that could be used to try to solve problems and implement solutions. This leads us into quite political territory. Your own view of the 'right' actions to take will depend on your view of capitalism as a system versus a more socialist model. You might think solutions are best implemented by governments, or believe actions should be small-scale and involve local decision making.

➤ What sort of **future** should we be aiming for? Can we continue as we are, aiming for a 'business as usual' future, or do we need to head for a future of sustainable development and environmental sustainability? Perhaps you feel sustainability has become just another buzzword, and something much more radical is needed to secure our future.

Players, actions and futures are key aspects of the Contested planet unit, as they are synoptic concepts. They cut across all the topics in this unit and will be assessed as part of the synoptic assessment in Section B of the exam paper. More details on synoptic assessment are given on the website: www.hodderplus.co.uk/philipallan.

Unit 4 Geographical research

Unit 4 is introduced in Chapter 8.

Unit 3

NASA

Contested planet

Energy security

In science, energy is the 'capacity to do work'. This work can take various forms and is vital to human survival and development. Energy powers our motor vehicles, trains, aircraft and rockets. Energy lights our homes and cities, plays our music, and produces pictures on television. Energy warms our houses and cooks our food. Energy converts minerals into metals and water into electricity. As societies become more sophisticated, they consume more energy, they exploit a wider range of energy types, and the **consumption** patterns in the various sectors change (Figure 1.1).

The great challenge today is to meet an ever-rising global demand for energy. A secure energy supply is crucial to human **wellbeing**, but there are considerable environmental costs in harnessing many forms of energy. This is an important issue as concern about **global warming** increases. The challenge is to reduce our dependence on fossil fuels, cut greenhouse gas emissions and find new and **sustainable** sources of energy. The era of cheap and unsustainable energy supply is coming to an end.

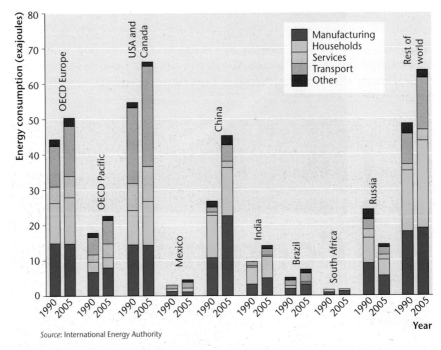

Source: International Energy Authority

Figure 1.1 World energy consumption by sector, 1990 and 2005

Energy supply, demand and security

To what extent is the world 'energy secure' at present?

By the end of this section you should:
➤ *be aware of the different sources of energy*
➤ *understand that access to and consumption of energy varies from place to place*
➤ *know the reasons for the growing demand for energy*
➤ *understand the factors affecting energy security*

Energy sources

Fossil fuels

All energy ultimately comes from either the sun or the Earth. **Fuel** is any material that is burned or altered in order to obtain energy. Food is clearly a fuel. Wood, dung and animal fat were early fuels, burned by our prehistoric ancestors to create heat and possibly light. **Fossil fuels** are those formed over geological time from the partly decayed remains of plants or animals. They include coal, oil and natural gas. They can be used (or combusted) only once and are therefore finite. They become exhausted because they can only be replaced over considerable periods of geological time. For this reason, they are classified as **non-renewable sources** of energy.

During combustion, fossil fuels produce carbon dioxide, which has an impact on climate because it contributes to the greenhouse effect. Exploiting fossil fuels by quarrying, mining and pumping has other environmental impacts, such as deforestation and the disruption of water tables and groundwater supplies. Nuclear energy falls into the category of non-renewable energy since supplies of the raw material, uranium, are finite.

Corel

Photograph 1.1
Oil is a fossil fuel

Renewable sources

By contrast, **renewable sources** of energy are those capable of natural regeneration on a human timescale. They provide almost continuous flows of energy. These sources include inland water, wind, the tides, ocean waves, geothermal heat and the sun's rays. **Sustainable sources** of energy include wood, which can be regrown, and the pumped-storage water of a hydroelectric power (HEP) plant, which can be used time and time again. Some would also put nuclear energy in this category, because the nuclear power industry is able to reprocess some spent fuel so that it can be reused.

Table 1.1 Primary energy sources and their characteristics. Renewable sources are on a green background (MJ = megajoules)

Primary energy sources

A distinction is made between primary and secondary energy. **Primary energy** is the energy found in **natural resources**. Examples include coal, crude oil, sunlight, wind, rivers, vegetation and uranium. **Secondary energy** is primary energy that has been converted into a more convenient form, usually electricity. Table 1.1 summarises information about the different sources of primary energy.

Primary energy type	Classification	Energy density (MJ kg^{-1})	Key concerns/issues
Coal A combustible, sedimentary rock formed of converted residual plant matter and solidified below overlying rock strata. There are several types of raw coal: hard/bituminous coal, brown coal (lignite) and peat	Non-renewable	14–19	Use releases large amounts of carbon dioxide and other pollutants, contributing to climate change and atmospheric pollution. Carbon capture technology for removing carbon dioxide from atmosphere unproven and complex
Natural gas A methane-rich gas found underground. It may also contain water vapour, sulphur compounds and other non-hydrogen gases such as carbon dioxide, nitrogen or helium	Non-renewable	50	Costs and security of supply, especially for countries that are largely importers. Releases carbon dioxide on use
Nuclear fission The division of a heavy nucleus into two parts, usually accompanied by the emission of neutrons (neutrally charged particles inside the nucleus), gamma radiation (high-energy radiation) and energy release. This energy is converted into heat that raises steam to drive turbines and generate electricity	Non-renewable (may be recyclable)	88,000,000	Possible health risks associated with power plants and accidents such as Chernobyl. Disposal of radioactive material raises safety issues and there are unknown long-term risks. Amount of raw material left globally
Crude oil (petroleum) A naturally occurring mineral oil consisting of many types of hydrocarbons. Crude oil may include small amounts of non-hydrocarbons	Non-renewable	47	Concerns that global supplies may have reached their peak, security of supply, geopolitical tensions and lack of alternatives, especially for transport. Releases carbon dioxide when burnt

Primary energy type	Classification	Energy density (MJ kg⁻¹)	Key concerns/issues
Solar energy Energy directly harnessed from solar radiation, as distinct from wind, water and biomass energies indirectly driven by the sun. Solar radiation is absorbed by a collector and converted to heat energy, or into electricity by photovoltaic cells	Renewable	n/a	Distribution and availability varies spatially and temporally. Photovoltaic technology still expensive compared with fossil fuels
Ocean energy Energy harnessed by using either the physical characteristics of oceans (tidal movement, wave motion, thermal gradients, ocean currents) or their chemical characteristics (saline gradients)	Renewable	n/a	Only certain locations are suitable for offshore tidal generation. Technology for large-scale generation is unproven. Ocean sources have low energy densities, and large devices are needed to harness this energy
Wind energy Directly related to solar activity, which causes differences in atmospheric pressure and temperature (and to Earth's rotation and gravity). Modern wind turbines range from 600 kW to 5 MW of rated power	Renewable	n/a	Only certain locations have enough wind to be viable. Wind energy is variable power, so it is difficult to manage power supply through a grid system without some back-up
Biomass Organic, non-fossil material of biological origin. Although the different forms of energy from biomass are considered renewable, their rates of renewability differ. Wood is an example of a biomass energy source	Recyclable	6–17	Relatively low energy densities mean limited potential for large-scale electricity generation. Biomass acts as a carbon sink, so combustion releases stored carbon dioxide
Hydrological energy Energy harnessed from the movement of water through rivers, lakes and dams (owing to gravity). A 'head' of water is stored and then released to drive turbines and generate electricity. HEP systems can range in capacity from thousands of megawatts to small micro-hydro schemes	Recyclable and renewable	n/a	Large-scale systems are costly to build. Dam-building also has social, political and environmental impacts. Smaller micro-hydro plants may not be economically viable
Geothermal energy Comes from rocks within the Earth and can be tapped in three ways: (1) as hot water or steam, (2) as hot dry rock energy and (3) by means of conduction. The first two are used to generate electricity while the third is used to heat water, buildings and greenhouses	Renewable	n/a	Geothermal heat in the outer 10 km of the Earth's crust is too diffuse to be exploitable worldwide. Availability is limited to a few locations such as Iceland and the Philippines

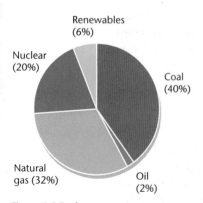

Renewables (6%)

Nuclear (20%)

Coal (40%)

Natural gas (32%)

Oil (2%)

Figure 1.2 Fuel used in electricity generation in the UK, 2006

Energy consumption

An important point you need to remember is that most of the energy sources considered above are used to generate electricity. In the UK, most of our domestic and imported supplies of coal and natural gas and all our nuclear energy are converted into electricity (Figure 1.2). This is done by burning them and using the heat to raise steam that turns electricity-generating turbines. Electricity is the largest 'consumer' of primary energies. As a **secondary energy** it is efficient, easy to transport and clean. Its main downside is that it cannot be stored. Demand and supply have to run in unison.

Moving to modern energy use

As poor families in developing countries increase their incomes, they can afford more modern appliances. These in turn demand more and better energy supplies (Figure 1.3). The three main factors that control the transition from traditional to modern energy use are:

➤ *Energy availability.* In many parts of the world modern types of energy are either not available, or remain inaccessible because the necessary infrastructure to deliver those energies has yet to be put in place.

➤ *Energy affordability.* Even when modern forms of energy are available, households may not use them if they are much more expensive than traditional sources such as burning wood or animal dung (biomass). In rural areas, biomass is often preferred because it is 'free' and readily available.

Figure 1.3 Household energy transition

➤ *Cultural preferences.* Tradition often slows the adoption of more modern energy sources. For example, in the UK today there are still many who prefer to use an open coal or wood fire rather than a gas or electric one.

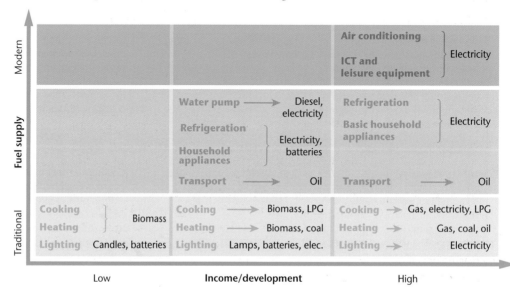

The influence of climate

At any point along the **transition** shown in Figure 1.3, the level of energy **consumption** will also be influenced by the prevailing climate. The need to keep warm in cold climates – and to keep cool in hot climates by means of air conditioning – increases consumption of energy. In both instances, there is a seasonal variation in energy consumption.

Global availability of energy resources

Fuel and energy resources (including renewables) are not evenly distributed round the globe. Table 1.2 shows proven reserves of energy sources, the regions with the richest non-renewable reserves and those with the highest consumption of renewable energy (it is debatable whether nuclear energy is renewable). The global distribution of energy availability depends on factors such as geology, physical geography, available **technology** and the costs of exploitation.

Energy resource (non-renewable)	Proven reserves			Regions with richest reserves
	1987	1997	2007	
Oil* (thousand million barrels)	910	1,069	1,239	Middle east and Africa
Gas (trillion m³)	106	146	177	Middle east, Europe and Eurasia
Coal (million tonnes)	(no data)	(no data)	847,488	North America, Pacific, Europe and Eurasia
Energy resource (renewable)	Consumption			Regions with highest consumption
Nuclear (million tonnes oil equivalent)	(no data)	541	622	Europe and Eurasia, North America
Hydroelectricity (million tonnes oil equivalent)	(no data)	588	709	Europe and Eurasia, North America, Asia-Pacific

Table 1.2 Energy availability and consumption

Source: BP Statistical Review of World Energy 2008
*Excludes oil-shales

Big players

Oil is the most widely used fuel for energy generation. Despite the search for new **reserves**, the middle east remains the biggest player, with huge output and immense reserves (Figure 1.4). Saudi Arabia alone accounts for 22% of the world's proven reserves. Oil gives the middle east great power on the geopolitical stage.

Other non-renewable energy resources have similarly uneven patterns of availability and access. China, for example, has great coal reserves, and builds the equivalent of two medium-sized coal-fired power stations each week (Figure 1.5). The country's coal consumption has more than doubled since 1900, but the increasing use of coal comes at a considerable environmental cost. China's carbon dioxide emissions now exceed those of the USA.

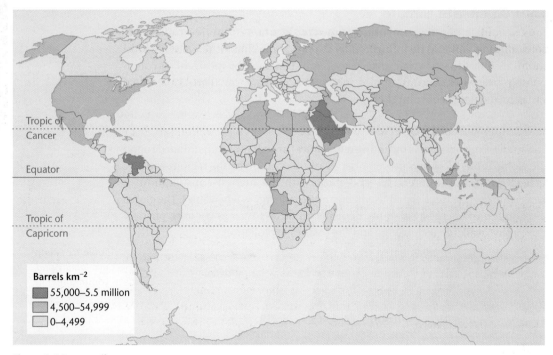

Figure 1.4 Proven oil reserves, 2007

Barrels km⁻²
- 55,000–5.5 million
- 4,500–54,999
- 0–4,499

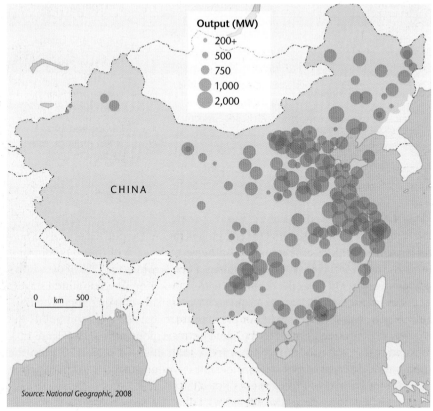

Output (MW)
- 200+
- 500
- 750
- 1,000
- 2,000

CHINA

0 km 500

Source: *National Geographic*, 2008

Figure 1.5 Coal-fired power stations in China

Local variations

The distribution of renewable energy also varies at a range of scales. The highest potential solar input occurs towards the equator, but it is also influenced by local factors such as the amount of cloud cover.

At a more local scale, it is possible to use an online estimation tool to calculate average wind speeds (see for example www.bwea.com/noabl/).

Access to energy resources also varies spatially. Poverty and access to electricity have been found to be inversely related. Today, more than 2.1 billion people or 425 million households are still without access to electricity.

Global demand for energy

The previous section discussed energy consumption, and now we turn to energy demand. Both terms are used throughout the rest of this chapter. What is the difference between them? **Energy demand** is the need or desire for energy. **Energy consumption** refers to the availability and use of energy. In many places, the demand for energy is fully met, in which case energy demand is matched by energy consumption. However, there are instances when energy demand is greater than the amount of energy available for use (consumption). This is a subtle difference, so be aware of it as you read the remainder of this chapter.

Case study — Energy poverty in two different worlds

Worldwide, some 2 billion people do not have access to a modern energy supply (Photograph 1.2). About 1.6 billion people live without electricity, either because they are in areas without a supply network or because they could not afford electricity even if it were available. Having no access to energy is just one aspect of the multiple deprivation that characterises extreme poverty. Alleviating this 'energy poverty' is a key factor in achieving most of the UN's Millennium Goals.

India is fast becoming one of the world's largest energy consumers, but only a small percentage of the population have access to clean, efficient energy systems. This is particularly the case in rural areas, where an estimated 70% of the country's population live. Here, most people burn hand-gathered solid fuels such as wood and dung for indoor cooking. This way of producing energy may be light in terms of its carbon footprint, but it is known to cause serious health problems.

In the UK, where energy is needed mainly for heating and lighting, energy poverty takes a rather

Photograph 1.2 Many people in poorer rural communities rely on wood or dung for energy, like this woman in Zimbabwe

different form. There are close to 5 million rural households not connected to the mains gas network. Most of these people have to rely on liquefied petroleum gas (LPG) for their heating and cooking, but in recent years this has been considerably more expensive than mains gas. Using oil for domestic heating is an alternative but can be expensive, and prices have risen significantly in recent years.

The winter heating allowance paid to pensioners by the government each year is official recognition that energy poverty exists in the UK, if only among elderly people.

Sources of demand

Energy is used for a wide variety of purposes: generating electricity, propelling transport, powering industry and homes. Figure 1.6 shows the demand patterns for all the main fuels. Transport takes nearly half of the world's oil production; homes and commercial properties use a little less than one-third of it, mainly for heating. Over two-thirds of coal production is used to generate electricity in thermal power stations. Much of the natural gas output is used for the same purpose, along with the heating of industrial, commercial and residential properties.

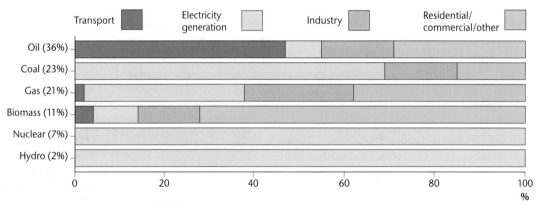

Figure 1.6 Global energy use, 2005

Rising consumption

Figure 1.7 shows the rising curve of global energy consumption. Remember that consumption is a function of demand: the greater the demand, the higher the consumption. During the twentieth century, energy demand increased tenfold. But see what is forecast to happen to that demand by 2050: it is expected to double and reach an annual level of around 900 exajoules. While much of that energy demand will be met by non-renewable sources, namely natural gas, oil and coal, the forecasts show an increasingly significant contribution by renewable energies. Why such a spectacular rise in energy consumption? The short answer lies in a combination of population growth, economic development (particularly industrialisation) and rising standards of living. The broad correlation between development (GDP per capita) and power consumed (kW per capita) is illustrated in Figure 1.8.

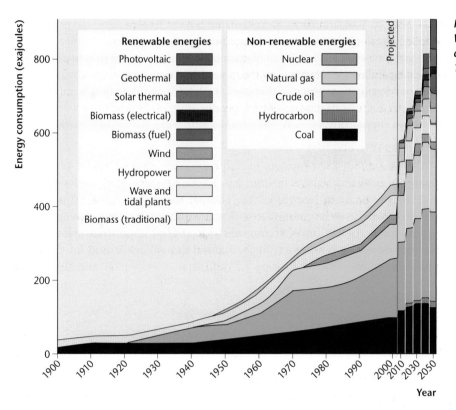

Figure 1.7
Worldwide energy
consumption,
1900–2050

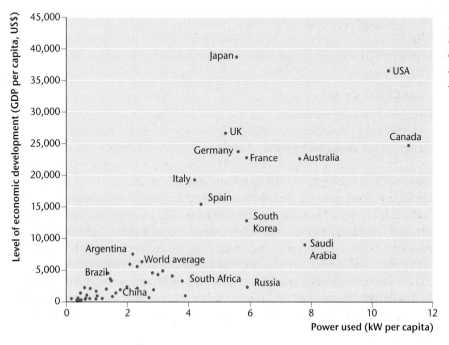

Figure 1.8 Power
used and level of
development in a
sample of countries,
2006

Future trends

Future increases in energy demand are unlikely to be even across the globe. China and India are expected to have the largest rises, while countries in western Europe may actually reduce their demands as a result of improved energy efficiency and rising energy costs. Energy consumption in the **developing world** is expected to double by 2020, while it increases by about one-third in the **developed world**. If this happens, energy consumption in the two 'worlds' will have become roughly equal.

Energy security

Energy security is vital to the functioning of a country, particularly for its economy and the wellbeing of its people. Any country that is self-sufficient in energy resources will be secure in the sense that it will have the energy needed for its development. For less fortunate countries which rely on imported supplies, energy security depends on whether there is uninterrupted availability of energy at affordable prices.

Risks

There are a number of risks to energy security:

➤ *Physical*. For example exhaustion of reserves or disruption of supply lines by natural hazards such as earthquakes.
➤ *Environmental*. For example protests about environmental damage caused by exploitation of energy resources.
➤ *Economic*. For example sudden rises in the cost of energy, or exhaustion of domestic supplies forcing increased imports of higher-priced energy.
➤ *Geopolitical*. For example political instability in energy-producing regions, disputes or conflict over sovereignty (ownership) of energy resources, or disputes over energy transmission by pipelines or cables across countries.

Energy security has risen to the top of the agenda of many governments, international organisations and businesses. The sustained growth in demand for energy (Figure 1.7) has led to serious concerns over the long-term availability of reliable and affordable supplies. Increasingly governments, industries and people are taking a more protectionist view of their own sources of energy.

Measuring energy security

Energy security is complex, but so great is concern about it that attempts have been made to measure it. The energy security index (ESI) is one such attempt. It assesses the extent to which a country may look forward to a reliable and affordable supply of energy. What is the risk that such a supply may be threatened? The higher the index, the lower the risk and therefore the greater the energy security.

Calculation of the degree of risk is based on information about:

➤ *Availability*. The amount and longevity of each country's domestic oil and gas supplies and its level of reliance on imported oil, gas and electricity.
➤ *Diversity*. The range of energy sources used in meeting each country's energy demand.

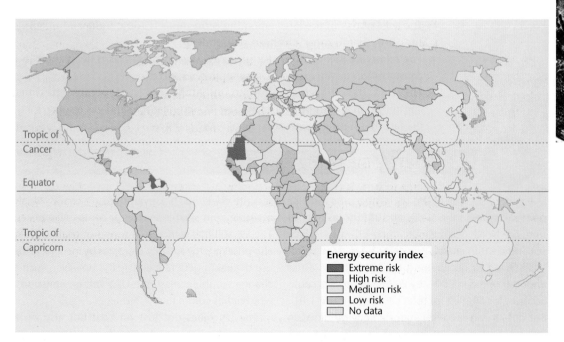

Energy security index
- Extreme risk
- High risk
- Medium risk
- Low risk
- No data

Figure 1.9 World map showing energy security risk

➤ *Intensity*. The degree to which the economy of each country is dependent on oil and gas.

Levels of risk

ESI values range from 0 to 10. Between these values four categories or degrees of **risk** are recognised (Figure 1.9):

➤ *Extreme risk*. ESI values less than 2.5. Most countries in this category are in northern Africa and northern South America. It is interesting to note the inclusion of South Korea, a newly-industrialised country.

➤ *High risk*. ESI values 2.5 to 5.0. Such countries are scattered across the globe and include a number of developed countries, most notably the USA and Japan.

➤ *Medium risk*. ESI value 5.0 to 7.5. A widespread category in Europe, south and southeast Asia, and Australasia.

➤ *Low risk*. ESI values greater than 7.5. Qualifying countries include Canada, Russia, Norway and the more stable middle eastern states – all are producers and exporters of oil and gas.

Characteristics of risk

The following conclusions may be drawn from Figure 1.9:

➤ Heavy importers of oil and gas show high levels of risk.

➤ Countries with substantial reserves show low levels of risk, regardless of their own levels of consumption.

➤ Medium-sized developed countries show medium levels of risk, partly because they use a diversity of energy sources.

➤ The level of risk in the large **emerging economies** (China, India and Brazil) is similar to that in most advanced economies.

➤ The relatively low level of risk in many African countries reflects their low consumption or the existence of untapped resources.

➤ The USA has a higher risk than might be expected because its huge consumption and imports overshadow its significant oil and gas resources and the fact that it uses a diverse range of energy sources.

Case study: UK energy security

The energy security of the UK has become a major political issue. In the 1980s and 1990s gas and oil from the North Sea meant that the UK was virtually self-sufficient in energy. Now North Sea production has started to decline and the UK became a net importer of gas in 2004. By 2020 gas imports could account for 80–90% of total demand (Figure 1.10). But does this reliance on imported energy translate into an energy security problem?

Not necessarily. Coal, for example, currently accounts for about 15% of the UK's primary energy supply and most of it is imported. This does not raise security concerns, however, because coal is widely available from reliable sources at competitive prices. The UK still has workable reserves of coal. It could also offset energy security concerns by increasing the use of coal to generate electricity. However, such a change would increase the UK's carbon emissions, which it has committed to reduce.

The UK relies not just on coal but also on a mixture of oil, gas and other forms of power. In general terms, the UK needs to minimise risks such as disrupted supplies and escalating prices. But each major source of energy has its own risks (Table 1.3).

Figure 1.10 Sources of UK gas, 2004 and 2020

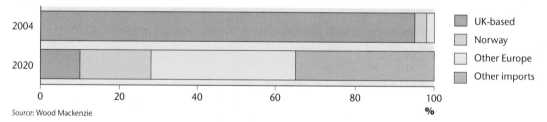

Source: Wood Mackenzie

Table 1.3 The energy security risks of oil and gas in the UK

Fuel	Share of UK primary energy supply	Risks
Oil	35%	Main security issues are rising and volatile oil prices, increasing demand from emerging economies such as China and India, and the rise of new national oil companies. The need is to create stable relations with oil-producing states and to assist in opening up new reserves
Gas	38%	The UK increasingly depends on importing gas, much of it through potentially vulnerable pipelines. Russia supplies 30% of EU gas: political uncertainty can affect UK energy security, as can problems in the international market and pipeline defects

The impacts of energy security

What are the potential impacts of an increasingly 'energy insecure' world?

At the end of this section you should

➤ *realise that there the are energy pathways connecting producers to consumers*

➤ *be aware of the economic and political risks if energy supplies are disrupted*

➤ *understand that energy insecurity is prompting the exploration of technically difficult and environmentally sensitive areas*

➤ *know who the major players are in the global supply of energy*

Energy pathways

The geographical mismatch between energy demand and the availability of energy resources means that many countries rely on energy imports. The flows of energy from producer to consumer are the **pathways**. In physical terms, the pathways take the form of gas and oil pipelines, the sea routes of tankers carrying oil and gas, and electricity power lines.

Since the early 1990s there has been a significant increase in the export of fuels (mainly oil and gas), particularly from the middle east, Africa and the former Soviet Union (Figure 1.11). Europe, Asia and the Asia-Pacific region are now heavily reliant on energy imports.

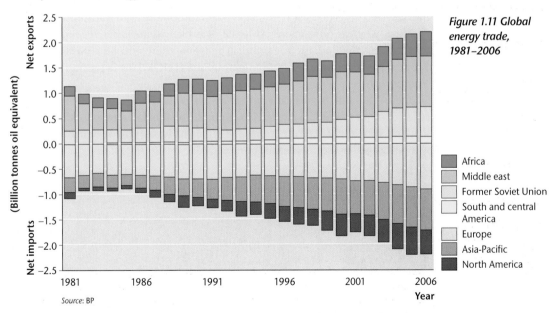

Figure 1.11 Global energy trade, 1981–2006

Source: BP

Oil and gas

In the case of oil, there is a complex global pattern of pathways and **players** (exporters and importers) (Figure 1.12). The middle east exports around 15,000 barrels per day, mainly to Japan, Europe and China. Substantial amounts flow from Africa, Europe, Canada and South and central America to the USA. Russia

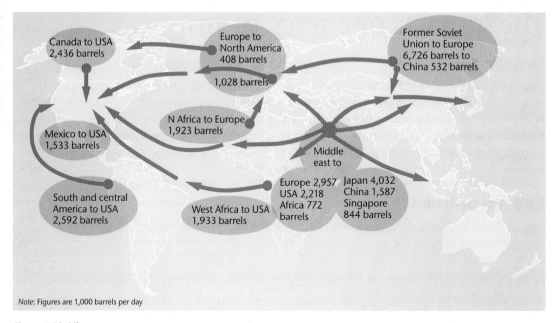

Note: Figures are 1,000 barrels per day

Figure 1.12 Oil movements by volume, 2007

supplies some oil to China, but the bulk of its exports now head in the direction of Europe.

Gas pathways are different in that they tend to be localised and regional rather than global. This is because natural gas has traditionally been transported through pipelines, whereas oil is mainly shipped. It is likely that, as delivery via pipelines becomes less dependable for political reasons, there will be a switch towards shipping gas in tankers as liquified natural gas (LNG). This is starting to happen (Photograph 1.3).

One of the most significant gas pathways is the trans-Siberian pipeline, the main conveyor of Russian natural gas exports. The Russian section of this pipeline is operated by the Gazprom corporation, but its monopoly is being challenged by a new pipeline (see case study).

Photograph 1.3 A tanker carrying liquefied natural gas

Europe's gas pipeline war

The European Union (EU) and Russia are involved in a battle over a pipeline aimed at diversifying Europe's energy imports. The Nabucco pipeline, first planned in 2004, will transport natural gas over 3,000 km from the Caspian region to Austria via Turkey, Bulgaria, Romania and Hungary. Construction is expected to start in 2010 and be completed by 2013 at a cost of €8 billion.

The Nabucco pipeline will be supplied with gas from Iran, Azerbaijan, Kazakhstan, Turkmenistan, Egypt and Syria. It will deliver a huge amount of gas, making the EU much less dependent on Russian supplies. Russia's reliability as a supplier has been in doubt since it temporarily shut off the gas supply to Ukraine in January 2006. Clearly, it is in the EU's interests to diversify its gas imports. However, the Nabucco project has already run into some problems. Iran and Syria remain politically unstable and the central Asian countries have also promised huge amounts of gas to China and Russia.

Coal

There are also coal pathways from countries as far apart as Australia and Poland. At the moment, far less coal is moved than oil and gas. However, there is a prospect of greater movements of coal, if only because supplies seem more dependable and less threatened by geopolitical considerations.

Risks of disruption

The so-called 'oil crises' of 1973 and the 1980s shocked many countries into developing national and international energy policies. These aimed to reduce the risks of disruption to supplies by geopolitical instability and unforeseen rises in energy prices. After those policies were put in place, most parts of the developed world enjoyed a period of more or less uninterrupted, and generally cheap, energy supplies.

More recently there has been a growing nervousness about energy security. What has happened to make importer countries such as the UK concerned about the risks associated with energy supply?

➤ First, there has been unprecedented growth in energy demand across the globe. For a long time governments disregarded the impact that the economic growth in countries such as China and India would have on demand and prices. There a huge demand for oil (Figure 1.13), leading to rising prices. There is a growing understanding that energy security is about relations not only with oil and gas producers but also with other competing consumers.

➤ Second, there is rising concern about the security of the energy supply infra-structure. Higher volumes of fuel than ever are being transported over longer distances. This is under threat from terrorism, lack of capacity, wear and tear to the infrastructure, piracy and political rivalries. In order to maintain and pay for the safe transport of energy across international borders, huge amounts of private investment are necessary.

➤ Third, energy markets do not always behave as expected. For example, the Iran–Iraq War of 1980–88 had a relatively limited impact on oil supplies and

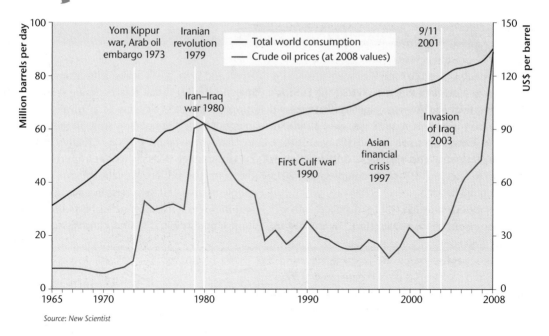

Source: New Scientist

Figure 1.13 Oil demand and oil prices, 1965–2008

prices, yet more recently oil prices have jumped at the mention of strikes in Nigeria, elections in Venezuela or cyclones in the Caribbean.

➤ Finally, speculation in the futures market for oil and gas has driven prices higher and increased the risk factor.

Looking for more energy

As oil and gas supplies become scarcer and more expensive, the hunt for new reserves is creating political alliances and the danger of fresh conflicts. China is moving aggressively to find sources of energy imports, potentially setting up a confrontation with the USA over the dwindling resources of the middle east and Africa.

One energy expert has said, 'To assume that high energy prices mean we'll switch to wind or solar or other renewables is simply unrealistic.' Instead, as fossil fuel prices rise, the option of exploiting resources previously considered uneconomic becomes more attractive. It is now possible to pull carbon out of the ground in forms that were once too expensive or too technically difficult to compete with cheap oil and gas. Governments around the world have re-examined their energy supplies, looking particularly at possible indigenous sources of 'unconventional oil'. A prime example is Canada's oil-shale (see case study).

Case study **Turning oil-shale and sands into oil**

Oil-sands are thick slurry composed of sand, water and a hydrocarbon tar called bitumen. Oil-shale is a sedimentary rock containing oil. Deposits of shale and oil sands have been known about for a long time, but until now have not been developed. However, oil-price rises and technological advances have now made their working feasible. Oil-sands can be refined into something very similar to the petroleum being pumped out of the Saudi Arabian desert but this is only viable if the oil price is above US$50 a barrel.

Geologists estimate that oil-sands in the province of Alberta contain up to 2.5 trillion barrels of oil (more than Saudi Arabia's reserves). A few hundred billion of these barrels are reckoned to be recoverable using current technology. Oil-shale buried deep in the western USA is estimated to contain 2 trillion barrels of oil (Figure 1.14). North America would seem to be the hotspot, but other countries are known to possess deposits.

Environmentalists see the exploitation of oil-shale and sands as a disaster in the making. The oil in the shale is not easily separated out, and the immense amount of heat required to do this is usually generated by burning natural gas. This gives the oil-sands industry a greenhouse gas footprint much larger than that of traditional oil. Using one fuel to create another does not necessarily add up. The process also uses enormous amounts of water: one study found that every barrel of oil produced required up to four barrels of water. During the process, the water becomes polluted. It is then returned to the drainage system, damaging ecosystems and groundwater supplies. There is also the problem of disposing of the shale once the oil has been extracted.

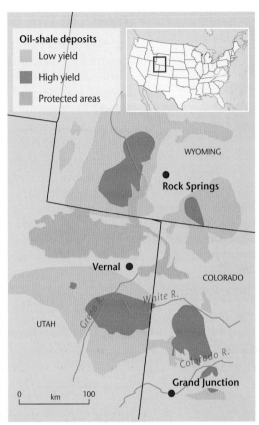

Figure 1.14 The oil-shale deposits of western USA

Environmental costs

Canada's oil-sands seem to offer a vast energy resource, but it can only be exploited at considerable cost to the environment. This is not only local (Photograph 1.4). Huge amounts of energy are consumed in heating the sands to extract the oil. The same is true of previously untapped reserves of oil. For example, the largest onshore oil reserves yet found in North America are in the Arctic National Wildlife Refuge in northern Alaska (USA). But the refuge is a huge area of wilderness inhabited by 45 species of land and marine mammals, ranging from the pygmy shrew to the bowhead whale. Should these vast oil reserves be exploited to help increase energy security or should they continue to be protected? Is oil a more important resource than wilderness?

Photograph 1.4 An opencast oil-sands mine in Alberta, Canada

Players in the energy game

The most powerful **players** or stakeholders in the global supply of energy are the oil-producing and exporting countries (OPEC), some of the oil-producing countries outside OPEC (e.g. the USA, Mexico and Russia) and a number of transnational corporations (TNCs), most notably oil giants such as Shell, Exxon Mobil and BP. Recently, however, some new players have emerged. They are not energy producers and suppliers, but major consumers. Newly industrialising economies such as China are beginning to flex their muscles in the global energy arena. China is a particularly interesting case in that its rapid industrialisation and voracious demand for energy have turned it from a net exporter of oil to a net importer (Figure 1.15).

Figure 1.15 China: oil production and consumption, 1980–2005

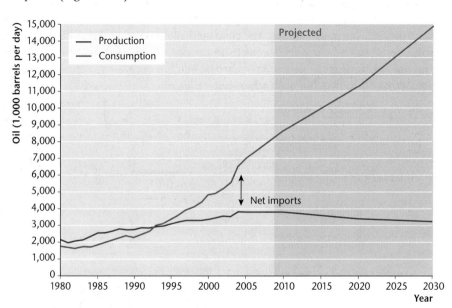

Case study OPEC

The Organisation of Petroleum Exporting Countries (**OPEC**) has 12 members: Iran, Iraq, Kuwait, Qatar, Saudi Arabia, the United Arab Emirates, Libya, Algeria, Nigeria, Angola, Venezuela and Ecuador.

The main declared aims of OPEC are:

- to protect the interests of member countries, individually and collectively
- to stabilise oil prices and eliminate harmful and unnecessary price fluctuations
- to ensure an efficient, economic and regular supply of oil to consuming nations

There are many who doubt whether OPEC has achieved more than the first of these aims. It has been accused of holding back production in order to drive up oil prices. But OPEC's influence is now weaker than it was in previous decades because some significant oil producers have decided not to join the organisation. These include Russia, Norway, Mexico and the USA. Even so, OPEC holds two-thirds of the world's oil reserves, and in 2008 accounted for 36% of the world's oil production. In short, it is still a powerful player.

Case study The top 20 oil companies

Table 1.4 shows the top 20 oil companies in the world in 2005. It compares them in terms of six criteria – oil reserves and production, natural gas reserves and output, refinery capacity and product sales volume. Companies are ranked according to each criterion, then the six individual rankings are added together to give the cumulative overall position. Each of the criteria are given equal weighting.

There are four important observations:

■ At least eight of them are state-owned companies, so they do not really qualify as transnational corporations. They are public rather than private-sector companies. They are government-controlled and are perhaps more active in the realms of **geopolitics**.

■ The remaining companies are relatively free of direct political influence and driven rather more by economic considerations and their share-holders.

■ Most of these 20 companies are involved in a range of operations of which pumping oil is only one. They are also engaged in transporting and refining oil and in petrochemical industries. Exploring for new reserves and looking for new sources of energy are also important. These companies have to plan for when the oil runs out.

■ Their diversity and presence in many countries ensures that TNCs, and others further down the rankings, will continue to be key players in an increasingly tough game.

You could do some research of your own and take a closer look a one nationalised company and one TNC. How different are they?

Table 1.4 The top 20 oil companies, 2005

Rank (2005)	Company	Country	State ownership (%)
1	Saudi Aramco	Saudi Arabia	100
2	Exxon Mobil	USA	
3	NIOC	Iran	100
4	PDV	Venezuela	100
5	BP	UK	
6	Royal Dutch Shell	UK/Netherlands	
7	PetroChina	China	90
8	Chevron	USA	
8	Total	France	
10	Pemex	Mexico	100
11	ConocoPhillips	USA	
12	Sonatrach	Algeria	100
13	KPC	Kuwait	100
14	Petrobras	Brazil	32
15	Gazprom	Russia	51
16	Lukoil	Russia	
17	Adnoc	UAE	100
18	Eni	Italy	
19	Petronas	Malaysia	100
20	NNPC	Nigeria	100

Energy security and the future

What might the world's energy future be?

At the end of this section you should:
➤ *know the reasons why there is uncertainty about future global energy supply and demand*
➤ *have evaluated different options for meeting the rise in energy demand*
➤ *be aware that energy insecurity might increase geopolitical tensions and lead to conflict*
➤ *understand the need for new approaches to energy supply that are radical and sustainable*

Future uncertainties

There is a growing realisation that a glitch in world energy supplies could trigger an economic catastrophe. In the case of oil, for instance, there are a number of factors that are increasing the likelihood of such an event:
➤ The spectacular rise in global oil consumption (see Figure 1.13).

Figure 1.16 World oil production: historical and forecast, 1990–2030

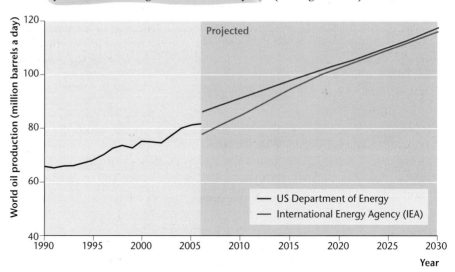

➤ The possibility that we may have reached '**peak oil**' (the point when the maximum rate of global oil production is reached), with the prospect of declining production and rising prices. Some scientists argue that global production of crude oil actually peaked in 2005, while other observers claim that peak oil will not occur until 2015 or even 2020.
➤ The concentration of oil production in fewer countries as oil wells elsewhere are pumped dry.
➤ The unpredictable actions of OPEC and other producer countries, notably Russia. They are still capable of holding the rest of the world to ransom.

Figure 1.17 shows a range of other factors contributing to the general uncertainty.

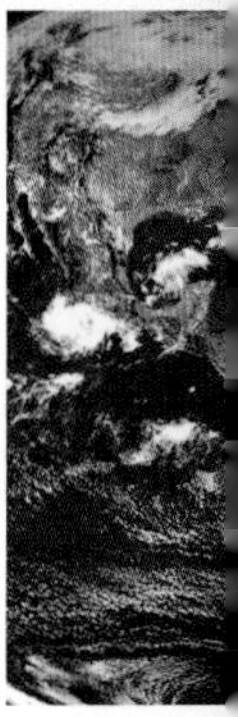

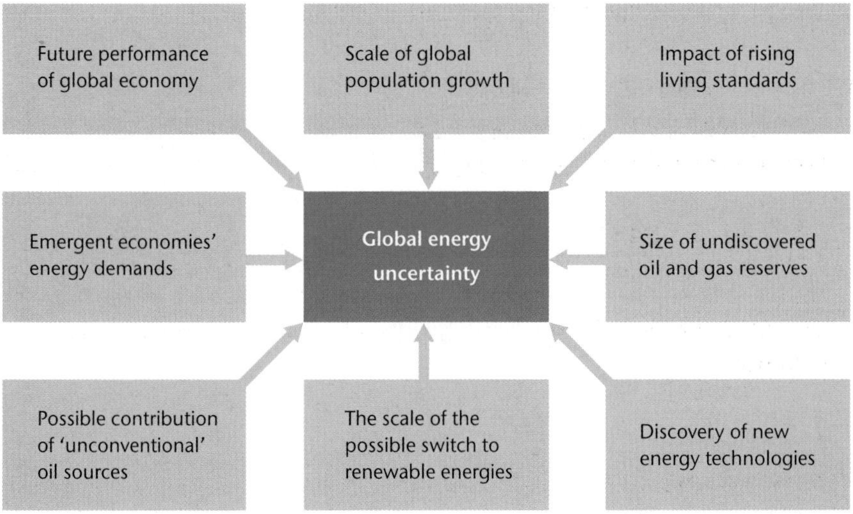

Future performance of global economy
Scale of global population growth
Impact of rising living standards
Emergent economies' energy demands
Global energy uncertainty
Size of undiscovered oil and gas reserves
Possible contribution of 'unconventional' oil sources
The scale of the possible switch to renewable energies
Discovery of new energy technologies

Figure 1.17 Factors contributing to the uncertainty over global energy supply

Responses to increasing energy demands

Despite the uncertainties about the future, the challenge facing the world is to meet the rising energy demand linked with further economic growth while moving towards a low-carbon economy. There are three possible future scenarios.

1 Business as usual

If we do nothing, forecasts suggest that between now and 2030:

- global primary energy demand will rise by 53%, leading to a 55% increase in global energy-related carbon dioxide emissions
- fossil fuels will remain the dominant source of energy worldwide
- as the demand for electricity rises, emissions from electricity generation will account for 44% of global energy-related emissions by 2030
- coal will provide the largest incremental source of power generation, with the majority of this increase likely to be in China (55%)
- over 70% of the increase in global primary energy demand will come from developing countries, reflecting rapid economic and population growth

2 Multi-energy solution

A **multi-energy solution** involves meeting future energy demands from a mixture of renewable, recyclable and non-renewable sources. A rich fuel mix is necessary to ensure energy security and to maintain an affordable supply for both individuals and industry. One controversial component of this future mix may be nuclear energy. **Nuclear power** is 'clean', but can it improve its popularity? Wind generators also have opponents (see case studies below).

There are other sources of renewable energy. Hydro power has been harnessed now for over a century. Solar power is increasingly used to power heating and air conditioning in homes, especially in the Mediterranean. Large-scale solar electricity generation is already occurring in Spain, Germany, Canada and the USA, and there are plans to take advantage of the cloudless skies of the Sahara. In the UK, landfill gas now contributes to electricity generation (see Figure 1.23, page 31).

Case study   Nuclear power's second chance?

Attitudes to nuclear power are shifting in response to climate change and fears over the security of fossil fuel supplies. China and India are building several reactors and intend to increase their nuclear generating capacity in the next 15 years. The USA has experienced a rush of applications to build new reactors, and in the UK there is now government support for a new generation of nuclear power plants.

By 2008, some 439 nuclear reactors in 31 countries were supplying 15% of the world's electricity, about 370 gigawatts a year. It is estimated that by 2030 this output will increase to 520 gigawatts. A big advantage of nuclear energy is that it does not produce greenhouse gas emissions (Figure 1.18), although there are some emissions associated with plant construction and uranium mining. Uranium is relatively cheap and easy to mine, and most commentators think that reserves are plentiful and will last for up to 150 years. Because it is used in small quantities uranium is also cost-effective to transport.

However there are problems associated with nuclear power, highlighted by the 1986 incident at Chernobyl. Modern power stations are designed to be safe, using 'passive safety' systems that operate automatically. But while new designs are safer, they still generate toxic waste in the form of radioactive materials, which have to be transported and stored. This is difficult to manage, politically as well as technically. Nuclear plants are also expensive – they can cost several billion pounds to design and build.

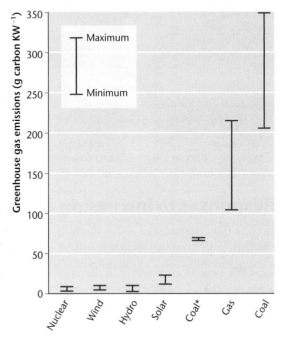

Note: Figures include indirect emissions from life cycle
* With carbon capture and storage

Source: IAEA

Figure 1.18 Greenhouse gas emissions of energy sources

The future of nuclear energy will depend on many factors, including successful waste management, improved economics and convincing the public that nuclear energy is safe.

Case study   Wind power

Wind generation produces about 1% of the global electricity supply. Large-scale wind farms are connected to electricity grids, while individual turbines can provide electricity in isolated locations.

In windpumps or mills, wind energy is used directly as mechanical energy for pumping water or grinding grain. Wind energy is plentiful, renewable, widely distributed and clean, and it can reduce greenhouse gas emissions by replacing fossil fuels as a source of electricity. Fluctuations in wind speeds seldom create problems when wind power is used to supply a low proportion of total demand.

Wind farms have met with local opposition. Some people believe they are unsightly, make a droning noise and pose danger to birds.

There is no one source of energy that ticks all the boxes for meeting rising energy demand without increasing emissions, but wind power must come close in terms of costs and sustainability. On the down side, it is claimed that much of the UK would be covered by wind farms if they were to completely replace fossil fuels as generators of electricity.

3 Energy conservation

The **energy conservation** response to increasing energy demands is based on decreasing the amount of energy used. Individuals and organisations that are direct consumers of energy may want to reduce consumption for a number of reasons – to reduce costs (or maximise profits), to reduce harmful emissions, or to promote energy security on a regional or national scale.

Energy usage	% of total consumption in the home
Heating or air conditioning	44
Water heating	13
Lighting	12
Refrigeration	8
Home electronics	6
Washing/tumble-drying	5
Kitchen appliances	4
Other uses	8

Table 1.5 Typical energy consumption in the home

Energy conservation has been high on the political agenda of the EU in recent years. Countries have targets to reduce their carbon emissions (largely by moving to renewable sources of energy) and cut their energy requirements by increasing the efficiency with which energy is consumed. For example, the UK is working towards a zero energy building standard for all new housing by 2016.

Energy insecurity and geopolitical tensions

It is in every country's interests to become as energy-secure as possible. The key to energy security lies in:

➤ making the greatest possible use of domestic sources of energy
➤ diversifying energy resources to minimise the use of fossil fuels and maximise the use of renewable sources
➤ ensuring guarantees of imported energy, namely reliable supplies and stable prices

The last of these presents the greatest challenge. There is increasing competition for energy, particularly oil and gas, and much of the world falls into one of two camps – the producers and the consumers. Producer countries are able to use their oil and gas resources as powerful bargaining tools, for example by forming international partnerships such as OPEC. Attempts to reduce OPEC's power have met with some success. Indonesia has been persuaded to leave the organisation, while other up-and-coming oil producers have been persuaded not to join. At the same time, there are high levels of military tension and activity around oil-related stress points (Figure 1.19).

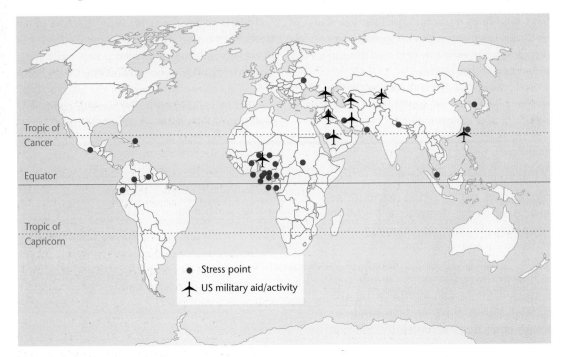

Figure 1.19 World energy-related tensions, 2005

Oil and conflict

Major consumers are concerned to ensure the reliability of their supplies. Some observers have claimed that this was a significant factor in the 2003 Allied invasion and occupation of Iraq, which has the world's second largest oil reserves. Oil was also seen as a driving force in earlier armed conflicts in the Gulf region: the Iran–Iraq war of 1980–88, Iraq's invasion of Kuwait in 1990 and the international operation to restore Kuwaiti sovereignty (known as the First Gulf War) that followed. In Africa, major consumers, especially China, have been competing to secure access to African oil with promises of economic aid and military protection. On the other side of the Atlantic, previously close relations between the USA and Venezuela became strained following the election of the left-wing President Chavez in 1998. He threatened to stop selling Venezuela's crude oil to the USA and further alienated his powerful neighbour by supplying oil to Cuba and China.

In short, much of the conflict in the world since the end of the Cold War (*c.*1990) has been triggered by strategic oil considerations. There is increasing interest in where the largest remaining reserves of oil are located. Figure 1.20 suggests that the middle east will continue to be a global energy hotspot.

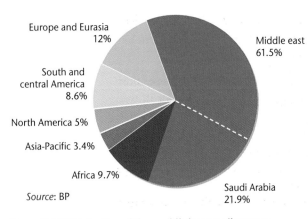

Source: BP

Figure 1.20 Distribution of the world's known oil reserves

India's need for energy has grown in the last decade owing to high economic growth rates, lack of energy-efficient technologies, reliance on heavy industry, and widespread cases of power being stolen from the system. Power shortages and black-outs have been a problem in India's major cities and undermine the confidence of investors and foreign companies operating in the country. Growing car ownership has added to India's need for oil.

In 2005 the Indian prime minister said, 'China is ahead of us in planning for its energy security – India can no longer be complacent'. Oil imports account for two-thirds of India's oil consumption, but only one-third of China's. Moreover, China's proven oil reserves stand at 18 billion barrels, compared with 5 billion barrels in India.

The Indian-owned Oil and Natural Gas Company (ONGC) invested US$3.5 billion in overseas exploration between 2000 and 2005, while the Chinese-owned China National Petroleum Corporation (CNPC) made overseas investments estimated at $40 billion.

Indian policymakers have come up with numerous policies to address the country's growing energy needs. In the short to medium term, India will have to rely increasingly on imported oil and gas. As a result, it is stepping up energy diplomacy with states in south Asia, as well as in central Asia, the middle east, Latin America and Africa. ONGC, for example, has invested in offshore gas fields in Vietnam, as well as energy projects in Algeria, Kazakhstan, Indonesia, Venezuela, Libya and Syria.

India's quest for energy security is impeded by its sometimes tense relations with energy suppliers, countries that supplies have to pass through and energy competitors. India and China have for centuries competed for leadership in Asia, and the need for energy security has raised the possibility of further competition and confrontation in the energy sphere.

Meeting future energy needs

Managing future energy needs is a daunting task. The world population is growing and nations which have been relatively low consumers of energy per capita in the past now seem to have an increasing appetite for energy in a variety of forms.

Global challenge

With the world's primary energy needs set to grow by 55% by 2030, and electricity consumption expected to double over the next few decades, managing future need is a global challenge, perhaps one of the most significant of our time. The International Energy Authority (IEA) estimates that $22 trillion of new investment will be needed by 2030. At the same time, there is the global challenge of climate change and the need to develop cleaner sources of energy in order to improve, or at the very least not worsen, the health of our environment.

There are two possible ways of achieving this:
➤ by applying various 'carrot and stick' measures such as emissions controls, carbon trading and **green taxation** to encourage a reduction in energy consumption and an increase in energy efficiency
➤ by developing new and radical technologies that are sustainable and bring energy security

Stick and carrot

Emission controls

The Kyoto Protocol, adopted in 1997, proposed emission controls at the international level for the first time, with the aim of reducing greenhouse gas emissions in an effort to prevent human-induced climate change. It came into force in 2005, and by May 2008 it had been ratified by 182 countries. Of these, 36 developed countries are required to achieve specific reductions in their greenhouse emissions, amounting to an average of 5% against 1990 levels over the 5-year period 2008–2012. Other signatories include the rapidly industrialising countries of Brazil, China and India, but they have no obligation beyond monitoring and reporting emissions. The refusal of the world's second largest greenhouse gas emitter, the USA, to ratify the agreement – alone among developed countries – substantially weakened the effect of the protocol.

In 2007, 13 countries agreed in principle to a global cap-and-trade system (see emissions trading below) that would apply to both industrialised and developing countries. The hope was that the system would be in place by 2009. It was not universally welcomed by developing countries that need to increase their energy consumption in order to develop and are currently not very fuel-efficient.

Emissions trading

Emissions trading is an arrangement allowing countries that have made greater reductions in their carbon emissions than set out in the Kyoto Protocol to sell their surplus savings to countries that are over their targets. This has created a new commodity in the form of emission reductions or removals. Since carbon dioxide is the principal greenhouse gas, the system is often described as carbon trading. Carbon emissions are now tracked and traded like any other commodity. This is known as the **'carbon market'**. It is a controversial system – it may be a good arrangement for more environmentally conscientious countries, but it can tend to let less committed countries off the hook.

Green taxes

In some countries taxation measures, known as 'green taxes', have been introduced with the aim of cutting the use of natural resources and encouraging waste recycling. In the UK these include new vehicle excise duties (VED) that tax vehicles according to their level of carbon dioxide emissions. Owners of so-called 'gas-guzzlers' or 'Chelsea tractors' pay more, as do those with older, less fuel-efficient vehicles. Other ideas for taxes aimed at reducing energy consumption include removing stamp duty on the sale of carbon neutral homes, raising the duty on petrol and diesel, and raising air passenger duty on flights out of the UK.

Radical new technologies

Greater use of renewable energy and advances in energy technology may be one answer to a more secure energy future. However, all the new technologies that have emerged so far have their own advantages and disadvantages. Four such technologies are described below.

Offshore wind turbines

Building wind turbines offshore (Photograph 1.5) costs at least 50% more than on land, but wind speeds at sea are generally double those on land, so offshore turbines can generate more electricity. Wind blowing at 10 m s^{-1} can produce five times as much electricity as a 5 m s^{-1} wind.

The fact that offshore turbines are less visible and audible than onshore wind farms is an argument in their favour in terms of public opposition. However, UK plans to meet up to one-third of future energy needs with offshore wind farms have led to objections from the Ministry of Defence on the grounds that they could interfere with radar and pose a threat to national security.

Horns Rev, in the North Sea off Denmark, is one the world's largest offshore wind farms. Opened in 2002, covering an area of 20 km^2 and costing €270 million to build, it generates 160 MW (equivalent to 4,000 kW per hour) through its 80 turbines (see www.vestas.com/en/wind-power-solutions). A prime factor in the selection of the site was the strength of winds from all points of the compass (Figure 1.21).

Photograph 1.5 An offshore wind farm in the Baltic Sea near Copenhagen

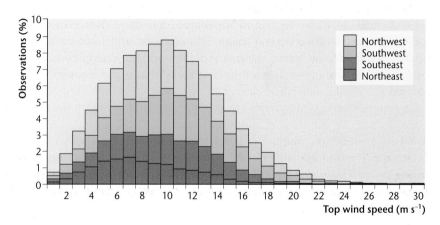

Figure 1.21 Wind speed distribution at Horns Rev

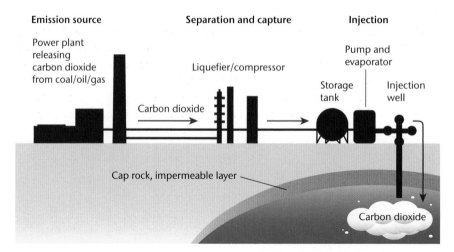

Emission source

Power plant
releasing
carbon dioxide
from coal/oil/gas

Carbon dioxide

Separation and capture

Liquefier/compressor

Injection

Pump and
evaporator

Storage
tank

Injection
well

Cap rock, impermeable layer

Carbon dioxide

*Figure 1.22 How
carbon capture
works*

Carbon storage

Whatever the future global energy mix proves to be, coal is unlikely to go away. On a world scale, it is cheap, abundant and can often be locally sourced, which makes it an attractive commodity. China has accounted for over 60% of the global growth in coal consumption since 1997.

Carbon capture and storage (CCS) involves 'capturing' the carbon dioxide released by burning coal and burying it deep underground. This technology potentially allows clean electricity to be produced from coal.

There are problems, however. No one knows whether CCS will really work and whether the carbon dioxide will stay trapped underground (Figure 1.22). Another problem is that it is expensive. A handful of pilot CCS projects have been conducted, but so far only one such project, in Spremberg, Germany, is linked to electricity generation.

Geothermal energy

In the Philippines 25% of the electricity supply is generated from underground heat. This renewable geothermal heat is free, inexhaustible and available day and night, due to local geology. The heat is used to turn water into steam, which generates electricity in turbines.

Geothermal energy has significant advantages over other renewable resources. There is no need to cover several square kilometres of land surface with wind turbines or photovoltaic arrays. Many parts of the world (for example, in the USA, south Australia and Iceland) have the 'hot rocks' that make recoverable heat possible.

However, extracting subterranean heat is not easy. In many locations the heat is too deep to be extracted economically, and the local geology can create problems. For example, the impermeable nature of granite and other igneous rocks makes it technically difficult and expensive to extract the heat using water. Current research is focused on finding ways of forcing open fissures to let the water flow from the injection hole to its final exit point, where it can be recovered in a super-heated form.

Biofuels

At a time of growing global demand for food and concerns about food security, growing crops for use as **biofuels** is controversial. There are three main types of biofuel: crops (such as grasses, maize and sugar cane), trees and algae. Grasses and trees need a lot of processing, but the whole of their biomass is converted into fuel – mostly ethanol. Aquatic algae are trickier to grow, but produce oil that requires less refining before it becomes useful biodiesel. A number of challenges must be overcome in order to improve the efficiency and acceptability of the biofuel industry:

➤ New (re-engineered) crops need to be developed, tailored specifically for fuel rather than food production.

➤ The supply chain for biofuels can be costly, making them uncompetitive with traditional fossil fuels.

➤ A range of small- and large-scale bio-refineries is needed to improve logistics within the supply chain.

➤ The competition between food crops and biofuel crops for agricultural space needs to be addressed, especially where it is likely to encourage large-scale deforestation (e.g. in Brazil and other tropical countries) and food shortages.

Sustainability

Offshore wind farms, carbon capture and geothermal energy all seem to promise a high degree of sustainability, but much remains to be done to make them economically viable. The last technology considered above, biofuels, is the most feasible of the four, but its sustainability is questionable in terms of its impact on the environment and human wellbeing. Figure 1.23 shows some progress in the use of renewables to generate electricity in the UK. However, by 2007 they still accounted for only 5% of the total.

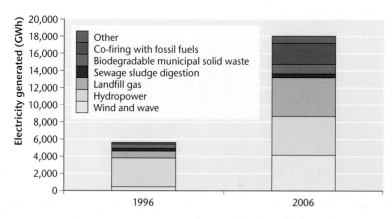

Figure 1.23
Electricity generated in UK from renewable sources, 1996 and 2006

The future

We need to spare a thought for the future, when oil and gas finally run out. What will be the impact on energy security? Will the world lie in ruins after the most powerful countries have fought bitterly for the last remaining reserves? Or will the world be a better place than now, with carbon emissions down to sustainable levels? In the future the energy needs of the world might have been met by a diversity of 'greener' energies. Countries might be less reliant on imported supplies and making greater use of domestic sources. Worries about energy security could be a thing of the past. What do you think?

Review questions

1 Explain the difference between: (a) renewable and non-renewable energy, (b) energy demand and energy consumption, and (c) primary and secondary energy.
2 Why is the global demand for energy increasing?
3 Examine the risks associated with the disruption of national energy supplies.
4 Describe and explain the role of TNCs in the energy business.
5 Suggest reasons why there is so much uncertainty about future global energy needs.
6 Which renewable source of energy do you see as having the most promising future? Give your reasons.

Chapter 2

Water conflicts

Water, like energy, is a fundamental human need, but water is not evenly available over the surface of the Earth. Population growth, economic development and rising standards of living all increase the demand for water. In many parts of the world, the rise in demand is outstripping supply. This is having serious consequences for human **wellbeing**. It is also a potential source of conflict between water users, as well as between those countries and regions with water deficits and those with surplus supplies. If the world is to ensure future water supplies it will need to develop management strategies to resolve these conflicts. Achieving more sustainable use of scarce water resources is another priority.

The geography of water supply

What is the geography of water supply and demand?

By the end of this section you should:
➤ *know the physical factors affecting the supply of freshwater*
➤ *be aware of the growing mismatch between water supply and demand, and the resulting stresses*
➤ *understand how human activities affect water availability*
➤ *appreciate how access to water is related to wealth and levels of economic development*

The familiar model of the hydrological system makes use of the terms **inputs**, **stores**, **outputs** and **flows** to explain how water moves through the environment. Within this framework, we are able to identify important elements such as precipitation, groundwater, evapotranspiration and surface runoff. Figure 2.1 shows the relative importance of these elements and introduces the concept of blue and green water flows. **Blue water flow** is the visible part of the system, namely water running on the surface and supplying rivers or travelling underground, recharging aquifers. This water is potentially available and recyclable. **Green water flow** involves either the interception and transpiration of water by vegetation or its evaporation from a variety of surfaces. These processes have important ecological as well as hydrological functions.

Water supply

Global water supplies are linked to three main physical factors: climate, river systems and geology.

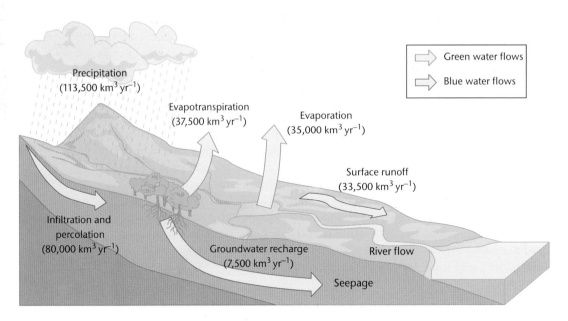

Figure 2.1 The hydrological system (global values)

Climate

The distribution of water globally is related to the Earth's climatic zones. For example, regions near to the equator receive high levels of annual precipitation, while some tropical areas suffer recurring drought. Rainfall may also vary with the seasons. Equatorial areas such as the Amazon lowlands have two distinct periods of wet weather per year, whereas the monsoon lands of southeast Asia have one very distinct wet season (Photograph 2.1). High mountains with snowpack hold vast reserves of water, some of which is released in late spring and during the summer.

Photograph 2.1 The monsoon in India

River systems

The world's major rivers store large quantities of water and **transfer** it across continents. The Amazon, for instance, produces an average **discharge** of 219,000 m³ s⁻¹ from a catchment area of 6,915,000 km². This is 20% of all the river water entering the world's oceans. River flow generally increases downstream as tributaries feed into the main river, though high temperatures can lead to considerable water loss by evaporation. Seasonal changes in climate can also create significant variations in discharge and produce distinctive **river regimes**.

Geology

Where the rocks underlying a river basin are **impermeable**, water will remain on the surface as runoff, creating a high **drainage density**. Permeable soils and rocks such as limestone may allow water to pass into underground drainage systems. **Aquifers** such as chalk and porous sandstones can store vast quantities of water underground. The Ogallala aquifer, in the High Plains region of the USA, is one such water source. Groundwater may create springs or provide the baseflow of rivers.

Figure 2.2 shows how these factors apply in the Indian subcontinent.

Figure 2.2 Factors affecting water supply in India

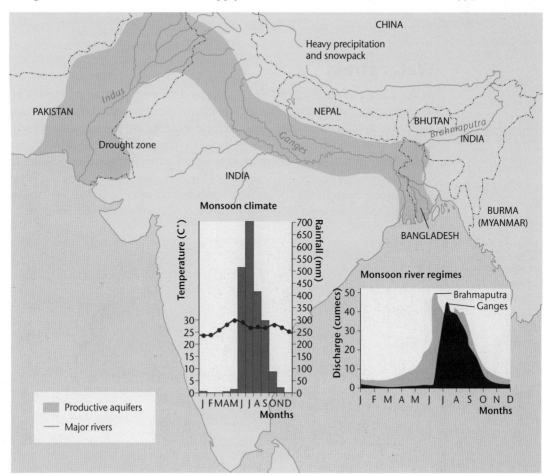

Finite resource

A fundamental issue for water supply is that the amount of water available is finite. The world's oceans hold an estimated 1,386 million km³ of water, and this accounts for 97.5% of the global water store (Figure 2.3). So only 2.5% of the store is potentially available as freshwater, and almost 80% of that is trapped in ice, snow and permafrost. Most of the remaining 20% is groundwater. Only 1% is easily accessible freshwater held in lakes, ecosystems, the atmosphere and rivers.

Figure 2.3 The availability of the world's water

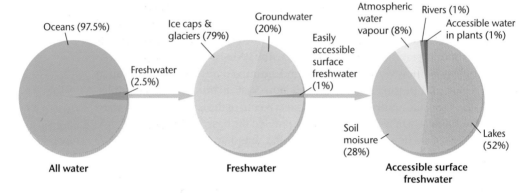

Water stress

As the global population grows and the demand for water increases, there will be less water per person. For water-rich countries such as Canada or Brazil this decrease is not a serious worry, but elsewhere it can be life-threatening. Globally, half a billion people – most of them living in Africa and the middle east – are chronically short of water. There are insufficient renewable supplies of water in China and parts of Europe, while India looks set to suffer considerable water stress in the future. Even in the USA, where water is relatively abundant, availability will have halved between 1955 and 2055, most obviously in the dry southwest.

Figure 2.4 The growing demand for, and use of, water, 1900–2025

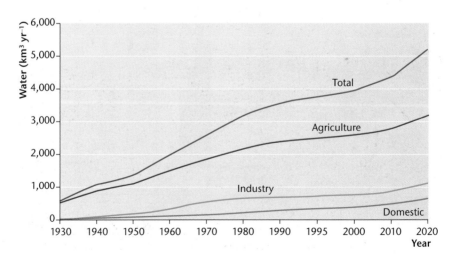

At present, more than one-third of the world's population is short of water, and it is estimated this will reach 45% by 2025. The United Nations Food and Agriculture Organisation (FAO) expects water demand to reach 5,235 km^3 per year by 2025. Figure 2.4 shows the rising demand for water for agriculture, industry and domestic uses.

Agriculture

Agriculture is the major user of water, particularly as we struggle to increase food supplies for a growing global population (Figure 2.4). Currently, agriculture uses 69% of the world's 4,430.7 km^3 a year freshwater supply. Some forms of agriculture are less water-efficient than others. A kilogram of beef, for example, is ten times more 'water-costly' to produce than a kilogram of rice. At present, 17% of the global area devoted to growing crops is irrigated (Photograph 2.2). While water storage and irrigation systems do make agriculture more productive, they can also be wasteful of water. Poor management of such systems can lead to problems of evaporation, seepage, salinisation and fertiliser pollution.

Industry

The proportion of water used globally by industry (21%) rose relatively slowly during the twentieth century, mainly in the developed countries of Europe, Russia, Canada and the USA. Estimates for the coming decade suggest a more rapid global rise, driven by large-scale industrialisation in countries such as India and China.

Hydroelectric power (HEP) continues to use huge amounts of water, but this water is available to other users once it has passed through the turbines. Industry is generally a much more efficient user of water than agriculture, but there are

Corbis

Photograph 2.2
Irrigation of crops
by spraying

some significant exceptions: paper manufacturing, for example, is one of the most extravagant users of water on the planet. Industry has also caused significant water pollution problems.

Domestic

Figure 2.4 shows that water usage in homes (labelled 'domestic' on the graph) is the smallest category of consumption, using only 10%. The amount used, however, varies enormously from country to country. Most developed countries need at least 100,000 litres of water per person per year, while in most African countries the figure is less than 50,000 litres. Global domestic demand seems to be doubling every 20 years and it is arguably only the poor access in Africa that is limiting growth in demand there. The quality of the water involved also varies considerably.

Water sources

Our water supply comes essentially from two sources: surface water and underground aquifers.

Surface water

Rivers, lakes and reservoirs provide large amounts of surface water for a wide variety of uses. So called 'mega-dams' are found on most of the world's major rivers. Half of all the world's dams (around 50,000) are in China, the USA, India and Japan, and their reservoirs account for a quarter of the global freshwater supply. The construction of reservoirs brings short-term economic gains in terms of water supply, hydroelectric power and flood control, but these must be measured against their longer-term environmental and social impacts. Large-scale river-water diversions and wetland drainage programmes also have costs and benefits.

Aquifers

Underground supplies from aquifers are the sole source of drinking water for about a quarter of the world's population. Three-quarters of Europe's drinking water comes from groundwater, while Bangladesh and India use most of their groundwater for irrigation. In many countries, for example the USA, China and India, as well as in much of the middle east, water is being abstracted from aquifers faster than it is being replaced. The long-term costs of this **over-abstraction** are dwindling supplies, falling water tables and seawater contamination.

Pressure on water supplies

In many parts of the world there is a growing mismatch between water supply and demand. This can be seen locally and across whole regions (see Figure 2.5).

Water stress is the term used when the annual supply of water per person falls below 1,700 m^3. When this figure drops below 1,000 m^3, the term used is **water scarcity**. There are two types of water scarcity:

➤ **Physical scarcity** occurs when more than 75% of a country or region's river flows are being used. A quarter of the world's population lives in such areas, which include parts of the USA and Australia.

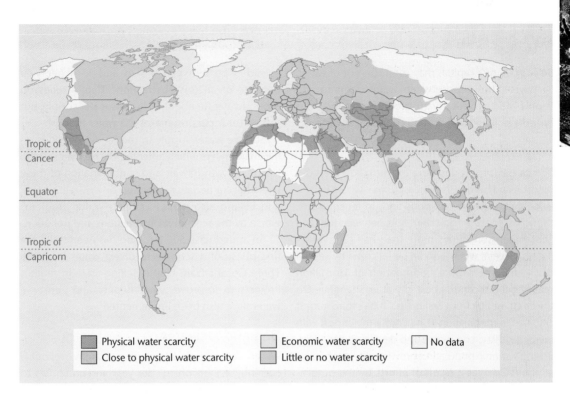

Physical water scarcity

Close to physical water scarcity

Economic water scarcity

Little or no water scarcity

No data

➤ **Economic scarcity** occurs when the development of blue water flow sources is limited by human and financial capacities. More than 1 billion people, in areas such as sub-Saharan Africa, use less than 25% of the river resources available.

Figure 2.5 Water stress and scarcity

Rapid economic growth in India and China is putting enormous pressure on water supplies.

India

India has 4% of the world's freshwater, but 16% of its population. Demand will probably exceed supply by 2020, as urban water demand is expected to double and industrial demand to triple. Hydrologists calculate that 43% of precipitation never reaches rivers or aquifers, and water tables are falling rapidly as 21 million wells abstract water.

China

China has 8% of the world's freshwater but must meet the needs of 22% of the world's population. Two-thirds of Chinese cities do not have enough water all year round, and national water supplies are likely to reach stress levels by 2030. China uses irrigation to produce 70% of its food, mostly in the north and northeast, where the Yellow River and major aquifers are running dry. Huge engineering projects will soon transfer vital water to this area from the water-rich south. An interactive map showing water issues in China can be found at **www.pbs.org/kqed/chinainside/nature/waterissues.html**

The water problems of the Beijing–Tianjin region

Beijing, China's capital, may soon run out of water. Each year, the gap between water demand and supply widens, wells dry up, groundwater and rivers become polluted and ground subsidence worsens.

Why is this happening?

The causes of this deteriorating situation are both physical and human. Northeast China, where Beijing is located, is prone to floods and, in recent years, droughts. Most precipitation falls between July and September, sometimes more than half of it within 3 days. Several wet years can be followed by several dry years. The capital's population of 16 million makes it the second largest city after Shanghai. On the coast, not far from Beijing, is China's third largest city, Tianjin (population 11 million), a major port with heavy industry, commerce and developing services. Beijing's annual population growth rate is stabilising at about 2.5% as a result of efforts by the government to restrict family size, but rural–urban migrants continue to arrive. The situation in Tianjin is similar.

Water supply

Beijing draws 60% of its water supply from aquifers. These are overexploited, but the water quality is still acceptable. In the late 1970s and early 1980s, a series of droughts led to increased demands for irrigation water. This lowered the water table in some areas by as much as 40 m, and some wells were pumped down to the bedrock. Much of Beijing has subsided by between 0.5 m and 1 m per year because of all this abstraction. Tianjin relies on groundwater for about 30% of its water supply, but **salt water incursion** makes the water brackish.

Surface water supply in the region depends on five major rivers which enter the Hai He river system. Upstream withdrawals and contamination of these rivers have a negative effect on downstream cities, and Beijing also makes Tianjin's water problems worse by the scale of its abstractions and pollution.

An aqueduct 2,500 km long has been built, the first phase of a scheme to divert water from the Three Gorges Dam to the Beijing–Tianjin region. Projects to improve water quality and conserve water have also been implemented.

Demand for water

Water demand in the Beijing–Tianjin region is currently 4.9 billion m^3 per year and continues to rise. Of this, agriculture accounts for about 65%, although the use of water-saving technologies means irrigation demands are levelling off. Industrial output in the region has increased more than sixfold in the last 20 years. Water demand has not risen as fast as this as industries have become more water-efficient and recycle their waste water and there has been a shift from heavy to high-tech industry. The fastest rate of increase is in domestic water use: consumption has risen tenfold in the last 50 years and now averages 240 litres per person per day.

Human impacts on water availability

Human activity can have a negative effect on the water environment (Figure 2.6). Pollution caused by human activity and excessive abstraction of water supplies can further increase water stress.

Pollution of groundwater is much less obvious than surface-water pollution, but is no less a problem:

➤ Sewage disposal in developing countries is expected to cause 135 million deaths by 2020 (World Health Organization). Diseases such as hepatitis, typhoid and cholera are common in areas with polluted water. In the UK we add 1,400 million litres of sewage to our rivers daily, though most of it has been treated.

➤ Chemical fertilisers used by farmers contaminate groundwater as well as rivers

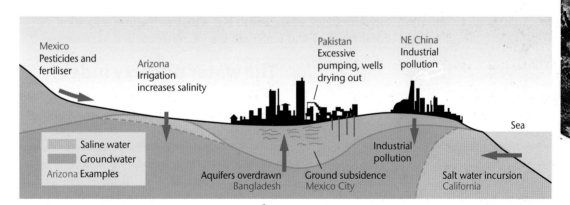

Figure 2.6 A model showing some human impacts on water supply and quality

and water supplies. In Yucatan, Mexico, the level of nitrate in the groundwater is 45 mg l^{-1}. Sewage and fertilisers add nutrients to the water and increase the growth of algae downstream. The algae remove oxygen from the water, for example along the shores of the Gulf of Mexico.

> Each year the world generates 400 billion tonnes of industrial waste, much of which is pumped untreated into rivers, oceans and other waterways. Heavy metals such as lead, cadmium and mercury also become concentrated in rivers. Chemical waste includes toxic and widely banned polychlorinated biphenyls (PCBs).

> Big dams trap sediment in reservoirs, which reduces floodplain fertility and the flow of nutrients from rivers into seas. This may damage coastal fish stocks and prevent beach formation, which in turn can expose coasts to greater erosion. Sediment disturbance during dam construction can also block the gills of river fish and suffocate them.

Abstraction

Removing water from rivers and groundwater sources, whether for drinking water or for irrigation, can have unintended consequences:

> Worldwide, water is being extracted from aquifers faster than it is being replaced. In arid areas, rainfall can never recharge these underground stores.

> The removal of freshwater from aquifers in coastal locations can upset the natural balance of saline and fresh groundwater and lead to **salt water incursion** and salinisation of wells, boreholes and wetlands.

Access to water

Water insecurity means not having access to sufficient, safe water. Despite efforts to improve supplies and sanitation ($30 billion is spent each year worldwide), there are 1.2 billion people without access to clean water, many of whom live in the 20 or so developing countries classified as 'water scarce'. Typically in these countries the poor are most water insecure, with few opportunities to escape from poverty and access the benefits of economic development. The problems of water insecurity are related to:

> *availability* – having a water supply and a distribution network

> *access* – freedom to use or income to buy water in a particular location
> *usage* – entitlement to, and understanding of, water use and health issues

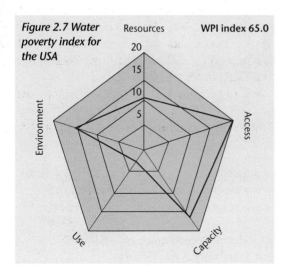

Figure 2.7 Water poverty index for the USA

The water poverty index

In 2002 the British Centre for Ecology and Hydrology published the first **water poverty index** (WPI). The index uses five parameters:

- *resources* – the quantity of surface and groundwater per person, and its quality
- *access* – the time and distance involved in obtaining sufficient safe water
- *capacity* – how well the community manages its water (and health)
- *use* – how economically water is used in the home and by agriculture and industry
- *environment* – ecological sustainability (green water)

Each of the parameters is scored out of 20, to give a maximum possible score of 100 (see Figure 2.7).

Poverty

Poverty and water poverty go hand in hand (Figure 2.8), but they are part of a wider equation. Lack of water hampers attempts to reduce poverty and encourage development. Improved water supply and sanitation can increase food production, bring better health and provide higher standards of wellbeing. Water wealth in developed countries brings cheap water, irrigation, energy and economic growth. Some commentators have dubbed water 'the lubricant of development'.

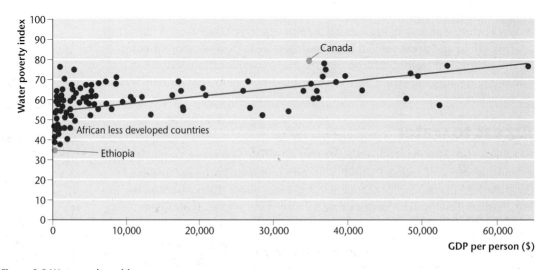

Figure 2.8 Water and wealth

Contrasting water extremes

Canada and Ethiopia represent the two extremes of the water and development **spectrum**. Canadian households use 800 litres per person per day to 'wash, cook and flush'. Water is also used for lawns, gardens, parks and swimming pools. Problems here are about rising water bills and leakages.

In Ethiopia the water consumption is 1 litre per person per day, much of it fetched daily from a shared source. This water has to meet all needs. Since Ethiopia is a poor country, its water problems relate to water shortages, pollution and the risk of disease. The fact that the population is concentrated in widely dispersed rural villages and overpopulated urban slums aggravates the problems.

Table 2.1 helps to explain the worsening water supply difficulties faced by Ethiopians, compared with the situation their Canadian counterparts are in.

Water indicators	Canada	Ethiopia
Water poverty index	78	45
Surface water resources (km³)	2,892	110
Groundwater resources (km³)	370	40
Renewable water resources in 2000 (m³ per person per year)	92,646	1,749
Renewable water resources by 2050 (m³ per person per year)	70,520	590
Water use: agricultural (%)	12	93
Water use: industrial (%)	69	6
Water use: domestic (%)	20	1
Access to improved water (% of population)	100	24
Access to improved sanitation (% of population)	100	12
Development indicators		
GNI ($ per person)	33,170	170
Population in 2000 (millions)	30	62.9
Estimated population in 2050 (millions)	42.3	169.4
Urban population (%)	77	18
Agriculture (% of GDP)	2	47
Industry (% of GDP)	35	14

Table 2.1 Water and development indicators for Canada and Ethiopia

The price of water

As demand begins to overtake supply in the global market, water costs look set to follow oil and food prices upwards. Who pays most for their water may surprise you. Homeowners in Washington DC (USA) pay about $350 for a year's water (72 cents per m³). In many developing countries, water is free in rural areas, but it often needs to be carried daily over long distances and is likely to be contaminated. In the largest cities, slum dwellers may have to buy water

Table 2.2 Costs (US cents per m³) of water supplies in selected cities

City	Tap connection	Informal vendor
Jakarta (Indonesia)	16	31
Dhaka (Bangladesh)	8	42
Karachi (Pakistan)	14	81
Ulaanbaatar (Mongolia)	4	151
Phnom Penh (Cambodia)	9	164
Manila (Philippines)	11	474

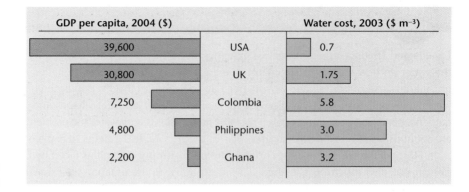

Figure 2.9 Water prices and GDP in selected countries

GDP per capita, 2004 ($)		Water cost, 2003 ($ m^{-3})
39,600	USA	0.7
30,800	UK	1.75
7,250	Colombia	5.8
4,800	Philippines	3.0
2,200	Ghana	3.2

from private vendors whose prices often exceed $1 per m^3. This can be many times the price of tap water elsewhere in the city (Table 2.2).

Figure 2.9 shows some interesting relationships between national water prices and GDP.

The price of freshwater depends upon transport costs and the level of demand, less any subsidy.

➤ Californian cities import water over hundreds of kilometres from the Colorado basin. Lifting water from depth and moving it over hills by pumps is energy-expensive.

➤ Water prices in Australia's markets peaked at nearly 75 cents per m^3 in December 2006, having increased twentyfold in the year as a result of prolonged drought.

➤ In India, water scarcity has prompted some farmers to profit by selling their abstracted water instead of using it themselves for irrigation.

➤ Water subsidies can be large. In the city of Delhi, they make up 80% of the cost of providing municipal water. Farmers in California use roughly one-fifth of the state's water, yet pay only 1 cent per m^3 for it.

The risks of water insecurity

What are the potential implications of an increasingly 'water insecure' world?

By the end of this section you should:

➤ *be aware that water availability affects human welfare and economic growth*
➤ *understand how the need for water can lead to tensions and conflict*
➤ *have some grasp of the politics of water supply and the role of agreements and treaties*
➤ *know the environmental and political risks of transferring water*

Water supply problems

Secure water supplies are essential to economic development. They are needed to support irrigation and food production, manufacturing and energy generation.

However, the development, extraction and use of water resources can lead to environmental and supply problems, and can have negative impacts on both economic activity and human welfare. During its 'Green Revolution' programme to increase food production, India put 45 million hectares of land into irrigation. The negative consequences of this were depletion of underground aquifers and salinisation of the soil. Perhaps the most severe example of damage inflicted by irrigation programmes can be seen in the large-scale diversion of rivers which once flowed into the Aral Sea (see case study).

Case study The Aral Sea

Once the world's fourth largest inland sea (68,000 km²), the Aral Sea has been steadily shrinking since the 1960s. In the late 1950s the Soviet government diverted much of the water from the rivers Amu Darya and Syr Darya, which fed into the Aral Sea, for irrigation of agriculture. By 2007 the sea had declined to just 10% of its original size and split into separate lakes, and its level had fallen by up to 40 m (Figure 2.10). This is an environmental catastrophe.

An interactive map and satellite photographs can be seen at: http://visearth.ucsd.edu/VisE_Int/aralsea/aral_map.html

The Aral Sea crisis has involved several stakeholders:

■ *The former Soviet government.* Communist leaders began an ambitious irrigation scheme designed to develop fruit and cotton farming in what had been an unproductive region and create jobs for millions of farm workers.

■ *The fishing community.* A once prosperous industry that employed 60,000 people in villages around the lakeshores has collapsed. Unemployment and economic hardship are everywhere. Ships lie useless on the exposed seabed (Photograph 2.3).

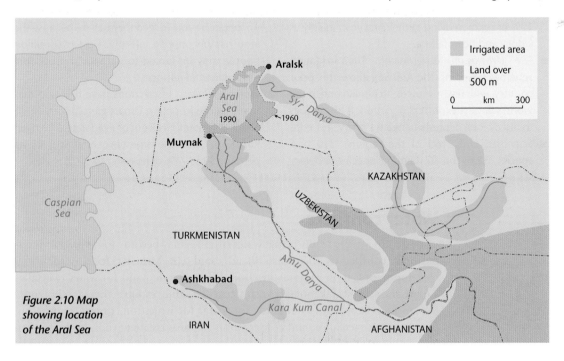

Figure 2.10 Map showing location of the Aral Sea

*Photograph 2.3
Abandoned fishing
boats on the Aral
seabed*

- *Local residents*. Health problems are caused by wind-blown salt and dust from the dried-out seabed. Drinking water and parts of the remaining sea have become heavily polluted as a result of weapons testing, industrial projects, and pesticide and fertiliser runoff. Infant mortality rates are among the highest in the world, with 10% of children dying in their first year, mainly of kidney and heart failure.
- *The Uzbekistan government*. The irrigation schemes based on the Aral Sea allow this poor country, with few resources, to remain one of the world's largest exporters of cotton. It also hopes to discover oil deposits beneath the dry seabed.
- *Scientists*. Only 160 of the region's 310 bird species, 32 of the 70 mammal species and very few of the 24 fish species remain. The climate has changed too, making the area even more arid and prone to greater extremes of temperature.
- *Kazakhstan farmers*. Irrigation has brought the water table to the surface, making drinking water and food crops salty and polluted.
- *International economists*. People in the region may no longer be able to feed themselves, because the land has become so infertile. Up to 10 million people may be forced to migrate and become environmental refugees.
- *Water engineers*. Inspections have revealed that many of the irrigation canals were poorly built, allowing water to leak out or evaporate. The main Kara Kum Canal, the largest in central Asia, allows perhaps 30 to 75% of its water to go to waste.

Water conflicts

'If we do not act, the reality is that water supplies may become the subject of international conflict in the years ahead,' said UK Minister for International Development Gareth Thomas in 2008. When the demand for water overtakes supply and several stakeholders wish to use the same resource, there is a potential for conflict. Competing demands for water for irrigation, power generation, domestic use, recreation and conservation can also create tension both between and within countries.

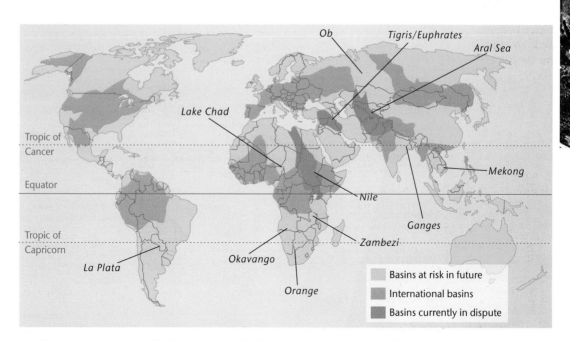

Figure 2.11
International
conflicts over water
in major river
basins

Conflict is perhaps more likely where developing countries are involved. Water is vital as they struggle to feed their growing populations and promote industrial development, and often they have to cope with a legacy of poor water management.

Just as oil resources have caused growing international tension over the last 50 years, many people see water resources as the next flashpoint. UN reports suggest there are around 300 potential water conflicts around the world as rivers, lakes and aquifers struggle to provide sufficient supplies for neighbouring countries (Figure 2.11). It should be noted that politicians and government map-makers have not always helped these situations, creating boundaries and borders which do not easily fit with the natural features of river catchments.

Case study   The middle east water conflicts

The middle east is already an area of significant conflict. The fact that it has relatively low seasonal rainfall and growing population is the root cause of the tensions over water resources (Figure 2.12).

■ In the western part of this region, Israelis, Syrians, Jordanians, Lebanese and Palestinians are in dispute over shrinking water supplies. Security of water supplies was not the cause of the Arab–Israeli war in 1967, but was a contributory factor. Water in this region comes primarily from two sources: the River Jordan (and its lakes) and

three important aquifers. The division of these water resources between the neighbouring states is an ongoing challenge. A detailed account can be found at www.mideastweb.org/Mew_water95.pdf

■ In the eastern part of the region, Turkey plans to build dams to store and use water in the headwaters of the Tigris and Euphrates Rivers. This is strongly opposed by Syria and Iraq, where reduced water supplies threaten to hold back economic development and food production.

Figure 2.12 Water conflicts in the middle east

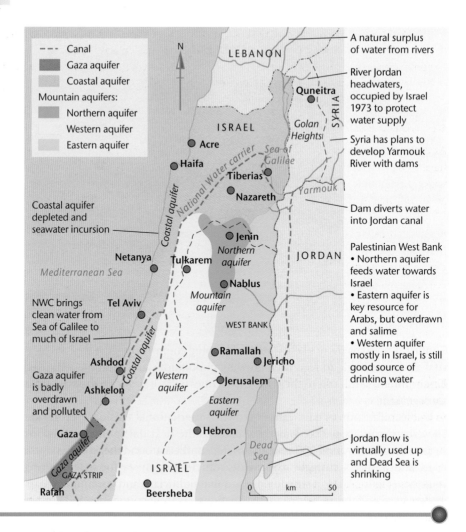

Map labels:

Legend:
- - - Canal
- Gaza aquifer
- Coastal aquifer
- Mountain aquifers:
  - Northern aquifer
  - Western aquifer
  - Eastern aquifer

N

LEBANON

Quneitra

SYRIA

ISRAEL

Golan Heights

Acre

Sea of Galilee

Haifa

Tiberias

Nazareth

Yarmouk

National Water carrier

Coastal aquifer

Jenin

Northern aquifer

JORDAN

Netanya   Tulkarem

Nablus

Mountain aquifer

Mediterranean Sea

Tel Aviv

WEST BANK

Ashdod

Coastal aquifer

Western aquifer

Ramallah

Jericho

Jerusalem

Ashkelon

Eastern aquifer

Gaza

Hebron

Gaza aquifer

GAZA STRIP

Dead Sea

ISRAEL

Rafah   Beersheba

0   km   50

Annotations:
- A natural surplus of water from rivers
- River Jordan headwaters, occupied by Israel 1973 to protect water supply
- Syria has plans to develop Yarmouk River with dams
- Dam diverts water into Jordan canal
- Palestinian West Bank
  - Northern aquifer feeds water towards Israel
  - Eastern aquifer is key resource for Arabs, but overdrawn and salime
  - Western aquifer mostly in Israel, is still good source of drinking water
- Jordan flow is virtually used up and Dead Sea is shrinking
- Coastal aquifer depleted and seawater incursion
- NWC brings clean water from Sea of Galilee to much of Israel
- Gaza aquifer is badly overdrawn and polluted

Case study   Tensions between India and Bangladesh

For much of its 2,500 km length, the Ganges flows through India. But the last part of its course takes it through Bangladesh, where it is known first as the Padma River. It is joined later by the Jamuna River, the largest distributary of the Brahmaputra, and takes on the name Meghna before flowing out into the Bay of Bengal. In 1974 India opened the huge Farakka Barrage, just 11 km from the Bangladeshi border. Further upstream, a series of dams divert water into irrigation systems and many of India's largest cities use the river to carry wastewater from domestic and industrial sources. So Bangladesh is effectively a double loser. It is being deprived of much-needed water and has to suffer the effects of India's pollution of the river. Although an agreement was signed in 1990 by the two countries about sharing the waters of the Ganges, India is very much in control of the situation. To make matters worse for Bangladesh, India now has plans to make greater use of the Brahmaputra, which also flows through India before reaching Bangladesh (see Figure 2.2, page 35).

Bangladeshi grievances include the following:
- reduced flow of the river is affecting irrigation and food production

- fish stocks and the fishing industry are declining
- navigation and water-borne trade are becoming harder because of lower river levels
- lower river flows are increasing salinisation
- the delta is eroding because less silt is being carried and deposited
- seawater incursion is increasing as the delta dries out

Water geopolitics

As countries compete for water resources international agreements and treaties have to be drawn up on how best to manage shared water supplies. Pacts about water supply, distribution and use are in place along many major rivers. However, as the political situation changes, these can flare up into disputes (**hydropolitics**).

As water resources take on a greater significance, new treaties may need to be negotiated using what might be called **water diplomacy**. Unfortunately, international law does not provide a clear solution to transboundary river disputes, except where navigable waterways are involved. In fact, present international law tends to make matters worse. Upstream countries usually assert their right of territorial sovereignty (it is our water, so it is our decision how it is used). Downstream countries claim territorial integrity (it is our right to receive the same amount and quality of water as we have in the past).

Sharing water

Under the **Helsinki Rules** there is general agreement that international treaties must include concepts such as 'equitable use' or 'equitable share' and be applied to whole drainage basins, not single countries. Ideally, the criteria for water sharing should be based upon the following:

➤ *natural factors* – rainfall amounts, water sources, share of drainage basin
➤ *social and economic needs* – population size, development and welfare
➤ *downstream impacts* – restricting flow, lowering water tables, pollution
➤ *dependency* – are alternative water sources (other rivers or aquifers) available to the country?
➤ *prior use* – the tricky question of existing (past) or potential (future) use
➤ *efficiency* – avoiding waste and mismanagement of water

In reality, of course, agreements are rarely equitable because the country with the greatest political, economic and even military power gets the better deal. This is true in the middle east, in many parts of southeast Asia, and arguably even between states in the USA (see case study of the Colorado River).

Case study The Colorado River

The basin of the Colorado River is the most heavily used source of irrigation water in the USA. Water rights between states were allocated by the Colorado Compact in 1922. Over the next 60 years a series of treaties were agreed between the seven US states with a direct interest in the river, and between the USA and Mexico. A 'giant plumbing system' has come into being, involving more than ten major dams to serve the water needs of 30 million people (Figure 2.14 and Photograph 2.4).

Figure 2.13 The Colorado basin

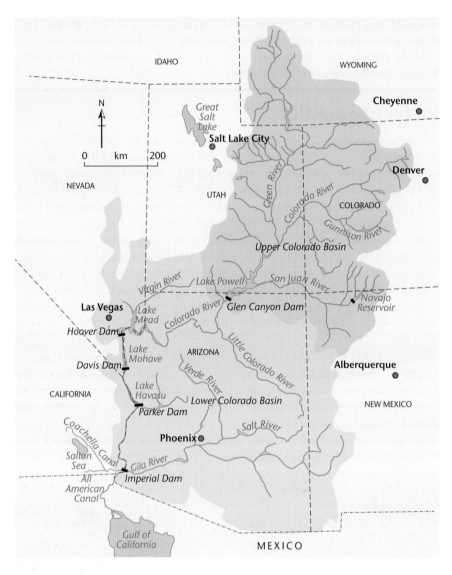

The 1920s 'Law of the River', based on the Colorado Compact, established the division of water between the upper basin states of Colorado, Wyoming, Utah and New Mexico and their responsibility to supply the lower basin states of Arizona, Nevada and California, together with Mexico, where the river meets the sea. Initial agreements allocated California the largest proportion of water because of its large population and considerable political power. This has since been reduced by new developments and legal challenges.

The 1920s, when these agreements were drawn up, was a period of higher rainfall and water surpluses. As demand and populations increase and less water is available they are a growing challenge for the states and players involved. The stakeholders include the following:

■ *Farmers*. Agriculture has always done well out of the Colorado River, receiving some 80% of the water allocation. This is because the farmers and ranchers got there first. In addition, to encourage agricultural development, the federal government supplied the water to farmers at low cost – as low as one-twentieth of the price in nearby cities. Much of this water is wasted in flood irrigation and inappropriate choices of crop (cotton and rice which need a lot of water). The sale of water rights by farmers to others is controversial.

- *City dwellers*. The southwest states have become increasingly urbanised. California is accused of using water that other states may need in the future. In recent years, against the background of a 5-year drought and continuing population growth, the conflict has become even angrier. In 2007, for the first time, Arizona began to take its full share of water for the cities of Phoenix and Tucson. To make up for this, California is squeezing farmers in the Imperial Valley to supply Los Angeles and San Diego.
- *Environmentalists and recreationalists*. The recreational development of lakes is of increasing concern to environmental groups which would prefer to see lower levels of recreational activity in wilderness and wetland areas. The heavy use of Lake Powell by tourists, for example, is threatening the lakeshore areas.
- *Indigenous groups*. Native Americans along the Colorado River have claims to water rights based

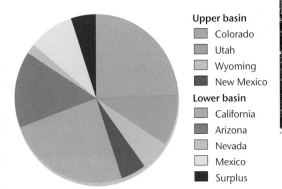

Upper basin
- Colorado
- Utah
- Wyoming
- New Mexico

Lower basin
- California
- Arizona
- Nevada
- Mexico
- Surplus

Figure 2.14 Water allocation from the Colorado River

on treaties and agreements made between their tribes and the federal government in the 1880s. They are engaged in prolonged legal battles over these claims.

- *Mexican people*. The Colorado River is used so heavily that it no longer reaches the sea – 90% of its water is extracted before it reaches Mexico. The wetlands that once existed in the river's delta are now a vast expanse of barren mudflats. Most of the local Cucupa fishermen have been forced to move elsewhere. The delta has reduced in size as water and sediment have been retained by the huge dams on the Colorado.

Photograph 2.4 The Hoover dam on the Colorado River

■ *US federal government.* This is under pressure from its own politicians not to change water allocations. Plans to line the canal which carries water to California's Imperial Valley with concrete seem a sensible water conservation project. However, seepage from the canal tops up groundwater along the border, so any change would reduce supplies in Mexico. On the other hand, it seems that Mexico is taking more than its allotted share from the Rio Grande. These water issues could affect US–Mexican relations on other matters, such as curbing cross-border drug smuggling and controlling illegal immigration from Mexico into the USA.

The measures taken to control the River Colorado in order to prevent floods, generate electricity and provide water for homes and agriculture were an engineering marvel at the time of their construction. There is a view now, however, that it has been a costly, inefficient, divisive and environmentally damaging operation (Table 2.3).

Table 2.3 Colorado River: the benefits and costs

Benefits	Costs
Flood control	Water loss through evaporation and seepage
Power to pump the water	Salinisation as a result of irrigation
Domestic water supply	Groundwater overdraft
Irrigation for agriculture	Water waste
Industrial development	Environmental damage
Sediment control	
Recreation opportunities	
Wildlife protection	

Water transfers

Many regions and countries faced with increasing populations are finding themselves short of water. One solution to water shortages is to divert water from one drainage basin to another. Large-scale **transfers** of water can be achieved by diverting a river or by constructing a large canal to carry available water from one basin to another. Two very different case studies illustrate the environmental and political risks of water transfer. The Snowy Mountains Scheme in Australia has followed a traditional path, while the Turkey/Israel case study shows how international proposals are easily derailed by environmental and political change.

Case study **The Snowy Mountains Scheme**

The Snowy Mountains Scheme in the Kosciuszko National Park is the largest engineering project in Australia and one of the most complex hydroelectric schemes in the world, with 16 major dams, seven power stations and a network of tunnels, pipelines and aqueducts. The scheme collects and diverts water so that it can be used by the power stations to create electricity. The water then flows west into the Murray and Murrumbidgee Rivers to irrigate farms and provide water for communities in New South Wales, Victoria and South Australia (Figure 2.15). Work began in 1949 and finished in 1974.

A number of negative consequences have gradually emerged. The creation of storage lakes, such as Lake Eucumbene, has destroyed valuable wildlife habitats, and in some places the Snowy River flow

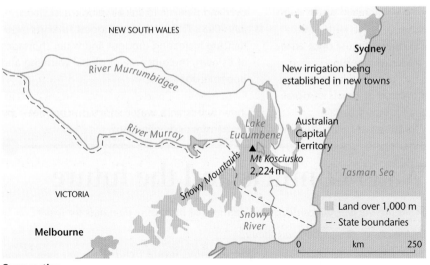

NEW SOUTH WALES

Sydney

New irrigation being established in new towns

River Murrumbidgee

River Murray

Lake Eucumbene

Australian Capital Territory

▲ Mt Kosciusko 2,224 m

Snowy Mountains

Tasman Sea

VICTORIA

Snowy River

Melbourne

Land over 1,000 m
- - State boundaries

0   km   250

Cross-section

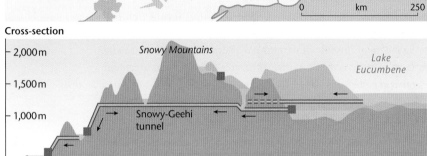

2,000 m

Snowy Mountains

Lake Eucumbene

1,500 m

1,000 m

Snowy-Geehi tunnel

Figure 2.15 The Snowy Mountains Scheme

has fallen to only 1% of its original discharge. Groundwater overdraft and salinisation problems resulting from this low flow and irrigation have adversely affected farming in the Murray lowlands. Water scarcity has set farmers against city dwellers as they compete for supplies. The political fallout has forced the governments of New South Wales and Victoria to restore some of the flow in the Snowy River and to invest in water-saving projects. The aim has been to protect farmers from the worst effects of water shortages. Record droughts in Australia in recent years triggered by El Niño events have all but used up the water allocations of the Snowy Mountains Scheme.

A useful reference is: www.cultureandrecreation.gov.au/articles/snowyscheme

Case study

Water transfers, Turkey to Israel

Israel's Hydrological Service has warned that the country's water reserves are being severely stretched as aquifers become salinised and water levels in the Sea of Galilee fall. Demand currently stands at 1.5 billion m³ per year. Turkey appears to have surplus water that could be taken from the Mangavat River and sold to Israel. The following chronology illustrates how the water transfer might be achieved:

■ *December 2001* – Israel and Turkey plan an undersea water pipeline link via Northern Cyprus.
■ *August 2002* – Israel begins talks with Turkey to import 50 million m³ of treated water each year using tankers.
■ *July 2004* – Syria objects to Turkish plans because

Turkey has built reservoirs that retain water along the Tigris and Euphrates.

- *May 2005* – Israel and Turkey discuss once again the possibility of an undersea pipeline.
- *April 2006* – the water pipeline deal is scrapped as fears of terrorism grow and the costs of desalinating seawater fall.
- *June 2007* – Turkey proposes a 'peace bridge'

overland pipeline to link all middle east states.

- *July 2008* – Official figures suggest Turkey is experiencing increasing drought and water shortages of its own, the outcome of global warming and poor management.

So how will Israel's water shortages be met – by water transfer or desalination?

Water conflicts and the future

What are the possible conflicts and solutions to increasing demands for water?

By the end of this section you should:

➤ *understand the uncertainties that surround future trends in water supply and demand*
➤ *be aware of the role of various players in decisions about water*
➤ *have investigated alternative strategies for water management*
➤ *have explored the role of technology in water supply and water security*

Trends in water demand

We have already looked at the current and forecast trends in global water supply and demand (Figures 2.4 and 2.5). By 2025, water withdrawal is projected to reach 5,235 km^3 per year, and this is likely to have considerable impact on food production, human welfare and the natural environment. Any predictions are tentative as they involve uncertain factors such as climate change.

Three alternative futures

In 2002 the International Food Policy and Research Institute used a computer model to examine the implications of three alternative futures for global water (and food) supply and demand. These futures calculated for 2025, are shown in Table 2.4. Clearly the business as usual scenario will be unsustainable in the long term. The most worrying scenario is that of water crisis, which shows how mismanagement of water resources or climate change could threaten our water and food supplies and lead to wider geographical problems including conflict. Some features of this scenario may be beginning to occur already.

Climate change

The impacts of global warming on water supply are easier to examine if we focus on the two most obvious features of current climate change – higher global temperatures and increasingly extreme weather events.

➤ Increases in mean annual temperature are already leading to earlier snowmelt in mountain areas and this is causing increase in spring discharge in major river basins. This water will be lost to the oceans or evaporated, as present water

Table 2.4 Alternative scenarios for water by 2025

Scenario	Water changes by 2025	Wider impacts
Business as usual	Water scarcity will reduce food production. Consumption of water will rise by over 50%. Household water use will increase by 70% (mostly in developing countries). Industrial water demand will increase in developing countries	Developing countries will become reliant on food imports and experience increased hunger and malnutrition. In sub-Saharan Africa, grain imports will more than triple. In parts of western USA., China, India, Egypt and north Africa, water will be pumped faster than aquifers can recharge
Water crisis	Global water consumption will increase, mostly for irrigation. Worldwide, demand for domestic water will fall. Demand for industrial water will increase by 33% over business as usual levels, yet industrial output will remain the same	Food production will decline and food prices, especially cereals, will increase rapidly. In developing countries malnutrition and food insecurity will increase. Dam building will decline and key aquifers in China, India and north Africa will fail. Conflict over water between and within countries will increase
Sustainable water	Global water consumption and industrial water use will have to fall considerably. Environmental flows could be increased dramatically compared to other scenarios. Global rain-fed crop yields could increase due to improvements in water harvesting and use of sustainable farming techniques. Agricultural and household water prices might double in developed countries and triple in the developing world	Food production could increase slightly and shifts occur in where it is grown. Prices could fall slowly. Investment in crop research, technology and water-management reforms will increase. Unsustainable pumping of groundwater should end. Governments could delegate farm management to community groups

management cannot store or use it effectively. Snowfields in the Andes are already disappearing as rainfall replaces snowfall – this means the loss of a primary source of water. Melting of Himalayan glaciers could threaten water supplies of nearly half the world's population in Asia.

➤ Cyclones and monsoon events threaten water supplies intermittently, but it is the shortages of water brought about by the increased frequency and intensity of drought that will have the most devastating impacts. Dried-up rivers, irrigation failure and depleted aquifers threaten the lives of millions of people in Asia and sub-Saharan Africa.

Water players and decision makers

A range of **players** are involved in any issue relating to water resources and their use. There are supporters and opponents, villains and victims, 'Davids' and 'Goliaths'. However, for almost all players, the conservation and **sustainable development** of water resources is an increasingly important priority.

The process of weighing up the motivations and perceptions of players is called **values analysis.** It is an important factor in the evaluation of issues and in decision-making.

Many of the issues examined in this chapter involve a range of specific players who are identified in particular case studies. Table 2.5 identifies and illustrates the more general categories of player.

Table 2.5 Some of the players involved in water issues

Category	Players
Political	International organisations (e.g. UN), government departments (e.g. DEFRA), regional and local councils, lobbyists and pressure groups
Economic (business)	World Bank, governments, developers, utility companies (e.g. Thames Water), agriculture, industry (esp. chemicals and food), TNCs and businesses (including energy companies)
Social (human welfare)	Individuals, residents, indigenous groups, landowners, farmers, consumers, health officials, scientists and NGOs (e.g. Water Aid)
Environmental (sustainable development)	Conservationists, scientists, planners, international organisations (e.g. FAO) and NGOs (e.g. WWF and People & Planet)

Case study   Water futures for India and its neighbours

The Indian subcontinent has an insecure water future because:

■ it has considerable supplies of water provided by three of the world's major rivers, but its monsoon climate creates extremes of flooding and drought

■ rapid population growth and urbanisation, the existence of a large rural population and recent industrialisation are creating an unsustainable demand for water (see Table 2.6)

■ the political division of some of its major drainage basins does not help water management, and disputes with neighbouring countries over water are ongoing

Figure 2.16 illustrates some of the pressures in the region.

Table 2.6 Current water-related projections

	1995	2025
Rural access to piped water (% of population)	11	47
Irrigated rice (million hectares)	18	22.5
Irrigated cereals (million hectares)	37.8	47.1
Rice yield (tonnes per hectare)	2.5	3.8
Ganges water used (km^3)	141	147
Domestic water used (km^3)	21	41

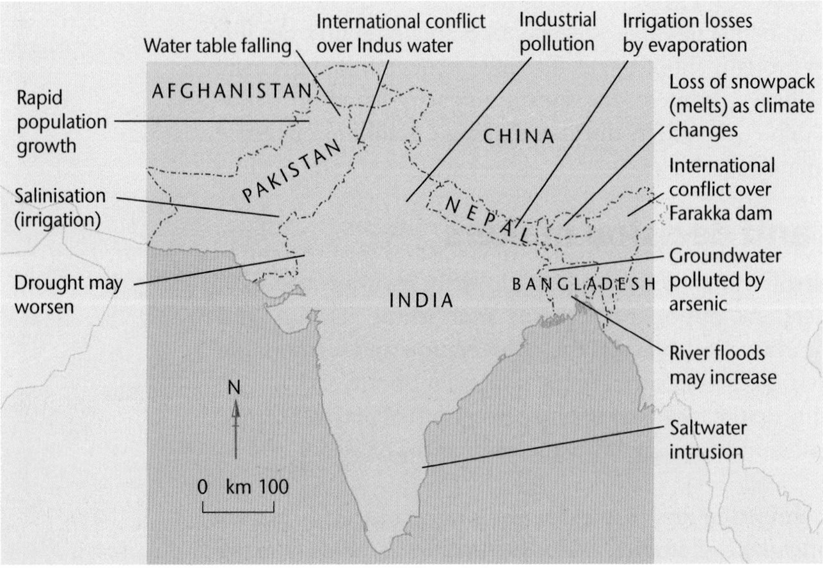

Figure 2.16
Human pressures in south Asia

Case study   The Ebro River in Spain

In July 2001 the Spanish government approved a scheme to divert water from the lower Ebro valley to supply cities, farmers and tourists in the parched southeast of the country (Figure 2.17). Three years later, the newly elected government cancelled the diversion project and replaced it with cheaper, more localised schemes, including desalination plants.

This decision was the outcome of a hotly contested debate between players in favour of and opposed to the diversion project.

■ *The case for.* Big international investors were concerned because they had marketed the south-east of Spain as the 'new Florida'. Vast tourist developments between Alicante and Almeria costing billions of euros, many based on new golf courses, were to be sited in areas supplied with Ebro water. People in Murcia and Almeria saw the Ebro scheme as the beginning of a new future, allowing the development of holiday homes, golf

resorts and Europe's biggest tourism complex at Cabo Cope. The head of the Murcia regional government claimed desalination was unproven and expensive. EU funding was available, but may not be in the future.

■ *The case against.* Environmentalists in the north protested that the diversion scheme was a misuse of a scarce resource and that it would have a drastic impact on the Ebro and its fragile delta. The Environment Minister claimed that the desalination plants would provide the same amount of water sooner and more cheaply. The new national government also promised to improve water recycling and make irrigation systems more efficient. Environmentalists claimed that the aquifers of the Ebro basin were already drying out because of over-extraction. They, and other critics, felt that the subsidies offered to farmers for irrigation encouraged the use of unsuitable land.

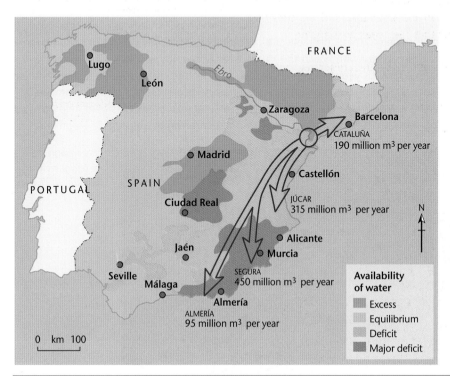

Figure 2.17
Diversion of the Ebro River

Responses to rising demands

Managing future water supplies will require action at a variety of levels, ranging from large-scale projects funded by governments down to changing consumers' attitudes to water use at a local level. Likely actions include:

➤ hard engineering projects to increase water storage and transfer, as for example in China's Three Gorges Project and its South–North Transfer Project (page 63)

➤ **restoration** of lost, mainly rural, water supplies, for example in the Aral Sea 'rescue' (see case study on page 60)

➤ water conservation in urban areas, involving such actions as rainwater harvesting and water recycling

The advantages and disadvantages of some of these actions have been discussed already. As demands for water rise tension is likely to increase. Major engineering projects will become too costly and their environmental impacts too great. Privatisation of water supply and sanitation services, together with the use of new **technology**, will change the economics of water use. People's concerns and priorities will change over time, as will their views of costs and benefits. There is the likelihood that water insecurity and water poverty will fuel major conflicts.

Case study The Three Gorges Project

China's Three Gorges Project along the Yangtze River, the world's largest hydroelectric scheme, is due to come fully on stream during 2009. Given its current reliance on coal-fired power stations (70%), China sees hydroelectric power as clean energy with which to support its rapid industrial growth. However, the social and environmental costs of using this source of energy are already apparent, well before the economic benefits are reaped.

Benefits

■ The 18,000 MW of water-generated electricity could save 50 million tonnes of coal each year.

■ The project will supply water to a region responsible for 22% of China's GDP.

■ Flood protection could save many lives and cut the financial losses created by flood damage.

■ Navigational improvements could help open up the interior region of China to development.

Photograph 2.5
An aerial view of the dam at Yichang

TopFoto

Benefits ($ billion)		Costs ($ billion)	
Economic growth	82	Construction	50
Power generation	31	Archaeological loss	15
Clean power – benefit of energy switch to HEP	17	Resettlement	12
Flood control	5	Organisational costs	5
Navigational improvements	3	Dam failure risks	3
		Downstream effects	3
		Fishery loss	0.7
		Tourism loss	0.4
		Land inundation	0.2
Total	138		89.3

Table 2.7
A possible cost–benefit analysis

Costs

- The dammed waters will drown 100,000 hectares of arable land, 13 cities, many smaller settlements and 1,500 factories.
- Some 1.9 million people will be displaced from their homes and lose their land.
- Dam failure, earthquakes, heavy rains and even terrorism pose serious safety risks.
- The ecological impacts on fisheries, biodiversity and habitats are considerable.
- Pollution will increase as abandoned mines and factories are flooded.
- Important archaeological and other heritage sites will be lost.
- The river has the world's fifth largest sediment load. Sediment could damage turbines and become trapped behind the dam, raising water levels and reducing soil fertility downstream.

Table 2.7 shows a cost–benefit analysis of the scheme. This gives a simple **benefit–cost ratio** of 138/89.3 = 1.55. This sort of value is considered a positive one in civil engineering proposals. Figure 2.18 suggests that after initial losses due to construction this project will return to profitability after 25 years.

The wider issues of China's South–North Transfer Project are considered in the final part of this chapter.

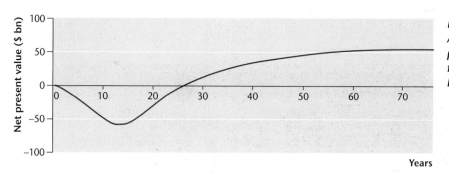

Figure 2.18
A cumulative net present value graph for the Three Gorges Project

Hard engineering

Most major dam construction in the future is likely to be limited to developing countries. Current global dam-building costs are between $22 and $31 billion each year. Half the world's large dams were built primarily for irrigation (contributing up to 16% of world food production). Hydroelectric power, flood control and domestic water supply are other benefits. But what are the real costs of such schemes? The World Commission on Dams report (November 2000) (to be found at www.dams.org) has some answers:

➤ *Economic costs.* The construction of large dams seems to overrun projected costs by an average of 50%. Water sales rarely cover the costs of water supply in developing countries. Even in the long term, multi-purpose schemes often fail in financial terms. The total global investment in dams between 1950 and 2000 was estimated at around $146 billion.

➤ *Ecological costs.* Dams, inter-basin transfers and water withdrawals for irrigation have fragmented 6% of the world's rivers, disrupting floodplain agriculture, fisheries, pasture, forestry and ecosystems. Many of these ecological impacts were not anticipated before the dams were built. Environmental impact assessments (EIAs) are relatively new.

➤ *Social costs.* During the construction phase local communities are starved of development and welfare investment. Communities and their livelihoods are severely disrupted. Construction of dams in India and China alone is reported to have displaced 58 million people in the last four decades.

River, lake and wetland restoration

A number of management strategies are being used to return water environments to their natural state. At a local scale, this can involve restoring meanders, replanting vegetation and using sustainable methods to manage watercourses for people and the environment. A good example is provided by the River Restoration Centre in the UK. It began its work on the rivers Cole and Skerne and has since tackled similar projects throughout the UK (for more information visit www.therrc.co.uk/rrc_case_studies_list.php).

On a larger scale, the US Army Corps of Engineers has begun restoring the Kissimmee River in Florida. When restoration is complete in 2011, more than 100 km^2 of floodplain ecosystem will be restored, including 8,000 ha of wetlands and 75 km of river channel. Restoration on an even grander scale is being planned in the Lower Danube basin, but perhaps the largest project currently being considered is the restoration of the Aral Sea.

Case study   Restoring the Aral Sea

Since the breaking up of the Soviet Union the northern part of the Aral Sea is in Kazakhstan and the southern part in Uzbekistan. In 2007 the Kazakhstan government secured a $126 million loan from the World Bank to help save the northern part of the Aral Sea (see the case study on page 45). It is an ambitious project aimed at reversing one of the world's worst environmental disasters.

The Kazakhstan government used an earlier $68 million loan to build a dam that has split the sea into two parts (Figure 2.19). Officials claim that the northern sea is already filling up, now that water from the Syr Darya is once again flowing into the Aral. The new loan will be used to build a second dam to bring the water back to the deserted port of Aralsk. Communities in the area are already feeling the impact. The fishermen are back in their boats, rain has returned and the future no longer looks hopeless. See http//:news.bbc.co.uk/2/hi/asia-pacific/7479760.stm

However, the actions taken so far have not solved the problem on the Uzbek side of the border. The southern part of the sea is still shrinking, and many experts believe it is too late to save it. The waters of the Amu Darya, which should be feeding into the sea, are desperately needed for growing cotton. The economy of Uzbekistan is heavily dependent on this cash crop. An additional problem with both this river and the Syr Darya is that their headwaters are controlled by other countries. Even worse is the fact that this is a part of the world where sensitive water developments could easily trigger conflict.

For a more radical proposal to solve the Aral Sea problem using major diversions of the Volga and Ob rivers, see www.ecoworld.com/home/articles2.cfm?tid=354

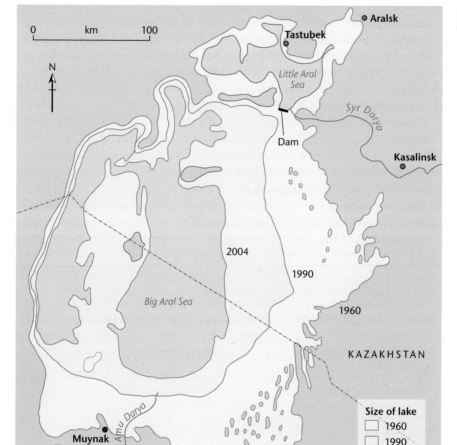

Figure 2.19 The shrinking Aral Sea

Water conservation

Water conservation involves reducing the amount of water used (i.e. demand) rather than trying to increase water supplies. In a world where the supply is finite, this is an important strategy.

Water conservation can be applied in a variety of situations. In agriculture, it can involve more efficient irrigation. In industry, water can be treated or recycled for further use. Domestically, water savings and water harvesting are beginning to move from a DIY basis to a more commercial footing.

In some places, efforts are being made to conserve wetlands, as part of a wider challenge to store water and develop a more eco-hydrological view of water resources and their management. At home, measures such as raising water prices and introducing water meters make consumers more careful about their consumption of water.

Effective use of water for food production is of crucial importance, and irrigation is a key area in this. In the past, flood irrigation has proved to be wasteful of water as it leads to high evaporation and seepage losses. Modern spray technology is more controllable, and the more advanced 'drip' irrigation, though expensive, is more effective. Fertigation, which uses small quantities of fertiliser with fine water sprinklers, has proved to be effective in Israel and the USA. For more information on the issues of water, agriculture, food security and poverty in developing countries, visit the FAO Water website 'Water at a glance' (www.fao.org/nr/water/art/2007/flash/glance/gallery1.html).

Conservation of industrial and domestic water is about recycling and re-use. Potable water is crucial for some purposes but grey water can be used for others. Water can be treated using filters or chemicals, but sewage and polluted water require strict disposal strategies. In and around the home, there is much that can be done to conserve water (Figure 2.20).

How many of these are part of your home action plan? Ten ways to save water...and money

In the bathroom

1 Fit a low-flush toilet, or put a water-filled plastic bottle in your toilet tank – saves 1,300 litres a month.
2 Shorten your showers by 1 or 2 minutes – saves up to 3,000 litres a month.
3 Don't waste water by waiting for hot water to reach the shower or sink. Catch the cold water in a container to use on your outside plants – saves 900 to 1,300 litres a month.
4 Turn off the water while brushing your teeth or shaving – saves 13 litres a day.

In the kitchen

5 When washing dishes by hand, don't leave the water running for rinsing – saves 900–2,000 litres a month.
6 Run only full loads in the washing machine and dishwasher – saves 1,300–1,800 litres a month.
7 Keep a bottle of drinking water in the fridge instead of running tap water to cool it for drinking – saves 900–1,300 litres a month.

Outside

8 Water the garden during the cool parts of the day.
9 Try water harvesting – catching rainwater from roofs in butts or ponds.
10 Drive your car onto the lawn to wash it: the rinse can help water the grass.

Figure 2.20 Water conservation at home

Water technology

The final part of this chapter focuses on the role of technology in managing and conserving future water supplies. Technology can help increase both water supply and access. Water transfer is now commonplace as civil engineering skills and construction technology continue to improve. The dams and canals of the Colorado Project, once the wonder of the world, are now dwarfed by developments in China and Brazil and on the Indian subcontinent. China's plans are both spectacular and controversial (see case study below).

Case study **China's South–North Transfer Project**

The south of China is rich in water resources but the north is not. To redistribute these resources and to even out the availability of water, a gigantic south–north water diversion project was begun in 2003. It is expected to take 50 years to complete and will cost $62 billion. The project involves building three canals which run 1,300 km across the eastern, middle and western parts of China and link the country's four major rivers: the Yangtze, Yellow, Huai and Han (Figure 2.21). The scale of engineering involved in this scheme is awesome. It will transfer a total of 44.8 billion m^3 of water per year. Central government will provide 60% of the cost of the scheme, with the rest coming from local authorities, which, in turn, will charge domestic and industrial

users. Water conservation, improved irrigation, pollution treatment and environmental protection are included in the plans.

Critics are concerned about the uncertainties and risks associated with the project. These include the likelihood of significant ecological and environmental impacts along the waterways, resettlement issues and worsening water quality. The pollution of the Yangtze River is already at alarming levels. Untreated industrial and city wastewater is being mixed unchecked with agricultural runoff containing pesticides and fertilisers. The Huai River is already severely polluted and the water of the Yellow River is undrinkable. Some experts fear an ecological disaster.

Will cut through the high Tibet plateau, linking the Mekong and Yangtze with the Yellow River. It is the most ambitious of the three canals

Will supply water for big cities like Beijing and Tianjin. Reservoir will be built to collect clean Yangtze water

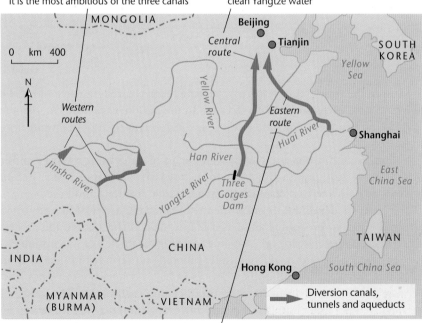

Wastewater treatment will be given top priority. Water taken from lower Yangtze basin where most polluting factories are

Figure 2.21 China's South–North Transfer Project

Desalination

The process of **desalination** (also known as desalinisation) is the removal of excess salt and other minerals from water. It produces freshwater suitable for human consumption or irrigation. For a long time, desalination was a technological success that failed to deliver in economic and environmental terms. However, as water costs and demand have increased, more countries are turning to desalination as part of their future water strategy (Figure 2.22).

Figure 2.22 The global growth of desalination

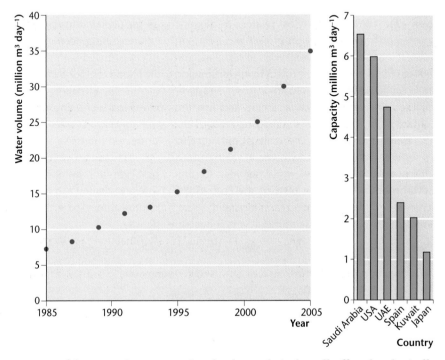

Many of the countries or states involved are relatively well off, technologically developed and increasingly water stressed. In the middle east, Saudi Arabia, the United Arab Emirates (UAE) and Kuwait use cheap energy to distil freshwater from seawater.

In the USA, California and Florida lead the list of states using reverse osmosis membrane technology to filter salt from brackish water and rivers. Recent newcomers to this technology include Spain, China, Australia and Israel.

The costs of desalination are difficult to calculate, as subsidies are often involved. Cheaper processing and larger plants make it cheaper but the process uses a lot of energy so rising oil costs are increasing the price. The water produced is of a high quality, although chemically different (in terms of minerals) from rainwater. Water intake and outflow processes have ecological effects, not least because concentrated brine is a by-product of desalination. The costs of desalinated water in California offer some interesting comparisons (see Table 2.8)

Remember that **water technology** includes not just desalination technologies, but also those associated with the diversion, transfer, storage, conservation and

Source	Lowest cost (cents per m³)
Desalination of seawater	95
Desalination of river/brackish water	60
Treated runoff	38
Untreated runoff	29
Subsidised water for agriculture	2

Table 2.8 Supply costs of water in California

restoration of water. The hope for a 'water-hungry' world free from water conflicts lies in a sensible, balanced and sustainable use of all these technologies.

Review questions

1 Examine the factors which can create water stress in some parts of the world.
2 Explain the links between (a) economic growth and water demand, and (b) water insecurity and water poverty.
3 Using examples, show how disputes over water can create tensions between countries.
4 Examine the risks associated with water transfer schemes.
5 Explain why there is so much uncertainty about future water demand and supply.
6 Evaluate the view that reducing water demand is better than trying to increase water supply.
7 Using examples, evaluate the economic and environmental benefits of different types of water technology.

Chapter 3

Biodiversity under threat

Biodiversity results from natural processes and so varies across the world. It is a key resource, providing valuable goods and services to people. It is increasingly recognised that human and ecological **wellbeing** are interlinked. Biodiversity and biological resources therefore need to be carefully managed. Threats are posed by the overexploitation of particular species, the introduction of exotic species into established ecosystems, and by the broader impacts of population growth, economic development and urbanisation.

Defining biodiversity

What is the nature and value of biodiversity?

By the end of this section you should:
➤ *be aware of the different ways of defining biodiversity*
➤ *understand the processes and factors influencing biodiversity*
➤ *recognise that biodiversity varies over the surface of the Earth*
➤ *appreciate the value of biodiversity as a provider of goods and services*

Defining biodiversity

Many ecologists define biodiversity as the totality of genes, species and ecosystems in a given area. One view is that it has three dimensions (Figure 3.1).

Figure 3.1 What is biodiversity?

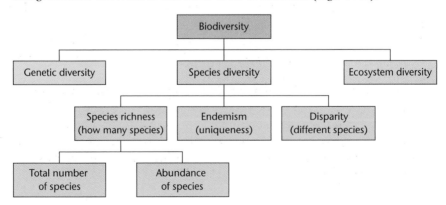

➤ **Genetic diversity** is the range of genes found within a particular species. Genetic diversity often determines the degree of resistance to pests and diseases. In agro-ecosystems, breeding new varieties of cereal, such as rice and wheat, has

Edexcel A2 Geography

led to **genetic erosion** and **genetic pollution**. These in turn have caused a narrowing of the genetic base and a general weakening of plant resistance to disease and climate change. This is likely to have a major adverse impact on future global **food security**.

➤ **Species diversity** refers to the variety of plant and animal species present in an ecosystem. Diversity is needed to enable the ecosystem to carry out its functions, such as carbon cycling, with maximum efficiency. Species diversity bolsters an ecosystem's resilience to withstand climate change. Removing species from the various **trophic levels** can have a huge impact on energy flows and nutrient cycling. Figure 3.1 shows that species diversity has several aspects, including the total number, abundance and richness of species, as well as their disparity. Another aspect is the rarity of some of the constituent species (**endemism**).

➤ **Ecosystem diversity** relates to the number of different ecosystems within a given area. This is partly controlled by physical conditions, particularly climate, geology, relief and soils. The ability of people to modify and eliminate ecosystems is a threat to ecosystem diversity.

Processes and factors influencing biodiversity

Numerous factors influence biodiversity, some at a global scale, others on a regional or local scale. Both physical and human factors are important, the latter increasingly so.

Global and continental factors

So-called primary ecological factors determine the broad framework within which other ecological factors operate.

➤ *Size of area*. Overall biodiversity increases with area, because large continuous **biomes** support a wider range of species and extensive boundaries encourage migration. Comparisons can only be made with similar ecosystems: for example, a large area of polar **habitat** contains far fewer species than a smaller area of rainforest or reef.

➤ *History and age*. In general, biodiversity is greatest in the oldest and least disturbed ecosystems, especially in the tropics, where there are few physical constraints on productivity.

➤ *Isolation*. Geographical isolation, particularly on remote islands, reduces the number of species but encourages endemism, as the remaining species develop in a distinctive way – for example, in the Galapagos islands or Madagascar.

➤ *Altitudinal range*. A large altitudinal range means a cross-section of different climates. The more climatic zones involved, the more diverse the habitats. The same principle applies to the ocean depths.

Regional factors

➤ *Productivity*. This is probably the most significant factor. High temperatures and humidity levels, rich supplies of nutrients and light for photosynthesis, and a lack of annual seasons all encourage high **primary productivity** and therefore abundant energy, as for example in rainforests and coral reefs. Conversely, factors limiting growth (cold and aridity) reduce the range and numbers of species.

➤ *Habitat architecture.* High primary productivity encourages the development of a complex trophic pyramid with many ecological niches. This system is capable of supporting high levels of biodiversity.

➤ *Habitat heterogeneity.* A varied physical environment will harbour greater biodiversity because it provides a wider range of habitats for a larger variety of species.

Local factors

➤ *Succession.* Biodiversity increases as species establish themselves, interact and subtly alter the environment. This is well illustrated by the successions that occur in sand dunes or a pond. In general, biodiversity increases over time with the immigration, establishment and development of species, leading to the creation of a succession or sequence.

➤ *Interaction between species.* This can lead to competition which in turn may drive certain species to extinction, particularly when exotic species are introduced.

➤ *Disturbance.* Major environmental disasters such as fires, flooding and storms can destroy biodiversity.

➤ *Dispersal and colonisation.* Individual species' dispersal and colonisation rates have an impact on biodiversity. High rates of efficiency enhance biodiversity.

Human factors

Undisturbed ecosystems provide a greater range of ecological niches and therefore higher levels of biodiversity. It is customary to think of human factors as entirely negative and threatening to biodiversity of ecosystems (Figure 3.2), but this is not always the case. Well-managed habitats combined with effective conservation strategies can have a positive impact on biodiversity. It is also possible for people to improve degraded and damaged ecosystems and so restore their biodiversity.

Figure 3.2 Drivers of change

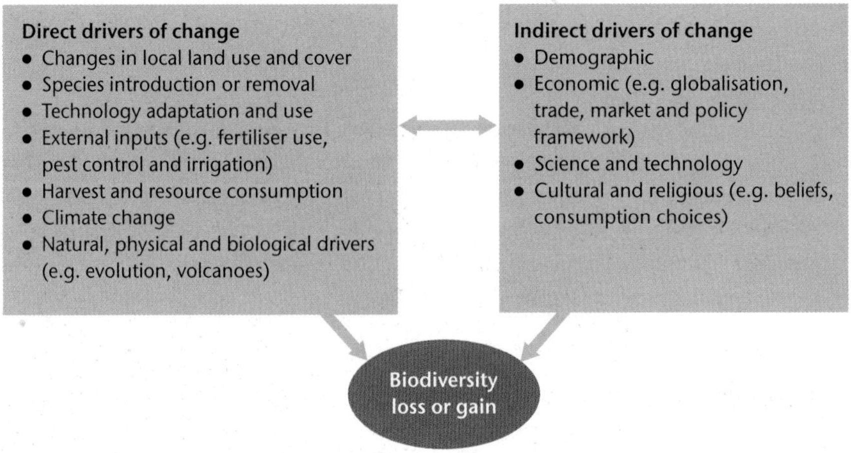

Direct drivers of change
- Changes in local land use and cover
- Species introduction or removal
- Technology adaptation and use
- External inputs (e.g. fertiliser use, pest control and irrigation)
- Harvest and resource consumption
- Climate change
- Natural, physical and biological drivers (e.g. evolution, volcanoes)

Indirect drivers of change
- Demographic
- Economic (e.g. globalisation, trade, market and policy framework)
- Science and technology
- Cultural and religious (e.g. beliefs, consumption choices)

Biodiversity loss or gain

The global distribution of biodiversity

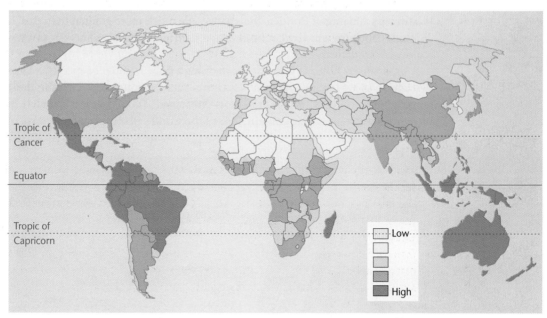

Tropic of Cancer

Equator

Tropic of Capricorn

Low

High

Figure 3.3 is a simplified map of biodiversity at a national level. Biodiversity is strongly correlated with latitude, the highest levels generally occurring in the tropical countries. These are nearly all developing countries, with the least resources to support sophisticated conservation strategies to tackle biodiversity loss. There is a gradual decrease in biodiversity towards higher latitudes. This spatial pattern is linked to the presence or absence of limiting factors controlling the amount of primary productivity. There are anomalies, such as the 'continental island' of Australia, which has high levels of endemism.

Figure 3.3 Global distribution of biodiversity

A ranking of countries according to their level of biodiversity puts Brazil at the top. This country has 55,000 species of flowering plant, 1,635 species of bird and nearly 400 species of mammal. It contains Amazonia, the largest rainforest in the world, which also has the highest biodiversity. Figure 3.4 illustrates this astonishing diversity in terms of what may be found in an area of 100 km^2.

60 species of amphibian

1,500 species of flowering plants

750 species of tree

400 types of birds

150 butterfly species

100 kinds of reptile

Figure 3.4 The biodiversity of 100 km^2 of rainforest

Hotspots

Figure 3.3 is a choropleth map and is misleading. It shows abrupt changes in biodiversity at national frontiers but changes are much more gradual than this. It also hides **hotspots** which occur both within individual countries and across international boundaries.

A **biodiversity hotspot** is an area containing a huge number of species, a large percentage of which are endemic. Hotspots have been described as 'the most remarkable places on Earth and the most threatened'. They cover less than 2% of the Earth's surface, yet they contain 44% of the world's plant species and 35% of its animal species.

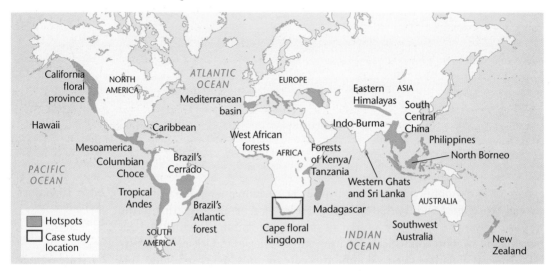

*Figure 3.5
Biodiversity
hotspots*

The world's 25 land-based top hotspots (Figure 3.5) are divided into three categories:

➤ *Continental hotspots.* These are the richest in terms of biodiversity. One example is the Cape floral region in South Africa (see case study).

➤ *Large island (or continental island) hotspots.* These harbour diverse and distinctive species, which can include **relict** fauna long extinct on the main continents.

➤ *Small island hotspots.* These are often low in species numbers, but contain a high proportion of endemics. Species on these islands are susceptible to extinction due to small populations, physical disturbances, human exploitation, and vulnerability to the introduction of alien species.

Recently marine hotspots have also been identified.

Case study — Fynbos, South Africa

Fynbos is the major vegetation type of the small botanical region in South Africa known as the Cape floral kingdom (Figure 3.6). Only five other floral kingdoms are recognised, and these cover huge areas, such as the whole of Australia and most of the northern hemisphere. The Cape floral kingdom is both the smallest and the richest, with the highest known concentration of plant species: 1,300 per

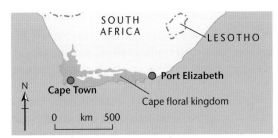

Figure 3.6 Location of the fynbos or Cape floral kingdom

10,000 km². Its nearest rival, the South American rainforest, has a concentration of only 400 species per 10,000 km². The region is home to over 7,700 plant species, 70% of which are endemics (i.e. confined to the Cape floral kingdom).

The word *fynbos* comes from the Dutch for fine-leaved plants. The woody plants have small, leathery leaves and include Cape reeds, *Proteas*, *Ericas* and members of seven plant families found nowhere else in the world. Fynbos plants are adapted to the Mediterranean climate of the Cape, particularly summer heat and drought. Unusual geology and soils, topography and a distinctive fire regime also play their part in the creation of this hotspot.

Conservation of the Cape floral kingdom has become a national priority. Current threats include:

- the spread of alien plants such as *Hakea* and Australian *Acacia*
- commercial forestry using non-native species such as European pines
- frequent bush fires (some attributed to arson)
- construction of housing estates around Cape Town
- intensification of agriculture

At present there are 12 nature reserves (51,000 ha) and four designated wilderness areas (123,000 ha) in the fynbos areas. No development (including the construction of power lines and roads) may be undertaken here without special approval.

The value of ecosystems

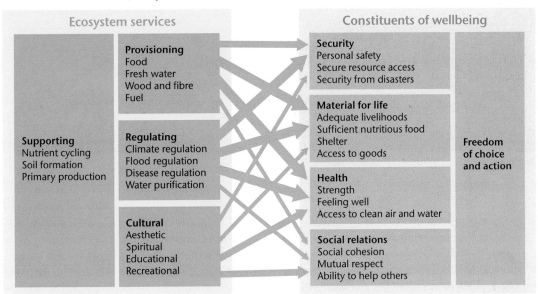

Figure 3.7 shows that the benefits people obtain from ecosystems have a significant impact on human wellbeing. The services provided by ecosystems are divided into four groups:

➤ **Provisioning services**, sometimes known as **goods**, are products derived

Figure 3.7 The relationship between ecosystem services and wellbeing

directly from the ecosystem, such as timber for fuel and building, or fruits, meat and fish for food. Some goods, such as fruit and nuts, are **sustainable**, but the exploitation of other goods, such as hardwood timber, can exhaust the supply. It is sometimes possible to place an economic value on goods, but difficult to do this for services.

➤ **Regulating services** are those which are vital to the functioning of the Earth's systems. For example, forests act as the 'green lungs' of the world and as important carbon sinks. Trees remove carbon dioxide from the atmosphere and release oxygen. They also protect against flooding and against soil erosion on slopes.

➤ **Cultural services** provided by ecosystems include the aesthetic and spiritual enjoyment that people draw from them and opportunities for recreation.

➤ **Supporting services** include processes such as nutrient cycling, soil formation and primary production that are vital to the wellbeing of the ecosystem itself. They also include the provision of wildlife habitats. These are *not* services that support people.

Case study   The value of coral reefs

Photograph 3.1

Coral reefs (Photograph 3.1) are of value in many ways.

■ *Biodiversity.* Although coral reefs occupy only 0.15% of the marine environment, they are home to over 25% of all known marine fish. They therefore rival rainforests in their biodiversity. Although 4,000 species of reef-living fish and 800 species of reef-building corals have been identified and catalogued, scientists think these are only a fraction of the total. Many species could become extinct without ever being discovered.

■ *Shoreline protection.* They 'buffer' coasts from wave erosion and the impact of storms at much lower cost than artificial defences. These natural self-repairing breakwaters will become even more critical as global warming causes sea levels to rise. Reefs have the ability to grow with rising sea levels, provided water conditions are 'healthy' for growth.

■ *Food.* Local people eat fish, conch, lobsters, sea urchins and sea cucumbers from reefs. Reefs also make a major contribution to commercial fishing. Globally, 20% of animal protein consumed by

Table 3.1 The value of coral reefs: tourism and recreation

	Direct spend (US$ million)	Indirect (boats, dive fees, etc.) (US$ million)	Local use (US$ million)	Total (US$ million)	% of GDP
Tobago	43	58–86	13–44	101–130	33%
St Lucia	91.6	68–102	52–109	160–194	24%

Table 3.2 The value of coral reefs: fisheries

	Direct spend (US$ million)	Indirect need for boats, nets (US$ million)	Total (US$ million)
Tobago	0.7–1.1	0.1–0.2	0.8–1.3
St Lucia	0.4–0.7	0.1–0.2	0.5–0.8

Table 3.3 The value of coral reefs: shoreline protection

	Protected length	% of coast	Potential avoidance of damage (US$ million)
Tobago	300 km	44%	18–33
St Lucia	610 km	50%	28–50

people comes from marine environments, with coral reefs providing 25% of the total fish catch. Population growth and the introduction of high-tech commercial fishing have put increasing pressure on reefs, especially in the far east, where reef fisheries feed 1 billion people.

■ *Medicine.* Algae and sponges yield bioactive compounds used by the pharmaceutical industry. Reef species support new treatments for bacterial infections, as well as some cancers, and corals are used for bone grafts.

■ *The aquarium trade.* Reefs contain resident animals, such as soft corals, sea anemones, sea horses and small tropical fish.

■ *Decorative objects.* Although international law regulates the use of black coral, the ornamental and jewellery trade still supports many indigenous craft industries.

■ *Building materials.* Coral reefs are mined for lime and stone in countries that lack alternative basic construction materials.

■ *Education and research.* They provide ideal habitats because of their shallow water and easy accessibility from the shore.

■ *Tourist magnets.* More than 100 of the 109 countries with reefs in their territorial waters have established tourist industries. Some Caribbean countries derive around half of their gross national product (GNP) from tourism.

In 2008, scientists attempted to put a monetary value on the contribution the coral reefs of Tobago and St Lucia make to the economies of these two small Caribbean islands. The results are summarised in Tables 3.1, 3.2 and 3.3.

The study concluded that the importance of coral reefs to local economies is complex and is often underestimated by government officials, coastal developers and the wider population. Decisions on land use, including the renewal of coastal mangrove plantations, the construction of roads and hotels and the improvement of agriculture, can all have significant negative effects on coastal water quality and therefore on coral reef health. Managing the pressures from fishing and tourism is a complex process with important consequences for reef condition (see www.wri.org/project/coral-reefs).

Biodiversity threats

What factors and processes threaten biodiversity?

By the end of this section you should:
➤ *be aware of the global pattern of threatened ecosystems and species*
➤ *understand the global and local factors which threaten biodiversity*
➤ *know how ecosystem processes can be disrupted by these threats*
➤ *appreciate the link between economic development and ecosystem destruction in a variety of eco-regions*

The distribution of threatened areas

Over geological time, species have become extinct as a result of climate change, random catastrophic events, predation, disease, and competition with other species. Geologists have identified five mass extinction events over the last 600 million years. Ecologists are concerned that there is the potential for another mass extinction event to occur, but this time the human population will play the key role. Audits of the Earth's ecosystems report an increasing rate of habitat destruction and species extinctions, and therefore widespread biodiversity loss.

There are various ways of auditing threatened ecosystems. None gives a complete picture, and they all produce differing results because they are measuring different things. The methods include:

➤ The *Economic Scorecard* produced for the World Resources Institute (WRI). This shows the ability of ecosystems to produce goods and services.
➤ The *Living Planet Index* developed by WWF. This monitors changes over time in the populations of representative animal species in forests, freshwater and marine ecosystems (see www.wwf.panda.org).

Figure 3.8
Status of terrestrial eco-regions

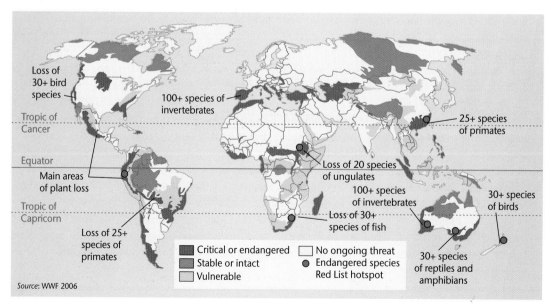

Edexcel A2 Geography

➤ The *ecological footprint*, a measure of the human impact on the planet.
➤ The *Red List of endangered species* compiled by the International Union for Conservation of Nature (IUCN). This has identified over 16,000 plant and animal species in danger of extinction.
➤ The *Millennium Ecosystem Assessment* (MEA), a multi-scale assessment commissioned by the UN (see www.millenniumassessment.org).

Figure 3.8 summarises findings derived by the above methods to show the status of **terrestrial eco-regions**. These are large areas of land containing geographically distinct assemblies of species, natural communities and habitats. Most significant is the distribution of the most threatened eco-regions — those classified as 'critical or endangered'. If you refer back to Figure 3.5 you will notice that many of the hotspots fall into this category. The broad latitudinal spread of these suggests that ecosystems of a wide diversity are involved. The 'vulnerable' category seems to account for roughly the same area as the 'critical and endangered'. It too shows a wide latitudinal spread. Further threats to these 'vulnerable' eco-regions could easily push them into the ranks of the 'critical and endangered'.

Figure 3.9 looks at the world's biomes and the losses they have suffered (and are expected to suffer) through being converted to economic land use. In 1990, the most converted and therefore most threatened biomes were in the temperate zone (Mediterranean forests, woodland and scrub; temperate forest, steppe and woodland; temperate broadleaf and mixed forests). This reflects the fact that these parts of the globe have a long history of human settlement and are the most

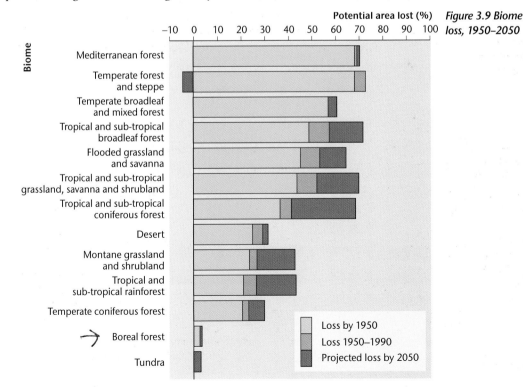

Figure 3.9 Biome loss, 1950–2050

economically developed. However, the projected losses by 2050 indicate that the threat is shifting to the tropics. This may be because of high rates of population growth and rising levels of resource exploitation (often for the benefit of other parts of the world). The very high latitude biomes (boreal forests and tundra) appear relatively unthreatened – but for how much longer?

Factors that threaten biodiversity

The WRI has identified factors that threaten biodiversity:

➤ An unsustainably high rate of human population growth and natural resource consumption.
➤ Inequality in the ownership, management and flow of benefits which threatens the livelihoods of the world's poorest people.
➤ The concentration of agriculture, forestry and fishing on a narrowing spectrum of products.
➤ Economic systems developed by governments and businesses that fail to value the environment and its resources.
➤ Legal and institutional systems that promote unsustainable exploitation at the expense of more sustainable strategies.
➤ Lack of knowledge and understanding in the management and conservation of biodiversity.

Global factors

Some factors have such a major and widespread impact that they are regarded as *global* threats to biodiversity (Figure 3.10).

Figure 3.10 The main direct drivers of change in biodiversity

Ecosystem	Driver Habitat change	Climate change	Invasive species	Over-exploitation	Pollution (nitrogen, phosphorus)	
Boreal forest	1	1	1	1	2	6
Temperate forest	3	1	1	2	2	9
Tropical forest	4	1	1	3	1	10
Temperate grassland	4	1	2	1	4	12
Mediterranean scrubland	3	1	3	2	1	10
Tropical grassland and savanna	3	2	1	4	2	12
Desert	1	2	2	1	1	7
Inland water	4	1	3	2	4	14
Coastal water	4	2	3	3	4	16
Marine	2	1	1	4	1	9
Island	3	1	4	3	1	12
Mountain	3	2	1	1	1	8
Polar	1	3	1	2	2	9
Total	36	19	24	29	26	

Example: Invasive species have high impact on island ecosystems and will continue to do so

Impact on biodiversity over the last century
1 Low
2 Moderate
3 High
4 Very high

Current trends
Decreasing impact
Continuing impact at current level
Increasing impact
Rapid increase of impact

Source: MEA

Climate change

The *Stern Review* on the economics of climate change (2005) argues that climate change is likely to occur too rapidly for many species to adapt. The global warming experienced during the last quarter of the twentieth century has already given a hint of ecosystem impacts. Species have been moving polewards by an average of 6 km per decade. **Phenological** studies show that seasonal events such as flowering, egg laying and fruiting have been advancing by several days each decade. Coral bleaching resulting from warming oceans has increased since the 1980s. This, combined with ocean acidification caused by rising levels of carbon dioxide in the oceans, poses a threat to the wellbeing of many coral reefs.

Of course, the degree to which biodiversity is threatened by climate change will depend on the scale and rate of the increase in global temperatures. Table 3.4 assesses the impacts of three different temperature rises.

Temperature rise	Impacts
1°C	Ten per cent of land species will face extinction. Coral-reef bleaching will be more frequent, especially in the southern Indian Ocean, Great Barrier Reef and Caribbean. Species-rich tropical mountain habitats are likely to lose many species
2°C	Between 15% and 40% of land species could face extinction, with most major species groups affected, including 25–60% of mammals in South Africa and 15–25% of butterflies in Australia. Coral reefs are expected to bleach annually in many areas. Almost 5% of the low tundra and 25% of coniferous forest could be lost
3°C	Anything between 20% and 50% of land species could face extinction. Massive losses in biodiversity expected in hotspots. Large areas of coastal wetlands will be lost as a result of rising sea levels. Mangroves will be flooded, removing a natural coastal defence. Coral reefs will die. Strong drying in the tropics could lead to destruction of rainforests

Table 3.4 Global temperature rises and their impacts on biodiversity

Source: Stern Review

As for the speed of climate change, recent research suggests that even a rise of 0.05 to 0.1°C per decade is more than most species would be able to withstand, as they would not be able to migrate polewards fast enough. The pace would certainly be too great for the evolutionary process of **in situ** adaptation.

Global warming will lead not only to increases in temperature and changes in rainfall but also to more damaging and frequent extreme weather events, such as floods, storms and droughts. It will also have indirect effects through sea-level rises and increased risks from pests and diseases. Vulnerable ecosystems, such as cloud forests on tropical mountain tops and the tundra, are likely to disappear almost completely even at quite modest levels of warming.

The threat of climate change and its potential impacts on biodiversity are made worse by the fact that human pressures, such as deforestation, pollution and over-exploitation, have already put many species on the verge of extinction. It will need only the smallest change in climate to tip them over the brink.

Case study: The impacts of global warming on biodiversity in the Arctic

The impacts of global warming on fragile arctic ecosystems include the following:

- There will be a localised shifting of ecosystems in a poleward direction. Coniferous forests will expand into the tundra zone, which in turn will spread into fragmented areas of polar desert.
- The tundra, with its rare arctic plants, will shrink as rising sea levels drown coastal areas.
- Increased forest fires and insect infestations are expected to ravage coniferous forests and reduce both biomass and biodiversity.
- Marine life will respond to warmer sea temperatures and reduced ice cover. Improved food supplies will mean bigger fish stocks and the appearance of new species.

- Fragile food webs could be easily damaged, leading to the loss of tundra mosses and lichens that provide the main food for animals such as reindeer (caribou). Declining deer numbers will affect species that hunt them, such as wolves, or scavenge on them, such as arctic foxes.

Changes in arctic ecosystems will have global impacts because of the links between the Arctic and ecosystems much further south. Many migrant bird species depend on summer feeding and breeding grounds in the Arctic. In the future migrant birds will have to fly further north and spend more time searching for suitable breeding and feeding areas. (See www.acia.uaf.edu for further research.)

Deforestation

The clearance of forest cover results in loss of biodiversity and resources for indigenous populations (Figure 3.10), with knock-on effects on the food web and nutrient cycling. There are also wider environmental impacts, as the removal of forest cover leads to increased soil erosion and flooding.

Pollution

Pollution takes many forms, but the most significant in terms of reducing biodiversity are:

- the acidification of oceans and acid precipitation on land
- nitrate and phosphate pollution in lakes and coastal waters
- airborne pollution, for example from the use of DDT
- ozone depletion by CFCs

Local factors

An enormous range of threats can affect ecosystems at a *local* scale. Their relative importance varies from place to place and over time.

Fire was once widely used in Europe and North America to clear forests for settlement and development, but today there is fierce opposition when it is used to clear rainforest for cattle grazing and soya bean production. Fire is an essential part of slash and burn farming practices, but large-scale burning causes a loss of biodiversity. Controlled fire, however, is used as a management tool on grazing land, for example in maintaining heather on the grouse moors of Scotland or managing ecosystems in National Parks to ensure succession. Arson poses a major threat, causing hazardous fires capable of destroying rare ecosystems and species.

Habitat change, for example developing natural habitats for agriculture, mineral working or urban growth, inevitably leads to loss of biodiversity (Figure 3.10).

Modern large-scale agriculture reduces biodiversity, but the impacts can be reduced by creating features such as hedgerows, ponds, copses and shelter belts. Overexploitation, such as overfishing in the North Sea, can easily unbalance food webs and lead to species extinctions.

Recreational use is often made of areas where ecosystems are fragile — plants are vulnerable to trampling and animals to disturbance. Its impact depends on the natural carrying capacity, the level of use and how recreational use is managed. There are many recorded examples of rapidly expanding recreation and tourist use damaging ecosystems in near-pristine environments such as Antarctica or the Galapagos. *Mineral exploitation* can be particularly damaging and disruptive, with open-cast extraction leaving huge holes and toxic spoil heaps scarring the landscape.

Disruption of ecosystem processes

Two processes are fundamental to ecosystem functioning:

➤ **Energy flows.** Primary producers (green plants) at trophic level 1 convert sunlight into energy by photosynthesis. As energy is lost through respiration at each stage of the process, the amount of **biomass** at each trophic level decreases (Figure 3.11). A food chain, or more usually a more complex food web, exists

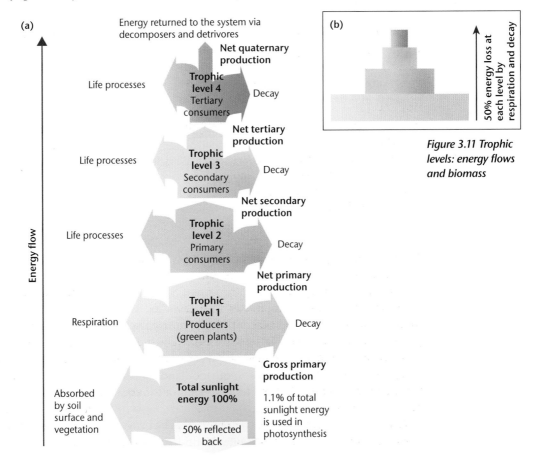

Figure 3.11 Trophic levels: energy flows and biomass

between the trophic levels. For example, caterpillars eat leaves, small birds eat caterpillars and birds of prey catch small birds. People catch or harvest various tertiary consumers (Figure 3.11).

➤ **Nutrient cycling.** This is the circulation of chemical elements from the environment to organisms and back again to the environment (Figure 3.12). Nutrients are stored in three parts of the ecosystem: in the soil, in the living biomass and in surface litter. They cycle between them via three main pathways. In the uptake or growth pathway, compounds of nitrogen, phosphorous, potassium etc are taken from the soil by plants. As plants or animals die, they contribute nutrients to the litter store via the fallout pathway. The decay pathway is formed by decomposition of litter to humus. Note that this is an open cycle, as nutrients can be added or removed by processes such as rock weathering or leaching. People can have an impact on the cycle by adding nutrients via fertilisers, by reducing the biomass through overharvesting and **deforestation**, and by degrading the soil. Once deprived of nutrients, soils are vulnerable to erosion.

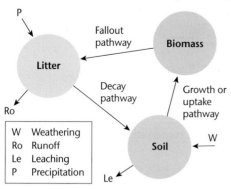

Figure 3.12 Nutrient flows

Movement of species

As the world becomes more globally connected, the movement of species from one part of the world to another, whether deliberately or by accident, poses an increasingly serious threat to ecosystems. **Alien or exotic species** may become established at any trophic level in the ecosystem. Such species usually share the following features:

➤ They have enhanced survival rates, because they are more efficient competitors than native species.
➤ As alien species, they lack any native predator.
➤ They are not susceptible to indigenous diseases.

As a result, introduced species can be difficult to control. They are easily established and spread fast. Many have harmful impacts on existing food webs as they take over.

The UK has some notable examples of *deliberate* introductions:

➤ Game species such as pheasants and rainbow trout, mainly for sporting purposes.
➤ Plant species for scenic purposes. The classic example is the rhododendron, brought from the Indian subcontinent in the eighteenth century to add colour to great English estates. Rhododendrons now flourish in many parts of the UK, but to such an extent that they hinder the development of natural vegetation and the regeneration of woodland. In National Parks and nature reserves there are now programmes to eradicate them and give the native flora a chance to flourish.
➤ Species brought in for a particular purpose. The hedgehog was imported from the Scottish mainland to the Outer Hebrides to deal with a plague of garden

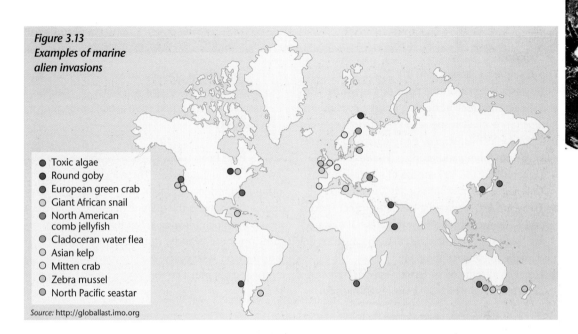

Figure 3.13
Examples of marine alien invasions

- Toxic algae
- Round goby
- European green crab
- Giant African snail
- North American comb jellyfish
- Cladoceran water flea
- Asian kelp
- Mitten crab
- Zebra mussel
- North Pacific seastar

Source: http://globallast.imo.org

slugs. Unfortunately, the hedgehogs developed a taste for the eggs of ground-nesting birds, populations of which dwindled at an alarming rate. The important point here is that although the hedgehog is a native species in mainland Britain, it did not colonise the Hebrides after the last ice age.

There are many more examples of *accidental* introductions which have profoundly host ecosystems.

➤ Some alien species arrive by ship (Figure 3.13). For example, the zebra mussel arrived in North America from the Caspian Sea in ships' ballast water or possibly clinging to the sides of ships. With the completion of the St Lawrence Seaway, ocean-going ships brought these mussels to the Great Lakes. In the absence of predators, they multiplied in Lake Erie to a staggering 70,000 individuals per m² and reduced phytoplankton by 80%. This allowed greater light penetration and led to algal blooms, which lower the quality of the lake water. As these mussels grow on each other and other shells such as clams, they block water intakes and outlets, causing power stations to shut down for cleaning.

➤ Air transport was responsible for introducing snakes to the Pacific Island of Guam, with disastrous results for the food web.

➤ Well-intentioned introductions can go wrong. The North American ruddy duck was brought to Slimbridge (Gloucestershire) as part of an international wildfowl collection. Some birds escaped and colonised ponds and lakes, not just in Britain but also on mainland Europe. This was not worrying until it was discovered that the ruddy duck was beginning to interbreed with one of Europe's endangered species, the white-headed duck. Since then, there has been a programme to eliminate this highly successful 'foreigner' which has caused outrage.

Case study   **Invasive species in the Galapagos**

The Galapagos Islands off the coast of Ecuador qualify as a hotspot on the basis of their endemism and the severe threat facing their unique ecosystems. A huge range of alien species were introduced from the Ecuadorian mainland by people seeking to make a living from fishing and tourism (Figure 3.14).

■ Up to 60% of the 180 species of endemic plant in Galapagos are now considered 'threatened'.

■ There are 490 recorded introduced insect species and 43 species of other invertebrates. Of these, 55 are 'high risk' with the potential to cause severe damage to native biodiversity.

■ Eighteen introduced vertebrate species have been detected, 13 of which are considered harmful.

■ New vertebrate species arrive every year, and aggressive invasive species, such as mainland snake predators, could soon establish themselves in Galapagos.

Actions have been taken to preserve the unique bio-diversity of the Galapagos. These include eradicating introduced rodents and feral cats, rounding up stray dogs and removing the quinine tree, one of the most serious alien plant invaders. But there are other pressures on these islands, not least the thousands of tourists who visit every year to marvel at what so impressed Charles Darwin when he first visited in 1835.

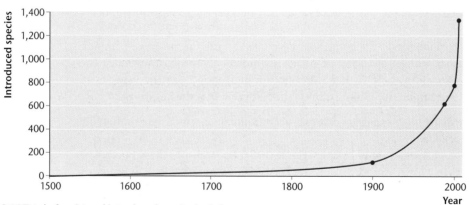

Figure 3.14 Total of registered introduced species in Galapagos

Nutrient overload

Nutrient loading has a significant impact on ecosystem processes. Excess nutrients in the soil, usually in the form of nitrates and phosphates, are washed into lakes and rivers. This is a natural process, but it has been increased by human activity, particularly the use of chemical fertilisers and detergents, the release of farmyard slurry and the removal of hedgerows, which causes increased soil erosion. Many lakes are now overloaded with nutrients.

The result of nutrient loading is **eutrophication**. Initially, the extra nutrients reaching ponds and lakes lead to increased growth of water plants. Microscopic plants proliferate, causing algal blooms. These block out light in the lower depths, reducing the number of large plants. Zooplankton (microscopic animals) are primary consumers and feed on the algae, but as the large plants die, fish take to eating more and more of the zooplankton. Algae consumption declines. Dead algae pile up and are gradually broken down by bacteria, but this uses up the oxygen

in the water. Falling oxygen levels lead to the death of both plants and animals, causing the food chain to collapse and the pond or lake to become almost lifeless.

This process is well documented in the Norfolk Broads, but is happening in over three-quarters of the world's lakes. Eutrophication can have a number of knock-on effects. It can lead to contaminated drinking water. Some algal blooms are harmful and can contaminate fish and shellfish and lead to gastrointestinal illness for humans. Eutrophication in east African lakes is threatening colonies of flamingos and other wetland birds.

Economic development and ecosystem degradation

It is important to distinguish the **destruction** of an area of an ecosystem (total clearance) from **degradation** (loss of quality). Usually the two are linked, but some large eco-regions have not decreased in extent but have become very degraded.

This is the case in many savanna areas of Africa and also in its rainforests, where secondary forest mosaic has replaced pristine forest. Figure 3.15 summarises the possible relationship between ecosystem state and economic development.

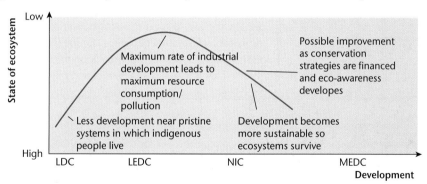

Figure 3.15 Possible relationship between ecosystem state and economic development

The reality is more complex, as so much depends on the players and pressures. This is reflected in the three case studies here, all of which are drawn from countries in early stages of development with a need for economic growth. Each describes a different type of environment – a pristine area (Udzungwa Mountains National Park, Tanzania), a degraded area (Masai Mara game reserve, Kenya) and a protected area (St Lucia in the Caribbean).

 Case study — **Udzungwa Mountains National Park: a pristine area**

While most forests in the east African mountains have experienced severe degradation, Udzungwa Mountains National Park has remained pristine, with a remarkable biodiversity (276 tree species, 50 endemic, and 55 recorded species of mammal, including leopards, lions, baboons and elephants) (Figure 3.16). It is also rich in birds and has a huge floral variety. It provides local villages with watershed protection, medicines and food. Villagers in the park are allowed limited and highly controlled

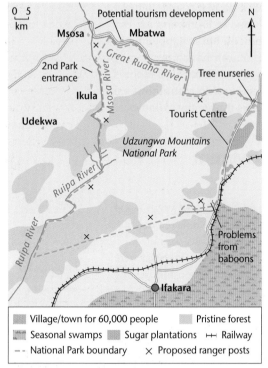

Village/town for 60,000 people ⬛ Pristine forest
Seasonal swamps ⬛ Sugar plantations ⊢⊣ Railway
-- National Park boundary ✕ Proposed ranger posts

Figure 3.16 Map of Udzungwa Mountains National Park

access for worship; collecting fuelwood and hunting have been prohibited. Pressures on the park include rapid population growth fuelled by immigration, with many people poor and short of land and employment.

The Tanzanian National Park authorities recognised at an early stage that they had to get the local people involved in sustainable bottom-up strategies. Crucial projects involved setting up tree nurseries and developing fuel-efficient stoves and rice husk technology to solve the fuelwood crisis. Agricultural diversification projects such as bee-keeping, poultry and vegetable farming, and cultivation of medicinal plants have provided much-needed employment. Non-farm projects have included establishing micro-business, promoting ecotourism and improving health and education services.

The Udzungwa experience shows that given the difficulty of policing a vast area with a skeletal ranger service, the way to succeed in conservation is to foster sustainable development projects for the local people so that they can see the potential long-term benefits. (For further research, visit www.panda.org.)

Case study **The Masai Mara game reserve: a degraded area**

This reserve, which belongs to the Masai people (Photograph 3.2), experienced a breakdown in management which led to a decline in the general state of its grassland ecosystems. The park fees paid by tourists were meant to go towards protecting the reserve and providing social services and support for local tribesmen living on adjacent land. Unfortunately, little of the money reached its intended destination. The park rangers were not properly paid and lacked basic equipment such as CB radio and four-wheel drive vehicles. They could do little to stop widespread and illegal hunting of the game – such as giraffes, zebras and antelopes – that tourists wanted to see.

In June 2008 the local councils that ran the park were replaced by a private organisation called Mara Conservation. A gift of $300,000 from two foreign donors purchased four new four-wheel drive

Photograph 3.2 Masai warrior

vehicles, repaired many of the roads and paid the rangers. The organisation will run on a non-profit basis but use 50% of the revenue to build roads and finance anti-poaching patrols, and ensure that the remaining 50% of revenue filters through to the local Masai tribes.

The support of the Masai people is crucial to the future of this reserve, as it requires them to give up some of the best cattle-grazing land in east Africa for the benefit of wildlife. It is difficult for them to see a future in tourism rather than cattle-rearing. One possible step might be to follow the experience of South Africa, Botswana and Zimbabwe and opt for 'game utilisation' (see the CAMPFIRE case study, page 88). This allowed for a small, tightly controlled amount of lucrative big-game hunting. Provided it can be undertaken at a sustainable level, it might help to stop the further degradation of the park's ecosystems.

Case study   Soufrière Marine Management Area (SMMA): protected

This management area is focused around the coastal town of Soufrière on the Caribbean island of St Lucia. Offshore there are magnificent coral reefs and much marine biodiversity. The people of Soufrière work in agriculture, fishing or tourism. The tension between the last two activities led to the creation of the SMMA in 1995. A range of environmental problems began get out of hand:

■ degradation of coastal water quality, with direct impacts on human health and the well-being of the reef ecosystem
■ depletion of near-shore fish resources
■ loss of the economic, scientific and recreational potential of coral reefs, particularly for diving tourism
■ degradation of beach landscapes and environmental quality by hotel developments
■ pollution from rubbish disposal in ravines or into the sea
■ yacht anchor damage to reefs
■ sedimentation of the reefs caused by runoff from rivers and storm damage

There were five main stakeholder conflicts:

■ between commercial dive operators and fishermen over the use of the coral reefs
■ between yachts and fishermen because of anchoring in fishing areas
■ between the local community and hoteliers over access to beaches
■ between fishermen and local and national authorities over the location of a jetty in a fishing priority area
■ between fishermen and hoteliers over the use of the beaches for commercial fishing or recreational, tourism-oriented activities

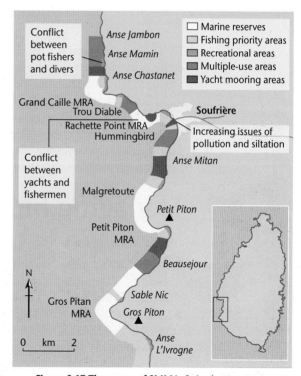

Figure 3.17 The zones of SMMA, St Lucia

After a number of consultations with all stakeholders, including government organisations, non-governmental organisations and users of the areas, the

SMMA was divided into five zones (Figure 3.16):

- marine reserves
- fishing priority areas
- yacht mooring areas
- recreational areas
- multiple-use areas

The SMMA has received funding from a number of agencies including the Caribbean Conservation Association, the ENCORE project and the French government. It is currently self-financing, although external funding occasionally finances additional projects.

The achievements of the SMMA are considerable:

- reduction of the conflicts among users
- increase in fish biomass within marine reserves
- increase in fish biodiversity (increased number of fish species observed per count in annual censuses)
- a self-financing management area
- a management team involving the continued participation of all stakeholders

Soufrière offers a good example of how an integrated approach to bottom-up management of natural resources has worked. It shows that if everyone feels they have been consulted and their interests protected, the chances of a successful outcome are considerable.

The Udzungwa, Masai Mara and SMMA case studies illustrate the inherent tension between pursuing economic development and protecting the biodiversity of environments. On the one hand, it is recognised that poor local people have a right to expect improvements in their standards of living and wellbeing. Equally, the wider world increasingly expects these people to sacrifice their needs in the cause of conserving biodiversity. Adopting a bottom-up approach that involves local people and promises them some practical rewards from playing their part in conservation programmes could help relax this tension.

Managing biodiversity

Can the threats to biodiversity be successfully managed?

By the end of this section you should:
- ➤ *understand the concept of sustainable yield and the role of sustainable management in determining the 'safe' use of ecosystems*
- ➤ *appreciate the role of different players and the extent to which their conflicting views of ecosystem management can be reconciled*
- ➤ *be aware of the spectrum of strategies and policies that are available to conserve biodiversity*
- ➤ *have explored a range of futures for biodiversity*

The concept of sustainable yield

Sustainable yield is a key part of sustainable management of ecosystems. It represents the 'safe' level of harvest that can be hunted/caught/utilised without harming the individual ecosystem (Figure 3.18).

Two measures are used to assess this yield:
- ➤ *Maximum sustainable yield (MSY)* is the greatest harvest that can be taken indefinitely while leaving the ecosystem intact. Harvesting wild plants, animals or

fish is part of the subsistence lifestyle of indigenous people and is usually sustainable. Overharvesting or overexploitation tend to be the result of commercial rather than subsistence activity. When activities such as shooting elephants for ivory, harvesting shellfish and logging in natural forests exceed maximum sustainable yields, the target species and their habitats become threatened.

➤ *Optimum sustained yield (OSY)* is the best compromise achievable in the light of all the economic and social considerations. This level of yield, unlike the MSY, will not destroy the aesthetic or recreational value of the ecosystem and will therefore allow multiple use for the maximum benefit to the community.

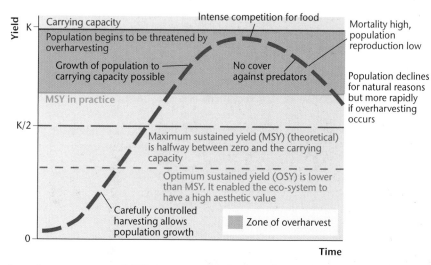

Figure 3.18
The concept of sustainable yield

In order to manage wildlife, or more usually fisheries, mathematical models have been developed to estimate the **carrying capacity**. This is the maximum human population that can exist in equilibrium with the available resources (food, nutrients etc.) The major problem is that carrying capacity varies seasonally, and over time may be reduced by climate change.

Case study | **Sustainable yield management in Southern Ocean fisheries**

The Southern Ocean encircles Antarctica and accounts for 10% of the world's ocean. Thanks to the Antarctic Treaty System (1961), the fisheries are now sustainably managed. Before this, the fishing grounds were overharvested by fleets of Soviet trawlers. This led to the extinction of several species of fin fish. The model used to calculate fishing yield is one of the most sophisticated because of its three-pronged approach:

■ The *single species approach* sets limits for harvesting individual species that are indefinitely sustainable.

■ The *ecosystem approach* involves considering harvested species both on their own and in relation to dependent species and the whole environment.

■ The *precautionary principle* aims to model the consequences of any planned expansion of catches before it is permitted.

See www.antarctica.ac.uk for further details.

The CAMPFIRE case study shows how the concept of sustainable yield can be developed to provide sustainable livelihoods for local people.

Case study — CAMPFIRE, Zimbabwe

Under British colonial rule large sections of the indigenous population in Zimbabwe were forced to live in communal areas known as tribal trust lands. The Communal Areas Management Programme for Indigenous Resources (CAMPFIRE) project was a pioneering scheme developed in the late 1980s, aimed at the long-term development, management and sustainable use of natural resources in each communal area. This was achieved by placing responsibility with local people and allowing communities to benefit directly from exploitation of the available resources such as wildlife. Because they were bottom-up, CAMPFIRE schemes varied locally, with administrative back-up and advice provided by the Zimbabwe Department of National Parks and Wildlife Management.

Details of wildlife species involved and how they were used (meat, live capture for sale, big-game hunting, photographic safari, fishing, etc.) varied. Many schemes made money from big-game hunting at sustainable yield levels, and this money was fed back into the community for the common good. This was controversial as environmentalists did not believe that hunting endangered species was a good way to protect them. The economic collapse of Zimbabwe undermined the scheme. Loss of staff, lack of funding, poaching, local hunger and land takeovers by 'war veterans' all contributed to its collapse.

Corel

Photograph 3.3 Under the CAMPFIRE scheme local communities were able to exploit wildlife

The key players

A range of **players** have a role in managing biodiversity (see Figure 3.19). They can operate at a variety of scales, with local players being most closely involved because of their likely dependency on biodiversity for their wellbeing. However, many people argue that the global or international players wield the greatest power. Some groups are committed to conservation, while others rely on exploiting the resource, although not always for the same purposes. Conflicts are thus inevitable.

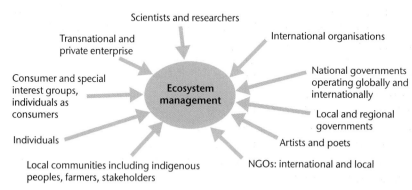

Figure 3.19 The range of players with an interest in ecosystem management

Global

On a global scale, countries get together to develop wildlife conservation treaties. There are now some 150 such treaties. They normally require an agreed number of country signatures before they become international law. International treaties are usually about funding conservation work, designating protected areas and regulating trade in endangered species. The five most influential international treaties in effect today but agreed before the Convention on Biological Diversity was established in 1992 are as follows:

➤ *The Ramsar Convention* to conserve wetlands was signed in Ramsar (Iran) in 1971. It is now adopted by 147 countries.

➤ *The World Heritage Convention* to designate and protect outstanding cultural and natural sites was signed in 1972 and is adopted by over 180 countries.

➤ *The Convention on International Trade in Endangered Species (CITES)* was signed in 1973 and is adopted by 166 countries. It has controlled trade in a range of species and their products.

➤ *The Convention on the Conservation of Migratory Species of Wild Animals* was signed in 1979, and by 2005 had been adopted by 90 countries to prevent shooting of birds in passage.

➤ *The UN Convention on the Law of the Sea (UNCLOS)* has been ratified by 148 countries.

Transnational corporations also operate on a global scale. They can determine which goods and services are produced and how (whether by environmentally friendly or detrimental methods). Increasingly they are favouring green strategies for reasons such as public image and long-term benefit. They are providing direct investment for a range of climate 'proofing' and renewable energy projects as well as for traditional exploitation. They also drive innovation and technology change by the process of technology transfer, sometimes with positive effects but more usually to the detriment of ecosystems.

There is a range of international institutions that are significant players on a global scale. They include UN agencies, the World Bank, the World Trade Organization and bodies such as ITTO (the International Tropical Timber Organization), a cartel of tropical timber producers and consumer countries which has developed mechanisms for forest conservation. Some of their activities can be controversial, as many are top-down in nature, and they initially favoured large, short-term projects, rather than ones that met long-term local needs in developing countries.

Non-governmental organisations (NGOs) play a vital role in biodiversity conservation. Some, like WWF and Greenpeace International, operate on a global scale: WWF, for example, operates in more than 100 countries. Its mission is to stop degradation of the planet's natural environment and build a future in which people live in harmony with nature. Others are smaller, one-issue organisations such as FAN (a Bolivian conservation NGO), whose mission is to conserve biodiversity by protecting sustainable and equitable use of natural resources in eastern Bolivia.

NGOs vary in their methods of action and do not always agree. Greenpeace captures public attention by taking direct action on conservation issues such as illegal whaling. It achieves wide media coverage and lobbies governments. Not all conservationists favour the direct action of Greenpeace ships, which intercept Japanese whalers.

National

On a national scale, governments play a vital role in the management of biodiversity, acting as both regulators and facilitators. In terms of regulation, they establish and enforce laws to conserve genetic biodiversity, protect various areas and species and regulate damaging activities such as using polluting agrochemicals or releasing invasive species. They also manage natural resources, providing clean air, water or open space. They fund preservation/conservation and development, often by a system of taxes and subsidies. Positive incentives to conserve are increasingly used, for example paying farmers to be stewards of the landscape and to farm in environmentally friendly ways.

Local

Local communities have diverse values. Indigenous peoples are often dependent on biodiversity for basic survival. For many, local biodiversity has spiritual significance as well as practical value, and they have great knowledge about local plants and their uses, for example in traditional medicine. Local communities of farmers or fishermen frequently have strong views about conservation, as it conflicts with their subsistence. With good management, however, local communities can form a vital force as conservation crusaders. There are numerous successful schemes you can research where people manage their own local resources for ecotourism (see case study, page 85). In the UK, county wildlife trusts (examples of small-scale NGOs) have developed their own biodiversity plans to involve local people in conservation.

Individual

Individuals are the most diverse group of all, in their demands as consumers of food, fuel, water, shelter etc. In the developed world **ethical consumerism** has led to people choosing to buy environmentally friendly products (e.g. dolphin-friendly tuna). Local food campaigns can challenge the 'food mile' aspects of supermarket operations and consumers can influence supermarket behaviour. Individuals also see ecosystems as places for spiritual renewal and recreation, and their behaviour has an enormous positive or negative impact. As fragile places such as the Galapagos or Antarctica begin to experience mass tourism, ecosystem management issues arise.

Individuals such as divers, birdwatchers, fishermen or mountaineers may unite to form special interest groups. Their collective actions can cause degradation and damage in high-quality eco-regions and hotspots.

Scientists and researchers work for a variety of international, national and non-governmental organisations. They play a vital role in monitoring the state of biodiversity and enhancing its quality. Some, however, are paid to find new products for pharmaceutical companies, which can lead to conflict with indigenous peoples.

Strategies and policies

Figure 3.20 shows the **spectrum** of conservation strategies available, from complete protection through various types of **sustainable development** to commercially exploited areas where limited parts are protected for publicity purposes (token protection).

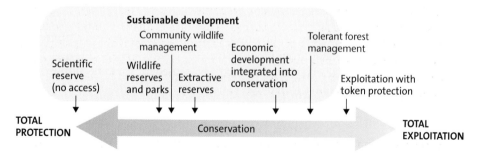

Figure 3.20 Spectrum of conservation strategies

Figure 3.21 shows that both the total area and the number of protected sites are steadily growing. Some countries, such as Tanzania, New Zealand, Ecuador and Poland, now have over 25% of their land area protected. At the same time, there has been a change in the type of conservation strategies used and therefore in the type of protected area.

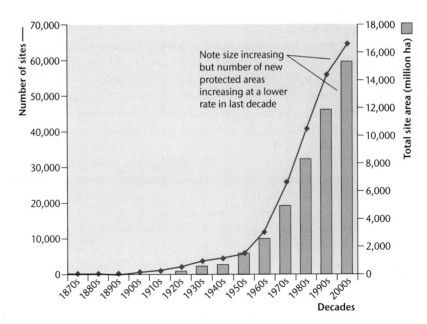

Figure 3.21 Global extent of protected areas

Total protection

In the 1960s total protection was the order of the day, with areas completely fenced off from local people, but in the 1980s concepts such as biosphere reserves surrounded by buffer zones for use by local people were developed. In the twenty-first century, conservation means much more than guarding rare species inside fenced, scientific reserves. Economic development is integrated with biodiversity conservation, using a huge variety of sustainable strategies such as tolerant forest management, extractive reserves and ecotourism, all adapted to suit the particular habitat and involve local people. This recognises that successful conservation is influenced by social, cultural, economic and political factors.

Total protection strategies have been criticised for a number of reasons, although they are still used.

➤ In the poorest countries of the world, there is a conflict between conservation and cutting people off from biodiversity.

➤ Totally protected reserves are often narrowly focused for scientific purposes, and there may be a failure to see that conservation is also influenced by social, economic, cultural and political factors.

➤ Many protection schemes were based on political and administrative boundaries, whereas ecosystems are defined by natural borders.

➤ Protection strategies often rely on coordination by outside agencies which are not always alert to the needs of the local people.

Although there is a general feeling that conservation has moved on from the days of total protection, today's fashion of integrating conservation with economic development is often criticised, mainly because conserving biodiversity is often the second rather than the first priority.

Biosphere reserves

Today, much more attention is given to the design and distribution of reserves. For example, in an era of climate change, current thinking favours the creation of large reserves connected by open corridors running in a north–south direction (Figure 3.22). Such a layout allows the maximum migration of species driven by polewards by global warming.

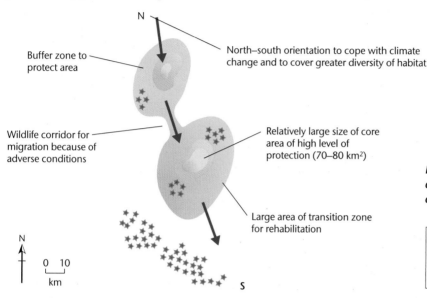

Figure 3.22 Designing a successful protected area

Buffer zone to protect area

North–south orientation to cope with climate change and to cover greater diversity of habitat

Wildlife corridor for migration because of adverse conditions

Relatively large size of core area of high level of protection (70–80 km²)

Large area of transition zone for rehabilitation

★	Human settlement
	Core area
	Buffer zone
	Transition area

There is also discussion about conservation priorities. Many argue that conservation should target the **hotspots**, because these contain maximum diversity or endemism and are under greatest threat. In contrast, WWF favours a broader approach in which representative areas of land and sea known as ecoregions are targeted to save a maximum variety of habitats and species. Still others argue that conservation should be focused on developing countries because the costs are lower and there is a greater chance of getting value for money. High-profile species such as whales, tigers and pandas tend to attract more interest and therefore funding, but this focus is questioned by some groups.

Restoration

The **restoration** of highly degraded ecosystems is the ultimate conservation challenge. Restoration can include recreating wetlands (river restoration) or linking up small fragmented reserves to produce a larger, more climate-proof reserve – for example the Great Fen project in East Anglia. These reconnection schemes require costly land purchases, so they have to emphasise local benefits such as recreation. Restoration of derelict sites such as spoil heaps, mines and quarries is even more expensive because the ecosystem and habitat have to be reconstructed virtually from scratch. A lot depends on how readily plants will reseed and how polluted the land is.

Conservation

So far the discussion has concentrated on **in situ** conservation, for which there is a huge variety of protected areas serving a multitude of purposes (Figure 3.23). An alternative for endangered species is to establish a captive population away from its natural habitat (**ex situ** conservation). This includes captive breeding with release schemes, and biodiversity banks such as genetic and seed banks in zoos and botanic gardens. Several species have been saved in this way, including the giant panda (Photograph 3.4) and the Nene or Hawaiian goose. Ex situ and in situ conservation are not rivals, but work together to increase endangered populations and re-establish near-extinct ones. Zoos can link directly with protected areas, providing stock to release and funds for conservation from ticket sales. Captive stock such as the panda can be used to educate people on hotspots, endemism and endangered species. Captive breeding buys time but releasing endangered species back into the environment is problematic.

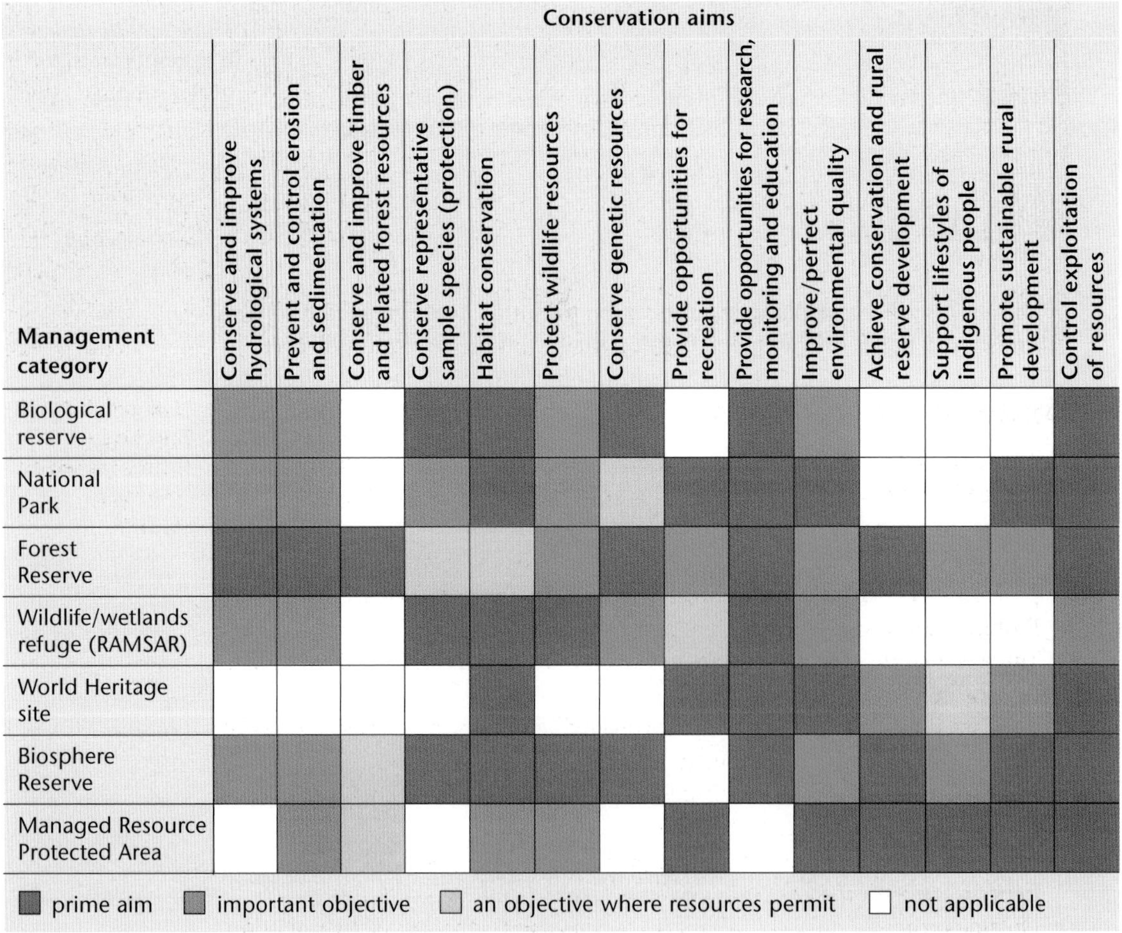

Conservation aims

Management category	Conserve and improve hydrological systems	Prevent and control erosion and sedimentation	Conserve and improve timber and related forest resources	Conserve representative sample species (protection)	Habitat conservation	Protect wildlife resources	Conserve genetic resources	Provide opportunities for recreation	Provide opportunities for research, monitoring and education	Improve/perfect environmental quality	Achieve conservation and rural reserve development	Support lifestyles of indigenous people	Promote sustainable rural development	Control exploitation of resources
Biological reserve														
National Park														
Forest Reserve														
Wildlife/wetlands refuge (RAMSAR)														
World Heritage site														
Biosphere Reserve														
Managed Resource Protected Area														

■ prime aim ■ important objective □ an objective where resources permit □ not applicable

Figure 3.23 Conservation aims of different types of protected area

Ingram

Biodiversity futures

There are several problems with the world's current protected areas which must be addressed in order to ensure that the Earth's diverse habitats are well managed and that their species are conserved:

➤ Only 12% of the Earth's land surface is designated as meriting some form of protection. Less than 1% of marine areas are currently protected.
➤ Protected areas are unevenly distributed and are fragmented.
➤ There is a shortage of funding for protection and conservation, especially in developing countries.
➤ The fact that an area is declared 'protected' does not guarantee successful conservation. Effective conservation needs an efficient, trained ranger service, scientific monitoring of habitat health and an understanding of the 'mechanisms' of habitats and their ecosystems.
➤ Protecting vast, remote areas from illegal human activity, be it poaching, felling trees or 'harvesting' particular species of plant or animal is a challenge.
➤ Outside protected areas, biodiversity continues to be threatened by pollution, climate change, invasive alien species and unsustainable development.

Photograph 3.4
The giant panda has been saved by breeding in captivity

Scenarios

There have been several attempts to explore plausible futures for ecosystems and human wellbeing in 2050. The millennium ecosystems assessments (MEA) explored:

> ➤ *two development pathways* – one in which the world becomes increasingly 'globalised' and the other in which it becomes increasingly 'regionalised' (1 and 2 in Table 3.5)
> ➤ *two different approaches* to ecosystem management – one in which actions are reactive and most problems are addressed only after they become obvious, and the other in which ecosystem management is proactive and policies seek to manage ecosystem services for the future (3 and 4 in Table 3.5)

All four scenarios predict rapid conversion of ecosystems, especially of grassland and forests to farmland or for urbanisation. The rates depend on the changes in population, consumption and overall wealth. Habitat losses will accelerate leading to loss of native species. On the other hand, Figure 3.24 shows that in three of the four scenarios there will be net improvements in at least one service category, in spite of continued biodiversity loss. The exception is scenario 2. Note the contrasts between the industrialised and developing world.

WWF's *Living Planet Report* (see www.panda.org) has also attempted to model ways of ending the ecological deficit ('overshoot') — the amount by which the ecological footprint exceeds the biological capacity of the space available to that population (Figure 3.25). Two possible pathways ('actions' and 'ways') are defined. On the basis of these pathways, WWF anticipates four possible scenarios:

> ➤ *Business as usual,* leading to an increased ecological footprint and no reduction in the 'overshoot' or the degree to which consumption exceeds biological capacities.
> ➤ *Slow shift,* gradually reducing the ecological footprint by developing many sustainable policies so that biological capacities recover by the year 2100.

Table 3.5 The MEA's four scenarios

(1) Global orchestration	(2) Order from strength
A globally connected society that focuses on global trade and economic liberalisation and takes a reactive approach to ecosystem problems. It takes strong steps to reduce poverty and inequality and invests in public goods such as infrastructure and education. Economic growth is highest in this scenario, and predicted population in 2050 is lowest	A regionalised and fragmented world that is concerned with security and protection, emphasises regional markets, pays little attention to public goods, and takes a reactive approach to ecosystem problems. Economic growth rates are lowest in this scenario (particularly in developing countries) and decrease with time, while population growth is the highest
(3) Adapting mosaic	**(4) Techno garden**
Regional watershed-scale ecosystems are the focus of political and economic activity. Local institutions are strengthened and local ecosystem management strategies are common; societies develop a proactive approach to the management of ecosystems. Economic growth rates are low initially but increase in time, and the population in 2050 is nearly as high as in the order from strength scenario	A globally connected world relying on environmentally sound technology, using highly managed, often engineered, ecosystems to deliver services, and taking a proactive approach to management of ecosystems. Economic growth is relatively high and accelerates, while population in 2050 is in the mid-range of the scenarios

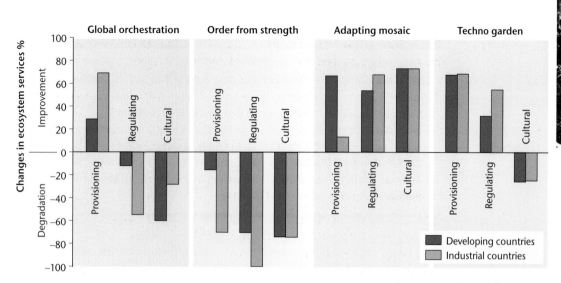

Figure 3.24 Number of ecosystem services enhanced or degraded in the four MEA scenarios

➤ *Rapid reduction*, with radical policies to control ecological footprints, leading to elimination of the overshoot by 2040.

➤ *Shrink and share*, breaking down the world into regions in order to share the responsibility of controlling the overshoot by global cooperation.

Defining scenarios such as these does not guarantee the future of global diversity. The future is full of unknowns, including the values, attitudes and perceptions of people, particularly the decision makers. There is no guarantee that they will be persuaded of the need to protect biodiversity. The tension between economic development and biodiversity may be irreconcilable, but can it be reduced?

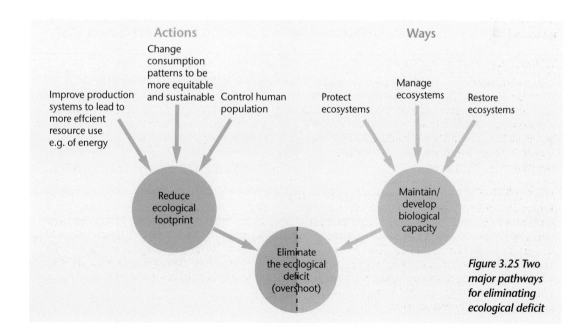

Figure 3.25 Two major pathways for eliminating ecological deficit

Review questions

1 Define and exemplify the term 'biodiversity'.
2 What is meant by the statement 'hotspots are the jewels in the biodiversity crown'?
3 Outline the different ways in which people disrupt ecosystems.
4 Explain what is meant by 'sustainable yield' and why it is important in the context of conserving biodiversity.
5 Who are the key players in the management of biodiversity?
6 To what extent do you think it is possible to reconcile the conservation of biodiversity and economic development?

Superpower geographies

Power – both economic and political – is not evenly distributed. Some nations and players have a disproportionate influence over regional and global decision making. The present geography of power is the outcome of complex processes with a considerable history. The pattern is constantly changing, as some nations gain power and others lose it. Equally, the nature of power has changed, from a direct to a more subtle control and influence. This power is exercised through trade and flows of capital and resources, as well as through culture.

Superpower geographies

Who are the superpowers and how does their power develop over time?

By the end of this section you should:
- ➤ *know what a superpower is*
- ➤ *understand how superpowers exert and extend their influence*
- ➤ *realise that patterns of power change over time*
- ➤ *appreciate the difference between the emerging powers and the existing superpowers*

Defining 'superpower'

The term **superpower** was first used during the Second World War to refer to the USA, the USSR and the British empire. It refers to a nation with the means to project its power and influence anywhere in the world, and to be a dominant global force. This demands huge resources, so true superpowers are rare (Figure 4.1). Some countries and country groupings are emerging as powerful forces and may attain superpower status in the future. The EU and China are key contenders, with Russia, India, Brazil and the oil-rich Gulf states powerful in particular ways. Other countries fulfil regional power roles.

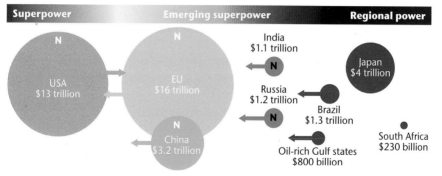

Figure 4.1 The power spectrum and current trajectories, GDP data, 2008

Superpowers exercise various forms of power:

➤ *Military power.* In the modern world, this essentially means access to nuclear weapons, although the ability to 'watch' the world using satellite and spy technology is important.

➤ *Economic power.* Wealth allows superpowers to export their power around the world, buy resources and influence trade patterns.

➤ *Cultural power.* This includes the projection of a particular 'way of life' and cultural values which influence the way others behave, and perhaps even think.

➤ *Geographical power.* This refers to the sphere of influence a superpower has. It might result from a physical or cultural presence in widespread locations.

Cameron Dunn

Photograph 4.1 Symbols of power: the Stars and Stripes inside the turbine hall of the Hoover Dam

Of these forms of power, economic power is the most important as it is required in order to maintain military power, spread cultural influence through trade and the media, and provide global geographical reach. Arguably the USA is today's only superpower. It is a major military force and the world's largest economy. Its cultural values have been spread globally and its cultural symbols (e.g. the Stars and Stripes, Coca-Cola, Ford vehicles) are found worldwide (Photograph 4.1).

Emerging and regional powers lack some forms of power. Japan has economic muscle, but lacks military power. In Latin America, Brazil acts as a regional power broker but its economic and military influence are confined to that region. China, as yet, lacks the cultural and geographical dominance of the USA.

Superpower societies

There are fundamental differences in the ways various superpower societies are organised.

➤ The British empire was organised as an **imperialist system**, with the culture, economy and politics of Britain dominating its subordinate colonies. Democracy, in a very limited form, existed only in Britain itself, not in the colonies.

➤ The USA functions within a **capitalist system**, albeit a democratic one. This means there is a division between people who own businesses and make profits, and those who work for them.

➤ In the USSR, under the **Communist system**, private ownership of the means of production (businesses and property) was not allowed. The philosopher Karl Marx developed the theory of communism. He argued that private ownership of businesses meant that the rich would seek to maximise profits at the expense of their workers, creating a society where the rich (the bourgeoisie) exploited the working class (the proletariat). Marx believed the means of production should be owned in common, as this would create a more equal society. In the USSR the state owned all businesses and property. Like other Communist states it was not a democracy.

 Case study **The Cold War superpowers**

The world today is uni-polar, with one major super-power. During the Cold War era, 1945–90, it was a bi-polar world, with two superpowers: the USA and the USSR. These two superpowers acted in different ways (Table 4.1). The USA followed a policy which globalised its sphere of influence. In the USA this was referred to as containment, as it sought to contain the influence of the USSR. The USSR created a strong core by invading or allying itself with its surrounding countries (Figure 4.2).

Table 4.1 The Cold War superpowers compared

	USA	USSR
Geography and resources	Population: 287 million (1989) Resources: self-sufficient in most raw materials	Population: 291 million (1991) Resources: self-sufficient in most raw materials
Economic system	Capitalist, free market economy	Socialist, centrally planned economy
Political system	Democracy with elections for president and Congress every 4 years Very little difference in political philosophy between the Republican and Democratic parties	Dictatorship with no free elections
Allies	Western Europe, through NATO Strong economic and military ties with Japan and South Korea Strong links with Latin America through trade Alliances with African, middle eastern and Asian developing nations, using military and development aid	Eastern Europe (the Warsaw Pact countries) Alliances worldwide with socialist governments (e.g. Cuba) Alliances with African, middle eastern and Asian developing nations, using military and development aid
Military power	Naval and air-based military power; established a 'ring' of bases to surround USSR Large nuclear arsenal and global network of nuclear bases Extensive global intelligence network (CIA)	Very large army, naval and air capabilities Nuclear weapons Troops stationed in eastern Europe Extensive global intelligence gathering network (KGB)
Cultural influence	Rapid growth in film and television industry was a powerful vehicle for conveying a positive view of the USA, especially its high standard of living Lack of direct censorship meant that negative views of the USA could be transmitted as well	Tried to sell a view of itself that emphasised high culture (as opposed to US popular culture), with ballet, music and art being central Very tight censorship that allowed no criticism

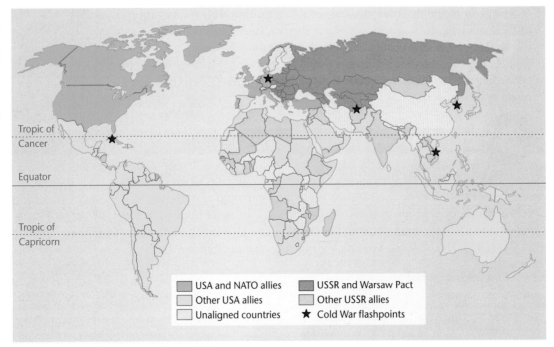

Figure 4.2 The Cold War geography, c.1980

The Cold War did not lead to direct military confrontation between the two superpowers. However, as each sought to exert its influence there were flashpoint periods of increased tension (Figure 4.2):

■ the Korean War, 1950–53
■ the Vietnam War, 1959–75
■ the blockade of Berlin in 1949 and the erection of the Berlin wall in 1961
■ the Cuban missile crisis in 1962
■ the USSR invasion of Afghanistan in 1980

In the early 1990s the political geography of the world was redrawn as the political systems of the USSR and the Warsaw Pact countries collapsed and the USSR broke up into its constituent republics. The USA emerged as the only superpower.

The geography of power

If we examine the only true superpower still in existence, the USA, we can identify several ways in which it maintains its global hegemony. The USA has the world's most powerful military machine on Earth and it is geographically widespread (Figure 4.3). The US armed forces consist of (2008 data):

➤ 540,000 army personnel
➤ 520,000 personnel in the navy and marines
➤ 330,000 personnel in the air force

This gives the USA huge military reach. The US Navy has 12 aircraft carriers and 70 submarines, allowing it to operate anywhere in the world. No other power has this capability at present.

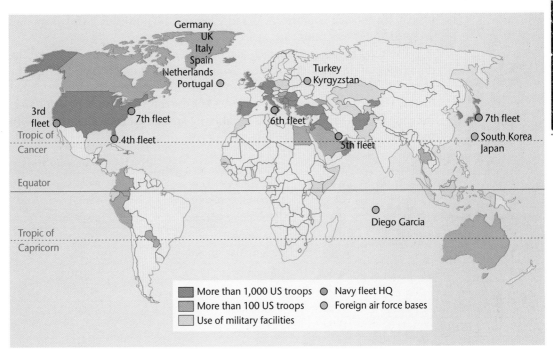

Figure 4.3 US military forces worldwide

The USA is also economically dominant and its companies are geographically widespread. The Forbes Global 2000 list identifies the 2,000 largest TNCs in the world. In 2008, US-based companies accounted for 776 of the top 2,000, followed by Japan with 331 and the UK with 132. The USA plays a major role in world trade, much of which is conducted in US dollars. The dollar is the world's reserve currency. This means that governments around the world hold reserves of dollars in their central banks. In fact, there are more US banknotes abroad than there are in the USA. Much of the world arguably has an interest in maintaining a stable USA, and friendly relations with the country, if only because of the importance of the dollar.

Cultural hegemony

The most obvious way of maintaining power is through direct force, usually in the form of police, army and security forces. However, power is not generally maintained in this way unless a society's leaders feel under threat of being overthrown by their people. The Italian Marxist philosopher Antonio Gramsci described a particular type of power which he referred to as **hegemony** or **cultural hegemony**. Gramsci, imprisoned in Mussolini's fascist Italy, was impressed by the way Mussolini maintained power without the need to resort to direct force. Gramsci believed power was maintained largely by consent. The values of those in power were accepted by people and this kept them in power. Education, religion and the media subtly reinforced the values of the powerful and maintained their hegemony. In such conditions, the ideology of the powerful simply becomes accepted as the 'way things are' and is rarely challenged.

US cultural hegemony is largely unchallenged, at least for the moment. The dominance of US consumer culture can be identified through 'brand value'. The annual *Business Week* Interbrand survey identifies the most valuable global brands (Table 4.2). In the 2008 survey, 53 of the top 100 brands by value were from the USA. Many of the brands in Table 4.2 are immediately identifiable with the USA.

Table 4.2 Global brand values, 2008

2008 rank	Brand	Country of origin	Sector	2008 brand value (US$m)
1	Coca-Cola	USA	Beverages	66,667
2	IBM	USA	Computer services	59,031
3	Microsoft	USA	Computer software	59,007
4	General Electric	USA	Diversified	53,086
5	Nokia	Finland	Consumer electronics	35,942
6	Toyota	Japan	Automotive	34,050
7	Intel	USA	Computer hardware	31,261
8	McDonald's	USA	Restaurants	31,049
9	Disney	USA	Media	29,251
10	Google	USA	Internet services	25,590

Source: Business Week/Interbrand

Changing patterns of power

Superpower status is not fixed. In the USA, there is concern that the country's superpower status is threatened. This is because the economic and population centre of gravity of the world is shifting towards Asia (Figure 4.4). In some ways it is inevitable that the USA will fall from its 'perch', if only because history suggests superpowers do not last for ever.

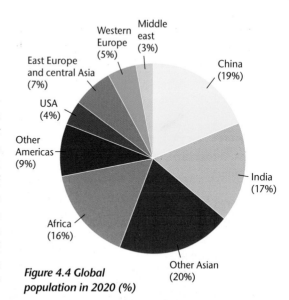

Western Europe (5%)
Middle east (3%)
East Europe and central Asia (7%)
USA (4%)
Other Americas (9%)
Africa (16%)
China (19%)
India (17%)
Other Asian (20%)

Figure 4.4 Global population in 2020 (%)

The nineteenth-century superpower was the British empire, which had emerged as the dominant global power during the eighteenth century. At its height, in 1921, the British empire held sway over about 458 million people, approximately one-quarter of the world's population. It covered about 36.7 million km², roughly a quarter of Earth's total land area (Figure 4.5).

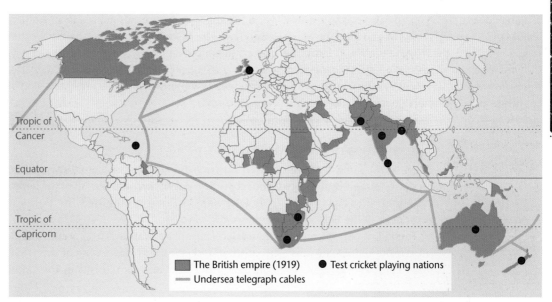

Figure 4.5 The network of undersea telegraph cables connecting the British empire in 1910: the internet of the Edwardian era

The rise and fall of the British empire

The British empire was founded on exploration and sea power. The Royal Navy dominated the high seas from around 1700 until the 1930s. The Navy provided a link between the home country and overseas colonies, and at the same time was a powerful 'keep off' symbol of military power. Three distinct phases of empire can be identified (Table 4.3).

Table 4.3 Three phases in the history of the British empire

The mercantilist phase (1600–1850)	Small colonies set up on coastal fringes and islands, e.g. New England, Jamaica, Accra, Bombay, defended by forts
	Focus on trade, including slaves and raw materials such as sugar
	Private trading companies such as the Royal African Company, Hudson's Bay Company and East India Company, defended by British forces
The imperial phase (1850–1945)	Coastal colonies extended inland; wholesale conquest of territories
	Religion and British culture (e.g. cricket) and language introduced to colonies
	Government and institutions set up to rule the colonial population
	Development of more complex trade networks
	Use of technology such as railways and telegraph (Figure 4.5) to connect distant parts of the empire
The decolonialisation phase (1945–)	After the Second World War the UK is effectively bankrupt and cannot support the empire as before
	Anti-colonial movements grow, e.g. in India, increasing tensions; some colonies are granted independence
	The focus on postwar reconstruction at home sees the majority of colonies independent by 1970

Britain does have a superpower legacy. It retains control of 14 overseas territories and fought a war to keep one of these, the Falkland Islands, in 1982. The Commonwealth is an association of 53 independent states (former British colonies) which consult and cooperate in the common interests of their peoples and in the promotion of international understanding. The association does not have a written constitution, but it does have a series of agreements setting out its beliefs and objectives. Given its size, should the Commonwealth be regarded as a kind of superpower?

The collapse of communism

The world changed dramatically following the collapse of communism. The process was rapid and pivoted around the key 'public' event of the fall of the Berlin Wall in 1989 (Figure 4.6). This wall had for long symbolised the political separation of the Cold War superpowers.

The fall of communism in the eastern European Warsaw Pact countries took little more than 4 months. The cultural and economic hegemony of the USSR disintegrated overnight. The causes of the collapse were reforms in the USSR

The union Solidarity is allowed to participate in Polish elections ending Communist Party rule, September 1989

EAST GERMANY

The 'Iron Curtain'

USSR

East Germans begin migrating west through Hungary's open border with Austria. The Berlin Wall falls, November 1989

POLAND

CZECHOSLOVAKIA

HUNGARY

Non-violent 'Velvet revolution' overthrows Communist Party in Czechoslovakia, November 1989

ROMANIA

BULGARIA

Hungarian parliament votes to establish a multi-party democracy, October 1989

Communist Party in Bulgaria gives up power, early 1990

Brief but violent clashes remove the Communist leaders of Romania, December 1989

Figure 4.6 The collapse of communism in eastern Europe

begun in 1985 by President Mikhail Gorbachev. These reforms were termed *glasnost* (openness, such as increased freedom of speech) and *perestroika* (economic liberalisation, such as private ownership of small businesses). Economic and social reform spread to the Warsaw Pact countries, where small freedoms quickly mushroomed into open revolt against the Communist system.

The USSR itself collapsed in February 1990 when the Communist Party gave up its monopoly on power. This led to the break-up of the entire country, as nationalist tensions, kept in check by the Communist system, split the country apart. In rapid succession the republics of the USSR, such as Latvia, Kazakhstan and Georgia, broke away to become independent nations. In retrospect, glasnost and perestroika acted as cracks in the Communist dam which quickly undermined the whole structure. The USSR portrayed its people as happy and healthy and willing to live within the Communist system because of the collective benefits it brought. The speed of collapse might suggest force, rather than consent, was more important in maintaining communism.

Emerging superpowers

While some superpowers have declined or collapsed, others are emerging to challenge the dominance of the USA. These are the BRICs (Brazil, Russia, India and China), the EU and the oil-rich nations of the middle east (Figure 4.7).

The emerging superpowers share one or more of the following:
➤ strong economic growth
➤ large populations

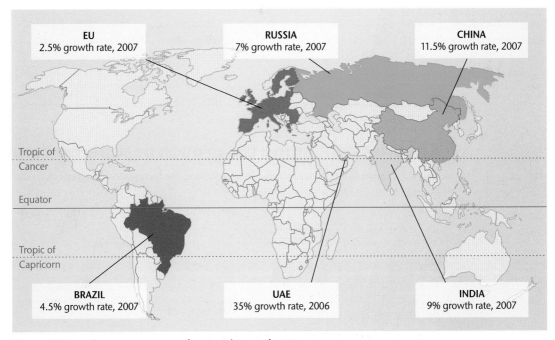

EU
2.5% growth rate, 2007

RUSSIA
7% growth rate, 2007

CHINA
11.5% growth rate, 2007

Tropic of Cancer

Equator

Tropic of Capricorn

BRAZIL
4.5% growth rate, 2007

UAE
35% growth rate, 2006

INDIA
9% growth rate, 2007

Figure 4.7 Emerging superpowers and economic growth rates

➤ access to key resources, especially fossil fuels
➤ market economies.
➤ regional power and influence.

In the next 20 years some are expected to increase their global power and influence. *Global Trends 2025: A Transformed World*, a report by the US National Intelligence Council in 2008, stated that:

➤ 'a global multi-polar system is emerging with the rise of China, India and others'
➤ 'the unprecedented shift in relative wealth and economic power roughly from West to East now under way will continue'
➤ 'the United States will remain the single most powerful country but will be less dominant'

Clearly the USA itself can feel its power weakening, especially in relation to China. There are many possible reasons for this that relate to both a weakening USA and a rising China (Table 4.4).

Table 4.4 The USA vs China

A weaker USA?	A more influential China?
Vulnerability to terrorist attacks, such as 9/11, removing its veneer of invincibility	The 2008 Beijing Olympic Games were a showcase of Chinese culture, ingenuity and technical prowess
Growing economic problems at home, such as the 2008 financial crisis, causing it to focus more on internal affairs	Chinese companies are beginning to become world players. In 2008, 70 of the world's largest companies were Chinese, compared to only 30 in 2002
A feeling that some of its foreign policy actions, such as the Iraq War and detention of terrorist suspects in Guantanamo Bay, were ill-conceived and have undermined its international authority	China's position as the world's biggest emitter of carbon dioxide gives it a new status and increasingly important role in the fight against global warming
Increased dependence on foreign oil and gas imports weakens its economic bargaining power	Chinese technology is advancing rapidly, as seen in the first Chinese space-walk in 2008

Theories explaining the growth of superpowers

Since the end of the Second World War in 1945, the most notable changes in the geography of superpowers have been:

➤ the superpower struggle for global superiority between the USA and the USSR
➤ the decline of the colonial superpowers, such as the UK
➤ the emergence of the BRICs and the EU as potential superpowers

Explanations of changing superpower geographies focus on a number of different theories.

Modernisation theory

In the 1960s W. W. Rostow's modernisation theory was used to explain the dominance of the British empire and the USA. These were the first nations to

experience the Industrial Revolution and this gave them an initial advantage over as yet unindustrialised countries and regions.

Rostow believed the economies of developed countries moved through five stages of economic development (see Figure 5.6, page 137) and that all countries would follow the same development pathway. Rostow was a strong believer in free trade and in a Western model of democracy and capitalism. Socialist and communist countries, such as the USSR, Cuba and at that time China, could not expect to develop unless they adopted this model. Rostow's model was influential and led to many developing countries attempting to create the preconditions for take-off by investing in key infrastructure and industries. Some of these countries, such as the Asian Tigers, succeeded, while others failed and found themselves burdened by debt.

Dependency theory

Dependency theory, based on the work of A. G. Frank, views the world as having an economically developed core and an underdeveloped periphery. According to the theory, the capitalist core deliberately keeps the periphery in a state of under-development by exploiting its cheap resources, taking its most skilled workers and selling it manufactured goods (Figure 4.8). By this argument, the developing world actually helps the developed world to become wealthier. Frank called this 'the development of underdevelopment'.

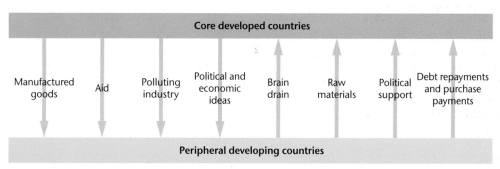

Figure 4.8 The mechanisms of dependency theory

Dependency theory argues that the developing world is placed in a position of selling its resources to the developed world for very little, while buying from it costly manufactured goods, technology and credit (loans). As the periphery remains underdeveloped, its most skilled people move to the developed world, further draining it of any chance to develop. Using this model, aid to the developing world could be seen as a way of preventing the periphery becoming too restless.

The rise of the newly industrialised countries (NICs), such as the Asian Tigers, seems to argue against dependency theory, as they are examples of countries that have developed. However, Taiwan, South Korea, Singapore and Japan all received huge economic support and aid from the USA, as it was felt that strong capitalist economies in Asia were a way of containing Communist China.

World systems theory

Wallerstein's world systems theory attempts to overcome the problem of a two-tier core and periphery world. More of an analysis of geographical patterns than a theory, Wallerstein's view is of a three-tier world (Figure 4.9). This is a more dynamic model, as it allows for change to take place, with some countries entering the semi-periphery and even emerging to be part of the core. Frank's dependency theory, based on Marxist ideas of 'the rich versus the poor', is much more static.

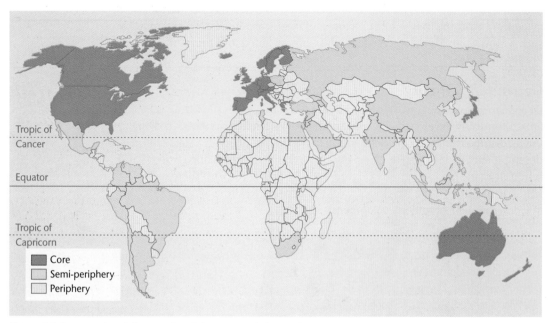

Figure 4.9 *Core, semi-periphery and periphery, 2000 (after Klak, 2002)*

There are two conflicting explanations of the recent rise of China and India. Wallerstein takes the view that industrial capitalism was born in Europe and that the rise of China and India simply represents another stage in the growth and spread of the global economy. In contrast, the US economist Frank sees the current situation as simply a shift back to a much older world order, when India and China were powerful economic forces. This global system was replaced for some 500 years by European hegemony. Frank views Britain and other European powers as the first NICs. What remains unexplained is why the global centre of gravity should swing, first from Asia to Europe, and then back again.

Case study **China and India compared**

China and India are two emerging superpowers, with vast populations: 1.3 billion in China and 1.2 billion in India. Both emerged as truly independent states in the 1940s, but have taken different paths to development.

Table 4.5 compares the two countries.

Table 4.5 India and China compared

	China	India
Population	1.3 billion	1.2 billion
Political and economic history	Early centre of civilisation Dominant global power for 2,000 years Decline in the nineteenth century, hastened by Japanese invasion and European interference Manufacturing impressed European visitors with its complexity and sophistication In 1985, 33% of global manufacturing production was Chinese	Early centre of civilisation Fell under the influence of European colonial powers in the eighteenth century Direct colonial rule by Britain in the nineteenth century During the nineteenth century, India was responsible for 15% of global manufacturing Active struggle for independence begins in the early twentieth century
Key date	Communist revolution, 1949	Independence from Britain, 1947
Path to development	State-led industrialisation and intensification of agriculture Largely cut off from rest of world, 1949–80 Increasing economic reform and liberalisation since 1980, leading to an explosion of foreign investment, manufacturing and trade	Policy of economic and political independence and home-grown technology High import tariffs, gradually lowered after 1990 Still a predominantly rural society, it has built a very powerful and increasingly global economy
Relations with other superpowers	Uneasy, sometimes hostile relationships with the former USSR, Russia and the USA Relations with the USA thawed in the early 1970s as the USA sought to prevent a communist alliance between China and the USSR In recent years, China has sought economic and political stability in Asia	Following independence India was 'neutral', steering a pathway between the USA and USSR Neither of the superpowers was happy with this policy India has worked hard to establish good relationships with other 'neutral' countries to enhance its role internationally

The role of superpowers

What impacts and influence do superpowers have?

By the end of this section you should:
- ➤ *know how power is exercised both directly and indirectly*
- ➤ *be aware of the role of superpowers in international decision making*
- ➤ *understand the importance of controlling trade*
- ➤ *have a feel for the idea of a developing 'global culture'*

The maintenance of power

Once gained, superpower status has to be maintained. How this is achieved has changed over time.

As recently as 1945, large parts of the world were under colonial rule. Most colonial powers were European, although the USA did maintain some colonies,

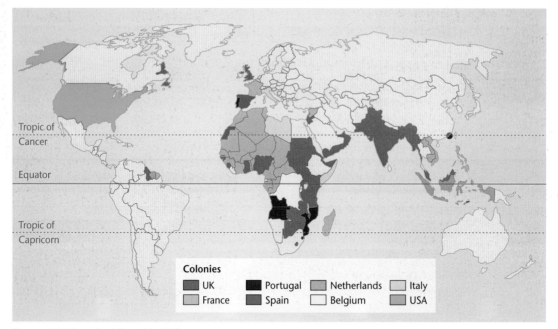

Figure 4.10 The colonial world, 1945

e.g. the Philippines (Figure 4.10). Colonial rule usually had a number of distinct phases:

➤ exploration, resulting in the 'discovery' of new lands
➤ initial settlement, usually on coasts, in defended forts
➤ the beginnings of trade in raw materials
➤ gradual extension of rule over larger territories by direct military action and conquest
➤ the development of political systems and institutions and transport and trade networks both to rule the colony and to exploit its resources

Some colonies became relatively peaceful places, but the threat of military action against insurgents was ever-present and indigenous people usually lacked freedoms, living mostly in poverty.

Case study — Colonial India

In India today it is possible to see the legacy of British rule. In order to maintain power, British military personnel, civil servants and businessmen emigrated to run the Raj. Symbols of power were built, such as the residence of the governor-general of India in Delhi. A process of acculturalisation was undertaken as British traditions such as cricket and tea-drinking, and crucially the English language, were introduced. A strict social order was maintained, differentiating between the ruling white British and the Indians.

India was 'modernised' so that its economy could better serve the needs of the mother country. Perhaps the most durable feature of this process was the railway system built by the British (Photograph 4.2). By 1880, 14,000 km of railway had been built:

Photograph 4.2 India's railways are a colonial legacy

by 1920, 61,000 km. This hugely improved transport and trade, but also allowed more efficient military transport – useful when putting down rebellions.

When independence was granted in 1947 there followed a period of chaos as colonial India was partitioned (Figure 4.11).

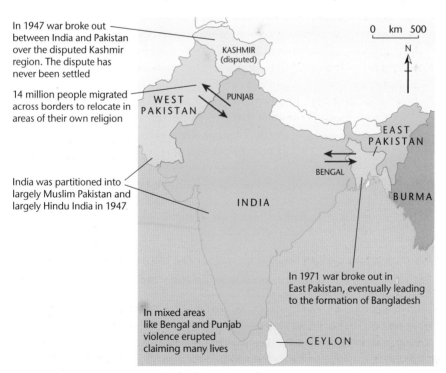

In 1947 war broke out between India and Pakistan over the disputed Kashmir region. The dispute has never been settled

14 million people migrated across borders to relocate in areas of their own religion

India was partitioned into largely Muslim Pakistan and largely Hindu India in 1947

In mixed areas like Bengal and Punjab violence erupted claiming many lives

In 1971 war broke out in East Pakistan, eventually leading to the formation of Bangladesh

Figure 4.11 The partition of India and its consequences

In many colonies, the era of decolonialisation and independence brought conflict and division rather than the immediate freedom and prosperity people hoped for.

➤ In many countries, colonial borders did not reflect religious and ethnic boundaries, which led to conflict over territory.

➤ Although colonies had government institutions, indigenous people had been excluded from running them, so experience in governance was lacking.

➤ As colonial powers packed up and left, insurgents took the opportunity to push them out, which resulted in violence.

Neo-colonialism

Neo-colonialism refers to a form of indirect control over developing countries, most of them former colonies. After decolonisation and independence, some new national leaders argued that their countries were being subjected to a new form of colonialism, waged by the former colonial powers and other developed nations.

The term neo-colonialism was first used by Kwame Nkrumah, the first president of independent Ghana. He regarded neo-colonialism as worse than colonialism because, as he put it,

> Neo-colonialism is...the worst form of imperialism. For those who practise it, it means power without responsibility and for those who suffer from it, it means exploitation without redress. In the days of old-fashioned colonialism, the imperial power had at least to explain and justify at home the actions it was taking abroad. In the colony those who served the ruling imperial power could at least look to its protection against any violent move by their opponents. With neo-colonialism neither is the case.

Figure 4.12 World trade shares, 2002

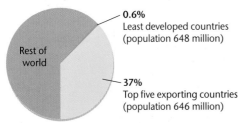

0.6%
Least developed countries (population 648 million)

Rest of world

37%
Top five exporting countries (population 646 million)

Neo-colonialism is most often linked to Africa and is used as an explanation for the lack of development in that continent. Proponents of neo-colonialism point to evidence such as the share of world trade that goes to the least developed countries (Figure 4.12) to argue that neo-colonialism has prevented any real development progress in the 40 years since colonies gained their independence.

Table 4.6 Possible mechanisms of neo-colonialism

Strategic alliances	The USA and USSR formed alliances with many developing nations to spread their global influence, often by means of foreign aid
Aid	Aid can be given with 'strings attached', forcing the recipients (developing countries) to spend the aid in the way the donors (developed countries) wish
TNCs	Foreign direct investment, e.g. locating low-tech manufacturing in the developing world, means big profits for TNCs but low wages and few skills for the developing world
Terms of trade	Low raw material and commodity export prices contrast with the high prices the developing world must pay for manufactured goods
Global finance and debt	Many developing nations pay huge sums to the developed world each year in debt interest payments, which often exceed aid receipts
Structural adjustment policies (SAPs)	Countries wishing to have their debt relieved have to apply Western economic policies devised by the World Bank and IMF, losing some of their economic sovereignty

Neo-colonialism is a theory which cannot be proved, but its supporters point to a number of mechanisms which work to allow the developed world to maintain control over parts of the developing world (Table 4.6). Neo-colonialism is really an extension of dependency theory.

International decision making

The leaders of the world's superpowers and emerging powers are frequently on the international stage making key decisions about the world economy, conflicts or environmental issues. Global economic and political power is in the hands of a small number of players in the form of **inter-governmental organisations (IGOs)**. These organisations have largely been created by the global powers. Many date from the Bretton Woods conference in 1944, when the allies set about creating postwar institutions that would prevent future wars and ensure the world economy ran more effectively than in the pre-war period (which included the Great Depression of the 1930s). Critics of IGOs argue that they were set up by superpowers, for superpowers. The key IGOs are shown in Table 4.7.

Table 4.7 Inter-governmental organisations

Organisation	Founding date	Headquarters	Function
International Monetary Fund (IMF)	1944	Washington DC	To monitor the economic and financial development of countries and to lend money when countries are facing financial difficulties
World Bank	1944	Washington DC	To give advice, loans and grants for the reduction of poverty and the promotion of economic development
United Nations (UN)	1945	New York	To prevent war and to arbitrate on international disputes. It has since developed a wide range of specialist agencies dealing with matters such as health and refugees
World Trade Organization (WTO)	1995	Geneva	Trade policy, agreements and settling disputes. It promotes global free trade. Formerly known as GATT (between 1947 and 1994)
North Atlantic Treaty Organization (NATO)	1949	Brussels	A military alliance between European countries and the USA. Recent new members include Poland
Organisation for Economic Co-operation and Development (OECD)	1961	Paris	Analysis of economic development. Forecasting and researching development issues. Most developed-world countries are members

The G8

Some global organisations are less formal and have a very restricted membership. The G8 (Group of 8) is a good example. It is a forum for the world's richest and most powerful nations. Annual summits are held, although these are informal meetings about the global policy direction the Western democracies should take. When G8 leaders meet they represent:

➤ 65% of global GNP, but only 14% of the world's population

> the holders of most of the world's nuclear weapons, with combined annual military spending of US$850 billion in 2007

Russia was first invited to a G7 meeting in 1997, thus forming the G8. This inclusion was an acceptance of Russia's importance as a nuclear and energy resource power.

Power in IGOs

There is a significant overlap in membership of IGOs which gives some powers, especially the EU and the USA, the ability to focus global policy and decision making in their own interests. Most IGOs operate some form of veto policy, and powers such as the EU and the USA tend to vote with each other. This gives them the opportunity to block policy they do not like, and force through their own policies. Table 4.8 shows that emerging powers such as China and India are less influential within IGOs at the moment, although this may change in the future.

Table 4.8 Membership of IGOs (green cells show members)

International organisation	Canada	Some EU countries	Japan	Russia	UK	USA	China	India
G8 member country								
Permanent member of the UN Security Council								
Member of NATO (North Atlantic Treaty Organization)								
Member of the OECD (Organisation for Economic Co-operation and Development)								
3% or more of votes at the IMF (International Monetary Fund)		30%	6%		5%	17%		

Few countries are capable of taking large-scale unilateral actions today. The Iraq War saw the USA effectively 'go it alone', with some support from the UK and other countries. More often IGOs are used, for instance:

> the NATO-led peacekeeping in former Yugoslavia in 1995–96 and from 2001 in Afghanistan
> G8-led attempts to focus on the issue of debt and poverty reduction in Africa
> EU attempts to force through deep carbon emissions cuts targets at the Bali summit in 2007

Emerging powers

While the 'old' powers of the EU and the USA still have considerable clout, there are signs that emerging powers are gaining ground. In November 2008 the G20 Leaders' Summit on Financial Markets and the World Economy was held in Washington DC. This summit discussed responses to the 2008 global financial crisis. The G20 includes Brazil, China, India, Russia and Saudi Arabia – perhaps reflecting an emerging new world economic order.

Davos Group

The World Economic Forum (WEF or Davos Group) is a Swiss-based non-profit-making foundation with the motto 'entrepreneurship in the global public interest'. As this might suggest, its focus is on business and profits. The WEF holds an annual invitation-only meeting in Davos, Switzerland. Those regularly attending the meetings at Davos include:

➤ business CEOs
➤ academics
➤ political leaders
➤ IGO representatives
➤ the media

The forum has come under fire from anti-globalisation campaigners and those who see capitalism as creating inequality. Rock singer Bono dubbed the annual meeting 'fat cats in the snow'. Some observers are suspicious of the Davos Group because it has no 'official' status yet is attended by presidents and prime ministers (as well as Hollywood A-listers).

The nature and control of trade

The nature of global trade is that free trade has come to dominate trading relations. The WTO has led a series of trade agreements since the 1950s which have removed:

➤ taxes and tariffs on imports
➤ quotas on imports
➤ subsidies for domestic producers

The result has been a huge growth in trade and wealth. Some parts of the world have benefited from trade growth (Figure 4.13), such as Asia, and in particular China and India. On the other hand, Africa's share of world trade has declined since 1970. These trends have several explanations.

➤ International trade is very much in the hands of the TNCs. These have chosen to invest heavily in India and China but not in Africa.
➤ In Asia, free trade zones have been used to attract investment by offering companies tax breaks, non-union areas and limited regulation.

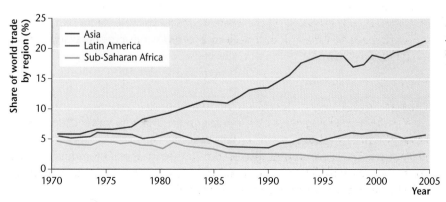

Figure 4.13 Trends in share of world trade, 1970–2005

➤ Africa will remain unattractive to much investment until it has more developed infrastructure, higher skills levels and greater political stability.

Free trade?

Trade has certainly become freer, but for some countries this is an illusion. Much trade takes place between countries which are members of trade blocs such as the EU, NAFTA and ASEAN. Trade within a bloc tends to be tariff-free. Trade between blocs may also have low tariffs if agreements have been reached. For developing countries outside any trade bloc, there can still be considerable trade barriers which prevent access to markets.

Many African countries are still trapped in a colonial trade pattern of exporting raw materials such as coffee, copper and timber to the developed world. The prices of commodities are set on the global stock exchanges and are prone to extreme volatility. Figure 4.14 shows how commodity prices rose steadily between November 2007 and July 2008 – good news for African exporters – only to collapse by November 2008, leaving exporters 20% worse off than they had been 12 months earlier.

Figure 4.14 The AIG commodity price index, November 2007–November 2008

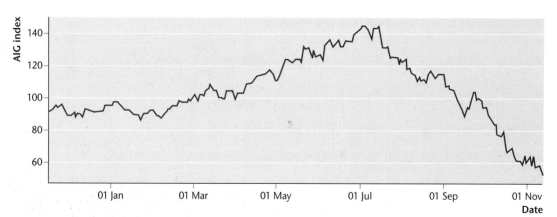

Control

The superpower economies also control innovation and technology. New inventions such as drugs, microchips and engines are patented, and users must pay a royalty or licence fee to use the technology. Figure 4.15 shows that 75% of these fees go to just three powers, with the USA dominating. This is another way in which the superpowers and developed economies control both trade and the availability of technology and innovation.

See the case study on Europe's gas pipeline war (Chapter 1, page 17) for a discussion of power struggles over energy supply.

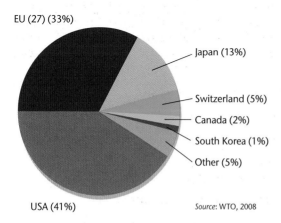

Source: WTO, 2008

Figure 4.15 Global receipt of royalties and licence fees, 2006

Global culture

We have seen how modernisation might be used to explain the position of the USA and the European colonial superpowers. Followers of modernisation theory viewed traditional cultures as 'pre-modern' and in some ways a barrier to development. From the standpoint of the USA and the EU, as powerful capitalist economies, the path to power was one where the relationship between businesses and workers was maximised. Traditional ethnic, religious and kinship cultural ties could be seen as largely irrelevant to the pursuit of profit and power.

The dominance of the USA as an unrivalled superpower since 1990, plus the growing power of the EU, has led some people to identify a global culture. It is difficult to define exactly what this global culture is, but some characteristics are commonly linked to it:

➤ A culture of consumerism.
➤ A culture of capitalism and the importance of attaining wealth.
➤ A white, Anglo-Saxon culture with English as the dominant language.
➤ A culture that 'cherry picks' and adapts selected parts of other world cultures and absorbs them.

Americanisation

Global culture is most often exemplified by the ubiquity of consumer icons such as Coca-Cola and McDonald's (Photograph 4.3). It is fair to say these symbols are global. In the case of McDonald's, 31,000 restaurants worldwide are serving about 50 million people every day (see Figure 12.10, page 337). The USA is seen as the most powerful force in cultural globalisation, and the process is often referred to as 'Americanisation'.

Cultural globalisation is not quite as straightforward as might first appear, however. In India, McDonald's has had to adapt its menu to suit local tastes and the Hindu and Muslim religions. It does not sell beef or pork and has more vegetarian options than in the West (Table 4.9). Throughout the world this process of local adaptation or hybridisation occurs as global trends reach new areas.

Photograph 4.3 McDonald's in Bangkok, Thailand

Table 4.9 Adapting to local tastes

Country	McDonald's adaptation
India	The Maharaja Mac, a Big Mac made of lamb or chicken meat McAloo Tikki, a vegetarian burger
Japan	Ebi Filet-O shrimp burgers Koroke Burger of mashed potato, cabbage and katsu sauce Ebi-Chiki, shrimp nuggets, and green tea-flavoured milkshake
Hong Kong	Rice Burger: burger sits between two rice patties rather than in a burger bun
Israel	Burgers are grilled over charcoal, not fried McKebab, with eastern seasoning, stuffed into a pita bread

Cultural traffic

Working against the idea of a global culture is the fact that the cultural traffic is not all one way, and neither are American or Western lifestyles adopted wholesale around the world:

➤ In the UK the curry, not the American burger, is the most popular takeaway food. There are six times as many curry restaurants in the UK as there are McDonald's.

➤ Sushi, from Japan, has become an increasingly popular food in the West.

➤ Some cornerstones of American culture, such as American football and baseball, have proved difficult to export to the rest of the world.

One area where Americanisation is strong is cinema, as Hollywood movies tend to dominate the market. Arguably this is an effective way of exporting Western culture to the rest of the world.

Despite cultural globalisation, people around the world hold very different views on the merits of Western global capitalism. Table 4.10 shows how US exports are viewed around the world.

	% of people expressing positive views		
	US television and films	US science and technology	US ideas and customs spreading
France	65	71	18
Venezuela	71	76	37
Turkey	22	37	4
China	42	80	38
India	23	64	29
Kenya	51	87	45
Bangladesh	14	81	25

Table 4.10 Differing views of American exports

Backlash

The cultural backlash against the world's major superpower is complex. Anti-Americanism rose in the aftermath of the invasion of Iraq and George W. Bush proved an unpopular president (both at home and abroad). The anti-globalisation movement is often linked with anti-American sentiment because many global cultural icons, such as Coca-Cola, originate in the USA. It is difficult to separate negative views of American culture from negative views of American politics and foreign policy. In Table 4.10, US science and technology are generally seen as positive, but cultural exports such as ideas and media are viewed more negatively.

Superpower futures

What are the implications of the continued rise of new superpowers?

By the end of this section you should:

➤ *be aware of the resource implications of the rise of the new superpowers*

> understand the impact that the new superpowers will have on the older core countries
> have considered the likely impact of the shifting distribution of power on the global periphery
> realise that shifts in the distribution of power may cause increased tensions

The impact on resources

In the last 20 years new global powers have emerged. The 'newcomers' are Brazil, Russia, India and China – collectively known as the BRICs. As the EU has expanded to include 27 nations, its power as a bloc has grown. There has been spectacular economic growth in Gulf states such as the UAE, Qatar and Bahrain. Economic growth in the emerging powers has had some obvious benefits: for example, China has lifted 200 million people out of poverty since 1990. In Brazil income growth has expanded the middle class and shrunk the number of people in poverty (Figure 4.16).

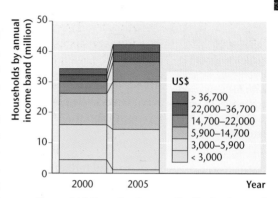

Figure 4.16 Changing income distribution in Brazil

However, this economic development is raising a number of concerns, including:

> the accelerating rise in the demand for energy and other resources
> the impact on the environment – from global warming to localised river pollution
> the uneven distribution of the benefits of economic growth, with growing inequality between the urban rich and rural poor

The last of these concerns could create internal tensions that might destabilise and derail economic growth.

Energy

The pressure on energy and other resources can be illustrated by car ownership. In 2003, 13.6 out of every 1,000 urban households in China had a car (Figure 4.17). The highest ownership rates were in Beijing (66 per 1,000) and Guangdong (43.7 per 1,000). In the same year, the car ownership rate in the USA was 750 per 1,000. If India and China achieve future car ownership levels even half of those in the USA, there will be double the current number of cars in the world.

The rapid rise in oil prices in 2007 and 2008 was the outcome of rising demand and stagnating supply. Oil may be being pumped out of the ground at a faster rate than new reserves are being discovered.

A key resource concern is the path India and China take as they continue to grow economically and gain power. If growth

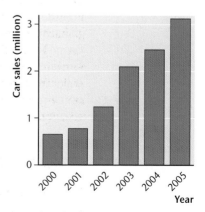

Figure 4.17 Growth in car sales in China

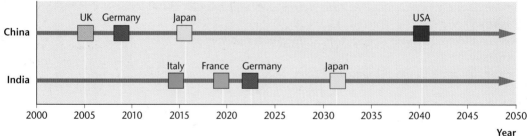

Figure 4.18
Achievement of income equivalence with the developed economies by India and China: projections

Source: National Intelligence Council, 2007

trends since 1990 continue, some time in the first half of this century the two emerging Asian powers will reach total GDP levels similar to those of the EU countries and the USA today (Figure 4.18).

Environment

Chinese and Indian ecological footprints might be similar to those of the EU and the USA by 2040, which would place huge pressure on water, energy and land resources. In reality this sort of future is probably unachievable, as current known oil, gas, water and farmland resources simply could not support such consumption levels. Such a level of global consumption might be possible with a dramatic shift toward use of renewable resources. This would involve radical restructuring of the way humans consume resources.

The impact on the older core regions

The rise of the emerging superpowers has enormous implications for the rest of the world, not least the citizens and governments of those countries that have enjoyed both political power and economic wealth. Until recently the emergence of new economic superpowers was seen by the established powers as more of an opportunity than a challenge. The EU, Japan and the USA have experienced economic growth and falling consumer prices driven by the explosion of economic activity in semi-peripheral NICs and RICs.

In the future there may be uncomfortable power shifts. One likely cause is dwindling fossil fuel supplies. As oil becomes scarcer and more expensive, tensions may begin to build. There may be potential for conflict between the major consumers of oil as they seek to secure supply (see Figure 1.4, page 8). Some of the powers, such as Russia and the Gulf states, have their own oil and gas reserves. In the future this could be a source of increased power.

Case study | **Russia and its energy exports**

Russia's economy relies on crude oil and natural gas exports. In the last 20 years it has uncovered significant reserves of both oil and gas in its Siberian provinces. These could add significantly to Russia's global power. Russia has developed important export partnerships to the east (China) and the west (Europe). Figure 4.19 shows Russia's present and proposed pipeline network. Russia depends on the

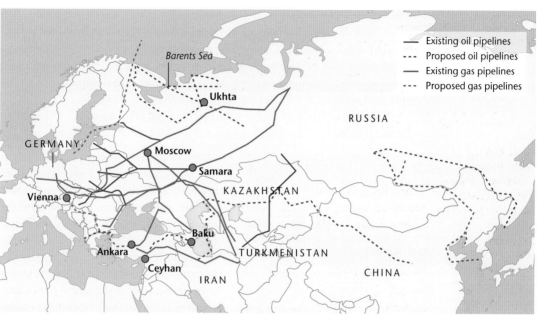

—	Existing oil pipelines
- - -	Proposed oil pipelines
—	Existing gas pipelines
- - -	Proposed gas pipelines

Figure 4.19 Russian oil and gas pipelines

European market to buy 80% of its oil exports, but the USA is keen to become a buyer and China's demand for oil is ever-growing.

During the past decade, China has joined Japan and South Korea as a major importer of crude oil from the middle east. This region supplies
- almost 50% of China's oil
- 80% of Japan and South Korea's oil

All three countries are in need of alternative crude oil sources and supply routes. Russia would seem to be the obvious source.

Asia's great cities need to reduce air pollution by switching to natural gas. Already the liquefied natural gas (LNG) imports of Japan, South Korea and Taiwan account for nearly 80% of all traded LNG. Much of this comes from south Asia and Australia. For mainland China, the cost of LNG has been a constraint, and it has been looking for more cost-effective ways of increasing its access to natural gas. An obvious source would be the large hydrocarbon reserves in nearby Siberia and Sakhalin Island.

In a world where energy resources are increasingly significant, the potentially vast fields of oil and gas that underlie Russia's Siberian provinces are a key card in international affairs.

Natural resource reserves have given Russia increased global significance and confidence. The impacts of this have been felt by several countries:
- In 2006 Russia cut its gas supplies to Ukraine for 3 days over a payment dispute, and in March 2008 it reduced supplies to its neighbour by 25%.
- In August 2008 Russian troops entered Georgia, leading to a short conflict and international crisis.
- In August 2007 Russian submarines planted two flags on the Arctic seabed, effectively claiming sovereignty over a large area of the Arctic thought to have oil reserves.
- Russia has repeatedly warned the USA not to expand NATO into eastern Europe or to site missiles there.
- Russian gas supplies to Ukraine and the EU were cut off in 2008–09.

All of these actions have raised international tensions and led some people to speak of a 'new Cold War'. Taken together, they warn the USA to keep out of what Russia considers its sphere of influence.

Preserving prosperity

Cheaper food, cheaper clothing and electronics from China have benefited people in the USA and the EU. They have come to terms with increasing dependence on the emerging power, believing that their own wealth is assured by their ownership of the quaternary industry, high-tech research facilities and dominance of global finance and services. This belief has been dealt a double blow by:

➤ increased outsourcing of research and technology jobs, especially to India
➤ financial turmoil in the banking sector during the 2008 credit crunch

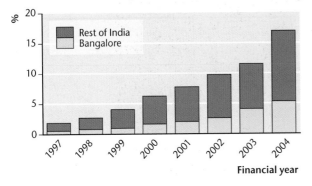

Figure 4.20 Growth of software exports from Bangalore and India

Major global technology players, such as Microsoft and Apple, have established research facilities in China and India (Figure 4.20). Rather than bring these countries' graduates to the 'global villages' of core countries, they have gone to the source of that innovative and imaginative labour force. The worry is that these mega-corporations owe no loyalty to their home country. Outsourcing of jobs has become a key concern for many Americans.

Restructuring

In the USA a painful period of economic restructuring is likely to continue for some time. The US car industry is a case in point. Once pre-eminent in the world, it has shrunk drastically since the 1970s. As Figure 4.21 shows, the USA is an important market for cars but the BRICs have caught up.

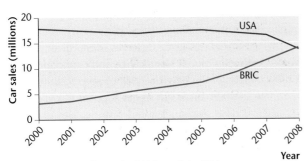

Figure 4.21 Car sales in the BRICs and the USA

Detroit's big three, Chrysler, Ford and General Motors, were begging the US government for financial help in December 2008 to avoid collapse. Lack of investment and a failure to compete with Japanese car technology brought Detroit to its knees. In 2008, the top five best-selling cars in the USA were Japanese in origin. Chinese car companies are gearing up to launch themselves on world markets.

➤ Dongfeng is investing US$1.3 billion in a research and development centre and factory in Wuhan with a capacity of 333,000 vehicles a year.
➤ FAW has committed US$1.8 billion to developing vehicles between now and 2015.
➤ By 2015 Geely will produce 1.7 million cars a year from nine factories in China and overseas plants planned in Mexico, South Africa, Indonesia, Ukraine and Russia.
➤ Chery is planning a fourth factory with a capacity of 200,000 cars, bringing its total capacity to 850,000 units by 2010.

Anthony Thompson

*Photograph 4.4
The future of the
US car industry?*

The future for the US car industry, once a symbol of the country's superpower might, is likely to be intensified global competition (Photograph 4.4).

Space

The EU and the USA may need to get used to competition from the emerging powers in other areas. A key area of US international prestige since the 1960s has been the exploration of space. The USSR won the first few rounds of the 'space race' by launching the first satellite in 1957 and completing the first manned space mission in 1961. The USA then threw the entire might of its military industrial complex behind a moon landing, which it achieved in 1969. By the 1970s the race fizzled out, and US dominance of space was ensured with the development of its space shuttle and the collapse of the USSR in 1991. In recent years, new competition has emerged to challenge NASA's number one position (Table 4.11).

Table 4.11 The twenty-first-century space race

USA	Europe	Russia	India	China	Japan
National Aeronautics and Space Administration (NASA)	European Space Agency (ESA)	Roskosmos (RKA)	Indian Space Research Organisation (ISRO)	China National Space Administration (CNSA)	Japan Aerospace Exploration Agency (JAXA)
Planning its *Orion* launch vehicle to replace the space shuttle Aims to build a moon base by 2020, and visit Mars by 2037	Focuses on unmanned exploration but may plan future manned missions	Planning a manned, reusable spacecraft called *Kliper* to begin missions in 2015	Planning manned missions to begin in 2015 using its GLSV–III rockets	Planning its own space station, and to land a probe on the moon by 2010. Plans manned Mars missions by 2040–60	Planning independent manned missions and a lunar base by 2030

The emerging powers and the majority of the world

Many developing nations, especially in Africa, could be forgiven for envying the rise of China and India. Despite the rise of the BRICs, the majority of the world still lives in the developing 'South'. The growing prosperity of the BRICs is unevenly distributed inside those countries. In China, the prosperous, urban coastal zone is in sharp contrast to the poor, rural interior (Figure 4.22). In India the growing middle class is concentrated in cities and the southern states.

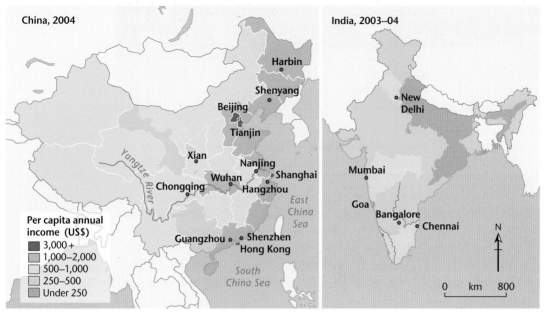

Figure 4.22 Income inequality in China and India, 2004

Opportunities

Will the emerging powers provide the developing world with new opportunities, or more of the same? Growing economies demand resources, some human and some physical. The growing Gulf state economies are rapidly diversifying away from oil and gas towards tourism, services, and research and development. This has generated a spectacular building boom in the UAE, Qatar and Bahrain (Photograph 4.5). The construction workers required come from Pakistan and India:

> It was the birth of his second daughter that finally forced Raju Singh's decision to leave home. The stonemason borrowed $2,500 from a labor recruiter in his village in Rajasthan to pay for an air ticket to Dubai. Three years on, his dream seems as elusive as a desert mirage. In February he finally paid off his debts to the labor recruiter in Rajasthan, including 42% interest on the loan. Sitting in a labor camp in the sprawling workers' district of Sonapur outside Dubai, Singh says he now spends most of his monthly income of about $190 feeding himself. Six days a week he wakes at 4 a.m. to travel to the building site, where he begins his 11-hour day at 6.30 a.m.
>
> (*Time Magazine*, 2008)

*Photograph 4.5
Building the future
in Dubai. The non-
airconditioned
buses transport
migrant
construction
workers from their
desert camps to the
building sites*

Raju might be forgiven for comparing himself to an Irish navvy building Britain's canals and railways in the eighteenth and nineteenth centuries. The low-skill migrant worker's story does not seem to change even if the superpowers do.

Resources

The BRICs are in need of physical as well as human resources to fuel their economic growth. It has been estimated that China alone accounted for over 40% of the total growth in the global demand for oil in 2003–08. Of all the global arenas, Africa is probably the most disputed today. As a continent it has huge mineral wealth. The Democratic Republic of Congo and Zambia possess 50% of the world's cobalt reserves, while 98% of the world's chrome reserves are located in Zimbabwe and South Africa. South Africa also accounts for 90% of the reserves of metals in the platinum group (platinum, palladium, rhodium, ruthenium, iridium and osmium).

 Case study **China in Africa: development or colonisation?**

China's search for oil and mineral resources has focused on Africa. Chinese companies are investing heavily in Africa, primarily in oil exploration projects and infrastructure to help exploit and export raw materials (Figure 4.23).

- Around 30% of all oil used in China comes from Africa.
- In 2007, Chinese investment in Africa totalled US$30 billion.

- China has invested US$8 billion building oil pipelines in Sudan.

There were estimated to be 750,000 Chinese working in Africa in 2008, and over 900 Chinese companies.

Critics argue that all China wants from Africa is its resources, and that it has no interest in African development. Most investment goes to African governments, TNCs and Chinese companies, not to ordinary Africans. China has been accused of overlooking human rights issues, for example:

- providing a huge increase in oil revenues to the government of Sudan, which has helped fund war in Darfur
- propping up the government of Robert Mugabe in Zimbabwe with arms shipments

In many cases large Chinese-funded infrastructure projects are built by Chinese workers, not local labour. It remains to be seen whether the financial benefits of such investment help some of the least developed countries out of poverty. In general, mining, quarrying and forestry bring few skilled jobs and pay low wages. The age-old problem of Africa's resources leaving the continent as cheap raw materials rather than expensive manufactured goods is likely to continue.

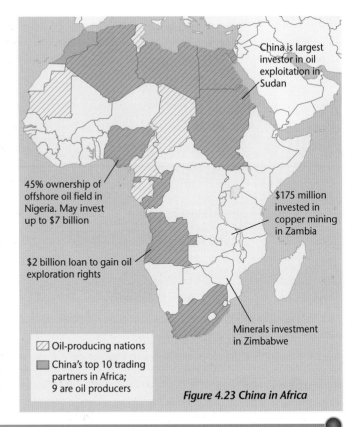

China is largest investor in oil exploitation in Sudan

45% ownership of offshore oil field in Nigeria. May invest up to $7 billion

$175 million invested in copper mining in Zambia

$2 billion loan to gain oil exploration rights

Minerals investment in Zimbabwe

Oil-producing nations

China's top 10 trading partners in Africa; 9 are oil producers

Figure 4.23 China in Africa

Oil

The US thirst for oil is also boosting the strategic importance of countries such as Angola and Nigeria. Experts agree that over the next 10 years Africa will become the USA's second most important supplier of oil, and possibly natural gas. US strategy in Africa has two main elements. The first is unlimited access to key markets, energy and other strategic resources, and the second is the military securing of transport routes along which raw materials will be moved to the USA. In July 2003 an attempted coup in São Tomé and Principe, a small west African state rich in oil reserves, triggered US intervention in the archipelago. Three months later, oil companies, mostly US ones, offered more than US$500m to explore the deep waters of the Gulf of Guinea, shared by Nigeria and São Tomé and Principe. That was double what the countries had hoped for.

Tensions between cultures

During the Cold War there was a huge cultural divide between the USA and the USSR. It was based on a profound difference in political ideologies (capitalism vs communism). Although Russia has since turned towards capitalism, the cultural tension remains. Differences in values are magnified by the mutual distrust and suspicion that persist between the two countries.

Even though they are allies, cultural tensions exist between the USA and Europeans. There are some key societal and cultural differences. Although generalising about cultural difference is notoriously hard (if not dangerous), Table 4.12 suggests some key European/American differences.

Table 4.12 European and American characteristics and attitudes

European	American
A stronger emphasis on the welfare state	Individual provision for healthcare and education
A tendency to eat as a family	
A lower legal age for alcohol consumption	Greater prevalence of fast food
A more liberal attitude to nudity in the media	Shopping malls rather than high streets and outdoor shopping areas
	More overtly religious
Generally not in favour of capital punishment	More concerned about 'being number one'

War

Support for the USA's war in Iraq was initially solid, with the UK, Spain, Italy, Georgia, South Korea, Australia and Ukraine all providing over 1,000 service personnel to the invasion force. The war was opposed by France and Germany, and by the UN secretary-general Kofi Annan. After the initial invasion of Iraq in 2003, many countries withdrew their troops, undermining the 'coalition'. The Iraq War and the drawn-out attempt to restore some form of peaceful, functioning government to Iraq undermined the USA's international status. Many Europeans believe the war was less about removing Saddam Hussein and his alleged weapons of mass destruction than about ensuring the USA had access to middle east oil supplies.

Terrorism

A feature of the twenty-first century has been a rise in global terrorism. Terrorism itself is not new. The UK experienced terrorism associated with Northern Ireland for decades, and Basque separatist terrorism is ongoing in Spain. Figure 4.24 shows terrorist attacks carried out by Islamist groups since 2001, as well as 'flashpoints'. These flashpoints are locations where the involvement of the USA and other countries is seen to be directly opposed to the interests of Islam and Muslims by extreme Islamist groups such as Al-Qaeda.

Islamic terrorism is most often directed against the USA, although it is questionable whether terrorism is motivated by a dislike of American culture. It is more likely to be directed against American military and political actions.

The future

Tensions between superpowers are only likely to increase in the future. As the emerging superpowers gain ground, there is the potential for a clash of cultures. Despite globalisation there are at least four cultural world views (Figure 4.25), and several of these are present in emerging powers. In the Muslim world the growth

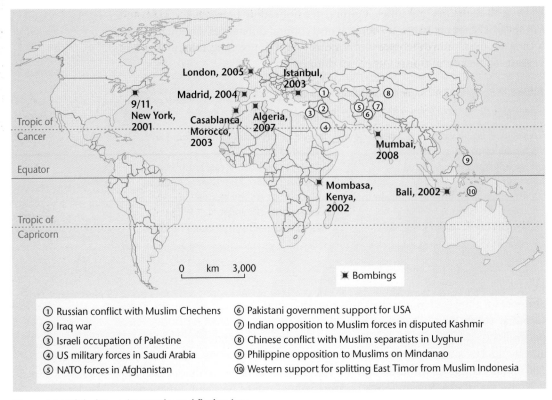

Figure 4.24 Global terrorist attacks and flashpoints

① Russian conflict with Muslim Chechens
② Iraq war
③ Israeli occupation of Palestine
④ US military forces in Saudi Arabia
⑤ NATO forces in Afghanistan
⑥ Pakistani government support for USA
⑦ Indian opposition to Muslim forces in disputed Kashmir
⑧ Chinese conflict with Muslim separatists in Uyghur
⑨ Philippine opposition to Muslims on Mindanao
⑩ Western support for splitting East Timor from Muslim Indonesia

of Islamic fundamentalism, with its opposition to what it sees as the moral corruption of the West, has created huge tensions and as China develops, demands for European-style freedoms there may grow.

It is difficult to know what the future will bring for the superpowers or emerging powers of today. The US National Intelligence Council report *Global Trends 2025: A Transformed World* puts forward a number of future scenarios. These are very much the world viewed from a US perspective, but they are worth consideration. Possible scenarios by 2025 include the following:

1 A multi-polar world replaces the current unipolar one, following the rise of China, India and other emerging powers. The USA remains the most powerful, but less dominant, superpower.

2 Increased risk of an arms race, possibly a nuclear one, in the middle east and east Asia if tensions and conflict in those regions cannot be resolved.

3 Increased resource nationalism and tension as resources such as oil and water run short and increase in price. Rising tensions develop between the BRICs as they search for new resources.

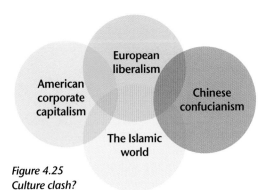

Figure 4.25
Culture clash?

4 Long-term decline of Europe and Japan if they fail to meet the challenges of rapidly ageing populations.

5 Resource-rich powers (Russia, the middle east) increasingly challenge the political and economic order.

Review questions

1 Suggest and justify a set of criteria for defining what is a superpower.
2 Examine the ways in which superpowers exert their influence.
3 To what extent have the ways of maintaining power changed over time?
4 Explain and illustrate what is meant by 'cultural imperialism'.
5 In what ways are the old core countries threatened by the new superpowers?
6 'The tensions between today's superpowers are economic rather than political.' Discuss.

Chapter

5

Bridging the development gap

The gap between the level of development of the world's richest and poorest countries is widening. This can be demonstrated by a variety of measures, and a range of theoretical concepts can help to explain the causes of the gap that was once referred to as the North–South divide, and its widening. Development gaps may be observed at spatial scales other than the global. There are divides between the regions of individual countries and between their urban and rural areas. Gaps also exist in the contexts of ethnicity and gender. A challenge facing us all, no matter where we live on the globe, is how to close these gaps.

The causes of the development gap

What is the nature of the development gap and how has it arisen?

By the end of this section you should:
➤ *have looked at different ways of measuring the development gap*
➤ *be familiar with the theories that explain why it is widening*
➤ *have identified the global players and their different roles in relation to the gap*
➤ *have examined the roles of trade and investment in maintaining the gap*

*Photograph 5.1
A school in Ethiopia.
Education is a
crucial factor in
development*

Jennifer Reynolds

Edexcel A2 Geography

Measuring the development gap

Development generally means the ways in which a country seeks to develop economically and to improve the standard of living for its inhabitants. The **development gap** describes the widening difference in level of development between the world's richest and poorest countries. It can also occur within countries, for example between regions or between urban and rural areas.

The global development gap can be measured in a variety of ways. Traditionally, a country's level of development has been shown by economic indicators of its wealth, such as gross domestic product (GDP) per capita. GDP is the total value of goods and services produced by a country during a year. Gross national income (GNI) is similar, but also includes income from overseas investment by organisations and residents. It therefore includes income from shares, and company profits from manufacturing or investment overseas (e.g. income from Coca-Cola returning to the parent company in the USA). For this reason, it is generally better to use GDP to measure income (Figure 5.1).

North and South

GDP is used to classify countries as more developed and less developed. In 1981 the Brandt Commission's report on world development emphasised what it saw as a division between the wealthy 'North', mainly in the northern hemisphere, and the poorer 'South', mainly in the southern hemisphere. The boundary separating them was known as the Brandt Line or the North–South divide (Figure 5.1). Later, this twofold classification was refined by the World Bank into three main

Figure 5.1 Global distribution of per capita GDP, 2004

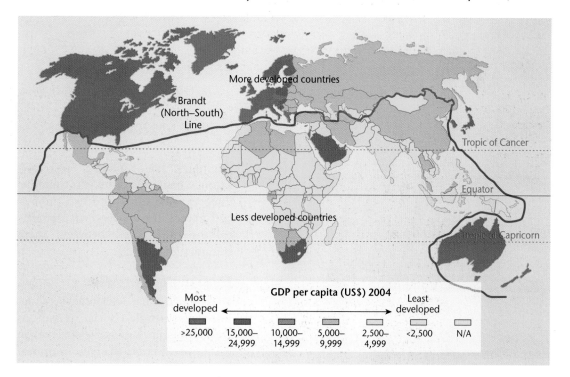

More developed countries

Brandt (North–South) Line

Tropic of Cancer

Equator

Less developed countries

Tropic of Capricorn

GDP per capita (US$) 2004

Most developed → Least developed

>25,000 | 15,000–24,999 | 10,000–14,999 | 5,000–9,999 | 2,500–4,999 | <2,500 | N/A

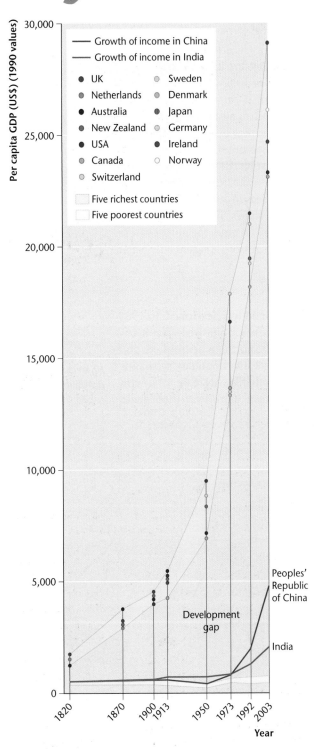

Figure 5.2 Changing per capita GDP

Table 5.1 Rankings based on per capita GDP and HDI values, 2002. 1 is most developed

	GDP per capita rank	HDI rank
Botswana	59	119
China	87	92
Costa Rica	53	41
Cuba	155	53
Iran	73	94
Poland	46	35
Saudi Arabia	48	68
South Africa	45	101
Sweden	16	2
UK	19	12

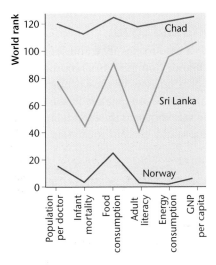

Figure 5.3 Development profiles

groupings: high-, middle- and low-income countries, with the 'middle' category subdivided into two ('upper' and 'lower'). The development gap refers to the differences between these countries (Figure 5.2).

Human development

The UN argues that development is about improving people's social as well as economic wellbeing – addressing human development rather than just economic

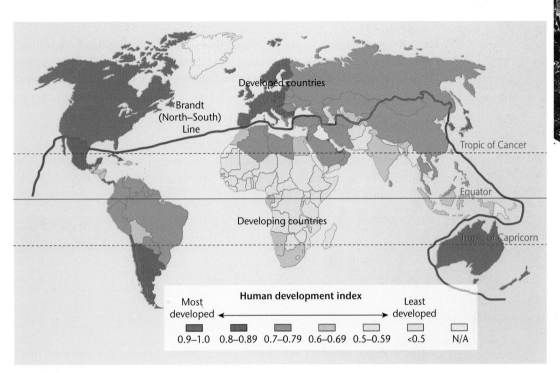

Figure 5.4 Global distribution of HDI, 2003

development. For example, people with low incomes may have a decent quality of life if they have access to free healthcare, free education and clean water (Photograph 5.1). More recent indicators of development have therefore focused on demographic and social factors such as literacy rates, life expectancy, number of people per doctor and infant mortality. These can be combined to reflect a broader picture of development. The human development index (HDI) was devised by the UN to describe human development (both economic and social) within countries. It is based on three factors: life expectancy, literacy, and per capita GDP. The HDI ranges from 0 (least developed) to 1 (most developed) (Figure 5.4).

It is interesting to compare the picture of development given by different indicators. Table 5.1 compares a country's ranking based on per capita GDP and HDI values. Development profiles can give a visual representation of a country's level of development according to its world ranking on different indicators (Figure 5.3).

Gender

The more recent gender-related development index (GDI) shows the inequalities between men and women in terms of life expectancy, education levels and income. It is one of the five indicators used in the UN Development Programme's annual *Human Development Report* (Table 5.2).

Table 5.2 Top and bottom 10 countries according to the GDI, 2007

Top 10	Bottom 10
1 Iceland	177 Sierra Leone
2 Norway	176 Burkina Faso
3 Australia	175 Guinea-Bissau
4 Canada	174 Niger
5 Ireland	173 Mali
6 Sweden	172 Mozambique
7 Switzerland	171 Central African
8 Japan	Republic
9 Netherlands	170 Chad
10 France	169 Ethiopia
[16 UK]	168 Congo (DR)

Continuum

The difference between countries is sometimes called a **development continuum** rather than a gap. Some people believe this better reflects reality: there is a gradation of countries at different levels of development rather than clusters in distinct groups.

Distribution

Table 5.3 Per cent shares of GNI and population by country groupings

Development data can also provide information about the distribution of inequality. Table 5.3 shows the unequal division of the world's wealth and population between the major economic regions identified by the World Bank, and the variety in their distribution.

Region (income per capita)	% share of GNI (2005)	% share of population (2005)
High-income countries (US$10,726 or more) e.g. UK, USA	78.9	15.7
Upper middle-income countries ($3,466–10,725) e.g. Turkey, Thailand	7.5	9.3
Lower middle-income countries ($876–3,465) e.g. Thailand, Brazil	10.6	38.4
Low-income countries ($875 or less) e.g. Bangladesh, Kenya	3.0	38.6

It is clear that whatever indicator is used to measure global development, there are large differences between countries. Table 5.4 shows a range of social, political, economic and physical factors that can affect levels of development. Figure 5.5 shows how key development factors can interact.

Table 5.4 Factors affecting differences in levels of development

Factors	Examples
Physical resources	Water availability Quality and location of mineral deposits Harsh environments Natural soil quality Agricultural potential
Social	Population levels and dependency levels Birth rates and population policies Education levels and workforce skills Infrastructure quality, e.g. roads, telephone/internet access
Economic	Stage of industrial development Dependency on particular industries and globalisation trends Location of transnational corporations (TNCs) Trade links Economic groupings, e.g. G8, EU, World Trade Organization, G77 (promotes South–South cooperation)
Political	Commitment of governments to take action Level and conditions of overseas investment Level of debt Corruption The legacy of colonialism

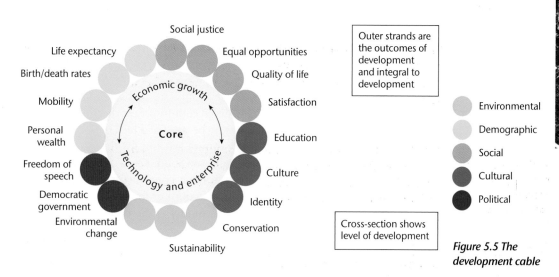

Outer strands are the outcomes of development and integral to development

Cross-section shows level of development

○ Environmental
○ Demographic
○ Social
● Cultural
● Political

Figure 5.5 The development cable

Theories of development

A number of theories have been put forward to explain the widening development gap between **developed** and **developing countries**. They all focus on the ways in which disparities in wealth can occur in different social, economic and political systems.

Rostow

Some theories are based on the economic development experienced by western Europe and North America. One of the first was Rostow's model of economic development (Figure 5.6), which argued that a country passes from underdevelopment to development through a series of stages of economic growth, similar to an aircraft taking off. In the 1960s Rostow believed that capital should be transferred from developed to developing countries to assist development. However, his theory did

Figure 5.6 Rostow's model of economic development

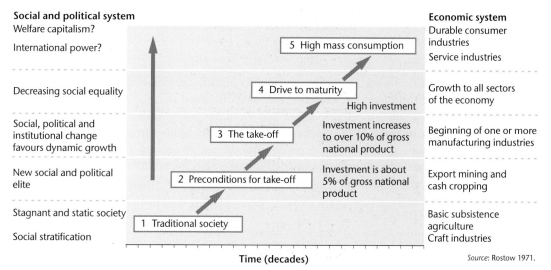

Source: Rostow 1971.

not take into account several important non-economic factors of development, such as high rates of population growth and political changes.

Poverty cycle

Other theories have focused on underdevelopment, using poverty and social deprivation to explain the inequality between countries. Less developed countries are trapped in a continuing cycle of poverty because of a lack of capital (money) and low incomes. However, this theory cannot account for the rapid economic emergence of countries such as China, India and South Korea. It also assumes that development takes place in isolation from other countries and is free of global interactions. Furthermore, it does not take account of foreign aid or loans from international banks. An extension of this model is the cycle of development (Figure 5.7), which takes a more positive view.

Figure 5.7 The development cycle

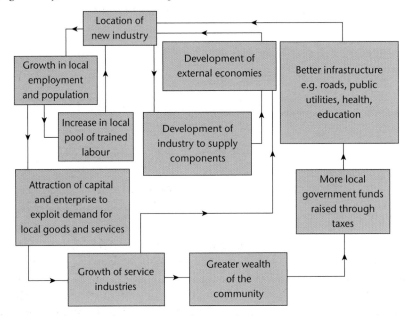

Politics

Political models examine the impact of different philosophies on equality and development. For example, Karl Marx believed that the capitalist free market economy caused exploitation and social inequality while communism, in which the state runs all key sectors of the economy, made the effects of development more equitable. Rostow's model of development also has a political aspect. It is a model of a capitalist society developing a high level of material wealth alongside economic growth.

Dependency

Gundar Frank's dependency theory of development suggested that developed countries, such as the USA, control and exploit less developed 'satellite' areas of the world. This produces a relationship of dominance and dependency possibly leading to poverty and underdevelopment in the less-developed countries. One example of this is colonialism, and its legacy.

Core–periphery

The relationship between regions or countries is a key focus of the core–periphery theories. Friedmann argued that beneficial effects can spread from developed core regions or countries to less developed, **peripheral** regions. Myrdal's model is similar (Figure 5.8), except that spread effects are outweighed by backwash effects which favour the core region. This widens the development gap. Many governments attempt to neutralise backwash effects with international aid or trade agreements.

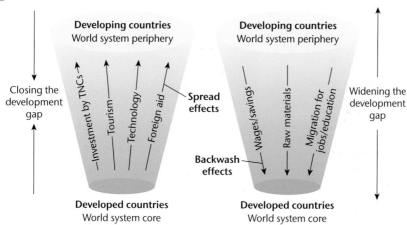

Figure 5.8
Myrdal's model

Globalisation

All these models illustrate that geographical disparities in wealth and development arise from different social, economic and political systems. More recent debates have focused on the effects of economic globalisation on development. Countries are becoming increasingly connected and interdependent at a global scale, in complex ways that are cheaper, faster and more efficient than previously. The main types of global flow that connect places around the world involve the movement of people (migrants, tourists, business people), capital, technology, ideas (including political ideologies) and information.

Debt

One other factor needs to be identified in this search for explanations of the development gap: the debt crisis. In the last 50 years, many poor countries have accepted loans from rich countries. Interest payments on the loans affect development as they put pressure on the already stretched financial situation of a country. Loans have to be repaid, plus interest, and some have strings attached. For example, developed countries give trade loans to enable poorer countries to buy their products or services.

The debt crisis largely concerns the poorest countries, causing even more

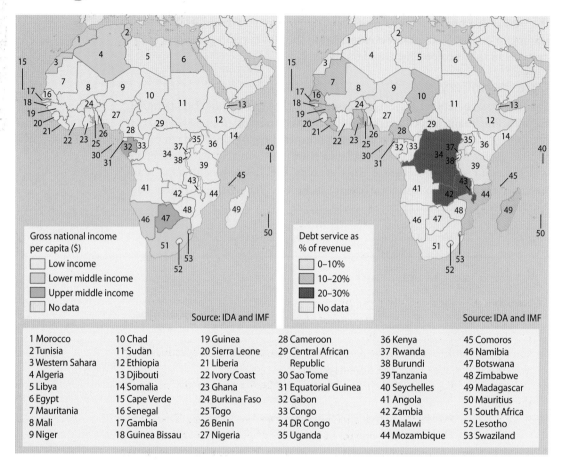

Figure 5.9 Africa's income and debt servicing, 2003

1 Morocco	10 Chad	19 Guinea	28 Cameroon	36 Kenya	45 Comoros
2 Tunisia	11 Sudan	20 Sierra Leone	29 Central African	37 Rwanda	46 Namibia
3 Western Sahara	12 Ethiopia	21 Liberia	Republic	38 Burundi	47 Botswana
4 Algeria	13 Djibouti	22 Ivory Coast	30 Sao Tome	39 Tanzania	48 Zimbabwe
5 Libya	14 Somalia	23 Ghana	31 Equatorial Guinea	40 Seychelles	49 Madagascar
6 Egypt	15 Cape Verde	24 Burkina Faso	32 Gabon	41 Angola	50 Mauritius
7 Mauritania	16 Senegal	25 Togo	33 Congo	42 Zambia	51 South Africa
8 Mali	17 Gambia	26 Benin	34 DR Congo	43 Malawi	52 Lesotho
9 Niger	18 Guinea Bissau	27 Nigeria	35 Uganda	44 Mozambique	53 Swaziland

hardship to their people and preventing the development gap closing. The problem is particularly severe in Africa (Figure 5.9).

The debt crisis was produced by a chain of events:

➤ The Arab–Israeli war of 1973–74 led to a sharp increase in oil prices.

➤ Individuals and governments in the oil-producing countries invested so-called petro-dollars (profits from oil sales) in rich countries' banks.

➤ These banks offered loans at low interest rates to recycle their large reserves of petro-dollars. Poor countries were encouraged to borrow to fund their development, and to exploit raw materials and grow cash crops so that they could pay back their loans with profits made from exports.

➤ In the 1980s, Western countries experienced recession and tried to combat rising inflation by increasing interest rates. At the same time crop surpluses led to a decline in prices. Demand for developing countries' goods fell. These factors, plus oil price increases, left developing countries unable to pay the interest on their debts.

Table 5.5 shows the external debts of a sample of countries. Debt-servicing as a percentage of exports of goods and services is taken to be a measure of the affordability of that debt.

Country	Total outstanding external debt (US$bn)	Debt servicing as % of exports of goods and services
Argentina	127.3	23
Brazil	240.5	19
Chile	58.2	14
Ghana	4.9	1
India	221.2	4
Indonesia	141.2	12
Kazakhstan	98.7	1
Kenya	6.7	7
Malawi	0.9	8
Malaysia	73.4	2
Mexico	205.3	14
Nigeria	8.0	17
Ukraine	92.5	5

Table 5.5 Debt and debt servicing in a sample of countries, 2005

The debt crisis continues because of:

➤ High interest rates charged by some banks; typically 10–25% higher than for projects in developed countries.

➤ Corruption within developing countries' governments and companies which diverts loan monies from the intended target.

➤ Political instability leading to loss of confidence that some countries can repay their loans.

➤ New IMF and World Bank loans to help pay back the old ones. These have conditions attached, e.g. allowing foreign imports which harm local industries.

➤ Trade barriers imposed by developed countries that make it hard for poorer countries to export their goods.

Global players

The actions of different global organisations can improve or exacerbate the development gap. Table 5.6 shows examples of such organisations.

TNCs

The most influential players in promoting economic development are the transnational corporations (TNCs). The largest of these companies now match some countries in terms of their wealth, power and trading. TNCs are driven by the need to maintain profitability to reward shareholders, so they constantly search for more 'efficient' methods of production and cheaper locations for that production. Traditionally, TNCs have located in developed countries or in the newly industrialised countries (e.g. South Korea, Taiwan, Singapore, Malaysia – Photograph 5.2). However, other areas of the world such as the emerging BRIC economies (Brazil, Russia, India and China) and South Africa are developing their own large corporations. We may see a second generation of globalisation, with companies from the South playing a significant role.

Table 5.6 Global players and organisations

Type and scale	Example organisations	Role/focus	Impact on development in developing countries
International organisations	The UN and its agencies World Bank International Monetary Fund (IMF)	Monitor and provide investment	Can provide investment for economic and social projects to improve standards Seen by some as 'top-down', with little regard for local needs
	World Trade Organization (WTO) Economic/trade blocs, e.g. European Union (EU), Association of Southeast Asian Nations (ASEAN)	Promote trade and economic cooperation between countries	Can promote trade between developed and developing countries Can raise standards of business practice and improve competitiveness of developed-country companies Can encourage trade dependency or create barriers to free and fair trade arrangements
International commercial	TNCs, e.g. Unilever, Nike, Nestlé, LG, Tata	Capitalist enterprises that create supply chains which spread across the world	Provide employment and investment in a country/region May exploit workers in developing countries to maximise cheap labour source and stay globally competitive Leakage of funds back to parent company
National political	Governments of particular countries	Influence economic and social conditions in their country (and sometimes globally)	Regulate the economy (e.g. by controlling interest rates) to make the most of market opportunities, attract inward investment and maintain economic competitiveness Create the right conditions for businesses to flourish Provide physical infrastructure (power, roads, technology) to support further development Supply public services such as health and education Decisions can be affected by politics and existing alliances
Non-governmental organisations (NGOs)	Humanitarian bodies and charities, e.g. Unicef, Oxfam	Raise awareness of concerns Give aid and practical assistance to developing countries	Non-biased assistance to development projects or relief programmes Can be involved where global politics keeps out governments A 'bottom-up' approach which takes account of local needs NGOs rely on funding which may be unreliable

Photograph 5.2
A Tesco store in
Malaysia

Indicators

Various indices can be used to measure how global or transnational a company is. The UN's transnationality index (TNI) is based on three ratios: foreign assets to total assets, foreign sales to total sales, and foreign employment to total employment. The geographical spread index (GSI) addresses the number of countries in which a company operates. The GSI is calculated as the square root of the internationalisation index (the number of foreign affiliates divided by the total number of affiliates) multiplied by the number of host countries. Table 5.7 illustrates these indicators.

Table 5.7 A sample of the world's TNCs

Company	Location of headquarters	Industry sector	TNI (%)	Number of host countries	GSI	Rank in top 100 TNCs
Thomson Corporation	Canada	Media	97.2	25	48.5	76
Roche Group	Switzerland	Pharmaceuticals	90.5	53	67.8	34
Philips Electronics	Netherlands	Electronics	87.4	62	67.7	44
Nestlé SA	Switzerland	Food and beverages	86.8	94	93.9	27
Vodafone	UK	Telecoms	82.4	19	26.4	2
Hutchinson Whampoa	Hong Kong	Various	80.8	15	36.8	20
Honda	Japan	Motor vehicles	80.3	34	44.9	19
BP	UK	Oil/petroleum	79.4	62	65.3	4
Coca-Cola	USA	Food and beverages	72.7	30	46.9	73
McDonald's	USA	Food and beverages	69.6	30	39.6	72
SingTel	Singapore	Telecoms	67.4	24	24.5	Below 100
Unilever	UK/Netherlands	Various	63.5	33	52.3	57
Sony	Japan	Electronics	57.9	42	56.2	39
Hon Hai	Taiwan	Electronics	53.8	13	32.1	Below 100
IBM	USA	Electronics	54.7	66	77.3	30
Lenovo Group	China	Computers	50.8	15	37.6	Below 100
LG	South Korea	Electronics	49.2	24	48.4	Below 100
Samsung	South Korea	Electronics	45.4	32	53.2	87

TNCs can provide opportunities for economic development and poverty alleviation in a country. Whether a TNC **invests** in a country depends on its resources, the size of the economy, the business environment, government policies and how skilled the workforce is. Figure 5.10 sets out the possible impacts of TNCs on host countries.

Figure 5.10 Impacts of TNCs on host countries

Transnational company (TNC)

Economic impacts		Social and political impacts	Environmental impacts
Direct	**Indirect**		
• Linkages between foreign and domestic companies – supply chains, service contracts, etc. • Competition for local companies • Foreign investment (FDI) • Leakage of profits/finance out of the country • Can help smaller companies reach economies of scale • May lead to dependency on TNC	• Multiplier effects in the local community • Infrastructure development • Affects macroeconomic performance of the host country – income distribution, economic growth, balance of payments • Financial linkages to the government via taxes, wages, shared profits • Exports help to generate foreign exchange	• Generates employment • Develops skills and knowledge • Management not often local • Disrupts traditional lifestyles • Cost of government incentives to attract this investment • Impact if TNC withdraws from the area: unemployment, cycle of poverty • Exploitation of workers • Health and safety concerns • Corruption of officials to allow further developments • Conflict with government • Influx of migrant workers	• Exploitation of local resources • Pollution and long-term health issues • Impact on local ecosystems, e.g. deforestation • Factories need large amounts of energy and water: may conflict with the needs of the local community • Planning for accidents/cleaning operations

Case study: The impact of TNC mining activity in Botswana

Between 1970 and 2000, Botswana was one of the fastest-growing economies in the world. At the time of the country's independence in 1966, agriculture accounted for 40% of GDP, while mining was virtually non-existent. By 2006 agriculture accounted for 2% of GDP and mining (mostly of diamonds) for 40%. As a result of this mineral-led economic growth, Botswana, once one of the world's poorest states, has become an upper middle-income country.

Almost all the mining companies are either wholly owned by TNCs or operated as joint ventures between the government and TNCs (e.g. De Beers). Over the period 1975–2006, the industry directly contributed 46% of total GDP growth. Diamonds accounted for about 80% of Botswana's total exports between 2001 and 2005. This made it the world's largest producer and exporter of diamonds in value terms. Per capita GDP in Botswana has increased from US$800 in 1975 to US$16,500 in 2007. This has meant rising living standards and investment in social and economic infrastructure, plus healthy financial and balance-of-payments positions.

Two major mining companies have invested in health and education facilities in local communities. Both operate hospitals that are open to company employees and the general public. One has been actively addressing HIV/AIDS – estimated to affect 37% of adults in Botswana (Figure 5.11) – and was the first company to provide anti-retroviral therapy (ART) to employees and family members free of charge.

However, outside the mining industry Botswana continues to have problems with unemployment (true figures are estimated as high as 30%) and conflict in areas where mining, cattle-rearing and tourism try to coexist. Much of the new employment is in urban areas, as the economy moves towards more mining, manufacturing (for example car assembly) and tourism.

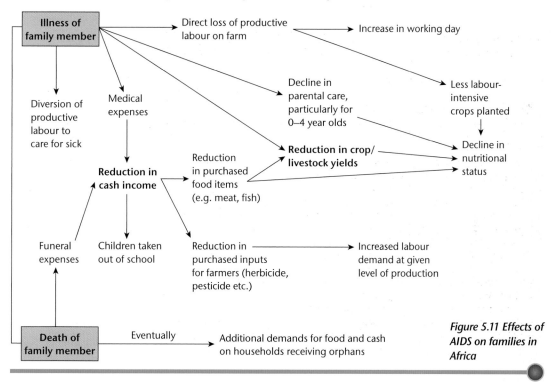

Figure 5.11 Effects of AIDS on families in Africa

Trade and investment

Trade flows

Increasing exports can help a country to narrow the development gap. Figure 5.12 highlights the distribution of international trade by value of exports. Traditionally, North–South trade flows have focused on developing countries exporting primary products such as minerals and agricultural produce. However, in the last 20 years developing countries have moved into manufacturing – about 80% of their merchandise exports are now manufactured products. There has also been a big increase in service exports from developing countries.

This has meant a change in the nature of North–South trade relations. Trade is often unequal, however. Some countries have trade surpluses (exports exceed imports), while others have trade deficits (imports exceed exports). Trade deficits may eventually lead to a 'debt trap' that inhibits investment and growth.

Economic globalisation has had a big impact on the flows of goods between countries. Some countries have had large increases in trade (e.g. China, India,

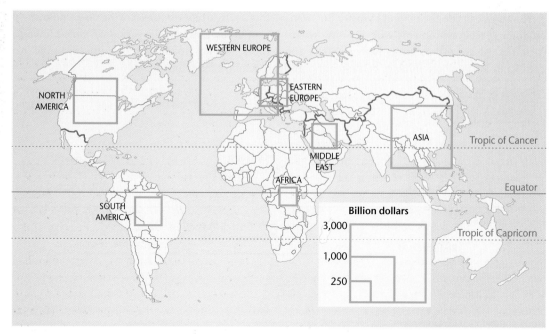

Figure 5.12 Distribution of international trade by value of exports, 2005

Mexico and Brazil), while others have had decreases. Inequality between rich and poor does not always change with increases in trade. In Uganda, inequality has decreased, with a good growth rate of 3.8% per capita. In Vietnam, however, there has been little change in inequality during the development of trade. Some argue that inequality in China has increased during its recent rapid economic growth. Some countries organise themselves into groups known as **trade blocs**. Although the volume of international trade increases each year, it is often dominated by wealthy countries in the EU, North America and east Asia. Over 80% (by value) of all exported goods come from these three regions. Only 2.5% originates from Africa.

Terms of trade

Another important consideration in international trade is the terms on which it takes place. A country's **terms of trade** is the ratio between the currencies earned from its exports (a unit price index is normally used) and the prices of imports. Generally speaking, world prices for raw materials have fallen over recent years in relation to the price of manufactured goods. Manufacturing adds value to commodities. Therefore, any countries that export raw materials and import manufactured goods are likely to have declining terms of trade. Often the poorest developing countries in this situation have to export even more as the world price falls. If all they have to export is cereals and other food products food becomes scarcer at home and prices rise. As a result there might be a decline in living standards and increased poverty. Recent rises in commodity prices have brought improved terms of trade for some countries, particularly those exporting minerals.

Case study — Trade patterns in coffee

Coffee is one of the most actively traded commodities in the world and is often known as 'black gold', second only to oil as a source of foreign exchange for some developing countries. It can account for as much as 80% of a country's foreign exchange earnings. Coffee is produced in tropical and subtropical climates in Latin America, Asia and Africa, largely by small landowners. Most of the world's coffee is exported to the high-income countries of Europe, North America, Japan and Australia (Table 5.8).

The traditional coffee industry's supply chain involves producers, middlemen, exporters, importers, roasters and retailers before the product reaches the consumer (Figure 5.13). This chain often works against coffee farmers in developing countries, who receive only a fraction of the final price paid by consumers. TNCs such as Nestlé dominate the industry, making it difficult for small farmers to negotiate better terms and prices. Moreover, the price of coffee on the global commodity market fluctuates quite wildly. The trend has been downward, which has had a significant economic, social and environmental impact on many developing countries:

- *Economic.* Farms abandoned, insecure land ownership, loss of jobs, reduced central revenue, knock-on effect on other economic sectors, reduced export earnings. Experienced in Cameroon, Central African Republic, Côte d'Ivoire, El Salvador, Ethiopia, Nicaragua.
- *Social.* Rural–urban migration, emigration, less money available for healthcare and education, increase in households living below the poverty line, increased malnutrition, increased indebtedness and growth in illicit crop production. Experienced in Cameroon, Central African

Producers: coffee farmers/plantation workers
Large coffee estates and plantations export their own harvests or have direct arrangements with a transnational coffee processing or distributing company

Collection centres/exporters: purchase the coffee below market price, keeping a high percentage for themselves

Importers: 'green' coffee is purchased by importers from exporters or plantation owners. They obtain coffee from around the world and have a strong influence on the supply train

Roasters: have the highest profit margin in the commodity chain. They sell pre-packaged coffee to companies such as Maxwell House

Suppliers: supermarkets, shops, cafés

Consumers

Typical fund distribution from a cappucino in a café

Producers, exporters, transporters (10%)

Retailers/café, roaster, importer (90%)

Figure 5.13 The coffee supply chain

Table 5.8 The global trade in coffee, 2007

Top ten export countries	
Country	**Production (1,000 bags) (% of world production)**
Brazil	36,070 (30.5)
Vietnam	17,500 (14.8)
Colombia	12,400 (10.5)
Indonesia	6,446 (5.5)
Ethiopia	5,733 (4.9)
India	4,850 (4.1)
Mexico	4,500 (3.8)
Guatemala	4,000 (3.4)
Honduras	3,833 (3.2)
Uganda	2,750 (2.3)

Top ten consumer countries	
Country	**Consumption (1,000 bags)**
USA	21,046
Brazil	16,900
Germany	8,624
Japan	7,282
Italy	5,799
France	5,594
Russian Federation	4,055
Canada	3,535
Spain	3,248
UK	2,824

Republic, Colombia, Costa Rica, Ecuador, El Salvador, Ethiopia, Nicaragua, Papua New Guinea and Vietnam.

■ *Environmental.* Abandonment of shaded plantations, cutting down shade trees for timber. Experienced in Ecuador, El Salvador and India.

The most effective way to achieve development through trade is to agree on improved trade conditions and better market access for developing countries. This can generate more gains for developing countries than any other area of international economic cooperation or aid. But it is not only unfair trade conditions that inhibit development. Other handicaps include rapid population growth, political instability and climatic disasters (such as drought) that reduce food supply.

The consequences of the development gap

What are the implications of the development gap at different scales for the world's poorest people?

By the end of this section you should:
➤ *understand what the development gap means to people in the most disadvantaged countries*
➤ *be aware that poverty is becoming increasingly concentrated in developing megacities*
➤ *appreciate that the development gap has ethnic and religious dimensions*
➤ *have evaluated the positive and negative consequences of countries moving out of poverty*

Impact on people in poor countries

The development gap has social, economic, environmental and political consequences for people in the most disadvantaged countries, but the precise impacts

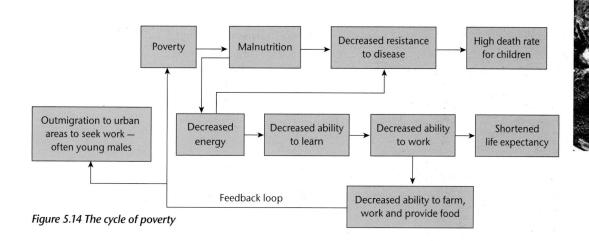

Figure 5.14 The cycle of poverty

vary. Urban and rural areas are often affected differently. Remote rural communities experience the worst effects of the cycle of poverty which is rooted in the inability to produce enough food (Figure 5.14).

The incidence of poverty in the developing world is declining in all regions except sub-Saharan Africa (Figure 5.15). But this does not mean the gap between rich and poor is narrowing. The statistics for individual countries show very high numbers of poor people – in some, as many as half the population is living in poverty (Figure 5.15). It is very difficult to find statistics about the incidence of rich people, or people who have a secure income.

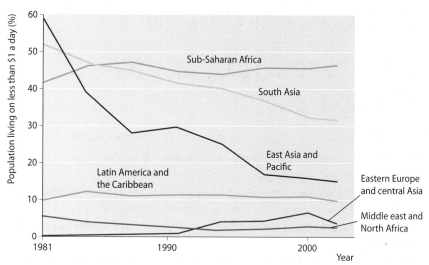

Figure 5.15 People living on less than US$1 per day

Castes

The development gap can create differences not just between the rich and poor, but also between groups such as castes in India or between males and females in the same country. A study of 300 people in rural villages in the coastal districts of Nellore and East Godavari, in India's Andhra Pradesh state, showed that caste is a key factor affecting who gets access to public facilities and services (Table 5.9).

Facility/service	Caste classification			
	High			Low
	Forward castes	Backward castes	Scheduled castes	Scheduled tribes
Access to a medical centre within 5 km (%)	67	22	51	9
Access to protected drinking water (%)	100	91	74	100
Completed primary education (%)	18	3	3	0
Own land (%)	32	6	0	0
Access to cyclone-resistant house (%)	67	32	18	41

Table 5.9 Access to facilities and services, by caste, 2007

Women

Women in developing countries are more likely than men to be unpaid family workers or occupy low-status jobs and have lower earnings. They often have limited participation in politics and government, which makes it difficult for them to influence policy. Although female literacy is seen as fundamental to improved health and development, 64% of illiterate adults are women, and 57% of children who receive no primary education are girls. In developing countries 1 in 61 women die during pregnancy or childbirth. In LDCs the figure is 1 in 17.

Megacities and the development gap

The fastest-growing economies generally show the highest rates of urbanisation, as much of the development in manufacturing and services occurs in urban areas. Cities in developing countries are growing rapidly in size and number as people migrate to them for work, access to public services, and a perceived higher standard of living (Figure 5.16).

Housing

The growth of large cities will have a considerable influence on future development. As cities grow, the cost of meeting basic needs such as housing, infrastructure and services increases, as does pressure on the environment. New migrants to a city often have little money, so they cannot rent a home or borrow money to buy one. Land and housing regulations make it difficult for poor people. As a result they either move in with friends or relatives, sleep on the streets or build a makeshift house on unused land, thus increasing the number of urban poor. These 'temporary' settlements tend to occur on land that is:

➤ too steep, marshy or polluted for building
➤ alongside transport routes
➤ close to the city centre but not developed because the owner is unknown or has left it empty, hoping it will increase in value
➤ on former farmland at the edge of the city, abandoned as the city spreads

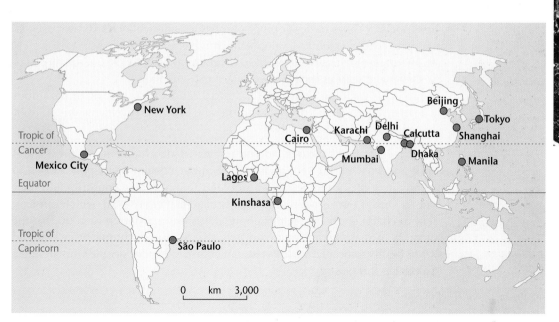

Figure 5.16 World megacities in 2025

Most of the urban poor do not have tenure security because their dwellings are illegal. Many people also rent in slums without formal contracts. As a result cities in developing countries often have high levels of inequality between rich and poor residents.

Deprivation

Urban poverty is a complex problem. The urban poor live with many hardships and face daily challenges, including:

➤ limited access to employment opportunities and income
➤ reliance on the informal economy
➤ inadequate, overcrowded and insecure housing and services
➤ violent and unhealthy environments due to the density and hazardous location of settlements and exposure to multiple pollutants
➤ little or no social protection mechanisms, with little support from the police or legal rights
➤ limited access to health and education opportunities or infrastructure such as telephone and internet services
➤ limited access to credit facilities

With such a high proportion of the population of many developing countries now living in cities, obtaining an accurate picture of where the poor are concentrated within those cities is an important requirement for targeting any management, which might improve the whole country's level of development.

Environment

Development and poverty reduction are often at the expense of the environment, unless there is careful management or significant efforts to promote sustainable

development. Cities in developing countries are affected by the 'brown agenda' associated with economic development. This has two components:

➤ environmental health issues linked to limited availability of good-quality land, shelter and services such as clean water and sanitation
➤ problems resulting from rapid industrialisation, such as toxic or hazardous waste; water, air and noise pollution, and industrial accidents due to poor standards of health and safety

The 'green agenda' focuses on the impact of development on the natural environment, while the 'blue agenda' looks at water quality and supply. Table 5.10 highlights some of the pollution problems in developing countries and their causes. One of the air pollutants is particulate matter (PM10s), which can have serious effects on health. For example, it was estimated even in 2000 that the megacity of Shanghai had approximately 15,100 cases of chronic bronchitis and 7,200 deaths associated with PM10s. Of course, it is poor people who are most exposed to this hazard.

Table 5.10 Pollution problems of developing country cities

Problem	Example	Causes
Air pollution	Air in cities such as Cairo is so poor that breathing it is the equivalent of smoking 60 cigarettes a day; major chemical and gas explosions, e.g. Bhopal, India	Traffic, factories, waste incineration plants and power plants, particularly where they are old and badly maintained Accidental spillages and explosions; poor health-and-safety standards
Water pollution	Untreated sewage in the River Ganges (from Varanasi and Kanpur)	Leaking sewers, landfill sites and industrial waste including oil and chemicals
Waste disposal	25% of all urban dwellers in the developing world have no adequate sanitation and no means of sewage disposal, especially in squatter settlements	Volumes of liquid sewage and industrial waste have increased considerably Contamination and health hazards arise from poor systems of disposal, rat infestation and waterborne diseases More solid wastes (paper and packaging) are being created as general levels of affluence rise
Water supply	The overuse of groundwater supplies has led to subsidence and flooding, e.g. in Bangkok	Cities consume huge amounts of water, especially as incomes and living standards rise; aquifers become depleted
Transport-related issues	Traffic queues in Mexico City are over 90 km each day; private car ownership in Taipei has increased 100-fold over a period of 20 years	Rising vehicle ownership leads to congestion, noise pollution, accidents and health issues related to the release of carbon monoxide, nitrogen oxides, ozone and particulates Under certain conditions, photochemical smog can develop

Case study   ## Dhaka, Bangladesh: a megacity under stress

By 2015 Dhaka is likely to have a population of 21 million and one of the highest population densities in the world (20,000 people per km²). Its rapid growth is due to high rates of natural increase and large

Table 5.11 Challenges and responses in Dhaka

	Challenge	Solutions or recent developments
Employment	Strong growth in manufacturing, finance, telecommunications and services. Dhaka, home to 80% of garment industry's 2 million employees, also attracts migrant workers: hawkers, roadside vendors, refuse recyclers. Unemployment remains high at 23% Women excluded from work in transport, services, trade. Thirty-three per cent of city's labour force is self-employed, mostly men. Child labour high in poorest households	Two export processing zones, home to 413 industries, set up to encourage export of garments, textiles etc. Bashundhara City: a developing economic area with high-tech industries, business corporations and one of the largest retail and leisure malls in Asia
Urban poor	Residential land too expensive for urban poor to purchase: 28% of Dhaka's population classified as poor, 12% as extremely poor. Only 5% live in permanent housing. Rents rise as demand outstrips supply. Many migrants end up in crowded slums in flood-risk areas (Photograph 5.3) About 4.2 million people live in slums; few slums have a clinic, only a quarter have a government school. One study found 58% of 6- to 7-year-olds did not attend school. Slums are controlled by gangs of mastaans who demand protection money and sell illegal connections to water and other services	Government improvements to drains and sanitation Ghore Fera (back to home programme) provides transportation, resettlement, income-generation loans, to help migrants return to village Micro-credit schemes, but low coverage Healthcare development, e.g. local community health volunteers Dormitory accommodation for female garment workers Work with local communities to rebuild trust in legal system and reduce violent crime
Environmental quality	Air pollution due to unregulated expansion and ineffective regulations exceeds national standards on more than 100 days of the year Most poor people lack clean water and sanitation, and rely on tube wells. Many live next to polluted water bodies, and depend on wood and dung for cooking. Result is poor air quality, respiratory infections, diarrhoea Only 27% of population connected to public sewer system. Pit latrines and septic tanks are used, but in densely populated areas these overflow into open drains. Almost all human, industrial and agricultural waste enters surface water untreated Poor management of water resources in Dhaka estimated to cost US$670 million annually, including impacts on human health	Promotion of cleaner gas-powered cooking stoves Ban on leaded petrol 2003 ban on two-stroke rickshaws cut particulate concentrations by a third; rickshaws now run on compressed natural gas Government's air quality management project reducing truck and bus emissions, reducing sulphur in diesel Work to improve water quality and supply, sanitation, flood management. Sewer and drainage system repairs to cost about US$100 million Public information to raise awareness of causes and impacts of poor air and water quality Stricter enforcement of waste disposal standards Investment in low-cost solutions to industrial effluent

volumes of migration from rural areas. This migration occurs because of insufficient job prospects in villages, extreme rural poverty, landlessness due to flooding, and large urban–rural wage differences, plus the perception that better education, health services and social amenities are to be found in the capital city. The situation in Dhaka is creating a number of management challenges (Table 5.11).

Photograph 5.3
Slums in Dhaka

Social and political unrest

It is easy to understand how disparities in wealth can generate uneasiness, discrimination and unrest between rich and poor, both between and within countries. Within countries, they are intensified when the distinction between the 'haves' and 'have nots' aligns with sociocultural differences such as ethnicity, religion, political allegiance and class. The Ecuador case study (page 156) illustrates some of these issues and underlines the fact that migration is both an outcome of disparities in development and a common cause of unrest.

The experience of two countries — South Africa and East Timor — illustrates the ethnic and religious dimensions of some development gaps.

Apartheid in South Africa

South Africa has an abundance of natural resources, including gold, diamonds and platinum, and fertile farmlands. Between 1948 and 1990 the government operated a policy known as apartheid. All South Africans were classified in one of three categories: white (European origin), black (African) or coloured (of mixed descent). The coloured category also included Indians and other Asians and formed the middle tier in the racial hierarchy. Apartheid segregated the three groups in all areas of life, including where they lived, and ensured that the vast economic differences between them were maintained, if not increased.

Black resentment of this injustice (Table 5.12) was strong, but kept in check by the white-controlled police and army. Since the ending of apartheid there has been some easing of the 'gaps' between the three ethnic groups. Since 1990 the country has had a succession of black presidents (starting with Nelson Mandela) and governments, but the whites are still very much in control of the economy and wealth.

	Blacks	Whites
Population (millions)	19	4.5
Land allocation (%)	13	87
Share of national income (%)	<20	75
Ratio of average earnings	1	14
Minimum taxable income (rand)	360	750
Number of people per doctor	44,000	400
Infant mortality rate (%)	20 (urban) 40 (rural)	2.7
Annual expenditure on education per pupil	$45	$696
Number of students per teacher	60	22

Table 5.12 The economic and social injustice of apartheid in South Africa, 1978

East Timor

East Timor, officially known as the Democratic Republic of Timor-Leste, is a small country in southeast Asia. It mainly comprises the eastern half of the island of Timor. From the sixteenth century until 1975 it was a Portuguese colony. Shortly after Portugal withdrew, East Timor was invaded by Indonesia.

The reasons for the Indonesian occupation of this poor, sparsely populated and undeveloped territory were not immediately obvious. Initially it was thought that Indonesia wanted to stop East Timor adopting a communist regime allied to China, and that it could use the island as a place to move people from the over-populated islands of Java, Bali and Madura. It later emerged that oil and natural gas fields had been discovered under the sea between East Timor and Indonesia.

In 1999, after a long guerrilla war, Indonesia agreed to let the East Timorese choose between independence and local autonomy. Militia loyal to Indonesia, tried to use terror to discourage a vote for independence. However more than three-quarters of the people voted in favour and in 2002 East Timor became the first new sovereign state of the twenty-first century.

Exploitation of the oil and gas has now begun with the help of Australia, and East Timor's economic future is beginning to look much brighter. Clearly this will affect the development gap that exists between it and Indonesia.

The consequences of development

It is easy to think of the positive outcomes of development: more employment opportunities, higher wages, more services (commercial and welfare) and a better quality of life. But of course those benefits are not shared equally by all levels of society. Often as a country undergoes economic development the wealthy become richer, while the poor become poorer and sometimes even greater in number. In short, the development gap becomes wider within the country.

Migration

Development changes that bring mixed results include migration. Increased migration flows appear to be an integral part of development and are of two kinds: international and internal. International migration involves both immigration to a country as it develops (e.g. business people, technicians and workers from less developed countries) and emigration (people now able to seek a better life elsewhere in the world). The internal flows are mostly one-way, from rural to urban and from periphery to core. Table 5.13 sets out the benefits and costs of migration as an outcome of development.

Table 5.13 Some costs and benefits of migration

	Source country or area	Host country or area
Benefits	Natural increase slows as young adults leave Less pressure on resources Remittances sent back Return migrants bring skills and money to invest	Declining populations boosted by migrants Human resources enhanced Labour-force needs (including unwanted jobs) filled Higher pay for skilled workers who then pay taxes Multicultural society – religions, languages, food, retailing, music
Costs	Population becomes older Fewer people to develop country's resources Loss of skilled workers Westernisation of returnees Diminished cultural diversity	Racial and social tensions 'White flight' of original population Gender concentrations, e.g. where only males migrate Increased pressure on resources unless their contribution to the economy raises living standards Social support if unemployed; educational demands Illegal and/or exploited labour; low pay if unskilled Areas dominated by a particular group – ghettoisation and segregation

Case study   Migration into and out of Ecuador

Ecuador is South America's fifth-largest oil producer and is also an important cocoa producer. According to USAID, 60% of the population live in poverty, and business people rate it the twentieth most corrupt country out of 133.

Emigration

- Ecuador experienced two major waves of emigration in the 1980s and 1990s – following oil price collapses and economic downturns 10–15% of Ecuadorians moved overseas, mostly to Spain, the USA, Italy, Venezuela and Chile.
- At least 75% of remittances (money sent back by migrants from overseas) are used for basic household needs (education, food and medicine), to build or repair homes and to reduce debts.

- Although most Ecuadorians who gain legal status in the USA remain there, their children are discriminated against and called *rezis*.
- In parts of Ecuador where people have emigrated by illegal routes, thousands of children have been left behind with the remaining parent or with other family members. Some of the children or adolescents suffer from depression and there is a high rate of suicide.
- The growing return of migrants from the USA has produced a cultural upheaval. It is difficult for returnees to reintegrate. Many of the migrants were originally rural peasants or urban working poor, with last names that lacked status and were associated with indigenous (Indian) identity. The economic success of these previously margin-

alised families has caused resentment among some of the families that stayed.

Immigration

- The number of immigrants to Ecuador, particularly Peruvians and Colombians, has increased in recent years. Most Peruvians are economic migrants attracted by the country's switch to the US dollar in 2000. Estimates vary, but it is likely that between 60,000 and 120,000 Peruvians now live in Ecuador, most without legal permission. Most Colombians are refugees escaping armed conflict and the hardships created by drug eradication programmes (spraying coca crops) in southern Colombia. They typically earn less than Ecuadorians.

- Colombians are often suspected of being rebels, paramilitaries, drug runners or criminals. This suspicion increased when, in January 2004, a prominent Colombian rebel was captured in Quito, Ecuador. Although Peruvians are generally not considered to be criminals, they face discrimination, prejudice and exploitation. Many lead hard lives and earn little money working in undesirable jobs. Some Ecuadorians accuse Peruvians of stealing Ecuadorian jobs, lowering wages and engaging in criminal activity, although there is little evidence to support this.

Environment

One of the greatest negatives of development is environmental pollution and the deepening of a country's **ecological footprint.** This is the amount of land and water required to provide a person (or society) with the energy, food and resources they consume and to absorb the waste they produce.

No country in history has emerged as a major industrial power without creating a legacy of environmental damage that can take decades and huge amounts of public wealth to undo.

Economic development raises demand for resources, particularly minerals and energy, and there is a strong temptation to exploit these as quickly and as cheaply as possible, regardless of the environmental costs. 'Growth comes first' tends to be the philosophy.

Case study **Pollution in China**

The speed and scale of China's growth as an economic power is matched by the growth of its pollution problem. Environmental degradation is creating a major long-term burden for the Chinese people. The main contributors to pollution include:
- large-scale working of coal and other minerals
- coal-fired power stations which discharge huge amounts of pollutants into the air
- heavy industry, which requires a lot of energy from the burning of fossil fuels, and creates other forms of pollution. The World Bank says that

Chinese steel-makers, on average, use one-fifth more energy per tonne than the international average. Cement manufacturers need 45% more power, and ethylene producers need 70% more than producers elsewhere. China's aluminium industry alone consumes as much energy as the country's commercial sector – all the hotels, restaurants, banks and shopping complexes combined.
- expanding car ownership, heavy traffic and low-grade petrol: only 1% of the country's 560 million

city dwellers breathe air considered safe by EU standards

■ indoor air pollution caused by poorly ventilated coal and wood stoves or toxic fumes from shoddy construction materials

■ dumping of waste into rivers and lakes by factories and farms: China's own environmental monitors say that one-third of all river water, and vast sections of China's great lakes (the Tai, Chao and Dianchi) have water rated at the most degraded level, unfit for industrial or agricultural use

The most obvious impact of such pollution is on the health of the Chinese people, particularly poor urban dwellers. It has been estimated that 300,000 people die each year from air pollution, mostly of heart disease and lung cancer. An additional 110,000 deaths each year could be attributed to indoor air pollution.

China's pollution picture looks bad today, but it is set to get much worse, because the country now relies on energy-intensive heavy industry and urbanisation to fuel economic growth. Politicians are reluctant to do anything that might curb China's economic development.

Reducing the development gap

How might the development gap be reduced and by whom?

By the end of this section you should:
➤ *understand a range of theories about reducing the development gap*
➤ *have considered contrasting strategies for giving aid*
➤ *have looked at the role of trade and investment in reducing the development gap*
➤ *appreciate that the future for many poor people is bleak unless difficult choices are made by key players*

Approaches

Table 5.14 Neo-liberalism, Marxism and populism

A number of strategies to improve living standards in the poorest countries have been proposed and attempted (Figure 5.17). Private, public and voluntary organisations often have different approaches to resolving the development gap and reducing poverty. Governments tend to think in large-scale, **top-down** terms, but

Theory	Essentials	Likely impact on development gap
Neo-liberalism	A set of economic policies that became popular towards the end of the twentieth century, under Thatcher and Reagan. It is based on market forces, privatisation and reducing state intervention in the economy. Its effects tend to be that the rich grow richer and the poor grow poorer	Unlikely to change
Marxism	A belief that capitalism is based on the exploitation of workers by the owners of the means of production and that history has been mainly a struggle between conflicting classes. It seeks to replace existing class structures with a system that manages society for the good of all	Likely to reduce
Populism	A philosophy that supports 'the people' in a struggle against society's elite. It is about urging change in economic, social and political systems, but it does not have a strong ideological identity in the sense of being either left- or right-wing	Unlikely to change

some of the most effective schemes have been developed at the grassroots level, by communities themselves, often working with non-governmental organisations (NGOs).

Philosophies

The more important theories relating to development were examined earlier in this chapter. A range of philosophies underpins development efforts (Table 5.14). Most theories are described as 'modernist' in that they are founded on the belief that development is all about transforming traditional countries into modern, Westernised states. They tend to assume that there is only one path to development, followed by all countries at different speeds. They stress the inter-dependence of developing and developed countries (Figure 5.18). However, it is now recognised that the route to development may be different in individual countries.

Figure 5.17 Routes to development

External approaches
- Global economy and economic growth
- Globalisation trends
- Aid and foreign investment
- Trade strategies
- Tourism development
- Debt reduction or cancellation
- International cooperation

Developing country → Increasing development → Developed country

Internal approaches
- Political stability
- Government investment in infrastructure, ICT, social services and local communities
- Food security
- Increased resources for healthcare and HIV/AIDS
- Addressing inequalities between regions, male/female, rural/urban
- Legal empowerment of the poor and pro-poor strategies

Figure 5.18 The interdependence of developing and developed countries

Developed countries

- Food and disaster aid, trade concessions
- Political support, strategic defence, military aid
- Technical knowledge, research, education
- Financial capital, machinery, semi-finished goods

- Political dependency, strategic concessions
- Cheap finished goods
- Cheap labour, students, illegal immigration
- Raw materials, foodstuffs, fuel supplies

Developing countries

Critique

A new 'anti-development' school of thought is emerging , based on the following criticisms:

➤ Development as we know it today is a 'eurocentric' idea based on material prosperity.
➤ It is a subordinating process creating dependency.
➤ It creates and widens spatial inequalities.
➤ It undermines local cultures and ways of life.
➤ It is environmentally unsustainable.
➤ It infringes human rights and undermines democracy.

Some people believe that countries should be left to determine their own paths. A minority of countries wish to define their own vision of a better future and take whatever actions (most likely **bottom-up**) are needed to achieve it. The majority wish to promote development and reduce both poverty and development gaps. The ways in which they approach this are discussed in the remainder of this chapter. They are largely top-down in the sense of being handed down by governments.

Aid strategies

There are different types of aid. **Humanitarian aid** aims to alleviate suffering in the short term, for example in response to disasters such as an earthquake or drought. **Development aid** aims to address poverty in the longer term. **Project**

Table 5.15 Largest aid donors, 2006

Donor country	% of total ODA	Net ODA (US$bn)	% of donor's GNI (UN target = 0.7)
USA	21	22.74	0.17
UK	12	12.61	0.52
Japan	11	11.61	0.25
France	10	10.45	0.47
Germany	10	10.35	0.36
Netherlands	5	5.45	0.81
Sweden	4	3.97	1.03
Spain	4	3.80	0.32
Canada	4	3.71	0.30
Italy	4	3.67	0.20
Norway	3	2.95	0.89
Denmark	2	2.23	0.80
Australia	2	2.13	0.30
Others	8	8.27	0.30
Total	100	103.94	n/a

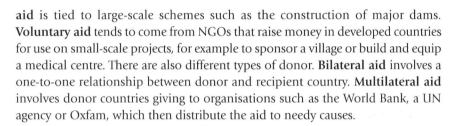

aid is tied to large-scale schemes such as the construction of major dams. **Voluntary aid** tends to come from NGOs that raise money in developed countries for use on small-scale projects, for example to sponsor a village or build and equip a medical centre. There are also different types of donor. **Bilateral aid** involves a one-to-one relationship between donor and recipient country. **Multilateral aid** involves donor countries giving to organisations such as the World Bank, a UN agency or Oxfam, which then distribute the aid to needy causes.

Official development aid

The developed countries that make up the Organisation for Economic Cooperation and Development (OECD) are committed to providing a certain level of development assistance to developing countries. This is called official development assistance (ODA) and is given either on a government-to-government basis through government aid agencies (i.e. bilateral aid) or through international institutions (i.e. multilateral aid). ODA is given to support the economic, social and political development of developing countries. In recent years the traditional view, in which the developed country was dominant in the relationship, has given way to the idea of partnership and development cooperation.

The largest donors of ODA are shown in Table 5.15. In 2006, developing countries received ODA totalling $104 billion, and this is growing year on year (Figure 5.19).

Top-down

Aid strategies, as distinct from types of aid, tend to be of two kinds. The first is **top-down**, capital-intensive and often government-led. ODA is often used to support

Figure 5.19 Per capita ODA received, 2002

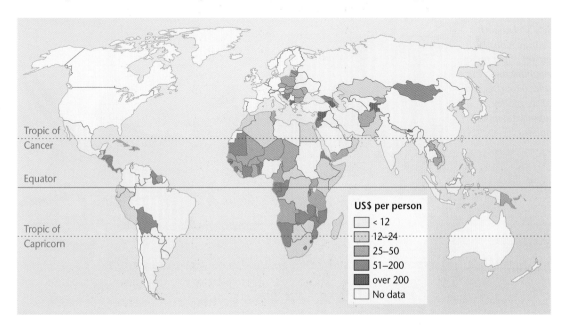

US$ per person
- < 12
- 12–24
- 25–50
- 51–200
- over 200
- No data

this type of strategy. It has been criticised as an inappropriate way of helping poor countries. The argument is that aid given to governments is fought over by different interest groups at the cost of investment in productive business activities, and the money is more likely to be diverted to rich people than benefiting poor people. So ODA creates a situation of winners and losers (Table 5.16).

Table 5.16 Aid winners and losers

Typical aid 'winners'	Typical aid 'losers'
Urban areas and high-profile projects, which attract large-scale funding	Rural areas and smaller-scale projects that rely on funding from NGOs or voluntary schemes
Topical issues such as global warming, HIV/AIDS	Recipients of tied aid, e.g. conditional on importing goods from donor country, often at high prices than local equivalents
Areas or projects of strategic or political interest to the donor	
Areas with historic ties between donor country and recipient, e.g. colonial ties or trading groups	Development programmes whose funds have to be diverted to other purposes
	Countries that have corrupt governments or systems of distribution
Major disaster areas that benefit from short-term aid	Countries that become dependent on long-term aid
Countries using aid to support their existing systems (seen as more effective)	

Bottom-up

The second type of aid follows a local and '**bottom-up**' approach. NGOs often work effectively at a local scale in collaboration with local communities (Photograph 5.4).

Photograph 5.4 This Sri-Lankan cottage industry makes paper out of elephant dung for sale to tourists and raises money to preserve elephant habitat

Dulcie Knifton

Forms of aid

A great deal of aid, particularly ODA, is in the form of loans. But loans attract interest and have to be repaid. It is easy for receiver countries to spiral down into a debt crisis. Developing countries need capital, but technical assistance in the form of expertise, technology and education can be more useful in supporting their development efforts. This is where 'bottom-up' aid projects score much more heavily than 'top-down'.

The links between developed and developing countries in the context of aid can easily lead to a situation of dependency. However, there is a general move to promote aid as a form of partnership and to encourage interdependence. Again, 'bottom-up' approaches to development are more likely to succeed in this direction.

Trade, investment and economic growth

Trade expansion is a key driver of economic growth. Developing countries' share of world trade tripled from 12% in 1995 to 36% in 2006. In 2006, average annual growth in economic output in developed countries was 2.4%, compared with 6.4% in developing countries, with China recording 10.5% and India 8.5%. Nearly half of developing country exports were sent to other developing countries. South–South trade flows are becoming increasingly important.

Developing countries are keen to attract foreign investment in order to help the development process and thereby reduce the global development gap. It follows a similar pattern to trade (Figure 5.20). In 2006, foreign direct investment (FDI) inflows to developing countries reached $334 billion (36% of the world total),

Figure 5.20 Foreign direct investment: net inflows, 2005

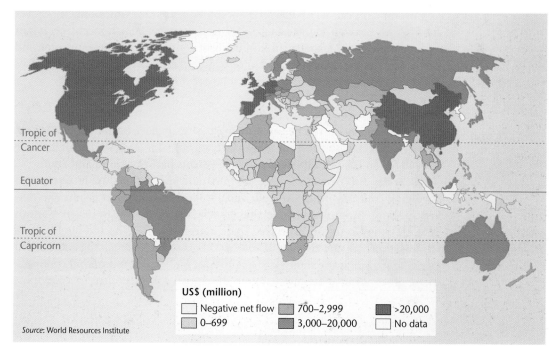

US$ (million)

- Negative net flow
- 0–699
- 700–2,999
- 3,000–20,000
- >20,000
- No data

Source: World Resources Institute

the highest level in history. In the same year, FDI outflows from developing countries climbed to $133 billion (17% of the total), much of which were directed to other countries in the South. In addition, TNCs from the South employed some 6 million workers worldwide.

Managing trade

Table 5.17 identifies ways in which governments try to manage trade. Free trade aims to remove trade barriers (protectionism) such as tariffs and quotas, and government subsidies. Of course, any form of trade intervention can distort patterns of exporting and importing. The World Trade Organization (WTO), which consists of 148 member states, is committed to increasing free trade. However, some people argue that the terms of free trade are unfair, as richer countries gain at the expense of developing countries.

Table 5.17 Major types of trade intervention

Influencing imports	Influencing exports
Tariffs: taxes levied on imports, which increase their price and make them less competitive	Incentives: financial help and tax concessions for producers of exports
Import quotas and licensing, which limit the volume of imports	Export credits and guarantees
Tight regulations, e.g. on labelling, making importing more difficult	Establishing export processing zones and free trade zones
Exchange rates: deliberate lowering of rates makes imports more expensive	Exchange rates: deliberate lowering of rates increases the competitiveness of exports
Formation of trade blocs	Embargoes on certain exports
	Formation of trade blocs

Governments can set up special economic zones (SEZs) which offer incentives for foreign companies, including TNCs, to locate there. Such incentives might include preferential tax rates. In turn the host country earns foreign income and often increases the skills of its workforce. China is one country that has set up SEZs (Figure 5.21).

Trade agreements

The trade agreements reached over the past 20 years have been mainly bilateral, between developing and developed countries. Table 5.18 highlights the advantages and disadvantages of such agreements between North and South.

There has also been an increase in free-trade and regional-trade agreements involving countries from different geographical locations, to produce a 'new regionalism'. Examples include the Association of Southeast Asian Nations (ASEAN), the North American Free Trade Agreement (NAFTA) and the EU. Such organisations are effectively trade blocs. They encourage free trade within their boundaries, but at the same time tend to put up barriers to external countries. These blocs afford more protection to developed countries than to developing countries.

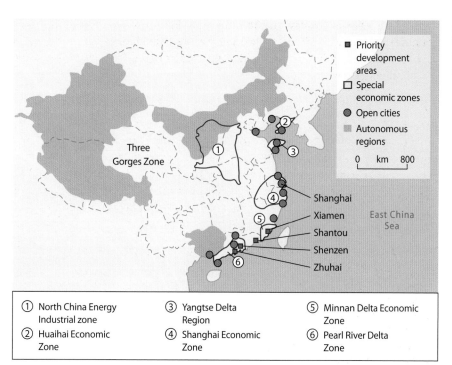

Figure 5.21
Economic
development
areas in China

Key:
- ■ Priority development areas
- □ Special economic zones
- ● Open cities
- ▨ Autonomous regions

0   km   800

Three Gorges Zone

Shanghai
Xiamen
Shantou
Shenzen
Zhuhai

East China Sea

① North China Energy Industrial zone
② Huaihai Economic Zone
③ Yangtse Delta Region
④ Shanghai Economic Zone
⑤ Minnan Delta Economic Zone
⑥ Pearl River Delta Zone

	Advantages	Disadvantages
Generally	Removal of trade barriers promotes expansion of trade, which increases wealth and benefits everyone Free trade concentrates production of goods and services where they are cheapest and most efficient, lowering prices to the benefit of consumers	Many agreements are biased towards rich countries' interests Agreements often require policy changes to allow foreign investment: new labour and environmental regulations, new competition rules Subsidies to farmers in some rich countries reduce the effect of agreements
For developing countries	Concessions that are not given to other countries, e.g. better market access for their products New trading opportunities, e.g. increase in Mexican manufacturing exports with NAFTA More foreign direct investment (FDI) attracted	Trade agreements often require something in return. If TNCs based in rich countries gain access to poor-country markets, local producers are put out of business Local firms often have difficulty complying with restrictive rules-of-origin regulations on goods for export to the rich-country partner Preference negotiated by one developing country with a rich country may be eroded if the latter makes agreements with other countries

Table 5.18
Advantages and
disadvantages of
trade between
developed and
developing
countries

*Photograph 5.5
A coffee farmer in
Uganda*

Simon Rawles/Fairtrade Foundation

*Photograph 5.6
Fairtrade coffee
products for sale in
the UK*

Sue Atkinson/Fairtrade Foundation

Fair trade

One initiative to improve the terms of trade between North and South is the Fairtrade Foundation. This NGO seeks to obtain a fair price for a wide variety of goods exported from developing to developed countries, including handicrafts, coffee, cocoa, sugar, tea, bananas, honey, wine and fresh fruit. The aim is to work with poor small-scale producers and make them more economically secure (Photographs 5.5 and 5.6).

The fair trade movement goes from strength to strength. In 2006, Fairtrade sales were valued at US$2.3 billion worldwide, a 40% increase on the previous year. As a result, 5 million people benefited from infrastructure and community development projects funded by Fairtrade.

Doha

The Doha development agenda negotiations, involving 153 countries, attempted between 2001 and 2008 to establish better trade conditions for developing countries by allowing them access to EU and US agricultural markets in return for opening their doors to more EU and US manufactured goods and services. However, several developing countries had concerns that this arrangement would not reduce poverty for their poorest farmers. At the same time, some developed countries were not prepared to give up farm subsidies. There were also disagreements about a sliding scale of tariffs that would have enabled emerging countries to impose higher duties if there were surges in imports of certain products from developed countries.

Future actions

Each of the proposed ways of reducing the development gap has its merits and advocates, and each is likely to conflict with other approaches. But there is no one approach that will work in all circumstances.

Debt cancellation

In recent decades there have been a number of attempts to reduce the debt burden of the poorest countries. In 2005, the Make Poverty History campaign called for the debts of the world's poorest countries to be cancelled in full. As a result, 14 African 'heavily indebted poor countries' (HIPCs) hope to have their debts totally written off under a plan drawn up by the G8 finance ministers in 2005. However, there are other non-HIPC countries with debt levels that exceed the World Bank and IMF debt sustainability thresholds: Bangladesh, Cambodia, the Comoros Islands, Haiti, Nepal and Samoa.

Debt reduction is not designed to cancel 100% of the accumulated debts of all countries but to make debt repayments more manageable. In December 2000, the UK government agreed to cancel the debt owed to the UK by 26 countries, but debts owed to other creditors, such as the Inter-American Development Bank, have not been cancelled. Many debt relief schemes still come with conditions, and there is no fair arbitration mechanism for resolving debt crises. Table 5.19 shows some of the strengths and weaknesses of debt reduction.

Table 5.19 Strengths and weaknesses of debt reduction schemes

Strengths	Weaknesses
Allows a country's loans to be rescheduled in order to make them more manageable	Is often accompanied by a shift from domestic food cultivation to production of cash crops or commodities for export
Makes the country's economy more competitive	Reduces government expenditure by cutting social programmes, e.g. health and education, and abolishing food and agricultural subsidies
Improves foreign investment potential by removing trade and/or investment restrictions	Privatisation of state enterprises to cut government expenditure results in assets being sold to TNCs
Boosts foreign exchange by promoting exports	Increases pressure on countries to generate exports to pay off debts. This is likely to increase deforestation, land degradation and other environmental damage
Reduces government deficits through cuts in spending	Some developed countries accused of protecting their own interests

Tourism

Developing countries often see tourism as a path to development. Many of them have biodiversity and scenery which can attract long-haul tourism from developed countries. However, there are conflicting views on whether this is effective (Table 5.20).

*Table 5.20
Tourism: a path
to development
or under-
development?*

Tourism as a path to development	Tourism as a path to underdevelopment
Tourism enables the less developed world to develop in the same way that the developed world has	Tourism helps the developed world to develop more than developing countries because profits go back to the rich countries — the less developed world becomes more dependent
Foreign investment, expertise and technology are brought to developing countries by TNCs	TNCs control tourism in their own interests, not those of the local community
Mass tourism brings holidaymakers from wealthy countries — they are attracted by advertisements showing idyllic resorts	Mass tourism may spoil the character of the resort and it could become a victim of its own success
Traditional local culture is an obstacle to tourism — it is replaced by modern Western culture, symbolised by McDonald's, Coca Cola etc.	The local community may be resentful if its culture is devalued — this can lead to crime and even terrorism
Tourism requires development of the local infrastructure (e.g. roads and airports), which may also benefit local people	Tourism can put too much pressure on local resources and reduce the quality of life for people through pollution
Tourism generates local employment and helps to increase wealth	Tourism exploits cheap local labour — the best-paid jobs often go to outsiders

Tourism can generate a **multiplier effect**. As profits from tourism increase and become more widespread, they begin to trickle down into the local economy. This can lead to the emergence of local suppliers of food, clothes, souvenirs and tourist services and a decrease in reliance on foreign imports. However, there are some concerns:

➤ Tourism is vulnerable to factors such as downturns in the world economy, changing fashions in destinations, terrorist incidents (such as the Bali bombing) and disasters (such as the 2004 Asian tsunami).

➤ If tourism is developed by foreign investors, most of the profits will go to developed countries.

➤ Tourism can be so effective in regenerating an area that it leads to localised inflation, making basic foods and services too expensive for local people.

➤ Problems can be caused for other sectors of the economy, for example if young people migrate from nearby rural areas to work in tourism, labour shortages can occur in farming.

➤ Tourism can overload the physical infrastructure of water, sewerage and road systems.

➤ Tourism can degrade the very environment the tourists come to see.

Some countries have tried to overcome such problems by developing ecotourism. This involves small-scale ventures based in local communities and with minimal environmental impact. At present, ecotourism can only meet a small part of the mass tourism market, and it is not what every tourist wants.

*Photograph 5.7
A mobile phone
shop in South Africa*

Technology

The spread of information and communications technology (ICT), including mobile phones and the internet, can play a significant part in promoting bottom-up socioeconomic development, even among the poorest communities (Figure 5.22). However, use of such technologies is still uneven. This is known as the **digital divide**.

Access to mobile phones in developing countries can also help bridge the digital divide. A mobile phone does not require the same literacy level as a computer, and it is a cheaper means of access to information. Africa is now the fastest-growing mobile market in the world (Photograph 5.7). The number of mobile users is often much higher than the actual number of phones, as many people allow family and friends to use their phones.

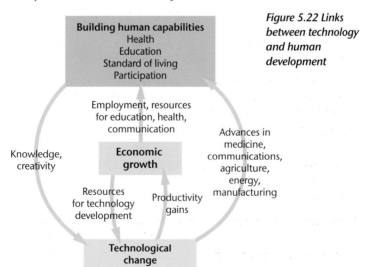

Figure 5.22 Links between technology and human development

Building human capabilities
Health
Education
Standard of living
Participation

Employment, resources for education, health, communication

Knowledge, creativity

Economic growth

Advances in medicine, communications, agriculture, energy, manufacturing

Resources for technology development

Productivity gains

Technological change

The population of Mongolia is sparsely distributed, per capita GDP is equivalent to £1,360 per annum and more than a third of the people live in poverty. Forty per cent of the population are nomadic herders living in *gers* (tents), just as they did 1,000 years ago. In addition, Mongolia has a poor infrastructure. The telephone density is 4.1 per 1,000 inhabitants and the radio density is 15.7. Traditional media therefore cannot reach more than a small proportion of the country's population, but there is a need for information.

Despite its disadvantages the country has a literacy rate of 96%. All these factors make development of the internet worthwhile, but the cost is a problem. The Asia-Pacific Development Information Programme (APDIP), a UN-funded organisation, has developed 'citizen information centres'. These contain computer workstations, a printer and a small library with reference material. The services are free. They also function as training centres, where visitors can learn basic computer skills and get help taking their first steps in the internet world.

Those in remote rural areas, including parts of the Gobi Desert, can now connect to the central government, apply for grants and receive news online. For example, Mongolian steppe nomads have access to information about weather and commodity prices by means of a 'cyber ger'. The programme's long-term aim is to encourage businesses and colleges to use IT, and to counteract the sense of remoteness and being 'peripheral' that prevails over much of the country.

Knowledge of latest prices in food markets, for example, can help small farmers and fishermen, who can cut out the middlemen and gain direct access to markets. In Kenya, Safaricom has introduced the Sokoni text messaging service, which transmits daily reports from the Kenyan agricultural commodity exchange. Users simply text the name of the commodity they are interested in, such as 'maize' or 'sheep', and receive an instant reply with an update on its price that morning at each market. This enables them to assess the best place and time to buy or sell. The service also allows traders to offer their goods for sale or place bids, as well as post short messages or agricultural questions.

Legal rights

The UN regards legal empowerment of the poor as a valuable way forward. This involves ensuring such things as property rights, access to justice and labour rights, and making it easier for people to start, own and pass on businesses. One important issue is to ensure that women as well as men gain these rights

South–South links

The idea of South–South cooperation stems from a growing realisation that poor nations might find appropriate, low-cost and sustainable solutions to their problems in other developing countries rather than in the 'rich' North. For example, if African farmers need boreholes to access water, it makes more sense to access India's huge pool of expertise than to send expensive European water engineers. The intention is to encourage recipient governments to spend aid more effectively.

A key example of South–South cooperation is China's presence in Africa. China has increased its aid to African governments, cancelled US$10 billion of debt and offered further debt relief to 31 African countries, as well as opening discussions on zero-tariff trade.

The reasoning behind China's new focus on Africa is simple. If its economic boom is to be sustained, it must find more raw materials and new markets for manufactured goods. In 2003 China overtook Japan to become the world's second-biggest consumer of petroleum products after the USA, and its oil consumption is forecast to grow by at least 10% every year for the foreseeable future. Africa has 90% of the world's cobalt, 90% of its platinum, 50% of its gold, 98% of its chromium, 64% of its manganese and one-third of its uranium. It is rich in diamonds, has more oil reserves than North America and has been estimated to hold 40% of the world's potential hydroelectric power.

China now buys about one-third of its oil from Africa, mainly from Angola, where it has invested £800 million to develop a new oilfield, and from Sudan, where it has built a 1,500-km pipeline and invested at least £8 billion. China is spending another £1.2 billion on a new offshore oilfield in Nigeria (Figure 5.23). However, this investment and trade generates advantages and disadvantages for both parties (Table 5.21).

Figure 5.23 China's foreign direct investment in Africa, 2005

1 Gambia
2 Guinea Bissau
3 Guinea
4 Sierra Leone
5 Liberia
6 Côte d'Ivoire
7 Ghana
8 Togo
9 Benin
10 Equatorial Guinea

US$ million
■ 50–300+
■ 20–49
□ 0–19
□ No data

Source: World Bank

Table 5.21 Advantages and disadvantages of Chinese investment in, and trade with, Africa

	Advantages	Disadvantages
To China	Increasing influence and expanding access to the natural resources China needs to support its development Development of new markets for Chinese goods There is no colonial history between China and African countries, only aid projects, so its investment is well received New links have been developed: trade between China and Africa totalled around £30 billion in 2008, a six-fold increase since 2000. It is expected to top $100 billion in 2010	Economic migration of people from China to some African countries to earn higher wages Deflection of resources away from projects in China Possible effects on the Chinese economy and employment sectors
To Africa	Chinese companies employ local workers Chinese investment is building new factories and infra-structure across Africa Workers are learning new skills China has tried to offset trade deficits by offering favourable terms of trade for African products and providing aid (e.g. scrapping tariffs on 190 kinds of imported goods from 28 of the least developed African countries) Nearly 700 Chinese companies operate in 49 African countries	Wages remain low Most African countries have a growing trade deficit with China, in spite of tax-free trading agreements Large-scale projects can lead to the displacement of significant numbers of people from their homes China sometimes insists that workers from China are used on large construction projects Evidence in some areas of health and safety regulations being ignored

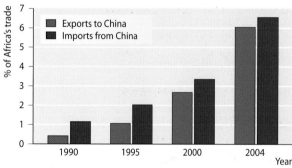

Figure 5.24 China's trade with Africa

Source: IMF/OECD

There seems to be a consensus that the exploitation of Africa's natural resources should be monitored by a UN agency to ensure that the wealth created in Africa is reinvested in development and not pocketed by corrupt officials and regimes. There is also a strong feeling that the terms of trade between China and Africa favour China and exploit Africa (Figure 5.24).

Millennium Development Goals

The Millennium Development Goals (MDGs) provide a vital framework for monitoring the development gap and measuring any progress towards reducing it. Most of the MDG targets were set in the 1990s by a series of conferences and summit meetings (Figure 5.25). With regard to the issues raised in this chapter, the most important goal is the first: the elimination of extreme poverty and hunger by the year 2015. The UN issues a yearly report on progress towards achieving these targets. There is still a long way to go before the development gap is narrowed once and for all.

MDGs	South Africa	Mexico	India	Bangladesh	Thailand	Malawi	Kenya
1 Eradicate extreme poverty and hunger							
2 Achieve universal primary education							
3 Promote gender equality and empower women							
4 Reduce child mortality							
5 Improve maternal health							
6 Combat HIV/AIDS, malaria and other diseases							
7 Ensure environmental sustainability							
8 Develop a global partnership for development							

Legend:
- Achieved
- Likely to achieve
- Possible to achieve
- No data

*Figure 5.25
Progress towards the Millennium Development Goals in selected countries, 2007*

Further research

www.un.org/millenniumgoals – up-to-date information and detail on the MDGs and progress towards them for particular countries.

Review questions

1 Identify the advantages and disadvantages of three different ways of measuring the development gap.
2 In what ways do TNCs hinder as well as help economic development?
3 Give reasons why the world's megacities have become poverty hotspots.
4 Explain why narrowing the development gap has its costs.
5 Outline at least two theories that help underpin attempts to reduce the development gap.
6 Outline the key arguments for and against cancelling the debts of the poorest countries.
7 Which single action do you think is likely to contribute most to the narrowing of the development gap? Give your reasons.

Chapter 6

The technological fix?

Who should have access to modern technology, and at what price, is one of the key questions facing the world. At present, access is largely determined by the level of development of the community or society concerned, and therefore it varies from place to place. Most societies look to technology to help them to achieve and sustain higher standards of living and to provide fixes for a whole range of problems. Indeed, there is a tendency to think of modern technology as having all the answers to contemporary issues and to suppose that its outcomes can only be positive and to the benefit of humanity. However, there is plenty of evidence that modern technology also carries real risks and that its use can generate considerable social and environmental costs. In some instances, the consequences of applying a new technology are quite unforeseen.

The geography of technology

Why is there inequality in access to technology?

By the end of this section you should:
➤ *understand what is meant by technology and how it has developed and spread*
➤ *be aware of the geographical distribution of technology use at a range of scales*
➤ *realise that access to technology varies in different parts of the world*
➤ *understand the reasons for this inequality of access*

Photograph 6.1 'Technology' includes new ways of communicating, like the iPhone 3G

Apple

The nature of technology

Although it is a word very much in everyday use, 'technology' is surprisingly difficult to define. Technology results from invention and the ability of people to innovate and find new and better ways of carrying out a task. It increases the ability of people to satisfy their needs, for example by developing:
➤ new tools, machines and systems of production in areas such as manufacturing and farming
➤ new ways of moving (by transport) and communicating (by information technology, Photograph 6.1)
➤ new ways of modifying the environment, by building, irrigation and flood control technology
➤ new means of prolonging and shortening life in the form of medical technology and weaponry

Solving problems

Ours is a **technocentric** world. There is a general optimism that technology can solve problems and improve lives.

Many people believe that for every problem there is a **technological fix** – an innovation waiting to be discovered that will solve it. A solution or 'cure' to problems such as global warming, HIV/AIDS or oil shortages is sought through science and engineering. But problems can also be solved by an attitudinal fix, which involves changing human behaviour. These two types of fix are not mutually exclusive. Indeed, both approaches are often to be found running in parallel (Table 6.1). Those in favour of attitudinal fixes argue that the technological fixers are looking for the 'silver bullet' that will solve the problem at a stroke.

Problem	Technological fix	Attitudinal fix
Global warming	Geo-engineering to reduce incoming solar radiation	Education and tax incentives to reduce personal carbon footprints
HIV/AIDS	Pharmaceutical research to find a vaccine or curative medicine	Public health education to prevent the spread of the disease
Oil shortages	A 'hydrogen economy' or similar alternative energy future	Energy efficiency, public transport and energy-efficient cars

Table 6.1 Three problems, each with two fixes

Development of technology

The process of technological development is widely perceived to be one of unending progress, with new and better technologies replacing older, obsolete ones. Figure 6.1 uses the development of music playback technology to illustrate this. As Figure 6.1 shows:

➤ New technologies have a life cycle.
➤ Decline begins when better technologies beome mainstream.
➤ Life cycles have become shorter over time.
➤ The speed of growth has increased.

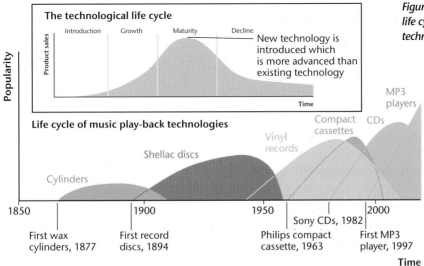

Figure 6.1 The technological life cycles of music playback technology

Some 2.4 million years ago in the Palaeolithic period, early humans such as *Homo habilis* discovered the use of stone tools. This revolutionised life and led to the development of stone axes, knives and arrowheads. This is the earliest known example of technological innovation. Much later – in Mesopotamia 10,000 years ago – the development of agricultural technology created a system of food supply that was no longer reliant on hunting and gathering. For much of human history, the development of technology has been gradual, punctuated by 'technological breakthroughs' such as the invention of metal tools, the use of antibiotics to treat infections, and more recently the creation of the internet.

Controlling nature

Over time, people have used technology to control nature, so that their lives are less determined by environmental factors. Examples include:
➤ using an umbrella when it is raining
➤ taking antibiotics to fight infection
➤ irrigating deserts to grow food crops

In the twenty-first century, in the developed world at least, technology has pervaded every aspect of life to the extent that we are entirely dependent on it in one way or another. Figure 6.2 illustrates just one everyday aspect of our dependence on technology.

Figure 6.2
The technological breakfast

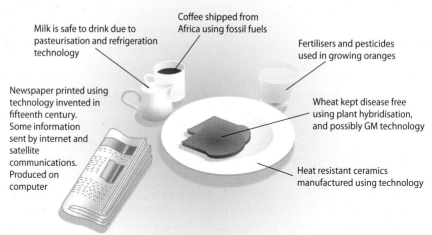

Coffee shipped from Africa using fossil fuels

Milk is safe to drink due to pasteurisation and refrigeration technology

Fertilisers and pesticides used in growing oranges

Newspaper printed using technology invented in fifteenth century. Some information sent by internet and satellite communications. Produced on computer

Wheat kept disease free using plant hybridisation, and possibly GM technology

Heat resistant ceramics manufactured using technology

Of course, not everyone in the world can enjoy a breakfast such as this. Strip away some of the technology and 'breakfast' would be very different. In rural sub-Saharan Africa, for example, 90% of people would be out gathering wood for fuel. Many would also be walking long distances to collect untreated water. In some places technologies such as refrigeration are virtually unknown.

Attitudes to technology

In general, people tend to accept new technology if they think it will improve their quality of life. At one end of the spectrum of adoption are the 'techies' who positively seek out and embrace developments: these are the 'early adopters' of

*Photograph 6.2
The Amish in the
USA reject many
modern
technologies*

new technologies. The majority of people – what might be called the mainstream – are more likely to adopt a new technology when its benefits are clear and its costs have fallen to an affordable level.

At the other end of the spectrum are the '**Luddites**' – people who are opposed to technological change. The name derives from Ned Ludd, who in 1811 organised opposition to the introduction of new textile looms in Nottingham. In the 1830s, Luddism spread to the rural workforce, and gangs of men destroyed threshing machines in England. In both instances, new technology was seen as threatening jobs.

In the USA there are some 200,000 Amish Christians who in general reject modern technology such as cars, electricity and telephones (Photograph 6.2). Their objection is a religious one and reflects their wish to live separately from non-Amish people. Telephones and power lines are avoided because they are seen as providing 'connection' with the wider world of non-Amish people.

In the UK there is growing concern over the widespread use of closed-circuit television (CCTV) cameras as a crime-fighting technology. The country has over 10 million CCTV cameras, and during a typical day you will be filmed dozens, possibly hundreds, of times. This development has raised issues concerning personal privacy. In 2008, the Metropolitan Police reported that only 3% of street robberies were solved by CCTV, but put this low figure down to poor image quality. Balancing the benefits of CCTV in reducing crime against the right of people to go about their business without being 'watched' is a difficult challenge for contemporary society.

Geographical distribution of technology

The distribution of, and dependence on, technology varies markedly across the planet. Access to electricity is one of our most basic expectations, but it is not universally available (Figure 6.3). Table 6.2 illustrates a relationship between levels of economic development and electricity consumption.

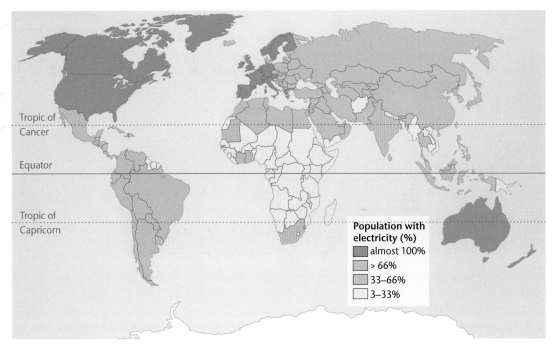

Figure 6.3 Global access to electricity, 2003

Table 6.2 Electricity use related to income and human development

Country	Classification	Electricity use (kWh per person), 2006	Per capita GNI ($), 2006	Human development index, 2007
USA	Developed	12,200	44,970	0.95
Brazil	NIC	2,000	4,730	0.80
Philippines	RIC	550	1,420	0.77
Ghana	Developing	240	520	0.55
Ethiopia	LDC	25	180	0.41

Digital technology

Countries at higher levels of development tend to have greater access to communications technology. The digital access index illustrates this (Figure 6.4). It combines data on:

➤ telephone landlines
➤ mobile phone subscribers
➤ cost of internet access
➤ adult literacy
➤ school enrolment
➤ internet bandwith available
➤ internet users and broadband subscribers

Countries with a digital access index of over 75 are hyperconnected. They have the infrastructure to support digital information transfer, and competition has lowered

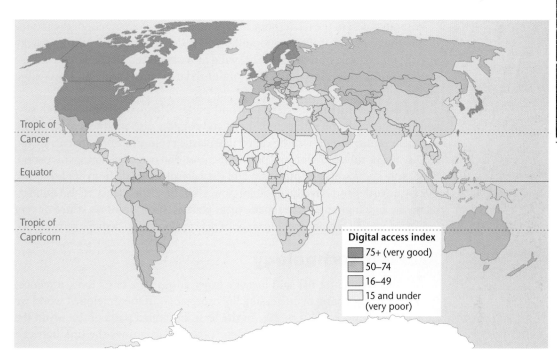

Figure 6.4 The digital access index, 2003

costs. Unsurprisingly, these countries correspond to the triad of economically wealthy areas – the powerhouse of the **knowledge economy** (east Asia, North America and the European Union). On the other side of the digital divide are countries with index scores of 15 or lower. These countries, largely in Africa, are still far from entering the digital age.

For such places, unfortunately, gaining access to digital technology is not simply a question of importing a lot of computers. For internet technology to work, a range of other technologies and systems have to be in place, for example:

➤ a wireless or hard-wired (telephone) network
➤ a reliable power supply
➤ internet service provider companies
➤ a sales, distribution and repair network
➤ useful websites and software in a familiar language

Consequently, the many benefits of the digital age have been slow to reach those who might have most to gain.

Fossil fuels

A key feature of the developed world is its dependence on fossil fuels. Coal, oil and gas store energy fixed by photosynthesis millions of years ago. Exploiting fossil fuels gives us access to the vast amounts of cheap energy on which modern technology depends. Large-scale exploitation of coal began around 200 years ago, oil has been used since about 1880 and natural gas only since the 1950s. In 2004, fossil fuels supplied 86% of global energy use.

Without access to the technology to exploit and burn fossil fuels, or the money to buy them, much of the developing world is dependent on capturing energy directly, for example by using biomass, wind or water power. Dependence on these sources restricts development. They are unreliable, small-scale and inflexible power sources.

Our dependence on oil extends beyond energy. The **petrochemicals** industry, which refines crude oil into petrol, diesel and paraffin, also produces plastics. The twentieth century could well be called the 'plastic century', as polystyrene, nylon, PVC, synthetic rubber, Teflon and polyethylene were all perfected during this period. Plastics are cheap, versatile materials, and virtually all are made from crude oil. The cars we drive depend directly on oil for power, but the dependency is also indirect: many car and engine parts are made from plastics. If oil becomes scarce or very expensive, we will require a whole range of new technologies, perhaps very quickly.

Access to technology

Technology can reduce risk and increase expectations. At a basic level, it reduces the risk of dying young by increasing life expectancy. In the developed world we expect to live into our 70s or 80s. In the least developed parts of the world the risk of dying in your 40s or 50s is high. Table 6.3 examines the link between technology and risk in Haiti, where people have a life expectancy of 52 years (compared with 82 years in Japan). Haiti is a high-risk society which lacks the technology to manage these risks and improve life expectancy.

Table 6.3 Technology and risk in Haiti

Risk	Impact on life expectancy	Key technologies required
Natural hazards	Flooding, usually associated with hurricanes, regularly kills. In 2004 Hurricane Jeanne killed 3,000 and destroyed crops. Storms cause landslides, destroying homes and roads	Warning and evacuation systems Storm shelters to provide temporary refuge Flood control and slope-stabilisation engineering to reduce landslide risk Afforestation programmes to reduce flooding and soil erosion
Disease	Only 54% of Haitians have access to improved water supply, and 30% to improved sanitation. Only 50% of children are immunised against measles. 300 per 100,000 people have TB. Around 6% of the population are HIV+	Clean water supply and sewage systems to decrease risk of disease Nationwide vaccination and immunisation programmes to reduce disease prevalence Medical technology, drugs and education
Malnutrition	Two-thirds of Haitians are farmers. 54% live on under $1 per day; 45% are undernourished. Infant mortality rate is high at 74 per 1,000 live births	Farming technology to raise yields and incomes, improve food security and reduce child malnutrition Better transport to improve food distribution systems

Haiti suffers from **environmental determinism**. Its people are more at the mercy of nature than those in the developed world. If a major hurricane struck Haiti, or drought led to crop failure, we would *expect* people to die. In the developed world, we would *assume* technology would come to our aid. Significant investment in technology in Haiti would improve the situation, but with a per capita GNI of only $1,600 in 2002, finding the money to pay for this is difficult.

Inequality of access to technology

Wealth is the reason why some parts of world are at the technological cutting edge whereas others lack even the most basic access to technology. However, wealth is not the only explanation for the geographical pattern of technology (Table 6.4).

Table 6.4 Access denied

Technology	Example
HIV/AIDS anti-retroviral (ARV) drugs	Used to treat HIV, prolong life by decades but are costly. Drugs are patented and protected by companies that develop them. This prevents cheap 'generic' copies being made that the developing world could afford. Some countries ignore patent laws, feeling they have no choice
Nuclear power	Thirty-one countries operated nuclear power plants in 2007. They can be used to manufacture plutonium for nuclear weapons. For this reason Western powers have used military force, economic sanctions and tied aid to prevent countries such as Iraq, Iran and North Korea from gaining access to nuclear technology
Communications	In North Korea, citizens have been banned from having private phones or mobiles since 2004. Access to the internet is restricted to government officials and tourists, and is filtered. There is a national intranet, with no connection to the outside world. The North Korean communist government fears political unrest if its citizens gain information about everyday life in the West
Contraception	Catholicism bans the use of contraception, such as condoms and the pill, on religious grounds. Italy, where 90% of the population is Catholic, has one of the lowest fertility rates in the world (1.30 in 2008) but access to contraception in less developed Catholic countries is much more restricted
GM crops	Genetically modified crops are not grown in the UK because of public opposition. In consumer surveys, 90% of the UK public are against them, because of concern about the ethics of transplanting genes into food crops, and their impacts on biodiversity

The examples in Table 6.4 raise difficult moral questions. Some drought-resistant GM crops (being developed by TNCs Monsanto and Syngenta) could increase food security in developing regions and save lives. ARVs can prolong life for people with HIV. Drug companies such as GlaxoSmithKline have invested millions of dollars in the development of ARV drugs and are reluctant to sell them cheaply. Making cheap copies of drugs is possible, but illegal. Two-thirds of all those infected with HIV live in sub-Saharan Africa and they cannot afford the $300–1,200 annual treatment costs of ARV therapy (Photograph 6.3).

Do individuals have a right to life-saving technologies, or do TNCs have a right to protect their investments and profits? In response to the moral outrage at the inability of developing nations to gain access to costly ARVs, the G8 summit in 2005 began the process of making access universal by 2010. The World Health Organization (WHO) is working towards this goal, but the cost in aid is expected to be $20 billion per year.

Technology and development

How far does technology determine development and resource use?

By the end of this section, you should:
- ➤ *understand the link between economic development and technological change*
- ➤ *be aware that technological leapfrogging is one way of overcoming the barriers to development*
- ➤ *realise that technological innovation may have unforeseen costs and benefits*
- ➤ *appreciate that the externalities of technology use are not always taken into account*

The link between technology and development

The developed world's **initial advantage** has been maintained by continual technological innovation. Development brings with it the infrastructure needed for technological advancement:
- ➤ educated populations, universities and research organisations
- ➤ government-sponsored research and development
- ➤ TNCs able to invest in new technologies, develop them and bring them to market
- ➤ an advanced legal system which protects research from theft and new products from patent infringement
- ➤ reliable energy, water, transport, health and communication systems

Building these systems is a major challenge. Countries such as China, South Korea and Taiwan have achieved this by a long-term commitment to investment in education, companies and infrastructure. Table 6.5 examines the link between education, innovation and development. Countries which invest some of their GDP in research and development and education tend to innovate and produce new technologies.

Table 6.5 Investment, innovation and wealth

| Country | Inputs | | | | Outputs | |
	% of age group enrolled in tertiary education (2006)	% GDP spent on R&D/ education (2004)	% of population connected to internet (2007)	Number of world's 500 largest TNCs (2007)	Patents in force (2005)	GDP per capita ($) (2005)
USA	82	3/14	75	162	1,214,556	41,850
South Korea	91	3/5	67	14	353,251	22,000
China	22	1.5/2	17	24	59,087	6,750
Vietnam	11	0.2/2	21	0	6	3,050

Source: UNESCO Institute for Statistics, *Fortune* magazine, WIPO 2007

Intellectual property

Intellectual property rights are rights given to people to protect the things they have created using their minds. They are of two types:
➤ **Copyright**. This protects the written word, music, performance, art and media productions. Normally, copyright is protected for 50 years after the death of the creator.
➤ **Industrial property**. This protects trademarks, geographical origins (for example, Scotch whisky), inventions, trade secrets and designs.

The inventions component of industrial property is protected by patents. A **patent** is a legal device to protect the intellectual property of an inventor of a new technology. Patents are normally enforced for 20 years after they are granted. Table 6.5 shows that patents are numerous in developed countries, but rare in the developing world. The degree of geographical concentration of patented new technologies is very high. The USA accounts for nearly 40% of new technology patents and roughly the same percentage of global research and development spending. The $288 billion spent on research and development in the USA in 2004 was equivalent to about half the total GDP for sub-Saharan Africa in the same year.

The patent system allows businesses and individuals to benefit from their inventions, but does it prevent access and innovation? The TNC Microsoft, based in Seattle, has often been accused of creating a **monopoly**. Around 90% of the world's computers use Microsoft software. In 2000 the US Department of Justice brought an anti-trust legal action against Microsoft, accusing it of preventing fair competition by installing Internet Explorer alongside the Windows operating system in new pcs, making it less likely that computer users would adopt competitors' internet browser products. The Department of Justice argued that this tied users in to using Microsoft products and prevented other software companies from innovating. Microsoft lost the case and was forced to allow other companies access to some of its software code. In addition, Microsoft has been fined €1.6 billion in the EU over similar anti-competition charges. Despite these legal actions, Microsoft remains the world's dominant software company, with revenues in 2007 of $57 billion.

Globally, the World Trade Organization (WTO) protects intellectual property rights through the Agreement on Trade-Related Aspects of Intellectual Property Rights (TRIPS) of 1994. All 152 WTO members are signatories. The agreement has been criticised for enforcing the movement of money from the developing to the developed world, where most copyrights and patents are held. It has also been accused of creating **artificial scarcity** – for example, a copy of Vista or Office 2007 costs a few pence to print onto a CD but sells for £100 or more. Software and drugs companies argue that they need to maintain high prices in order to cover the huge costs of research and development. Supporters of intellectual property rights argue that without such rights there would be no reward for innovation.

Leapfrogging

For countries trying to develop, **technological leapfrogging** may provide a 'quick fix' or short-cut route. Twentieth-century technology was hard-wired. Telephones relied on a network of exchanges physically linked by cables. Such networks are time-consuming and costly to build and maintain. Leapfrogging is possible because new technologies are increasingly wireless and mobile. Wireless nodes, such as mobile phone masts and solar power systems, can be built very quickly, almost anywhere. This has allowed efficient, long-distance, digital communication to develop rapidly in places where before there was no telecommunications system at all. It has eroded the digital divide in some areas.

 Case study **India: a mobile nation**

In 1998 India had 22 telephone landlines per 1,000 people, compared with 70 in China, 440 in South Korea and 554 in the UK. Landlines are expensive and the wait for a telephone in India in the 1990s was several years. This was an unacceptable delay for any start-up business. Mobile phone services were introduced in 1994. Since 2000, mobile phone use has grown from 3.5 mobiles per 1,000 Indians to 230. By 2007, some 7 million Indians were signing up for mobile phones each month and the number of users doubled from 100 to 200 million in a year. The growth has been fuelled by:

- cheap handsets costing as little as $40 and sign-up costs of around $20
- low-price calls and 'top ups' costing as little as 10 rupees (about 12p)
- lack of competition because the landline network was undeveloped
- a growing middle class which has benefited from outsourced jobs in call centres and IT
- fake accessories and batteries that cost under $1 (much of rural India has no electricity)
- bottom-up innovation, such as villagers using car batteries to charge mobiles where electricity is absent
- major expansion of networks into the untapped rural market (70% of the population) by Airtel and Reliance Communications

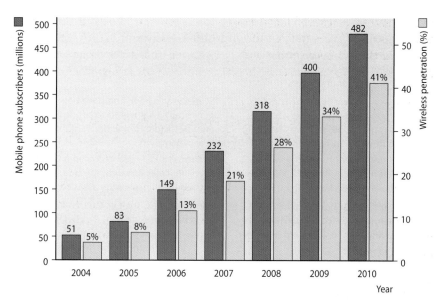

Figure 6.5 Growth of the Indian mobile phone market, 2004–2010

Why has India taken to the mobile phone so rapidly? There are many benefits underlying the take-off:

- Families, many of them split up by rural–urban migration, can stay in touch.
- Farmers, who used to be isolated, can check prices before going to market to buy fertilisers or sell crops, ensuring they get the best price.
- Small businesses can keep in touch with customers, suppliers and services such as banks.
- Key information such as weather forecasts and hazard warnings can be sent to farmers and businesses by SMS.

Mobile phones have the potential to narrow the digital divide by providing the poor in India with access to the information they need in order to maximise their economic output and minimise their risks.

The challenge of feeding increasing numbers of people in the developing world has been the target of large-scale technological fixes. The Green Revolution of the 1960s and the Gene Revolution of the 1990s both sought to bring about a dramatic rise in food production. Developing world farmers were encouraged to leapfrog from centuries-old farming systems into a high-tech world.

In the **Green Revolution** high-yielding varieties (HYVs) of crops such as rice and wheat were selectively bred (hybridised) from thousands of varieties to increase yields. In order to achieve maximum yields a new farming system involving fertilisers, irrigation and pesticides had to be adopted.

The **Gene Revolution** is based on genetically modified varieties of cotton, rice, maize and soybean. The DNA of the crop is altered by genetic engineering to produce new characteristics such as tolerance to drought and resistance to pesticides, herbicides and pests.

The two revolutions involved different technologies, and also have different origins and geographies (Table 6.6).

Table 6.6 The Green and Gene Revolutions compared

	Green Revolution	Gene Revolution
Who developed the crops?	Research institutes such as the International Rice Research Institute, funded by donors such as the Ford, Rockefeller and Gates foundations	TNCs and bio-tech companies such as Monsanto, Bayer and Syngenta
Which crops are grown?	The first crop, a rice variety known as IR8, was dubbed 'miracle rice'. Other varieties (IR36, IR72) replaced IR8 as it was found to succumb to diseases and pests	Bt maize and Bt cotton have been genetically engineered to produce their own pesticide. Herbicide-resistant soybean is widely grown
Where are they grown?	HYV rice is grown extensively in Asia. HYV wheat is grown in Latin America. Very few HYV crops have succeeded in Africa	The most widely planted crop is GM soybean. Latin America, Canada, the USA and China all have large areas of GM crops
What are the benefits?	Rapid-growing varieties of rice allow two crops per year, with yields up to 10 times those for traditional rice. HYVs are now bred to be resistant to pests and diseases such as the stem borer and blast disease. HYV rice allowed India to become self-sufficient in rice by 1980	Some varieties, such as Golden Rice, have been bred for nutrition. Golden Rice contains high levels of vitamin A. Many crops are resistant to the herbicide Roundup, so weeds can be killed without crop damage
Have they increased food production?	Yields of wheat, rice and maize grew by over 2% per year between 1967 and 1996, although yield growth slowed to 1–1.5% between 1997 and 2006	Possibly, although most GM crops are fed to animals, not people. Research in the USA suggests soybean yields are similar to those of non-GM crops

Unforeseen consequences

Both the Green and Gene Revolutions have had consequences beyond those envisaged when the technologies were first launched. The Green Revolution has been accused of creating a number of issues:

➤ *Social polarisation.* Larger farmers who could afford fertilisers, machinery and labour benefited most. Smaller farmers lost out and many became landless labourers.

➤ *Monocultures.* HYVs are vulnerable to new strains of disease, such as Ug99, a variety of black stem rust fungus discovered in Uganda in 1999, to which no known wheat variety is resistant.

➤ *Dependency.* Without high inputs of fertiliser, water and machinery, HYV yields are very low. Farmers become dependent on purchasing these inputs.

➤ *Environmental problems.* The widespread use of agrochemicals has led to **eutrophication**, while overuse of irrigation in arid areas has created salinisation of soils and water shortages.

In Argentina the huge expansion of GM soybean production led to an export boom and helped the economy recover from a serious crash in 2001. However, increased yields and exports have been accompanied by significant unforeseen changes:

➤ The number of farms fell by 60,000 as the area of GM soybean tripled. Large farms benefited from economies of scale, whereas small ones did not.

➤ The cultivated area of maize and sunflower fell by more than 5 million hectares, reducing food security among the poor.

Technology such as the Green and Gene Revolutions and GM crops might be said to fit Kranzberg's first law of technology: 'Technology is neither good nor bad, nor is it neutral.' The introduction of significant new technologies will have consequences, and these cannot always be foreseen. Texting, for example, was originally added to early mobile phones as a feature for people with hearing difficulties, and was often not advertised. No one guessed it would become the most common way of communicating via mobile phone. By 2004, over 500 billion texts were being sent per year. This was arguably a 'good' consequence, but an apparently 'good' technology can also lead directly or indirectly to negative consequences. It is unrealistic, however, to assume that all the consequences of new technologies can be identified in advance.

 Case study **Death by DDT**

A notorious example of unforeseen consequences is provided by the synthetic pesticide DDT (dichloro-diphenyl-trichloroethane). From 1939 DDT was used to control malarial mosquitoes and was quickly adopted as a farm pesticide. In 1955 the WHO started a global malaria eradication programme based on the use of DDT. Initial results were excellent, but DDT resistance began to appear in mosquitoes. The bombshell came in 1962 when the environmentalist Rachel Carson published *Silent Spring*, which blamed DDT for a growing toll of wildlife deaths through the process of **biomagnification**. Birds of prey appeared to be especially vulnerable, as DDT ingested by creatures they fed on built up in their own systems, restricting their ability to lay viable eggs.

DDT was banned in the USA in 1972 and in the UK in 1984. The pesticide still has a limited role in mosquito eradication in a handful of countries, but is no longer used in agriculture.

Case study **The ozone hole**

The synthetic compounds known as chlorofluorocarbons (CFCs) were developed in the 1920s as refrigerants. CFCs are essentially non-toxic and non-reactive and were ideal for use in fridges and cooling equipment. They also proved to be a good propellant for aerosol spray cans, invented in 1949. CFCs had a range of consequences:

- affordable fridges, which offered better food, vaccine and medicine storage and contributed to the improvement of human health
- the beehive hairstyles and improved personal hygiene of the 1960s
- the spread of graffiti in the late 1960s

By the early 1970s, concern was growing that CFCs were depleting stratospheric ozone, and they were

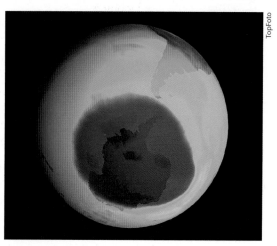

Photograph 6.4 The ozone hole over the Antarctic, 2003

Unit 3 Contested planet

banned from use in spray cans in the USA in 1976. In 1985 British scientists discovered the ozone hole in the stratosphere above Antarctica (Photograph 6.4) and the world was galvanised into action: the Montreal Protocol of 1987 phased out the use of ozone-depleting CFCs.

Externalities

Both DDT and CFCs produced negative **externalities**. These are the costs or benefits that use of a technology creates for a third party. Consider, for example, the 2008 Glastonbury Festival. Tickets cost £155, the proceeds being used to pay for the bands, the portaloos, rent for the land and all the other costs. However, if you do not want to pay £155 you might be able to hear the bands for free by standing nearby (a positive externality). If you live close by, you might hear the bands even though you do not want to (a negative externality). Local residents are not compensated for noise pollution, and therefore not all the 'costs' are paid for.

Pollution sink

Many technologies which we use on an everyday basis produce these externalitiess which are unaccounted for. The largest of these is the carbon dioxide we produce when burning fossil fuels to heat our homes, drive our cars and make our consumer goods. This is released into the atmosphere, which we treat as a large **pollution** sink. For decades it was assumed that this sink was large enough to cope. Only recently have people begun to realise that there may be significant costs to the pollution they produce. The WWF living planet index (LPI) has tracked the health of 1,313 terrestrial, marine and freshwater vertebrate species since 1970. It shows a significant decline in planet health (Figure 6.6). The LPI suggests that using the environment as a sink for pollution has serious consequences which humanity needs to address.

Figure 6.6 The living planet index, 1970–2003

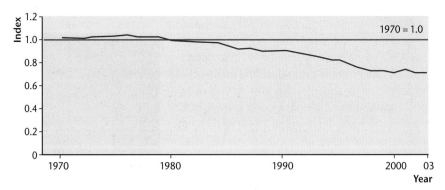

Polluter pays

One way of accounting for the pollution which is a negative externality of the use of technology is to implement the **polluter pays principle** (PPP). This approach quantifies the cost of pollution and passes it back to the producer, or user, of a technology. This is most commonly in the form of a tax or a fine. In Europe, PPP has gradually been applied to cars, perhaps our most pervasive technology and

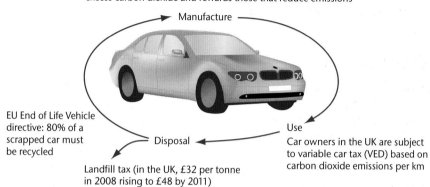

Car manufacturers are subject to EU 'cap and trade' Emissions Trading Scheme (ETS) which fines businesses that produce excess carbon dioxide and rewards those that reduce emissions

Manufacture

EU End of Life Vehicle directive: 80% of a scrapped car must be recycled

Disposal

Landfill tax (in the UK, £32 per tonne in 2008 rising to £48 by 2011)

Use

Car owners in the UK are subject to variable car tax (VED) based on carbon dioxide emissions per km

Figure 6.7 The externalities of car production and use

one of the biggest polluters (Figure 6.7). However, while PPP might reduce pollution, it does not prevent it. There is evidence in the UK that variable vehicle excise duty ('road tax') and higher fuel prices have encouraged people to buy less polluting cars. Nevertheless, carbon dioxide levels have remained high. Transport's contribution to EU carbon emissions rose from 21% to 28% between 1990 and 2004. The EU is proposing that car manufacturers be forced to reduce the average emissions of new cars to 130 g km^{-1} by 2012. This would be relatively easy for producers who make many small cars (for example, Fiat, Renault), but much harder for manufacturers of large, luxury vehicles such as BMW and Mercedes (Figure 6.8).

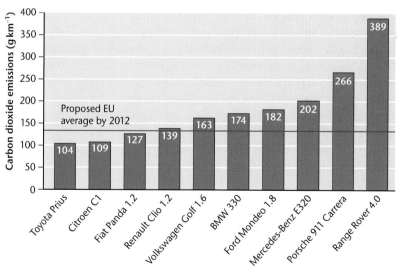

Figure 6.8 Carbon dioxide emissions for selected cars, 2007

Capturing pollutants

Road transport produces highly diffuse pollutants. For this reason, reducing emissions is a more realistic approach than trying to prevent them. For large, single-point polluters, such as power stations fuelled by coal and gas, it may be

realistic to capture and store pollutants before they enter the atmosphere. This technology has a long history. Flue gas desulphurisation (FGD) and selective catalytic reduction (SCR) have been used to remove the sulphur dioxide and nitrogen oxides – a cause of acid rain – from power station emissions.

Attention has recently turned to removing carbon dioxide emissions by using **carbon capture and storage (CCS)** technology (see Chapter 1). CCS is a current technology. Norway's Statoil has **geosequestered** around 1 million tonnes of carbon dioxide per year into the Sleipner gas field. In Weyburn, Canada, carbon dioxide from coal gasification plants in the USA will be used for enhanced oil recovery. This technology will require a huge upscaling if it is to have a significant impact on global carbon dioxide concentrations.

Technology, environment and the future

What is the role of technology in the management of the contested planet?

By the end of this section you should:

➤ *appreciate the difference between appropriate intermediate technology and the megaproject approach*
➤ *realise that some technological fixes may not be feasible or desirable*
➤ *question whether an increasing use of technology and achievement of a sustainable future can be reconciled*
➤ *have explored the two global technological futures of divergence or convergence*

Pessimism about the future of the world is not new. In 1798 Thomas Malthus forecast a world where food would run short as population outstripped supply. This 'Malthusian crisis' was revisited in 1972 by the Club of Rome with the publication of its report *Limits to Growth*. This suggested that a general resource crisis would occur as water, food and fossil fuels ran short and pollution increased. More recently, in his book *The 2030 Spike* (2003), Colin Mason suggested that six factors would combine around the year 2030 to create a global catastrophe:

➤ shortages of fossil fuels (as 'peak oil' is passed)
➤ global population growth (likely to be over 8 billion)
➤ persistent poverty (1.1 billion people lived on less than $1 per day in 2001)
➤ climate change (a 1–2°C warming is predicted by 2030)
➤ water shortages (the UN predicts that by 2030, people will have access to 30% less water than they do today)
➤ famine (with a greatly increased percentage of the global population suffering from food insecurity)

Countering these rather gloomy views are the optimists who believe that the human ability to innovate will come to our aid. In 1965 the Danish economist Ester Boserup argued that as population rises, agricultural technology develops to ensure food production can keep up. The Green and Gene Revolutions are cited as two such significant steps. In other words, technology prevents a resource crisis and ensures that **carrying capacity** keeps pace with the needs of the population. The phrase 'Necessity is the mother of invention' sums up this optimistic, technocentric view. At this time, we cannot tell whether the pessimists or the optimists will be proved right, but we can examine the technologies that might help manage our increasingly crowded and contested planet.

Types of technological fix

Technological fixes can take a variety of forms, as there is a wide range of levels and types of technology available, each with its own distinguishing characteristics (Figure 6.9).

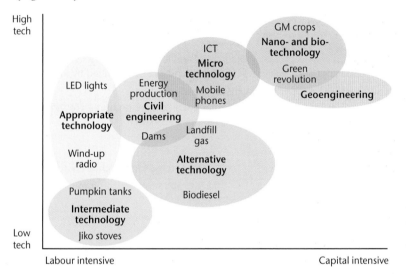

Figure 6.9 Contrasting technologies

It can be difficult to pigeon-hole particular technologies. **Intermediate technology** refers to relatively low, usually labour-intensive technology that can be mastered by local people, especially in the developing world. The Sri Lankan pumpkin tank water storage system is a classic example of this (Figure 6.10).

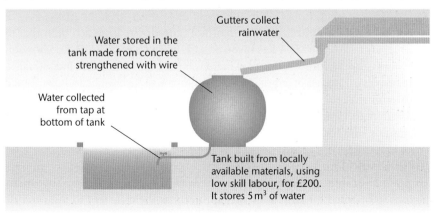

Figure 6.10 The Sri Lankan pumpkin tank, an example of intermediate technology

Appropriate technology

The pumpkin tank can also be classified as **appropriate technology** because it is appropriate to the level of income, skill and needs of the local population. Appropriate technology, however, does not necessarily mean low-tech. For instance, both the Freeplay wind-up radio and the XO-1 OLPC (one laptop per child) computer are examples of communication technology designed specifically for the developing world (Table 6.8). These two technologies also have social and environmental benefits.

Table 6.7 Contrasting technologies

Decision making	Top down	Bottom up
	Organised and controlled by TNCs, central government and international organisations such as the World Bank	Organised by local groups and NGOs, with dialogue between the funder and the recipient, and the ability to adapt technology to local needs
Development level	High tech	Low tech
	Reliant on sophisticated systems, specialist skills and advanced materials	Older, tried and tested technology which uses generic skills and can be mastered by local people
Inputs	Capital and energy intensive	Labour intensive
	Technology which is powered, and complex to produce and maintain	Technology which relies on human (or animal) energy to build and run it

Table 6.8 Two examples of appropriate technology

	Freeplay wind-up radio	XO-1 One laptop per child computer
Cost	Around $40. A similar Lifeline radio is available for children in the developing world	$188, although the aim is to lower this to $100
Details	Human powered, no pollution or energy costs Integrated torch Can be used to hear news, weather forecasts, hazard warnings and farm prices, and for education	Specifically designed for the developing world Minimal power consumption, and simple and rugged design Wireless mesh networking
Advantages/disadvantages	Increases independence and access to critical information, especially in isolated rural areas	Increases information flow and could be a powerful education tool. Laptops are sold to governments, not individuals, and a power source is required

The XO-1 OLPC reflects a somewhat more top-down approach than that of the Freeplay radio. The XO-1 has involved various TNCs, such as AMD, Microsoft and News Corporation. The Freeplay radio was the brainchild of an individual — Trevor Bayliss, a British inventor. As XO-1 laptops will be bought and distributed by governments, they may not get to everyone who could benefit. OLPC has been criticised for using a Western model of technology and development, based on the assumption that high-tech is best.

Megaprojects

Using small-scale technology can go some way in solving problems, but many nations have opted for large-scale **megaprojects** as the only way to industrialise and develop a high-income, consumer economy. Most commonly, these are civil engineering projects (dams, airports, motorways, power stations) which reflect a top-down approach. Individual citizens rarely have a say in their planning and construction and opponents argue that individuals' rights are often abused. China's development is an example of the megaproject approach to problem solving (see case study below).

Case study: China: fixed on technology

China has a long history of innovation, including the invention of paper, porcelain, gunpowder, printing and the compass. The communist People's Republic of China has been transformed in the last few decades by impressive technological megaprojects (Table 6.9). The policy of favouring the large-scale use of technology results from:

- a desire to quickly modernise the Chinese economy

- the vast scale of the country
- the fact that China's leaders are trained engineers

China's drive to modernise has reaped enormous gains in terms of annual GDP growth of between 8% and 10%. However, top-down megaprojects cannot avoid significant human and environmental impacts (Table 6.9).

Table 6.9 Some of China's megaprojects

Project, cost and timescale	Aims	Social and environmental impacts
Three Gorges Dam $25 billion 1994–2011	Multi-purpose navigation, hydropower (23,000 MW) and flood control scheme on the Yangtze River	Increased pollution, as the river can no longer 'flush' itself 1,300 historic sites flooded Up to 4 million people displaced Several species, such as the Chinese river dolphin and Siberian crane, are threatened and may become extinct
Green Wall $8 billion 1978–2050	4,500 km long, 3 million hectare planted forest belt to prevent further spread of the Gobi Desert. The desert increases in area by 3,500 km² each year	If it works, it will prevent annual $50 billion losses due to crop damage, soil erosion and dust storms Food security will increase as farming will be more sustainable Major doubts about whether the project can stop desertification Some land has been taken from herders to plant the tree belt
Shanghai Maglev $1.3 billion 2001–2004	The world's first commercial magnetically levitating train, capable of 435 km h^{-1} on a 30-km track between Shanghai's CBD and its airport	Maglev trains are pollution-free, although they use electricity Significant international prestige when the Maglev opened Protests in 2007 against an extension to the system were based on health concerns over electromagnetic radiation
South–North water transfer project $62 billion 2002–2050	To divert up to 45 billion m³ of water from the Yangtze River to the Yellow and Hai rivers for agricultural and industrial use	The project will displace 250,000+ people Could damage biodiversity in the Yangtze drainage basin by lowering water levels Promotes industrial development but also industrial pollution

Overcoming global environmental issues

Some technologies are more science fiction than science fact. The hypothetical technology of **terraforming** (modifying another planet to make it habitable by humans) became a popular idea in the 1970s and early 1980s, because finding a new planet to inhabit seemed a necessity to some in an age when there was much pessimism about the Earth's carrying capacity. Social revolution and unrest were common in the late 1960s, and photographs of the Earth taken from the *Apollo* spacecraft showed a tiny, vulnerable planet. The 1973 and 1979 oil crises added to the sense of economic gloom.

More recently, attention has turned to 'engineering' our own planet rather than finding a new one. Planetary-scale engineering, referred to as **geoengineering**, is seen by some as the way out of the global warming crisis (Table 6.10). On a small scale, the $32 million artificial island of Hulhumalé in the Maldives, built between 1997 and 2002, is an example of geoengineering. Built 2 metres above sea level, it is designed to reduce overcrowding on existing islands, but also to replace them as they are inundated by the sea-level rise generated by global warming. Geoengineering is perhaps the ultimate technological fix, as it seeks to control the nature of the entire planet.

Table 6.10 Geoengineering to prevent global warming

Idea	How it would work	Problems
Sulphur aerosols	Sulphate particles scattered in the stratosphere from balloons or planes block incoming solar radiation and cool the planet. A similar effect occurs naturally after a major volcanic eruption	Estimated cost: $50 billion every 2 years Sulphur could damage the ozone layer Polluting the atmosphere to solve a problem caused by pollution can be seen as unethical Acid rain could occur Global rainfall patterns might be disrupted
Space mirrors	Launching giant mirrors into geo-stationary orbit to reflect solar radiation away from Earth, creating a cooling effect	A Russian attempt in 1999 failed The technology for huge lightweight mirrors needs to be developed Models suggest that this would create warmer high latitudes and cooler tropics – not a pre-industrial climate Cost estimates exceed $1 trillion
Ocean fertilisation	Iron particles added to oceans to encourage plankton, which sequesters carbon dioxide as it grows. When plankton dies it sinks to the ocean floor. The company Planktos began trials in 2007 but abandoned them a year later	The UN agreed a moratorium on this technology in 2008, fearing biodiversity would be harmed Oceans could become acidified by the sequestered carbon dioxide It could cost $5 per tonne of carbon sequestered. Up to 6 billion tones per year would need to be sequestered at 2008 emissions levels
Synthetic trees	The 'trees', designed by Klaus Lackner, are intended to sequester 90,000 tonnes of carbon dioxide per year. They would use sodium hydroxide to capture carbon directly from the atmosphere, which would then need to be buried	Hundreds of thousands of trees would be needed, taking up large amounts of space Costs are estimated at $30 per tonne of carbon dioxide Trees would need to be powered Deep burial sites for the captured carbon dioxide need to be found

Sustainable futures?

Many environmentalists argue against geoengineering because it allows pollution to continue, then applies a 'fix' to clean it up. Environmentalists argue that a change in attitude is required, whereby we stop polluting in the first place. Many advocate the use of alternative energy technologies such as solar, wind (Photograph 6.5) and geothermal power. Technology and environmental sustainability are not mutually exclusive. It is possible to harness technology to maintain our lifestyles and the environment, for example through the use of microgeneration.

Photograph 6.5 Alternative energy technologies can help us stop polluting

Case study — Energy microgeneration

Renewable **microgeneration** includes energy gained from small-scale solar, wind, biomass and geothermal sources. In most cases, energy is generated for an individual building such as a house. These are small-scale, bottom-up projects, as householders themselves decide to install such systems. The systems themselves are relatively high-tech. In 2008 around 100,000 micro-generation systems were installed in the UK, compared with over 1 million in Germany.

Solar thermal systems accounted for 90% of installed capacity in 2008. Usually roof-mounted, these use the energy from sunlight to heat water (Figure 6.11). Direct generation of electricity from solar (photovoltaic) panels is popular in Germany, but less so in the UK. The potential to reduce greenhouse gas emissions and fossil fuel dependency is huge, but take-up of microgeneration in the UK is low:

■ Initial costs are high, often similar to the cost of buying a car, and savings are made over many years. These are not technologies for families on low incomes.

■ Many sites are not suitable for micro wind turbines or solar power systems.

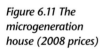

- Government grants to help with initial costs stopped in 2007 because demand was so high.
- The technology is not widely known about or is assumed to be unsuitable.

Some estimates suggest there are 10 million sites in the UK that could benefit from some form of micro-generation and that this could cut carbon emissions by 5%, or 30 million tonnes per year.

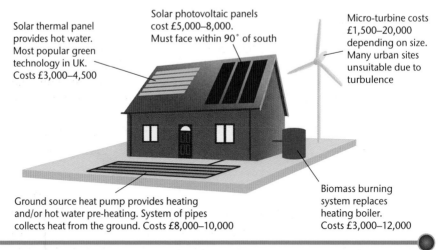

Figure 6.11 The microgeneration house (2008 prices)

Solar thermal panel provides hot water. Most popular green technology in UK. Costs £3,000–4,500

Solar photovoltaic panels cost £5,000–8,000. Must face within 90° of south

Micro-turbine costs £1,500–20,000 depending on size. Many urban sites unsuitable due to turbulence

Ground source heat pump provides heating and/or hot water pre-heating. System of pipes collects heat from the ground. Costs £8,000–10,000

Biomass burning system replaces heating boiler. Costs £3,000–12,000

Assessing sustainability

In order to judge which technologies we might use to solve global environmental and resource problems, we require a framework. The sustainability quadrant (Figure 6.12) allows us to assess technology against well-known criteria. How does the microgeneration house in Figure 6.11 measure up against the sustainability tests?

➤ *Futurity.* Most installations have a 30-year design life and should perform well over this whole period.

➤ *Equity.* The installations are expensive and there is a risk that only the wealthy benefit. Some installations, such as wind turbines, may have negative external-ities for neighbours.

Figure 6.12 Assessing technology on the sustainability quadrant

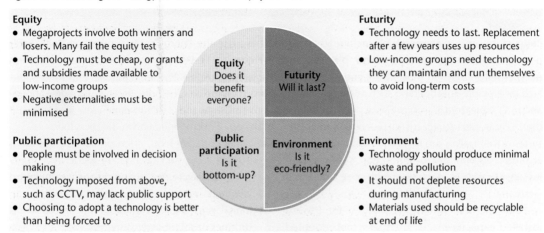

Equity
- Megaprojects involve both winners and losers. Many fail the equity test
- Technology must be cheap, or grants and subsidies made available to low-income groups
- Negative externalities must be minimised

Futurity
- Technology needs to last. Replacement after a few years uses up resources
- Low-income groups need technology they can maintain and run themselves to avoid long-term costs

Public participation
- People must be involved in decision making
- Technology imposed from above, such as CCTV, may lack public support
- Choosing to adopt a technology is better than being forced to

Environment
- Technology should produce minimal waste and pollution
- It should not deplete resources during manufacturing
- Materials used should be recyclable at end of life

Equity — Does it benefit everyone?
Futurity — Will it last?
Public participation — Is it bottom-up?
Environment — Is it eco-friendly?

> *Public participation.* As the installations are small scale, home-owners can decide which suit them best.
> *Environment.* The installations are zero carbon or carbon neutral (biomass), but they use resources and energy during manufacturing.

Technology for all?

The challenge facing the world at the start of the twenty-first century is enormous. Arguably there are two huge and seemingly contradictory global challenges:

> To use technology and changes in attitude to reduce resource consumption and pollution to more sustainable levels. This is necessary to avoid an environmental crisis.
> To use technology and resources to develop parts of the world where poverty, ill-health, illiteracy and food insecurity are growing concerns. This is necessary to avoid a humanitarian crisis.

Business as usual

Our current model of technological development, with its dependence on fossil fuels, seems incapable of meeting either of these challenges. A business as usual approach is likely to lead to further increases in greenhouse gas emissions, land

---

Case study   A Green Revolution for Africa?

The Green Revolution of the 1960s and 1970s bypassed Africa, so now agricultural research is looking for a way to bring such a change to this continent. The Alliance for a Green Revolution in Africa (AGRA), an organisation funded by the Gates Foundation ($150 million) and the Rockefeller Foundation ($50 million), is one body seeking solutions. The need is critical, as Africa's population growth rate of 3% per annum since the 1960s has exceeded its agricultural production growth rate of 2%. Low levels of agricultural investment mean that maize yields in Africa are typically 1–1.5 tonnes per hectare, compared to 2.5–4.5 in field trials where the best available technology is used.

There have been some successes, such as the rice variety Nerica, which has a short growing cycle, resists weeds and doubles yields. Much more investment is needed if a Green Revolution is to spread to Africa's 180 million small farmers.

Current research is focused on developing drought-resistant crops, such as maize and cassava, capable of tolerating Africa's variable and infrequent rainfall. Unfortunately, the right seeds are only the start:

■ Water for irrigation will be required.
■ Fertilisers will be needed, but if new crops require large quantities, input costs will spiral.
■ Improved storage of crops is required to prevent rot and rodent damage, so that surpluses can be stored until sale.
■ Access to markets requires better roads, as well as communication systems to check prices. Farmers who cannot get their surplus production to market will be no better off.
■ Education is needed in crop management, pest control, water management and the impact of climate change.

In short, a Green Revolution for Africa needs not only a range of GM or HYV crops, but a whole set of supporting technologies to ensure farmers can produce surpluses and sell them.

---

*Photograph 6.6
Cyclone shelter in
Bangladesh*

Joerg Boethling/Still Pictures

degradation and water shortages. Global inequality is likely to continue to grow, leaving many parts of the world, such as sub-Saharan Africa, technologically impoverished.

Poor countries such as Bangladesh face stark choices and limited options in the future. Some 10 million Bangladeshis live on land less than 1 metre above sea level. If sea levels rise this far, 15% of the country could be lost. In many areas, groundwater has already turned salty, forcing farmers to switch from growing rice (a vital food crop) to the aquaculture of shrimps and prawns (a profitable export). Food security could be affected if this trend continues. Bangladesh's 130 million people produced 0.1% of global greenhouse gas emissions in 2004, as opposed to 22.2% produced by the USA's 300 million people. Can technology come to Bangladesh's aid?

➤ Sea level might be slowed or halted if the developed world used technology to reduce carbon emissions.
➤ Coastal populations might be relocated inland, but farm technology (such as HYV crops) would be needed to boost yields and feed the people.
➤ Sea defences could be constructed, but the estimated cost runs to billions of dollars, well beyond Bangladesh's means.
➤ Flood warning technology and cyclone shelters and flood platforms would save lives (Photograph 6.6), but not crops. Aid might be required more frequently in the future if tropical cyclones and river flooding become more common.

A country like Bangladesh can only realistically use technology to cope with the frequent flood disasters that afflict it. Longer-term solutions that prevent disaster are out of its hands without either massive aid from the developed world or action to tackle global warming.

Technological convergence

Of all the technologies invented in modern times, the one which people have come to depend on most is probably the internal combustion engine, developed in the 1870s and 1880s. When Karl Benz used this engine to power the first automobile in 1885, our love affair with the car began. More than 120 years later

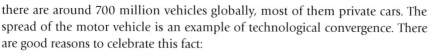

there are around 700 million vehicles globally, most of them private cars. The spread of the motor vehicle is an example of technological convergence. There are good reasons to celebrate this fact:

➤ Cars allow individual mobility, creating choice and allowing people to live and work where they wish.
➤ Road transport plays a key role in development, allowing markets and networks to operate.
➤ Transport is an industry, typically accounting for 5–10% of GNP and providing jobs and income growth.

It is no surprise that as a country develops, people seek to buy cars both as a status symbol and to increase their mobility. The launch of the Indian-built Tata Nano in 2008, priced at $2,500 (the world's cheapest car) shows how keen developing nations are to get mobile. But there is a problem, in that more cars mean more carbon dioxide emissions and a higher risk of serious climate change. In China the rapidly expanding economy has led to a soaring demand for cars. Sales grew by 56% in 2002 and 75% in 2003. China's 22 million private cars in 2007 were expected to grow to 140 million by 2020.

Energy efficiency

Adoption of automobile technology by the **BRIC** economies has serious environmental implications. Globally, 12% of greenhouse gas emissions come from transport, and this is likely to rise as car numbers grow. Forcing people not to buy cars is politically unrealistic. The price of fuel may reduce demand, but in many developing countries fuel is subsidised. The answer may lie with technology.

Launched in 2007, the Automotive X-Prize is a global competition to find a 100 mpg four-passenger car. The winner will receive $7.5 million in prize money from the X-Prize Foundation. This non-profit foundation is well known for its competitive challenges which seek to encourage technological breakthroughs. Already a German company, Loremo AG, has demonstrated a car with fuel efficiency well in excess of 100 mpg (Figure 6.13). Figure 6.14 shows how it compares with existing low-energy cars.

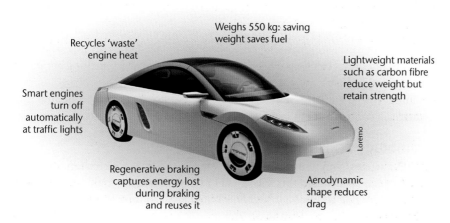

Recycles 'waste' engine heat

Weighs 550 kg: saving weight saves fuel

Lightweight materials such as carbon fibre reduce weight but retain strength

Smart engines turn off automatically at traffic lights

Regenerative braking captures energy lost during braking and reuses it

Aerodynamic shape reduces drag

Figure 6.13
Low-energy car technologies: the Loremo LS

Figure 6.14 Fuel economy in low-energy cars

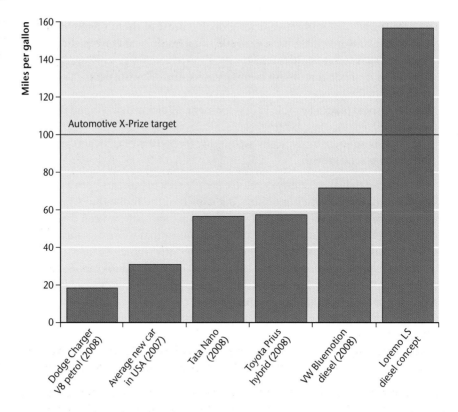

If widely adopted, cars such as the Loremo could have a dramatic impact on greenhouse gas emissions. The Loremo is planned to sell for only €15,000, so perhaps here is a case of energy efficiency not costing the earth. Other automobile technologies may help reduce the environmental impact of the car, but they need further development:

➤ Electric cars could reduce emissions if they use renewable sources of electricity. Conventional batteries are heavy and lightweight lithium-ion batteries are expensive. Only a limited distance can be covered at present by a single charge of the batteries.

➤ Hydrogen cars, either burning hydrogen or using a hydrogen fuel cell to produce electricity, would only emit water vapour. Producing hydrogen is energy-intensive, so renewable energy would be needed to do this. There are also major safety challenges in transporting hydrogen and refuelling because it is highly flammable.

➤ Biofuel (bio-diesel and bio-ethanol) is in theory close to carbon-neutral, but there are concerns about using land to grow plants for fuel instead of food.

Technology transfer

In 2007 a report by the International Monetary Fund (IMF), *Technology Widening Rich–Poor Gap*, concluded that the world has become increasingly unequal since 1980. It stated that technology has contributed most to this rising inequality and technological divergence (Figure 6.15).

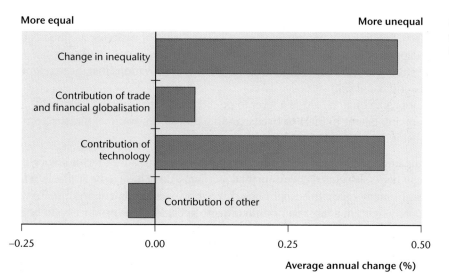

Figure 6.15 Annual change in global inequality since 1980

More equal ... **More unequal**

Change in inequality

Contribution of trade and financial globalisation

Contribution of technology

Contribution of other

−0.25   0.00   0.25   0.50

Average annual change (%)

The IMF study suggested that this was because:

➤ rising levels of technology require a workforce with skills and education that the poorest lack

➤ manufacturing plants in Asia have trained a skilled workforce, allowing them to benefit much more than unskilled workers in Africa and Latin America

The report concluded that education was the key to ensuring people in the least developed parts of the world could benefit from new technology. Without this, they will continue to be left behind.

In order to prevent the technology gap widening even further, significant **technology transfer** to the developing world is required. The commitment to development technology index, produced by the Centre for Global Development, measures the developed world's willingness to allow this technology transfer (Figure 6.16).

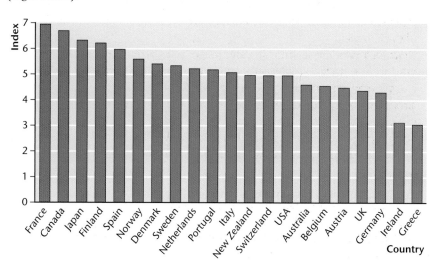

Figure 6.16 Commitment to development technology index, 2007

Countries with high index scores, such as France, are characterised as:
➤ refusing to grant patents for new plant and animal varieties, as these could deprive poor countries of new food crops
➤ refusing to allow patents on some ICT software innovations that the developing world could use
➤ not using bilateral aid as a lever to extend intellectual property rights
➤ forcing patent holders to license production of innovations that are seen as being for the public good

If the developed world wants the developing world to adopt technologies that might help solve global environmental problems, these have to be available at low cost. In many cases, this might be achieved by waiving patent and intellectual property rights in some countries in order to allow low-cost production to begin. Solar power is one such technology. If this is to be used extensively in the developing world, it will need to cost less than power from fossil fuels. Such technology transfers do happen, but they often rely on NGOs to provide the funding required to purchase and install the technology. Practical Action is a UK NGO which has installed 6,000 solar-powered water pumps across the developing world, at a cost of around $6,000 each (Figure 6.17). Solar water pumps are designed to:
➤ provide 40 litres of water per person per day
➤ provide water for people, livestock or crops, and therefore improve health and food security
➤ store 3–5 days' supply of water as a buffer against cloudy periods

Figure 6.17 A typical Practical Action solar water pump

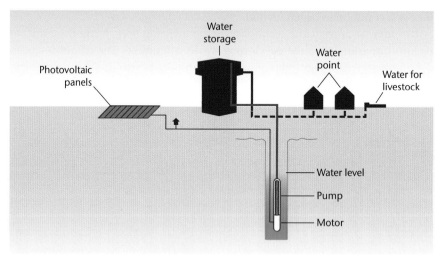

The future

The contested planet's environmental problems are partly a result of our addiction to technology, particularly those technologies powered by fossil fuels. The widening development gap is to some extent caused by the different levels of access to technology that different groups experience. Technology has a role to

play in narrowing the development gap and addressing key global concerns such as global warming. But this will only happen if we develop environmentally sustainable technologies and make them available to all. We have to face difficult technological, economic and moral choices if we are to successfully reconcile the urgent need for global environmental sustainability and human development.

Review questions

1 Using examples, explain the meaning of the terms 'technological fix' and 'access to technology'.
2 Evaluate the reasons for the unequal spatial distribution of technology.
3 Examine the relationship between technology and development.
4 'Technology may have unforeseen consequences.' Discuss, with reference to examples.
5 Explain how both technological and attitudinal fixes might contribute to solving global environmental concerns.
6 How do you see the technological future? Will it be one of convergence or divergence? Give your reasons.

Managing the contested planet: synoptic themes and links

By the end of this chapter you should:
➤ *be aware of links between the key topics and themes in Unit 3*
➤ *understand the relationship between key themes from your AS geography and the more in-depth, complex topics covered at A2*
➤ *realise that overarching global themes (such as poverty and sustainability) are a way of linking content and seeing the 'big picture'*
➤ *understand that groups and individuals across the world have different views about the future of the contested planet*

What is synopticity?

Synopticity means being able to see 'the big picture'. In class, topics are usually presented and investigated in a linear order. First, you may study biodiversity, then move on to development, then water conflicts and so on. This approach allows you to develop a detailed knowledge and understanding of each topic in turn. However, in order to convert this understanding into 'being synoptic', you need to start to see the links between separate topics (Figure 7.1).

Figure 7.1 Linear learning versus synoptic links

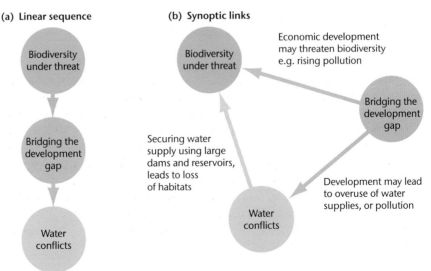

(a) Linear sequence

- Biodiversity under threat
- Bridging the development gap
- Water conflicts

(b) Synoptic links

Economic development may threaten biodiversity e.g. rising pollution

Securing water supply using large dams and reservoirs, leads to loss of habitats

Development may lead to overuse of water supplies, or pollution

- Biodiversity under threat
- Bridging the development gap
- Water conflicts

Synopticity can be taken further than just your A2 course. Links may be explored between the topics covered at AS and your present A2 options. The search for links may even be extended to other subjects you are currently studying. Figure 7.2 shows how these wider linkages might be developed.

Some AS topics, such as climate change, globalisation and migration, link to most of the A2 topics. For example, global warming (one of your AS topics) is having an impact on water availability. This in turn is affecting both development and biodiversity. Sustainability is a more general and popular theme in modern geography. It could be used as the arch under which to consider different management strategies aimed at balancing the need to develop against the need to maintain sustainable water supplies and to conserve biodiversity.

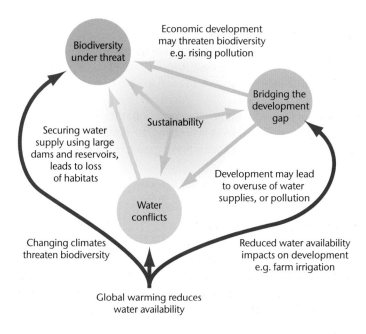

Figure 7.2 Development of synoptic links and overarching themes

Comparing approaches

Synopticity can also be approached by using comparative and parallel examples. The aim is to examine a particular issue by comparing it with another similar issue. For example, GM crops are one outcome of modern technology aimed at increasing food production. GM crops have a range of advantages and disadvantages which need to be weighed up. However, there are alternative ways of achieving increased food production. For example, Green Revolution crop varieties could be used to raise yields. These use existing technology with a long development history, and many of the lessons have already been learnt. Another possibility is organic farming, which is strongly backed by environmentalists. Comparing these three farming systems and assessing their relative merits would be an exercise in synopticity.

'Out of the box' thinking

It is also possible to be synoptic by turning an issue on its head. For example, instead of increasing food supply, the problem of food shortage could be tackled by reducing demand. This might be achieved through population policies aimed at reducing the number of people requiring food. The concept of synopticity includes 'beyond the obvious' or 'out of the box' thinking that enables us to make links between what might at first appear to be very separate topics.

Synoptic assessment

In the Unit 3 examination, Section B will directly assess your synoptic skills. You will be given synoptic pre-released resources to study for 4 working weeks before the examination. These will be related to one of the six topics in Unit 3. Examples of appropriate topics include:

➤ energy options for the Cumbrian coast (Energy security – Chapter 1)
➤ water resources in China (Water conflicts – Chapter 2)
➤ conservation and management in the Galapagos Islands (Biodiversity under threat – Chapter 3)
➤ the rise of India (Superpower geographies – Chapter 4)
➤ development options in Sri Lanka (Bridging the development gap – Chapter 5)
➤ GM crops in Latin America (The technological fix? – Chapter 6)

Figure 7.3 Synoptic skills to use with pre-release material

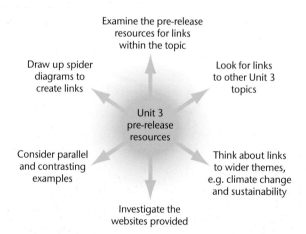

As well as a particular issue, the resources are likely to relate to one region or country. Your task will be to look for the wider links to other topics, global themes and contrasting situations.

When you receive the pre-release materials, it is important to study them and draw out the synoptic links before the examination. Figure 7.3 shows how this might be done. It is also important for you to know that synoptic links are written into the mark schemes for Section B of Unit 3. Candidates aiming for a top A-level grade will need to be aware of this, and work to make sure synoptic links are fully developed.

Approaches to synopticity

There are many possible approaches to synopticity. One way is to consider what geography is about. This allows us to identify themes which cut across the entire subject and all its sub-disciplines. Three examples follow.

Time and change

Change is a key theme in geography. The focus is on the processes that change one scenario into a new one, and the outcomes of those processes. Some processes and their outcomes are known and therefore can be predicted. Consider urban regeneration. With careful planning, we can build up a detailed picture of what a run-down area such as Salford Quays will look like after it has been subjected to the processes of regeneration and re-imaging. We will also have a good idea of what the economic impacts of those processes will be. In other words, known processes lead to predictable changes.

This predictability is not always so easy to achieve. As part of the development process in Bangladesh, more than 10 million tube-wells have been drilled to supply groundwater to 90% of the population. The United Nations Children's Fund (UNICEF) backed this development with millions of dollars from the 1970s onwards. Up to 50% of these tube-wells have become contaminated with arsenic that occurs naturally in sediments and in the bedrock. This has led to a huge health crisis which has been described as 'the biggest mass poisoning in history' (Photograph 7.1). Ignorance of the geology and the arsenic hazard meant that the outcome was completely unforeseen.

Many processes in geography have an inherent uncertainty. This often leads to conflict between different groups or players. Each group tends to believe that it is better able than the others to predict the consequences of a particular change or set of changes. They believe they are better informed, or they are in a better

Photograph 7.1
Lesions caused by arsenic poisoning, Bangladesh

Shehzad Noorani/Still Pictures

position to weigh up costs and benefits. Take, for example, some of the 'hot' issues of the day:

➤ GM crops – increased food security versus ecological disaster
➤ globalisation – increased wealth and prosperity versus exploitation
➤ migration – increased cultural diversity versus rising ethnic tensions

Geography is about examining physical and human processes, monitoring change, identifying consequences and suggesting how best to manage new situations. Its unique strength is its focus on places and the often complex processes that form and change locations. Geographers have a particularly broad interest in the perceptions of a huge range of different players in changing situations.

Pace

A striking feature of the late twentieth and early twenty-first centuries is the pace of change. There is evidence that time is being 'compressed' by the pace of technological, social and environmental change.

Figure 7.4 shows that change is rapid and extensive. Computer processing power follows Moore's Law. The power of computer chips doubles about every 18 months. On current trends, by around 2025, computers will be equal to human brains in terms of processing power. People will have access to unprecedented technological power. At the same time, the gathering pace of urbanisation is rapidly converting the world into an urban planet. Following hard on the heels of the growth of computing power and cities are rising sea levels and their frightening environmental threats.

It is worth noting your own experience of accelerating change. If you were born in the early 1990s you will have witnessed the following changes in the broad realm of communications:

➤ The death of the audio cassette, the peak of the CD, the first MP3 player (1998) and the first iPod (2001).
➤ The rise of the mobile phone. Before the mid-1990s, mobile phones were rare and very big. The first text message was sent in 1993. Today, how many of your friends and family do not have a mobile?
➤ The proliferation of the internet. Back in 1995, only 16 million people had access, compared to 1.2 billion in 2008.
➤ The first digital camera was launched in 1990, costing US$13,000 for a 1.3 megapixel image.

This is not an exhaustive list, but it demonstrates the pace of present change and hints at future accelerations.

Space and place

The technologies listed above have all contributed to what is known as either **time–distance convergence** or **time–space convergence**. Developments in both transport and communications have contributed to this. These are key features of globalisation. Arguably, the process of time–distance convergence began with the revolution in transport that took place after the Second World War (1939–45).

(a) Environmental: sea-level change past, present and future

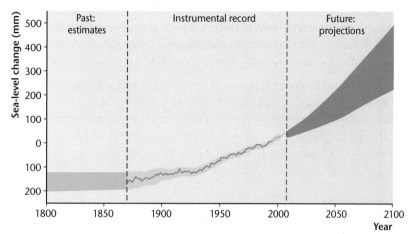

(b) Technological: processing power of Intel microprocessors

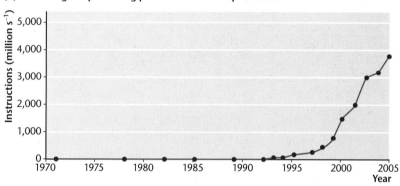

(c) Social: urban population in the developing world

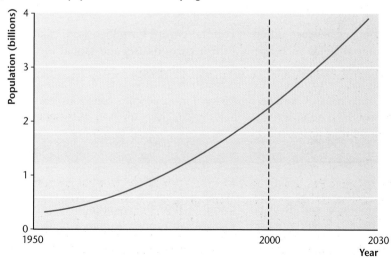

Figure 7.4
Environmental,
technological and
social change

Significant advances included the advent of jet-propelled air travel and the refinement and widespread use of the motor vehicle. The communications revolution of the 1990s, led by the internet, has undoubtedly accelerated the process. These two revolutions have overcome the friction of distance (Figure 7.5). Space and distance have 'shrunk', so that places no longer seem very far apart or out of reach.

Figure 7.5
The friction of
distance concept

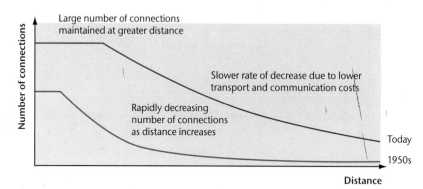

Before these revolutions, the slogan had been 'distance = money' – a blunt reference to the high costs of transporting and communicating over long distances. This meant that connections with distant places were few. Today, the costs of overcoming distance are much lower. Air travel is relatively cheap, as is ocean-going freight. The cost of telephone connections is low, and internet communication costs are not related to distance at all. Add to this satellite television, rising incomes spent on foreign holidays, and supermarket shelves stocked with goods from every part of the globe, and it is not surprising that today's world seems increasingly small. Changes such as these have had a fundamental impact on people:

➤ Information about places, even very remote ones, flows as never before. This has combined with increased travel and tourism to erode the 'exoticness' of such places.

➤ Contacts between different cultural groups have increased, creating hybrid cultural styles such as the British curry house, and global media such as YouTube and MySpace.

➤ Global environmental concerns such as biodiversity, climate change and natural hazards have become part of most people's consciousness.

Case study   Credit crunch

During the 1980s and early 1990s, developing countries such as Malaysia, Indonesia and Thailand enjoyed rapid economic growth. Credit (borrowed money) was easy to obtain and was used to sustain even more growth. The result was a rapid inflation of wages and salaries, property prices and the cost of living. In 1997 the credit 'bubble' burst, sending many Asian economies into a period of slow or negative economic growth known as the 'Asian financial crisis' (Figure 7.6).

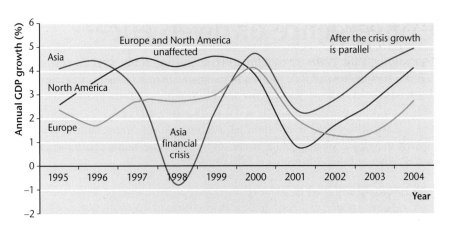

Figure 7.6
The 1997–98 Asian financial crisis

Economies in Europe and North America were not really affected by the crisis. It was a regional rather than a global crisis. Ten years later, in 2007, another crisis began – the global credit crunch. Its origins were in the USA. Banks lent money to homebuyers whose income barely covered their mortgage loan repayments (sub-prime mortgages). The new crisis was triggered by a fall in US house prices. As banks realised that many of their loans were bad, interest rates rose and people began to default on (fail to pay) their mortgages. The crisis was not extinguished but quickly spread:

- Bear Stearns, a major US bank, collapsed.
- Northern Rock in the UK went into receivership and was nationalised.
- Major banks began to write off the debts, realising that they would never be repaid or resold on.
- Borrowing money became much harder globally.
- Housing markets in many other countries, particularly the UK, crashed.

By late 2008, investment confidence was almost totally lost and the world found itself slipping towards economic recession.

How is it that some bad loans in the USA could have such a global impact? The answer is that the bad loans were 'resold' between banks on the global financial markets. This had become common practice since 1998, as the internet made instant global financial dealings possible. It no longer matters where banks are physically based – they can all trade as if they were in the same room. Unfortunately, the volume of sub-prime mortgages had become so great that the global financial markets were overwhelmed and unable to cope. Institutions were no longer prepared to take on sub-prime mortgages, so great had the financial risks become.

The credit crunch shows how much space has shrunk, and how globally connected the world has become. Table 7.1 shows some of the bank losses that occurred in 2008.

Bank	Country of HQ	Losses ($ billion)
UBS	Switzerland	37.7
Citigroup	USA	39.1
Crédit Agricole	France	4.8
HSBC	UK	20.4
CIBC	Canada	3.2
Deutsche Bank	Germany	7.7
Mizuho Financial Group	Japan	5.5
ICICI Bank	India	0.3
Bank of China	China	2.0

Table 7.1 Bank losses around the world resulting from the credit crunch, 2008

Convergence or divergence?

Events such as the 2007–09 credit crunch might suggest the world is converging, that it is moving towards a common state. There are good reasons to believe that this is not the case. If we examine the distribution of per capita income, the world is clearly a more unequal place than it was 20 or 30 years ago. Many people have become wealthier, and some nations, such as China, India and Brazil, have entered the global wealthy club. Some convergence has taken place, but there is also divergence both culturally and economically.

Table 7.2 Comparison of key issues facing countries at different levels of development

Country grouping	Examples	Analysis
OECD developed countries	USA EU 25 Australia Japan Singapore	The most globalised nations Development has led to high HDI (human development index) levels Populations have access to resources Ecosystems are increasingly conserved
Latin America and Caribbean	Brazil Mexico Chile Trinidad and Tobago	Many of these countries are approaching developed world HDI levels and access to services They lack the levels of globalisation of the developed world Income inequality is a key issue
Asian industrialising countries (NICs and RICs)	China India Malaysia Thailand	Improving countries, which are becoming globalised with rising HDI levels Access to resources is improving but with some negative impacts in water availability and ecosystem health Pollution and poor income distribution are key issues
Middle east and North Africa	UAE Saudi Arabia Tunisia Egypt	Many are rapidly growing, which is improving HDI levels and service access Water stress is a key issue in these arid regions as demand soars Gender and freedom/democracy are issues
Developing countries	Kenya Bangladesh Malawi Laos	Low HDI levels and access to electricity reveal countries that are struggling to develop They are not well connected with the wider global economy Ecosystems are healthy, often because of a lack of rural development Poverty is the key issue
Failed states	Burma Iraq Somalia Haiti	Isolated and insular states with failing human development The least globalised nations with little in the way of international trade Their populations live in fear and danger Ecosystems are damaged by conflict

Data sources (2005–07): University of Columbia environmental performance index, United Nations Development Programme, Foreign Policy globalization index

Edexcel A2 Geography

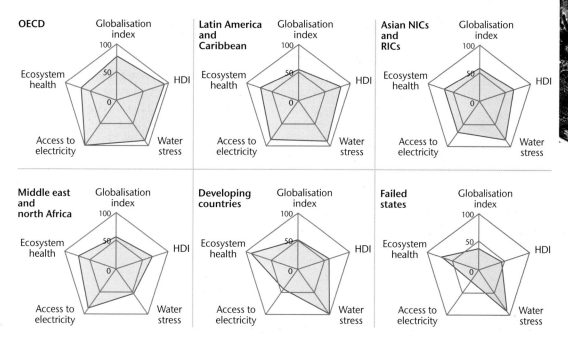

Figure 7.7 compares the profiles for the six groups of countries described in Table 7.2:

➤ The *globalisation index* (GI) measures how connected and open a country is, on a scale of 0 (least connected) to 100 (most connected).

➤ The *human development index* (HDI) is based on three social development measures (life expectancy, income and education level). The HDI ranges from 0 (least developed) to 100 (most developed).

➤ *Water stress* measures the percentage of a country's area using sustainable water sources: the lower the value, the greater the water stress.

➤ *Access to electricity* measures the percentage of households that have an electricity connection.

➤ *Ecosystem health* involves an index of 0 to 100 that indicates the degree of conservation and protection of natural areas.

Figure 7.7
Profiles of countries in Table 7.2

States of failure?

A number of countries in the world are described by the Fund for Peace (a USA-based non-profit organisation) as failed states. These are countries where all or large parts of the territory are no longer controlled by the government. Failed states are characterised by:

➤ corruption, which deters investment and makes it impossible to deliver aid effectively

➤ tribal divisions and rival warlord rulers instead of unified national government

➤ an ineffective legal system open to bribery and abuse

➤ abject poverty

➤ violence, conflict and civil war, often linked to ethnic and/or religious divisions

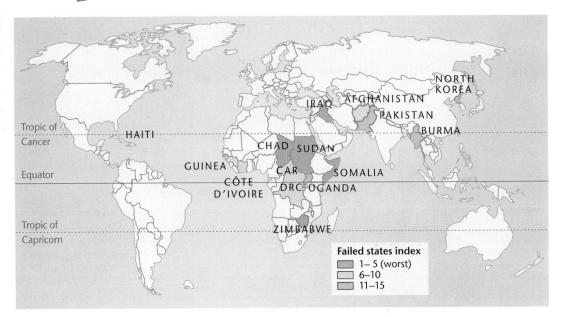

Failed states index
- 1– 5 (worst)
- 6–10
- 11–15

Figure 7.8
The top 15 failed
states, 2007

Failed-state geography reveals a clear pattern. Qualifying countries are concentrated in Africa and the middle/near east. Why should this be? There is no one reason, of course, but many failed states have a number of factors in common:

➤ Some are geographically landlocked, which makes trade difficult and dependent on neighbouring states.

➤ Some have harsh and hazardous physical environments characterised by unreliable rainfall, drought, floods or earthquakes.

➤ Most have rapidly growing populations, leaving scarce resources continually stretched.

➤ Most are divided in the sense of having both external and internal borders that cut across ethnic and religious boundaries – a recipe for territorial conflict.

➤ Many suffer from external interference in their internal affairs by more powerful countries.

It is interesting to note that the international borders of most European countries have been gradually honed by centuries of fighting and squabbling. In contrast, the borders of many African and Asian nations were drawn on a map by colonial powers with the stroke of a pen. It is hardly surprising that sometimes such boundaries divide people rather than uniting them.

Case study **Somalia**

Somalia, in the Horn of Africa, is home to 9.5 million people who scrape out a meagre existence. In 2008, 20% of them needed urgent humanitarian aid. An ancient people, the Somalis gained their independence from Britain in 1960. Somalia comprises one ethnic group which is divided into six clans, with numerous sub-clans (Figure 7.9).

Somalia has experienced almost continual conflict since independence (Table 7.3 and Photograph 7.2). The country became a pawn of the superpowers in

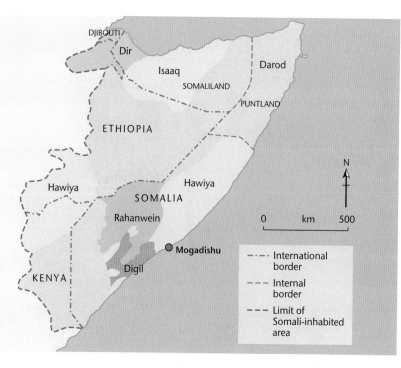

Figure 7.9 The clans of Somalia

Table 7.3 Forty years of unrest in Somalia

Timeline	External interference
Inter-clan rivalry persisted during the 1960s and 1970s	The country's strategic position at the entrance to the Red Sea and its Marxist government under Siad Barre attracted help from the USSR
In 1977 Somalia invaded the Ogaden, a predominantly Somali region of neighbouring Ethiopia. The Ogaden war ensued	The USSR and Cuba backed Ethiopia in the conflict, as Ethiopia was a fellow communist state
Civil war broke out in 1986. Five years later the north of the country declared itself a separate state, Somaliland	The UN, led by US troops, occupied parts of Somalia in 1992 as peacekeepers; it withdrew in 1995 but with no peace in place
Puntland declared autonomy in 1998, followed by other clan regions as Somalia split apart	The world largely ignored the break-up of Somalia during this 'warlord' period
A power struggle between various groups ended in conflict between the Islamic Courts Union (ICU) and the Alliance for the Restoration of Peace and Counter-Terrorism (ARPCT)	The ARPCT was backed by the US CIA. ICU had links to Al-Qaeda and Eritrea
2006 war	Ethiopia invaded Somalia in 2006 in support of the Somali Transitional Federal Government (TFG) and against the ICU and Eritrea. The USA provided some air support for the TFG

the 1960s and 1970s, and more recently the USA has backed attempts to rid it of the influence of Islamic fundamentalism and Al-Qaeda. Regional rivalries keep Ethiopia and Eritrea involved, and there is always a danger that the conflict will spill over the border into Kenya.

Photograph 7.2
Militia in Somalia

Should the world care?

A key question about failed states such as Somalia is: should we care about them? The answer is likely to be yes, we should.

➤ For at least a decade, Somalia has gone backwards in terms of development. Many people would feel morally obliged to try to help this and other failed states.

➤ Further increases in violence could destabilise the entire Horn of Africa region, with huge consequences. The middle east is a geopolitical hotspot posing similar threats to peace.

➤ Piracy off the Somali coast already threatens the safety of the key Red Sea shipping route.

➤ Somalia may have oil and gas reserves. BP, Chevron, Phillips and Mobil had exploration rights in Somalia in the 1980s, and the Chinese oil giant CNOOC was granted exploration rights in 2006. Some might argue that we only become interested in failed states when there are natural resources, especially oil, up for grabs.

➤ Displaced populations are a major problem. Refugees from war-torn states often move towards developed countries, where they are a cost, at least initially.

Living in a failed state is a gamble. The threat of death from disease, starvation and conflict is ever present. Many failed states have life expectancies of around 40 years, just half of the best achieved in developed countries.

One step forward, two steps back

There are many countries in the world that are developing, but not very quickly or steadily. These nations are better governed than failed states, although government is often weak and political crises are common. They include the least developed countries (LDCs), the majority of which are located in sub-Saharan Africa.

LDCs are classified as such because they have:

➤ low per capita income, less than US$750 a year
➤ poor human resources, due to malnutrition, low adult literacy and minimal healthcare

Many LDCs suffer from what could be called the 'one step forward, two steps back' syndrome. They have highly volatile economies that are vulnerable to external shocks, such as:

➤ changes in the demand for commodities that they produce for export
➤ global price rises, especially food and oil prices
➤ natural hazards
➤ fluctuations in debt relief, aid receipts and foreign investment

Figure 7.10 compares annual GDP growth for Niger and the UK since 1970. Within this period, GDP growth in the UK has varied by 9% compared with more than 30% in Niger. Such volatility makes long-term planning difficult.

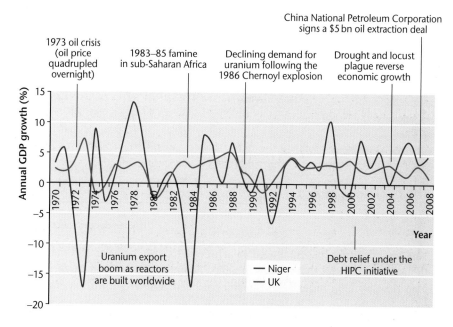

Figure 7.10 Volatility of the Niger economy compared with that of the UK, 1970–2008

Niger is one of the countries that could benefit greatly if the Millennium Development Goals were achieved. Debt relief, greater foreign investment and success in diversifying the economy could eventually enable Niger to take two steps forward.

Catching up?

Some of the newly industrialised countries have managed to break free of the great external shocks that bedevil the least developed countries, and are catching up with the developed world. Some, like Singapore and South Korea, have attained the magic goal of fully-fledged developed world status. But catch-up brings both benefits and costs. On the positive side, increased wealth and prosperity improve human wellbeing. The downside is that the desire to increase economic growth can encourage a country to take risks with the environment, leading to pollution and degradation.

Figure 7.11 The egg of wellbeing

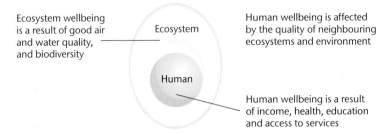

Ecosystem wellbeing is a result of good air and water quality, and biodiversity

Ecosystem

Human wellbeing is affected by the quality of neighbouring ecosystems and environment

Human

Human wellbeing is a result of income, health, education and access to services

Figure 7.12 The relationship between HDI and per capita ecological footprints for global regions

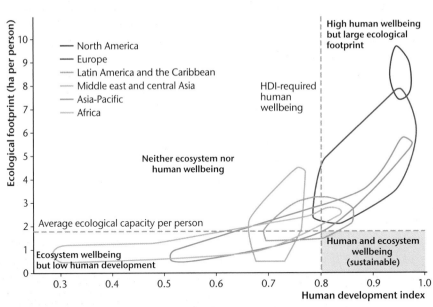

Very few countries have managed to achieve a balance between the wellbeing of their ecosytems and that of their people (Figure 7.12). In most cases, a high human development index (HDI) rating has been achieved at the expense of a deep ecological footprint. A deep footprint means that people are exceeding the biocapacity of the planet through an excessive use of non-renewable resources. A rising HDI might suggest that all is well with regard to human wellbeing. However, the HDI only measures three variables (income, education and life expectancy), and it gives no indication of the potential polarisation that exists within a country between the rich and the poor.

Table 7.4 The price of development

		Income inequality (Gini coefficient: higher value = greater inequality)	Obesity (% of the adult population)	Urban air pollution (deaths per million people per year)
Developed countries	Sweden	23	10.5	30–60
	UK	34	22	30–60
	Spain	32	16	30–60
Developing countries	South Korea	35	7	200–230
	China	47	2	200–230
	Brazil	57	13.5	60–100
	India	37	1.5	100–150

Table 7.4 compares some developing and developed countries in terms of income inequality, obesity and urban air pollution.

The rapidly developing economies have very unequal income distributions. Some people benefit from economic growth but others do not, which opens up a rich–poor divide. Developed economies tend to have more advanced welfare states that create a safety net and redistribute income through tax and benefits systems.

Obesity is a growing epidemic in the developed world, but the developing world is catching up. High-income lifestyles tend to be high in fat and processed food and low in physical activity.

Air pollution in cities is worst in industrialising economies. There tends to be a greater desire to generate economic growth than to clean up the pollution this causes. In developed countries, steps have been taken to clean up pollution, or to 'export' polluting industries abroad.

Tough at the top?

Developed economies, the OECD and the G8 countries face their own problems. Being top of the pile has its price (Table 7.5).

Figure 7.13 Public opinion on globalisation and the influence of nations, 2007

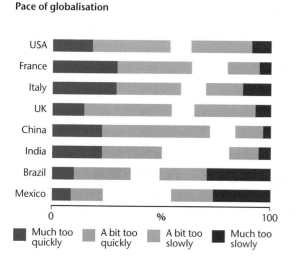

Pace of globalisation

USA, France, Italy, UK, China, India, Brazil, Mexico

0   %   100

Much too quickly | A bit too quickly | A bit too slowly | Much too slowly

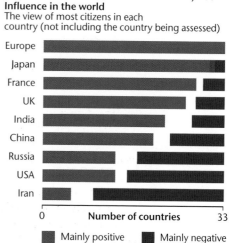

Influence in the world
The view of most citizens in each country (not including the country being assessed)

Europe, Japan, France, UK, India, China, Russia, USA, Iran

0   Number of countries   33

Mainly positive | Mainly negative

Table 7.5 The price of being developed

Life expectancy	Longevity has soared; some predictions suggest life expectancy could rise to more than 100 by 2070. Meanwhile fertility has plummeted. Together these trends present serious challenges: • ageing populations and shrinking workforces • rising healthcare and pensions costs
Lifestyle and diet	The obesity epidemic in the developed world has led to a huge increase in diabetes. Cancer and heart disease rates have risen sharply: • healthcare costs rise continually, as medical technology advances • difficult decisions may have to be made about state health systems such as the NHS
Migration	Economic success makes developed economies a magnet for migration, both legal and illegal, but with risks: • border controls are costly and politically contentious • the economic benefits and social costs of migration are finely balanced
Confidence	Confidence within the EU and USA has fallen: • terrorist attacks such as 9/11 and 7/7 have undermined confidence in security forces • China and Russia threaten the top political and economic slots
Consumer costs	The mass-consumption societies of North America and Europe are used to low-cost, high-quality produce, but this may not last. In 2007–08 there were: • rising gas, oil and petrol costs • rising food prices • collapsing property prices
Energy	One of the most uncomfortable prospects facing the developed world is its rising dependence on foreign oil and gas sources: • 'peak' oil was reached in the USA in 1970, in the UK in 1999 and in Norway in 2000 • dependence on Russian and middle eastern supplies can only increase

There is also uncertainty about some of the key forces that maintain the wealth of the richer countries. Globalisation is viewed with suspicion in the developed world (Figure 7.13), while even in some countries which appear to have benefited most from globalisation (China and India), many people believe the pace of globalisation is too rapid. Around the world, the USA is viewed as a negative influence on world affairs, whereas the emerging powers in Asia are seen as more positive. Conflict in Iraq and Afghanistan and tense relations between the USA and Russia, Iran, North Korea and Venezuela have probably all contributed to the perception of a country with too much power.

Players, actions and futures

Part of being synoptic is recognising that whatever geographical issue is being investigated, there are common elements. These are players, actions and futures (Figure 7.14).

- **Players** are the individuals, groups and organisations involved in an issue. They are sometimes called stakeholders.
- **Actions** involve the range of strategies and management methods that might be used to solve an issue or reduce its negative impacts.
- **Futures** are to do with what type of future people are aiming for – a sustainable future, one much like today, or something radically new?

Figure 7.14 Players, actions and futures

Actions and viewpoints

Geographical issues generate considerable debate. Many contested planet issues divide people on the basis of their viewpoints. A person's viewpoint on an issue is determined by, among other things, their politics. Your political viewpoint, in its turn, is influenced by your priorities. To some extent, this can be determined by considering how important different aspects of life are to you. For example:

- the environment
- culture and people
- individual rights and responsibilities
- the economy and wealth
- society and equality

Those who prioritise people, society and responsibility tend to be on the left wing of the political spectrum. Those who rank wealth creation and individual rights highly tend to be on the right wing. Figure 7.15 shows the range of political viewpoints using a diagram called a Nolan chart.

Perspectives on water

It might appear that political viewpoints have little relevance in geography. However, they

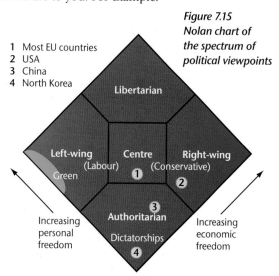

Figure 7.15 Nolan chart of the spectrum of political viewpoints

strongly influence decision making. Consider an issue such as the need to increase water supplies. The method chosen will be influenced by political viewpoint.

➤ Authoritarian political systems will tend to favour large, government-planned and government-built, top-down schemes such as dams and reservoirs. These will be seen as increasing the prestige of the government concerned and as benefiting the whole nation. Environmental and individual social costs will tend not to be considered to the same degree. The Three Gorges Dam in China is an example of this approach in practice.

➤ Left-wing (sometimes called 'socialist') political systems might focus on smaller-scale, local schemes using intermediate technology and local decision making (bottom-up). Individual needs are more likely to be considered. The government would build and own the schemes on the grounds that they are deemed to be for the social good of the people.

➤ By contrast, right-wing political systems (sometimes called 'liberal' or 'neo-liberal') are likely to look for a market-led solution, inviting private business and TNCs to increase water supply. These businesses would pick the most economic solution and make a profit. Individual rights would be respected, for instance, by paying compensation to landowners. Environmental issues could be largely overlooked.

➤ Lastly, in a libertarian system, anyone would be able to get water from anywhere without any interference from government. Most people fear this would lead to chaos and anarchy.

In many EU countries, including the UK, politics has recently drifted towards the centre. Water supply in the UK is privatised, but the government sets minimum supply standards and uses the regulating body OFWAT to protect water consumers from excessive price rises. If water prices rise too high, individuals have the right to switch to another water company. This political centre 'mix' of private economic freedom, individual choice and government protection is now common.

Players and conflicts

Inevitably, any issue facing the contested planet generates a wide range of viewpoints. This has the potential to create conflict. The issues range in scale from local (a third runway for Heathrow airport?) to national (what should the UK's future energy mix be?), right up to global (how best to tackle global warming). The roles of different players and the scale of their focus tend to vary. This can be illustrated using the analogy of a tree (Figure 7.16).

The roots

➤ Concern may arise on a local scale, with individuals focused on a single issue. These people may join together to form community action groups. Sometimes these grow into more formal organisations and join forces with other groups, for example larger environmental pressure groups.

➤ More formal groups with a local/national focus include umbrella organisations such as local chambers of commerce and professional bodies.

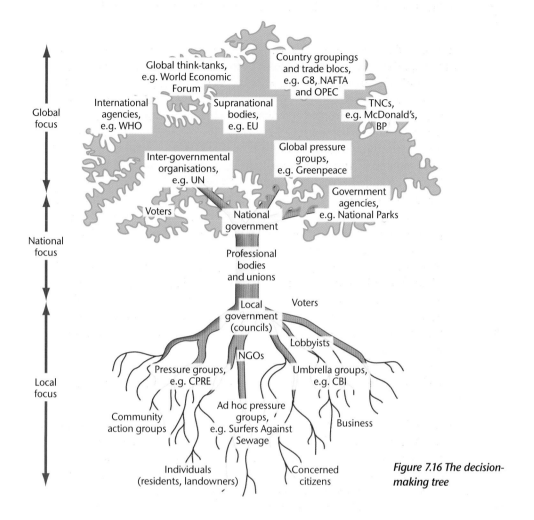

Figure 7.16 The decision-making tree

> Many organisations are national, but campaign on local and national issues, for example the Council for the Protection of Rural England.

The trunk

> Many decisions are made by government, both local and national. In democracies these are elected bodies, and voters can decide to remove them from office. This is a 'safety valve' to guard against unpopular decisions.

The canopy

> Decision makers in the 'trunk' take account of players who have a more global outlook. Government decisions are influenced by international treaties and agreements, such as the Kyoto protocol.
> In the UK, the supranational EU is a powerful player in national decisions.
> At a global level, there are inter-governmental organisations, think tanks, pressure groups, business organisations and TNCs. Many of these have power to influence government thinking and decision making.

Case study Heathrow's third runway

The case for a third runway at Heathrow airport near London illustrates how players can come into conflict with each other. In 2007, the government's transport secretary announced plans for Heathrow's expansion. Key to these plans are a proposed sixth terminal and a 2,200 m long third runway (Figure 7.17).

Local concerns

Not surprisingly, the plans met with outrage from local people. A spokesman for 12 local councils said: 'Expanding Heathrow may be good business for the airport operator BAA but that's small comfort to the 2 million people living around the airport who will pay the environmental price.' Local residents formed an action group, NOTRAG (No To Third Runway Action Group). Protests gained a national profile in 2007 when a Camp for Climate Action (a campaign peace camp) was set up near the village of Sipson.

This campaign group opposes a third runway, linking it with the global issue of climate change.

National interests

The transport secretary argued that 'Heathrow supports 170,000 jobs, billions of pounds of British exports and is our main gateway to the global economy. If nothing changes, Heathrow's status as a world-class airport will be gradually eroded – jobs will be lost and the economy will suffer.' The Conservative Party leader David Cameron has argued against Heathrow expansion on the grounds that the UK should be leading the way in reducing dependency on fossil fuels and reducing greenhouse gas emissions.

Global players

The airport's owner, BAA, and a large number of pro-

Figure 7.17 Proposed expansion of Heathrow airport

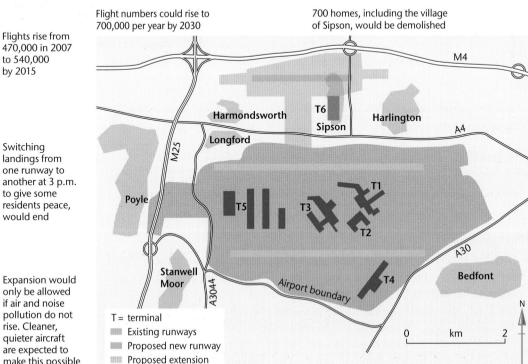

aviation companies such as British Airways, Virgin, Easyjet and DHL, as well as the Transport and General Workers' Union, launched Flying Matters in 2007. This is an umbrella and lobbying group pushing for support for a third runway. Aviation's link to climate change has led a number of global environmental players to become involved. These include World Development Movement (WDM), which claims it is not calling for an end to flying but for the government to stop further growth in emissions from UK aviation. Friends of the Earth is also campaigning against the airport expansion.

What appears to be a mainly local issue is in fact much broader. Local environmental concerns tie in with broader issues of carbon emissions and global warming. This has prompted national and international campaigning groups to become involved. Arguments that the expansion is in the national economic interest are supported by global corporations which believe the expansion is in their interests too. Heathrow is a classic geographical issue, pitting development against conservation. Those on either side of the debate are in effect involved in the global issue of progress versus sustainability.

It should be recognised that players have fundamentally different views on many issues and these views are unlikely to be easily changed. In the end, it comes down to what people and groups value the most.

Decisions and futures

Making decisions about the future is not an easy task. One of three broad paths may be taken. Each will reflect a different assessment of the underlying issue of development versus sustainability (Figure 7.18).

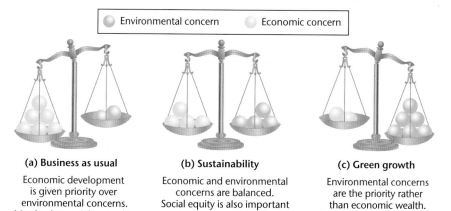

Figure 7.18 Three different futures

| Environmental concern | Economic concern |

(a) Business as usual
Economic development is given priority over environmental concerns. May lead to social inequality

(b) Sustainability
Economic and environmental concerns are balanced. Social equity is also important

(c) Green growth
Environmental concerns are the priority rather than economic wealth. Social equality is important

Business as usual

This approach implies that the future will be similar to the present – a world which continues:

➤ to rely on fossil fuels
➤ to use non-renewable resources and generate waste and pollution
➤ to move further along the globalisation path, with increasing wealth for some and poverty for others
➤ to cause **environmental degradation** to water supplies, ecosystems, soils and the atmosphere

Sustainability

To many, from individual consumers and governments to figures such as Al Gore and international organisations such as the Intergovernmental Panel on Climate Change (IPCC) and WWF, this type of future is too risky. Many focus on global climate change as the key threat. A more sustainable future could mean:

➤ a move towards renewable energy sources
➤ a switch to reuse, recycling and efficient resource use, with pollution increasingly paid for (the polluter pays principle)
➤ a more guarded approach to globalisation, using systems such as fair trade to ensure greater equality and social good
➤ a global effort to reduce environmental damage such as carbon emissions and deforestation

Green growth

Some players would argue that the sustainability approach does not go far enough. Green growth, as advocated by 'green' political parties, would go further, including:

➤ a wholesale switch to renewable energy and to low-energy production systems such as organic farming
➤ ethical consumerism including the consumption of locally sourced, renewable, fairly traded products
➤ a widespread use of (high) green taxes to reduce pollution and protect the biosphere
➤ a decentralisation of government and greater reliance on local decision making

Green growth emphasises the link between ecosystem wellbeing and human wellbeing. Activities that disrupt ecosystems will ultimately harm people. The polluter pays principle and the precautionary principle are at the heart of green political decision making. The precautionary principle states that people should exercise caution when introducing new technology (such as GM crops), until the technology can be demonstrated to have no negative impact on human and ecosystem wellbeing.

Global themes and issues

Some topics in geography might be referred to as overarching themes – they link to a large number of other topics. As such, they are synoptic. Some of these themes, such as global warming and globalisation, are context themes, in that they have the potential to affect almost every branch of geography you can think of. In this final section, we take a look at four overarching synoptic issues.

Overcoming poverty: think local?

The persistence of poverty is remarkable. Despite decades of economic growth, aid, debt relief and investment, and repeated global calls to action (e.g. Live Aid in 1984 and Live 8 in 2005, Photograph 7.3), more than 1 billion people live on

TopFoto

Photograph 7.3 Despite campaigns like Live 8, global poverty continues

less than $1 per day. Poverty is heavily concentrated in sub-Saharan Africa and south Asia, where 40% and 30% of the population respectively were living on less than $1 a day in 2005.

In 2000, the UN launched the Millennium Development Goals (MDGs), aimed at halving poverty (and hunger) by 2015. This was a tall order. The economist Jeffrey Sachs has argued that the least developed countries need 'clinical diagnosis'. By this he means each individual country needs to be studied carefully and the reasons for its lack of development identified. Only then can a 'prescription' be found that is tailored to that country's needs. It is dangerous to think that there might be a single cure-all. Each country is different.

Sachs argues that many of the barriers to development can be overcome (Figure 7.19), but only with a huge increase in aid – from $65 billion to $195 billion by 2015. The aid needs to be 'smart' in the sense of being tailored to suit the diagnosed needs in a particular country or region.

Some progress had been made towards the MDGs by 2008, but that year also saw a major setback, the 'food crisis', which illustrates the complexity of the situation. The food crisis arose from dramatic rises in the price of basic foods. Maize, rice, wheat

Figure 7.19 Barriers to development and overcoming poverty

- Low agricultural production leads to malnutrition and low incomes
- Corruption siphons off aid and investment
- Gender, race and caste inequality reduce human potential
- Physical barriers (landlocked, mountains) create isolation
- Barriers to development in least developed nations
- HIV/AIDS and malaria use up resources and restrict capacity to work
- Trade barriers restrict opportunities for income growth
- Unstable politics create an uncertain climate for investment
- Lack of physical infrastructure prevents investment and trade

Unit 3 Contested planet

and soya all more than doubled in price between 2006 and 2008. The reasons for this included:

➤ an increase in the amount of land used for growing biofuels rather than food, which reduced total food output
➤ growing populations, especially in the developing world, which have to buy food rather than producing it themselves
➤ rising oil prices which in turn increased fuel and fertiliser costs and therefore the costs of food production
➤ a shift, especially in Asia, towards eating meat, which is often grain-fed on land that once grew basic food crops
➤ severe drought in the breadbaskets of Australia and stem rust in much of Asia's rice crop

The UN warned that progress towards the MDGs was in danger of being wiped out by this global food crisis.

Resource exhaustion

As populations grow and wealth increases, so the prospect of resource shortages looms. The ideas of 'peak oil' and 'peak gas' are well known, but could other resources have passed their peak production? History shows that increasing resource use has gone hand in hand with population growth (Table 7.6). There is very little reason to believe that this relationship will change in the foreseeable future. Some resources, such as forests, are disappearing at an alarming rate. Others, such as fish stocks on the Grand Banks and in the North Sea, already seem to have been fatally degraded by overexploitation.

Table 7.6 Rising global resource consumption, 1970–2005

	1970	2005
Fish	67 million tonnes	160 million tonnes
Wood	2.6 billion m^3	3.4 billion m^3
Oil	44 million barrels day^{-1}	84 million barrels day^{-1}
Meat	100 million tonnes	263 million tonnes
Water	2,600 km^3 y^{-1}	5,500 km^3 y^{-1}

High-tech societies have come to depend heavily on a few metals to make their technologies work. Estimates suggest that it may not be long before these metals are exhausted (Table 7.7).

The figures for per capita use in Table 7.7 may seem small, but multiplied by the number of people in the USA (more than 300 million), and the number of other people in the developed world, they quickly become huge. Add to this the fact that more common metals are used in greater quantity (the average American uses over 8,000 kg of phosphorus, 1,500 kg of aluminium and 600 kg of copper in a lifetime), and the scale of the supply challenge becomes clear. Recycling is generally low (typically 15–25%, even for common metals such as copper and tin), so many of the world's resources are being dumped in landfill sites.

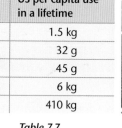

Metal	Used for	Global reserves at 2006 consumption rate	% recycled	US per capita use in a lifetime
Silver	Catalytic converters	30 years	16	1.5 kg
Indium	LCD televisions	13 years	0	32 g
Platinum	Catalytic converters	15 years	0	45 g
Uranium	Nuclear power	60 years	0	6 kg
Lead	Pipes, batteries	45 years	72	410 kg

Table 7.7
Exhaustion of key metals

Perhaps the big question is: how can global demand for metals in 2050, with a projected world population of more than 9 billion, be met without either a huge increase in recycling and efficiency or the extraction of new resources with potentially devastating consequences for the environment?

Global warming: difficult to agree

Preventing resource consumption, or even reducing it, is difficult. Taxes might be used in an attempt to reduce consumption, or alternative materials might be found. But there is no agreement that this should happen.

Increasingly there is agreement that global warming is a serious risk that deserves our attention. Some actions have been taken, for example the 1997 Kyoto Protocol. This was a bold attempt to take decisive international action to reduce carbon dioxide emissions, but it failed to convince the USA and Canada (and until recently Russia and China). Many business groups and TNCs also opposed restrictions on carbon dioxide emissions. 'Son of Kyoto', the planned follow-on global agreement, began its long journey in Bali in 2007. Many developing nations remain unconvinced that they should reduce emissions. Why is agreement so difficult to reach on this key global issue?

➤ International issues are dogged by rivalries and tensions; negotiators may bring 'baggage' to the table which clouds the issue being discussed.
➤ Agreement may need funding for monitoring; where does the cash come from?
➤ There is a lack of clear agreement on the science, for example concerning predictions of climate change.
➤ The scale of the problem may simply seem too daunting.
➤ There may be sharply conflicting ideas on what the solution should be.
➤ Cutting emissions will bring costs; some governments believe the costs will destroy jobs.
➤ Developing nations see global warming as not their problem, as they have not emitted very much of the carbon dioxide.

In 1992, at the Rio Earth Summit, there was general agreement on the Local Agenda 21 principle (think global, act local). Many local solutions have been put into place, such as recycling schemes, bus lanes and congestion charging (Photograph 7.4). It is relatively easy to gain agreement on local-scale solutions, but agreement on the national scale is much harder. For example,

Photograph 7.4 Local solutions are easier to implement than global ones

there is no agreement on the UK's future energy mix. The number of players is greater at this scale, and agreement that much harder to reach. At a global level the chances of agreement may seem slim.

Environmental sustainability

Sustainability has become a geographical buzzword. It was first used in the context of sustainable development to mean 'development that meets the needs of the present without compromising the ability of future generations to meet their own needs'. Figure 7.21 illustrates the three pillars of sustainability. According to this model, sustainability is achieved if economic development is equitable (fair) and viable (does not damage the environment). In addition, it has to be bearable, in the sense that the environment itself meets people's needs through the resources it provides.

More recently, the term sustainability has become incorporated into the concept of 'environmental sustainability'. This implies that people need to reduce their impact on the planet to a sustainable level – one that prevents irreversible environmental damage. Sustainability can be quite a difficult concept. A common misconception is that sustainability means a solution will last a long time. This is not necessarily the case. Large dams and reservoirs are designed to last a long time, but because they use huge quantities of concrete and frequently displace people and flood ecosystems they may not be sustainable. Conversely, a large number of small earth dams designed to last 10 years may be much more sustainable if they are built with local rock and soil using manual labour. Judging whether something meets the criteria for sustainability (Figure 7.21) is therefore a complex task.

Figure 7.20 The three pillars of sustainability

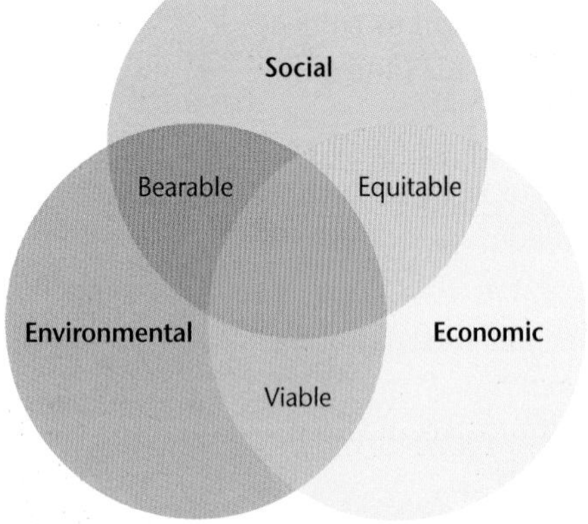

Assuming that the world decides to seek a more sustainable future, how would we measure our progress towards that objective? A number of potential measures have been proposed (Table 7.8).

Perhaps the most interesting and promising of these measures is the **happy planet index (HPI)** produced by the New Economics Foundation and Friends of the Earth in 2006. It is crucial to understand that this index does not measure how happy people are. It is a measure of how efficiently countries use resources to create human wellbeing. Efficient resource use should maintain ecosystem health, and therefore enhance human wellbeing. The 2006 index for selected countries is shown in Table 7.9.

The HPI produces some interesting patterns.

➤ Middle-income countries tend to score best overall, for example China, Malaysia and the Dominican Republic. Some economic development has improved life expectancy and wellbeing, but ecological footprints are low. Although not rich, people have reasonable income levels and are satisfied with life.

Table 7.8 Measuring sustainability

Sustainability measure (and origin)	How it works	Current situation	Comments
Ecological footprint (EF) (University of British Columbia)	Measures the biologically productive land needed to support resource consumption Measured in global hectares per person	Quantifies huge differences in resource consumption. Suggests consumption exceeds the planet's carrying capacity by 20%	The complexity of consumption, especially over the entire life cycle of products, is hard to quantify
Living planet index (LPI) (WWF)	Measures the state of biodiversity by monitoring key species in marine, freshwater and terrestrial ecosystems Uses an index where 1970 = 1.0	LPI has declined by about 30% since 1970 as a result of ecosystem degradation and extinction	The index only monitors vertebrate species, and data from remote parts of the world are patchy
Environmental performance index (EPI) (Yale and Columbia Universities)	Monitors 25 indicators relating to human health, ecosystems, natural resources and climate change Ranges from 0 to 100 (where 100 = best)	European, especially Scandinavian, countries score highly. Least developed countries have low scores	Tends to be very closely related to level of development, so may underestimate environmental damage
Happy planet index (HPI) (New Economics Foundation/Friends of the Earth)	Measures human wellbeing and ecosystem health, using a combined measure of ecological footprint, life satisfaction and life expectancy Measured using an index of 0–100 (where 100 = best)	Some highly developed and least developed countries have low scores. The former are ecologically destructive, while the latter fail to meet human needs	Is not a measure of human 'happiness', which has led to confusion. Its calculation is complex

Table 7.9 The happy planet index and per capita GDP, 2006

Country	Components of the HPI			Happy planet index (HPI)	Real GDP per capita ($)
	Life satisfaction (score)	Life expectancy (years)	Ecological footprint (hectares)		
Honduras	7.2	67.8	1.4	67.2	4,000
Dominican Republic	7.7	67.2	1.6	57.1	7,000
China	6.3	71.6	1.5	56.0	5,300
Malaysia	7.4	73.2	3.0	52.7	13,000
Malta	7.5	78.4	3.5	53.3	22,000
Egypt	4.8	69.8	1.5	41.6	5,500
France	6.6	79.5	5.8	36.4	33,000
Nigeria	5.5	43.4	1.2	31.1	2,000
USA	7.4	77.4	9.5	28.8	45,000
Sudan	3.6	56.4	1.0	27.7	2,100
Ukraine	3.6	66.1	3.3	22.2	6,900

Very good	Good	Medium	Poor	Very poor

➤ In general, islands and small states (Malta, Honduras, the Dominican Republic) score well. Is this because they are happily isolated from the wider world, or is it because they live within their limited resource base?

➤ Nations which are unstable (due to civil wars or the transition from communism to capitalism) score poorly.
➤ Countries with very low human development ratings (reflected in low life expectancy) such as Nigeria and Sudan score poorly.
➤ Surprisingly, developed nations (France and the USA) have low HPI scores. This is mainly a result of their deep ecological footprints, although in France it is significant that people are not satisfied with their lives.

Are there lessons for the future of the contested planet in the HPI scores? Perhaps the future we should be aiming for is one which:

➤ works to meet basic needs in the least developed nations
➤ attempts to produce stable, good governance
➤ reduces resource consumption to more sustainable levels

Planning for this future might maximise the wellbeing of both people and ecosystems, and the planet could perhaps move towards the situation found on the small Pacific island state of Vanuatu, which despite its isolation achieved the world's highest HPI score. Is this where the synoptic rainbow ends?

Review questions

1 Explain what is meant by 'synopticity'.
2 Distinguish between and exemplify the three different approaches to synopticity.
3 Assess the view that the world is experiencing 'accelerating change'.
4 Examine the relationship between ecological footprint size and level of development.
5 Use the information in the Heathrow case study to complete a conflict matrix of the views of the players involved.
6 Evaluate the different measures of sustainability shown in Table 7.8.

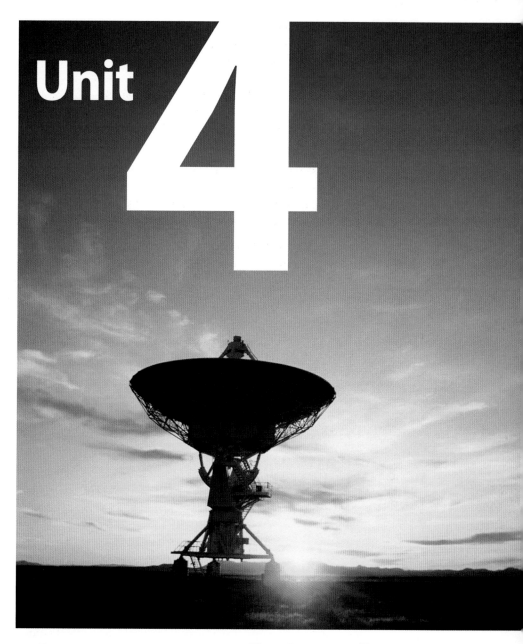

Unit 4

Geographical research

Chapter 8

The research process

Introducing Unit 4

Unit 4 is designed to allow you to enjoy some flexibility in your geographical studies. It provides you with the opportunity not only to acquire subject content, but also to master a range of independent learning skills (particularly selection and synthesis) which you may have only touched on in your other units. In this unit, you will focus on one option for a period of several months (Figure 8.1). During this time, you will be expected to have investigated four 'enquiry questions' (Figure 8.2).

Figure 8.1 The spectrum of option choice in Unit 4

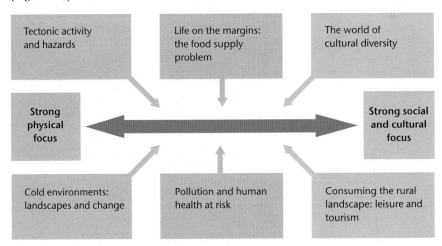

The assessment of your work will take the form of a 90-minute examination, during which you will write a long essay to show the depth and quality of your research into one overarching geographical topic. The examination paper will only offer you one essay title, but it will span several of the enquiry questions. For this reason, it is important that you cover all the prescribed content of your chosen option. A few weeks before the examination, and in order to help your preparation, Edexcel will publish a short, simple piece of guidance. This will 'steer' you to concentrate on particular aspects of the option. You will need to learn the relevant content thoroughly as you will not be permitted to take notes into the examination room.

Uniting your chosen option is what is termed the 'global synoptic content'. This puts the spotlight not just on *places*, but on the *people* and *players* in those places (Figure 8.3). In gathering the information for any case study, you should be aware

Tectonic activity and hazards
Risk, vulnerability, patterns, players
(1) Definitions, causes, event profiles, role of plate margins
(2) Impacts on landscape
(3) Impacts on people
(4) Responses and issues

Life on the margins: the food supply problem
Food insecurity and range of management methods: trade, high-tech, organic debates
(1) Issues and spatial patterns: deserts to megacities
(2) Causes of inequalities
(3) Desertification and dryland ecosystems
(4) Management techniques

The world of cultural diversity
Diversity in cultures and geographical patterns. Conflicts between consumerism, environmentalism, conservation, protection. Role of globalisation
(1) Nature and value of culture
(2) Spatial patterns, rural/urban, role of governments
(3) Impacts of globalisation
(4) Cultural values impact on landscapes, consumers vs Greens

*Figure 8.2
Details of the spectrum of choice*

Strong physical focus

Strong social and cultural focus

Cold environments: landscapes and change
Changing distribution, role of climate-active and relict landforms, challenges and opportunities, threats and management
(1) What and where
(2) Climatic and meteorological processes
(3) Geomorphological processes and distinctive landscapes
(4) Challenges, opportunities, management

Pollution and human health at risk
Health risk, link to economic development, geographical patterns and role of pollution. Management options
(1) Range of health risks, patterns, epidemiology model, impacts
(2) Causes of health risk, including pollution, role of geographical features, models
(3) Link between health risk and pollution, role of economic development, pollution fatigue
(4) Managing health risks local–global, sustainability

Consuming the rural landscape: leisure and tourism
Shifts from production to tourism and leisure from urban fringe to wilderness. Threats and fragility. Management: preservation to ecotourism
(1) Relationship between leisure and tourism and rural landscape: growth of pleasure periphery, attitudes, conflicts
(2) Physical significance and fragility of some landscapes, carrying capacity and resilience models
(3) Changing impacts of leisure and tourism, hotspots
(4) Management or not! Effectiveness and sustainability

of these three interlinked components. Their relative importance will vary according to the key question you are researching. For example, an investigation of the causes of tectonic activity or the physical processes affecting cold environments should focus on specific *places*. On the other hand, an investigation of challenges and responses should highlight *people* and *players*.

Figure 8.3
*Places, people,
players and power*

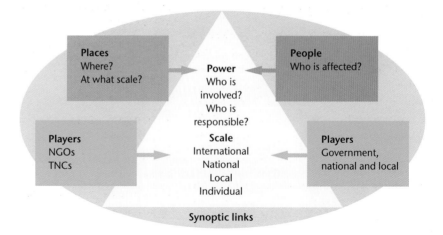

If your teacher allows you to choose your option, the following 'interest audit' might help you arrive at a suitable choice.

➤ If you found 'World at risk' interesting at AS, **Option 1: Tectonic activity and hazards** will provide you with the opportunity to study some hazards in greater depth.

➤ If you enjoyed studying glaciation way back in your GCSE course, **Option 2: Cold environments** will give you the chance to take the study further.

➤ If you have already studied A2 Unit 3, some of the content of the six topics will have introduced you to issues associated with poverty and the consumption of resources. If this interests you, **Option 3: Life on the margins** is a natural extension. This is a topical issue in the context of rising global food prices. It will also give you a chance to investigate semi-desert environments, which may be new to you.

➤ If you enjoyed 'Unequal spaces' or 'Rebranding' at AS, you might consider **Option 4: The world of cultural diversity**. This should make you challenge your present views on societies. It also builds on some topics, such as globalisation, that were only touched on in AS Unit 2.

➤ For a very different focus at A2, **Option 5: Pollution and human health at risk** may catch your attention. Its content ranges from HIV/AIDS to diseases linked with obesity and pollution. Indeed, you will need to be selective in this option, because the range of human health risks is enormous.

➤ We all have some experience of using the rural landscape as a recreation and tourism resource, whether it is on the urban fringe or in a more exotic location. If you have been on a field trip or visited a National Park or some other designated area for recreation and tourism, you might be able to quote your experiences as primary evidence in the examination of **Option 6: Consuming the rural landscape**.

You will see from Figure 8.2 that some options have a focus on traditional physical processes, such as tectonics and glaciation, whereas the more human-orientated options focus on cultural and rural landscapes.

The research process

If you go on to university you will undertake more research projects. A common complaint from universities is that their new undergraduates lack independent learning and research skills. These are highly valued. How would you rate yourself (Table 8.1)? Unit 4 should give you a good opportunity to hone these skills and gain valuable experience, as long as you follow the seven steps in the research process set out below. It should be clear from Table 8.2 that much more depends on you than on your teacher or the examiner.

Table 8.1 How do you rate your skills? (Copy this table and complete)

Skill	Score (0–5)
Time management	
Meeting deadlines	
Self-discipline	
Working outside class	
Organisation	
Taking the initiative	
Problem solving	
Effective research from a range of sources	
Being flexible	

Table 8.2 Who has the most work to do?

Examiner	Teacher	Student
Write clear specification	Facilitator: interpret and demystify the specification	Take ownership of all work without waiting to be told what to do
Set accessible questions allowing access for all A2 abilities	Give guidance on report style	Act on advice
		Keep to deadlines
Provide stretch and challenge for A* level	Provide basic information	Carry out independent research both in and outside lessons
Provide consistent fair marking	Mentor: set goals, check file organisation and content, help improve examination technique and overall progress	Prepare for test questions
		Keep an orderly file under the key questions
		Create content fact-files
		Learn a glossary of key terms

Planning

You need a structure for your research. Choose your option and stick with it. As you research, keep reminding yourself of the key aims. It may be a good idea to divide your file into sections based on the four key questions in the specification for your option. This will ensure that you cover the following:

➤ Create a *case-study grid* to ensure you have wide coverage of examples and that there are no overlaps or missed areas in the specification. This will also allow you to swap research with other students you trust to produce accurate, focused work. You might structure the grid by scale, impact or location. If economic groupings are appropriate to your topic, try to cover the complex range of economic development which exists globally. The simplistic North–South divide is now regarded as outdated and should be used with great care. The World Bank classification is widely used (Figure 8.4). This does more justice to the emerging 'BRIC' economies – Brazil, Russia, India and China.

➤ Compile *case-study fact-files*, including appropriate topical information, for example on tectonic hazards and health risks.

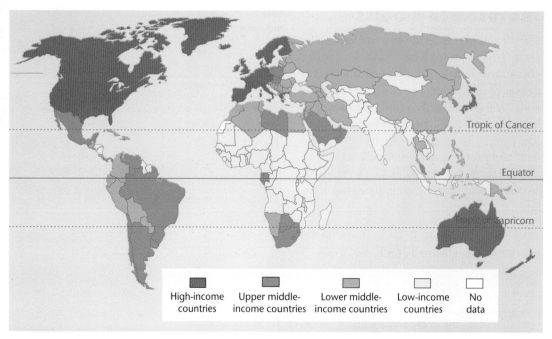

Figure 8.4 World Bank economic groupings

➤ Compile a *glossary* for each part of an option. Table 8.3 shows some examples of the range of key terms you need to command in each option. The glossary at the back of this book will be useful for this.

➤ The *key concepts, theories and models* relevant to your chosen topic should be fully noted (Table 8.4). You might use these to structure your examination report.

➤ You need to show you are aware of the differing *values and attitudes* of people. Remember your 'Western' viewpoint may be very different from that of someone in Asia or Africa. This applies to all options. Do not oversimplify complex situations.

Table 8.3 Glossary hints

Topic	Key terms (examples)
Tectonic activity and hazards	Igneous, liquefaction, tsunami, vulnerability, Richter and Mercalli scales...
Cold environments	Quaternary, glacial, periglacial, relict landforms, permafrost, hydroelectric power...
Life on the margins	Food security, organic, food miles, margin, famine, desertification, salinisation, dryland...
The world of cultural diversity	McDonaldisation, cultural landscape, ethnicity, ethnoscapes, cultural imperialism...
Pollution and human health at risk	Chronic disease, epidemiology, pollution incident, sustained pollution, pollution fatigue...
Consuming the rural landscape	Fringe, fragility, hotspot, stewardship, pleasure periphery, conservation, preservation, ecotourism...

Table 8.4 Possible key concepts, theories and models

Topic	Key concepts (examples)
Tectonic activity and hazards	Tectonic event, plate tectonic theory
Cold environments	Systems, equifinality, glacial erosion
Life on the margins	Food security, development gap, nutrition spectrum, desertification
The world of cultural diversity	Cultural globalisation, diversity
Pollution and human health at risk	Diffusion models, pollution
Consuming the rural landscape	Carrying capacity, resilience/fragility, rural–urban continuum

Reading and research

Be independent of your teacher. For each specific topic being studied, ask yourself:
➤ Is this overall article/piece of information relevant to the topic?
➤ What is its bias?
➤ How old are the data ?
➤ Are they from a reliable source?
➤ How does this answer specific aspects of the topic being studied?
➤ What other data do I still need?

Information sources

Be varied – gather information from available resources (Table 8.5) to maximise the range of your research. Be especially careful when using internet sources. Always ask: how do I know this source is authentic and reliable? Look for the date, the author and the organisation owning the site. The material could be biased, out of date or even false. Is there a bibliography to support the source? There are other research engines besides Google. Wikipedia has been shown to carry flawed entries. The internet offers over 6 billion pages of information and it is easy to get into a state of 'information overload'.

Creating a useful file

Use the key questions for your topic as the main divisions, and then structure your material as either 'theory' or 'case study'. We all have preferred ways of doing things, but some sort of fact-files and a glossary are essential to help your final revision. The fact-files may be in the form of spider diagrams or linear bullet points, or possibly colour-coded with images to help you remember. Ensure you have paper copies in a real file, and do not depend on a virtual IT environment – you cannot use 'a crashed computer' as an excuse for not being able to revise.

Foundation stones

➤ Keep a record of where your notes/articles originate from – you may need to return to them during revision. A bibliography may help, divided into books, magazines, internet, other.

Table 8.5 Research sources

Local authority/ city websites	These may have information on earthquakes, cultural equality, country parks, obesity, pollution or melting glaciers
GIS systems	Simple free ones, e.g. Google Earth, can be a rich source of information about an area, whether glaciated, a city, a National Park, a fault zone, a polluted river or an HIV/AIDS hotspot
Textbooks	Books aimed at the current specification and older ones. May be good for hazards, pollution and cities
Geography department videos and DVDs	These may be on your intranet if your school or college has one
Magazine articles	Local magazines and newspapers may give different perspectives on an area, especially in the 'World of cultural diversity' option
Geographical magazines	*Geography Review*, *Geofact* sheets, *Geofiles* – many of these are available in electronic form
Internet Athens	Your school or college may buy in to the Athens system, which makes a host of online materials available, from books to the *New Scientist* and *The Economist*, as well as daily newspapers (*Guardian* and *Independent* famed for their geographical articles). It includes access to the sophisticated GALE database. If you have this facility, use it instead of Wikipedia and Google
Internet metasearch engines	Allow research across several search engines in one hit, e.g. www.search.com
Internet search engines	Use keywords and phrases, quote marks and + symbols between words, add as much as you can to narrow the search. Most famous is www.google.co.uk
Internet gateways	Good for researching issues, e.g. INTUTE for arts and humanities (www.humbul.ac.uk). Try the online guide to how to use this geographical gateway: www.vts.intute.ac.uk/he/tutorial/geographer BUBL LINK catalogue of internet resources: http://bubl.ac.uk
YouTube	Has a good search engine for its video clips. Choose from more reputable sources, e.g. Unicef, national governments and pressure groups rather than individuals who may have a hidden agenda

➤ Skim-read all sources to get a feel for content, then reject/accept accordingly.

➤ Ensure any notes relate directly to the specification to reduce your workload. Reading around the subject is desirable, but you do not want to get lost in a mire of information.

➤ If your material overlaps different key questions on the specification, note as a header/footer other areas supported.

➤ Beware 'mind theft', i.e. plagiarism, even if unintentional. Create a habit of reading information then putting it into your own words rather than making a straight copy.

Practising timed reports in exam conditions

This is an essential part of your work. It can be a challenge to have to write so much content and fulfil the mark criteria in such a short time-frame. Try to practise at least four or five timed pieces, either open- or closed-book, before the real examination.

Treat any such exercise seriously. Your teacher will have to spend anything up to half an hour going through your work to give advice and indicate areas for improvement. He/she will not be impressed by lack of commitment and preparation on your part.

Working with the rest of your class can be helpful when it comes to brainstorming ideas on possible questions. Similarly, marking each other's work is useful, because you need to have a clear idea of the mark scheme (Table 8.6). You should be confident about the main command words, e.g. *discuss*, *evaluate* and *critically examine*, as well as key words such as *factors*, *impacts* and *challenges*. You can find detailed information about best practice in examinations and tips on examination technique on the website that accompanies this book (www.hodderplus.co.uk/philipallan).

The pre-release phase

Make sure you take advantage of support given at your centre. Once the research focus is released, showing which key areas in the options are to be examined, you should have a few lessons to help you prepare for them, and possibly sit a final mock examination. This will be your last chance to practise structuring your report, arguing a case and making the most of your case study material.

The examination

Stay calm and prove the value of your research over the past few months. This is the time for showcasing not just your knowledge but also how you can apply it to the specific question set. Do not be tempted to apply a pre-learnt answer, which is unlikely to have the focus required by the question in front of you. The key in the examination is to stay flexible and be prepared to reject material, not just write all you know.

Your examination answer will be marked out of a total of 70 marks (Table 8.6). It is worth 40% of the A2 award. How close can you get to maximum marks?

Table 8.6 Summary of the mark scheme for any report in Unit 4

		Marks
D	Introducing, defining, focus	10
R	Research and methodology	15
A	Analysis, application, understanding	20
C	Conclusions and evaluation	15
Q	Quality of written expression and sourcing	10
Total		70

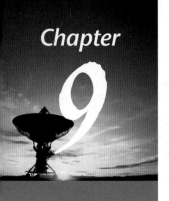

Tectonic activity and hazards

There is a range of tectonic hazards, many of them posing significant risks to people and their possessions. The level of risk varies according to a number of factors. The main physical factors include the magnitude, frequency, duration and areal extent of the hazard event. Of no less significance is the vulnerability of the population to the hazard. This is conditioned by their level of economic development and general preparedness, as well as by education and access to technology. The impacts of tectonic hazards may be reduced by understanding their causes, anticipating likely future events and taking 'evasive' actions.

Tectonic hazards and causes

What are tectonic hazards and what causes them?

By the end of this section you should:
➤ *have identified the range of tectonic hazards and explored their causes*
➤ *be aware that tectonic hazards have different profiles*
➤ *understand the link between tectonic hazards and plate tectonics*
➤ *understand that tectonic hazards vary with the type of plate margin*

What makes tectonic activity hazardous?

Tectonic activity generates a wide range of natural hazards, from lava flows and ash falls to ground-shaking and tsunamis. The fundamental cause of these is plate tectonics, the movement of the **lithospheric plates** that form the surface of the Earth, and so the associated hazards have a distinct geography, linked to different tectonic settings, such as the various types of plate margin and 'hot spots'.

A **tectonic event** is a physical occurrence resulting from the movement or deformation of the Earth's crust. Events are predominantly **earthquakes** or **volcanic eruptions**. Such events become tectonic hazards when they have the potential to cause loss of life and damage to property. Not all tectonic events, therefore, are hazardous. Many earthquakes in active areas are low in magnitude and may occur deep below the surface. People living in the area may not feel them. For example, during one week in April 2008 there were 161 earthquakes in the Los Angeles area, but virtually all were below 3.0 on the Richter scale. This meant that they passed almost unnoticed and were of no danger to local people.

Main hazards

Earthquakes

The hazards associated with earthquakes may be summarised as follows:

➤ *Ground displacement* is not life-threatening in itself, but its impact on buildings and other structures such as bridges and roads most certainly is. Displacement of gas and electricity supply systems can lead to a secondary hazard: *fire* (Photograph 9.1).

➤ *Landslides* are movements of masses of rock, earth or **debris** down a slope. Slope failure can be triggered by a number of events, including earthquake tremors.

➤ *Liquefaction* occurs when the shaking of silts, sands and gravels causes them to lose their load-bearing capacity. As a result, buildings and other structures may sink into the ground.

➤ *Tsunamis* are ocean waves with extremely long wavelengths, generated by earthquake tremors.

Photograph 9.1 The Kobe earthquake in 1995 caused many fires in the city

Further research

The *National Geographic* website covers all aspects of earthquake hazards:

www.nationalgeographic.com/forcesofnature/interactive/index.html?section=v

The Savage Earth website has good animations:

www.pbs.org/wnet/savageearth/animations/earthquakes/main.html

Volcanoes

The main hazards associated with volcanic activity (Figure 9.1) are as follows:

➤ *Lava flows* are sheets and tongues of liquid rock expelled from the crown or flank of an erupting volcano. Although some lava flows can travel at 80–100 km h^{-1} others move at human walking pace or more slowly. The speed of a flow depends on the viscosity of the lava, which itself is influenced by the temperature, the silica content and the incline of the volcano's slope.

➤ *Explosive blasts* are outbursts of fragments of rock and lava driven by gases expanding at great depths. These blasts may throw great blocks of rock many kilometres. However, the superheated blast cloud expelled by the volcano is more destructive.

Figure 9.1 Types of volcano hazard

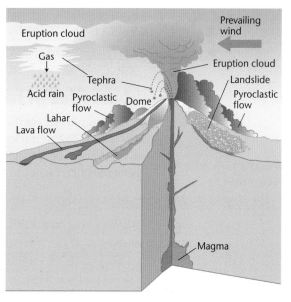

> *Ash flows* are dense masses of gas and fragments of lava that flow down the sides of volcanoes at great speeds. They form when gas-saturated lava comes near the surface of the Earth: as the pressure falls, the gas forms bubbles which break the lava into tiny fragments of liquid rock (called ash). If the ratio of gas to ash is low (i.e. there are lots of fragments), the ash can drag the gas downward into red-hot flows. Also called **pyroclastic flows**, these are partially controlled by gravity, and since the gas reduces the friction between the ash particles, they can flow very far (up to hundreds of kilometres) and very fast (over 150 km h^{-1}).

> *Ash falls* are less devastating than ash flows but can be very disruptive. Explosive volcanoes throw clouds of ash into the atmosphere which then fall to Earth downwind. The heavy ash can collapse roofs, break branches and coat the leaves of plants.

> *Mudflows* commonly occur on volcanoes with large deposits of ice and snow on their summits. As meltwater flows down the volcano's flank, it mixes with loose soil and ash to form a muddy liquid the consistency of wet cement. The Asian term for a volcanic mudflow, **lahar**, is widely used.

> *Glacial outbursts* are masses of water or ice suddenly released from a glacier by the heat from lava inside a volcano. Glacial outbursts are primarily water, but they can turn into mudflows if they flow over ground with abundant soil or gravel. The Icelandic term **jökulhlaup** is commonly used.

> *Poisonous gases* are released in and around volcanoes before, during, and for many years after volcanic eruptions. The most abundant gases, water vapour and carbon dioxide, are not poisonous, but smaller quantities of more toxic gases are released, including sulphur dioxide and sulphur trioxide.

Further research

Hazards of the volcano website :

www.vulkaner.no/v/vulkinfo/tomhaz/manyhaz.html

http://library.thinkquest.org/17457/volcanoes – gives plenty of detail of all volcanic hazards.

Event profiles of hazards

Tectonic hazards can be described in terms of their frequency, magnitude, duration and areal extent. The frequency of an event is often expressed as a recurrence interval, the number of years that can be expected to pass before the event recurs. The magnitude of an event can be described in a number of ways.

Table 9.1 The Richter scale

Magnitude	Earthquake effects
2.5 or less	Usually not felt, but can be recorded by seismograph
2.5 to 5.4	Often felt, but only causes minor damage
5.5 to 6.0	Slight damage to buildings and other structures
6.1 to 6.9	May cause a lot of damage in very populated areas
7.0 to 7.9	Serious structural damage
8.0 or greater	Can totally destroy communities near the epicentre

Earthquake scales

The magnitude of most earthquakes is reported using the **Richter scale**. It is calculated from the amplitude (not the strength) of the largest seismic wave recorded during the event, no matter what type of wave was the strongest. It is a base-10 logarithmic scale, so an earthquake that measures 5.0 on the Richter scale has a shaking amplitude ten times larger than one that measures 4.0. Seismologists use the more accurate but complex seismic moment magnitude scale.

An alternative is the Mercalli scale which measures intensity, not magnitude. It quantifies the effects of an earthquake on the Earth's surface, humans, natural and manmade structures on a scale of I (weak) to XII (causing almost complete destruction).

Volcanic explosivity index

The volcanic **explosivity** index (VEI) was devised to provide a relative measure of the explosiveness of volcanic eruptions (Figure 9.2). Each interval on the scale represents a tenfold increase in observed eruption criteria.

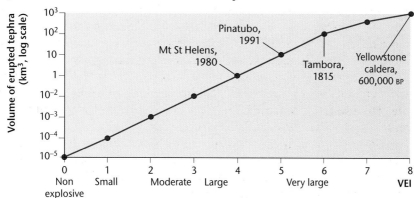

Figure 9.2
The volcanic
explosivity index

Frequency and magnitude

There is a relationship between the **frequency** and **magnitude** of tectonic hazard events. Generally, high-magnitude events have a low frequency and low-magnitude events have a high frequency (Figure 9.3).

Duration

The duration of an event is the length of time it lasts. This can be the time it takes for the fault to rupture, or the period for which shaking is felt at any given point. Volcanic eruptions can last anything from a few hours to several decades, as with those from the lava lakes of Kilauea, Hawaii. A recent simulation suggested that the so-called **supervolcano** of Yellowstone National Park would erupt for over a year.

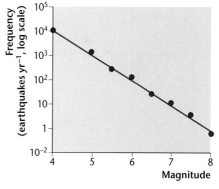

Figure 9.3 Earth-
quake frequency–
magnitude
relationship

Areal extent

The areal extent of an event refers to the surrounding area that it directly affects. This varies enormously according to the magnitude and location of the hazard. Small earthquakes may be felt only in the immediate locality, as energy from the shock waves created is absorbed by surrounding geology. Minor volcanic eruptions on the seabed do not affect wide areas, as the lava cools quickly in contact with the exceptionally cold water found at great depths.

Unit 4 *Geographical research*

The causes of tectonic hazards

Plate tectonic theory is now widely accepted. The Earth's crust is believed to be divided into a number of plates of different sizes. These plates move slowly and irregularly in relation to each other, typically at rates of a few centimetres a year. In some locations plates move towards each other, in others away from each other, while in a few cases they move past each other, either in opposite directions or in the same direction but at different speeds. Figure 9.4 shows the distribution of plates, their direction and, for the major plates, their rate of movement.

Figure 9.4 Global distribution of tectonic plates

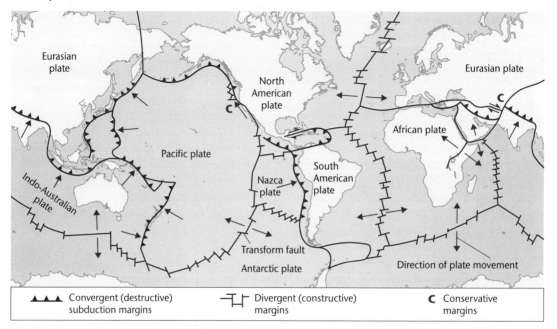

Crust types

The plates are made up of one or both of two different types of crust: continental and oceanic (Table 9.2).

It is now known that the Earth's outer layers cannot simply be divided into crust and mantle. Rather, the outer part of the mantle consists of rigid material that is attached to the crust. Together, these two elements form the **lithosphere**. The upper, semi-molten part of the mantle is known as the **asthenosphere**.

Table 9.2 Characteristics of the two types of crust

	Oceanic	Continental
Thickness (km)	5–9	30–70
Density (g cm^{-3})	3.0	2.7
Main rock type	Basalt	Granite

Heat

The most likely cause of plate movement is **convection cell** currents in the mantle, caused by heat from the core (Figure 9.5). This heat comes from a combination of radioactive decay and residual primary heat and its currents cause the lithosphere to move. There is uncertainty about the forces involved but the movement is thought to be due to the pushing apart of plates at places where two rising limbs of convection cells diverge below the surface, and the pulling downwards (known as drag) of the edges of plates at places where descending limbs exist. The downward drag seems to have the greater strength.

Plates are at their hottest near the mid-ocean ridges and cool as they move away. This increases their density and so they sink lower into the partially melted rock beneath and are dragged downwards into the subduction zone.

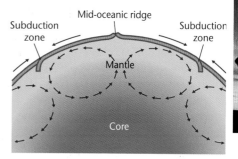

Figure 9.5 Convection currents and plate movements

Plate margins

The movement of plates produces different types of plate margin.

Divergent

Divergent plate margins occur where plates are moving away from each other. This may be a divergence of two oceanic plates, such as along the mid-Atlantic ridge, or of continental crust, as in the east African rift valley. The movement is due to the divergence of two convection cells beneath the surface, which bring magma from the mantle towards the surface. Pressure from the rising magma leads to a doming-up of the surface and the formation of a ridge. As the plates move apart, tensional faults are produced, into which the rising magma can enter. This cools and solidifies, producing new crust, either within the existing crust or on the surface following volcanic eruptions, either at individual vents or along the plate margin as a fissure eruption. The subsidence of sections of crust between the fault lines creates a rift valley within the ridge.

Earthquake activity occurs at all plate margins, as it is the mechanism which releases the stress built up by the friction between moving plates. The exact nature of earthquake activity varies with the type of plate margin. At divergent margins most earthquake activity is shallow focus, low magnitude and high frequency. This is because the movements are at or near the surface, and the pressure is easily released as the plates diverge.

 Case study **A divergent plate margin**

The divergence of the Eurasian plate and the North American plate in the mid-Atlantic is a good example of a divergent margin (Figure 9.6). A ridge and rift system extends along the mid-Atlantic for about 10,000 km, initially created about 60 million years ago as Greenland (on the North American plate) and northwest Scotland (on the Eurasian plate) separated to form the Atlantic Ocean. A series of submarine volcanoes exists along the margin, occasionally appearing above sea level as volcanic islands such as Iceland.

Much of Iceland is a lava plateau up to 200 m above sea level, with none of its rocks more than 3 million years old. The rift valley is clearly visible, while active volcanoes such as Hekla and Grimsvötn have erupted within the last 30 years. These volcanoes produce largely basaltic lava with magma rising from the asthenosphere, either due to the ascending limbs of convection currents, or perhaps as hot spot plumes. The eruptions typically have a low level of **explosivity**, as the plates are diverging and opening fractures in the relatively thin crust, which allows magma to escape easily before great pressure builds up below the surface.

Earthquakes are also common. Most of these are low magnitude, with three or four occurring each week, but seldom exceeding 3.0 on the Richter scale. Occasionally, greater magnitude events occur. A significant earthquake, 6.5 on the Richter scale, occurred on the south coast on 17 June 2000, while in February 2008 a 6.1 scale earthquake happened near Selfoss, again on the south coast. The focus of

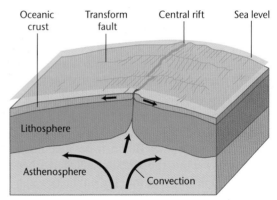

Figure 9.6 Cross-section of the mid-Atlantic constructive margin

these earthquakes is usually quite shallow, as no subduction is taking place.

Convergent

Convergent plate margins occur where two plates move towards each other. The movement is due to descending limbs of convection cell currents in the mantle beneath the lithosphere. This can happen when oceanic crust meets continental crust, such as at the convergence of the Nazca plate and the South American plate, or when two oceanic plates converge, as where the Pacific and Philippine plates converge.

Oceanic crust is denser than continental crust, and when the two converge the denser is subducted down into the asthenosphere beneath the less dense. This forms an ocean trench on the sea floor at the point of subduction. The continental crust, being more buoyant, is not subducted but is uplifted, buckled and folded, forming a range of fold mountains.

The subducted plate is heated and partially melts under pressure about 100 km below the surface. This melt is less dense than the surrounding rocks and so rises through any lines of weakness towards the surface. It may cool and solidify beneath the surface, forming intrusive igneous rocks such as granite, or eventually reach the surface under great pressure, forming violent, infrequent volcanic eruptions.

Earthquakes are also a common feature, occurring at a range of depths along the **Benioff zone**, the boundary between the subducting plate and the overlying crustal rocks, from shallow focus events at the ocean trench down to 700 km.

Case study   **A convergent plate margin**

The oceanic Nazca plate converges with and subducts beneath the continental South American plate (Figure 9.7). The Andes fold mountain chain, rising to nearly 7,000 m above sea level, has been formed here as the continental crust has been buckled and uplifted. Volcanoes such as Cotopaxi occur along the chain. These tend to erupt quite silicic, often andesitic, lava. The source of this is the melted edge of the

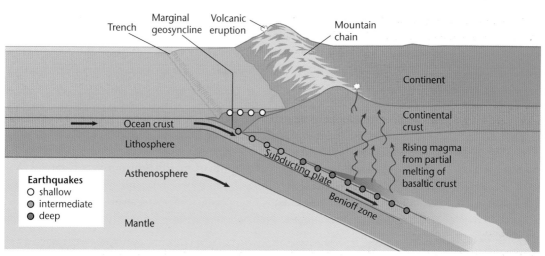

Figure 9.7 Cross-section of an oceanic/continental destructive margin

subducting Nazca plate. As this magma rises through the continental crust of the South American plate, it reacts with the rock and becomes increasingly high in silica and hence very viscous. The eruptions tend to be very explosive: the magma is rising under pressure through a great thickness of continental crust, so does not always find easy routeways to the surface. The Peru–Chile trench, reaching depths of 8,000 m, occurs at the point of subduction.

Earthquakes, such as the one in northern Peru in 1970 which killed 67,000 people, are common and often of high magnitude. Pressure builds up during convergence, much more so than during divergence, where it tends to be easily and frequently released. The focus of these earthquakes is often quite deep in the subduction zone.

Where oceanic crust converges with oceanic crust, subduction still occurs, as one plate is likely to be slightly colder and denser than the other (Figure 9.8). The landforms and features that result are similar, except that volcanic activity leads to the formation of a chain of volcanic islands above the subduction zone, known as an island arc. The Mariana Islands have been formed in this way as a result of the convergence of the Pacific plate and the Philippine plate with the subduction of the former below the latter.

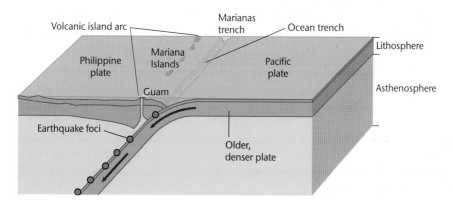

Figure 9.8 Cross-section of an oceanic/oceanic destructive margin

Volcanoes there tend to erupt intermediate lava with a silica content of around 50%. Although the source of this is the melted edge of the subducted plate, it passes through little overlying crust on its way to the surface, as the oceanic crust is fairly thin, often only a few kilometres.

Collision margin

The convergence of two plates of continental crust is known as a **collision margin**. No subduction occurs, as both plates are buoyant and low-density. However, intervening oceanic sediments trapped between the two converging plates will be heaved upwards, resulting in the uplift of major fold mountain ranges. No volcanic activity is found at this type of margin, as no crust is being destroyed by subduction and no new crust is being created by rising magma. Earthquakes do occur, although they are often deep-focus and have limited surface impact.

Case study   A collision plate margin

The Indo-Australian plate is moving northwards at a rate of about 5 cm per year (Figure 9.9). It collides with the Eurasian plate, which is moving southeast at a slightly slower rate. Prior to their collision, the two continental land masses were separated by the remnants of the Tethys Sea, which originated at the time of the break-up of **Pangea** 300 million years ago. The fold mountain chain of the Himalayas was thrust upwards to a height of over 9,000 m. Rocks found at the top contain fossils of small sea creatures, confirming the existence of the previously inter-vening ocean.

Such margins do not exhibit regular or significant volcanic activity. No magma is rising towards the surface, either due to the melting of a subducted plate edge or the ascending limb of a convection current or hot spot plume. Earthquakes are common, and although their focus is often quite deep below the surface, their magnitude can be very high as a result of the intense compressional forces exerted by the collision. In October 2005 a 7.6

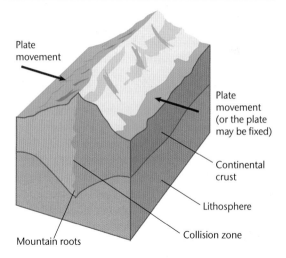

Figure 9.9 Cross-section of a collision margin

magnitude earthquake struck the Kashmir region of Pakistan. More than 75,000 people were killed, the death toll aggravated by the poorly built homes on steep slopes. The remoteness of the region and the poor emergency services were another major factor.

Transform margin

A **transform margin** occurs when two plates move laterally past each other. This is also known as a **conservative margin**. No volcanic activity is found here either, for the same reasons: no crust is being destroyed by subduction and no new crust is being created by rising magma. Shallow-focus earthquakes of varying frequency and magnitude are found. Low-magnitude, high-frequency events occur when pressure along the margin is easily released. Occasional major events take place after a significant build-up of pressure, typically when high levels of friction restrict movement of the crust along fault lines.

Most plates have a constructive margin at one edge and a destructive margin at the other, with conservative margins making up the other two sides.

Case study A transform plate margin

By far the best-known example of a conservative margin is the one between the Pacific plate and the North American plate along the coast of California (Figure 9.10). The Pacific plate is moving northwest at between 5 and 10 cm per year, while the North American plate is moving in the same broad direction at about 2–3 cm per year. The relative forces exerted by this movement are the same as those where plates slide past each other in opposite directions.

Movements of the crust occur along fault lines such as the San Andreas and Hayward faults. Low-magnitude earthquakes occur very frequently, with 20 per day being common. Major events such as those of 1906 and 1989 with magnitudes over 6.0 happen occasionally. The focus of these earthquakes is very shallow, as the build-up and release of pressure comes from friction between the two plates sliding past each other. Three earthquakes in excess of 3.0 occurred on 11 July 2008, at depths of 5, 6 and 10 km.

As with collision margins, transform margins do not exhibit regular or significant volcanic activity. No magma is rising towards the surface due to the melting of a subducted plate edge or the ascending limb of a convection current or hot spot plume.

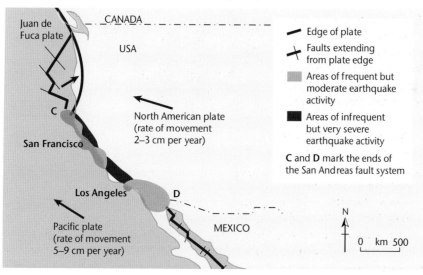

Juan de Fuca plate
CANADA
USA
C
San Francisco
Los Angeles
D
Pacific plate (rate of movement 5–9 cm per year)
MEXICO
North American plate (rate of movement 2–3 cm per year)

— Edge of plate

✛ Faults extending from plate edge

▨ Areas of frequent but moderate earthquake activity

▮ Areas of infrequent but very severe earthquake activity

C and D mark the ends of the San Andreas fault system

N

0　km　500

Figure 9.10
The San Andreas fault system

Hot spots

Hot spots are places where plumes of magma are rising from the asthenosphere, even though they are not necessarily near a plate margin. If the crust is particularly thin or weak, the magma may escape onto the surface as a volcanic eruption. Lava may build up over time until it is above present-day sea level, giving rise to a volcanic island.

Case study   A hot spot

The Hawaiian Islands are a chain of volcanic islands lying over a stable hot spot. The Pacific plate has been moving over the hot spot for about 70 million years and a succession of volcanic islands and submarine volcanoes has formed during that time. As the plate has moved, so the volcanoes have been carried away from the hot spot in a northwesterly direction, forming a chain of extinct submarine volcanoes called seamounts, often eroded into flat-topped remnants called guyots, extending all the way to the Aleutian Islands.

A new volcano is currently erupting 35 km southeast of Hawaii. Loihi is only 3,000 m tall at the moment and 2,000 m below sea level, but it is predicted to reach the sea surface in 10,000 to 100,000 years. As the volcanic eruptions are caused by the hot spot plume, the lava erupted is very basaltic and free-flowing. It has come directly from the asthenosphere and is typically over 1,000°C.

Earthquakes also occur in Hawaii, as the movement of the Pacific plate across the hot spot is not smooth and regular. The 2006 Hawaii event was an offshore earthquake occurring 10 km southwest from Puakō, at a depth of 38.9 km, at 7 a.m. on 15 October. It measured 6.7 on the Richter scale and produced several aftershocks, including one 7 minutes after the main shock that had a magnitude of 6.0. The Pacific Tsunami Warning Center in Ewa Beach, Hawaii measured a 10 cm tsunami on the coast of the Big Island. Sixty-one houses were destroyed, and while there were no fatalities, the cost was estimated at over $200 million.

Figure 9.11 The Hawaiian hot spot

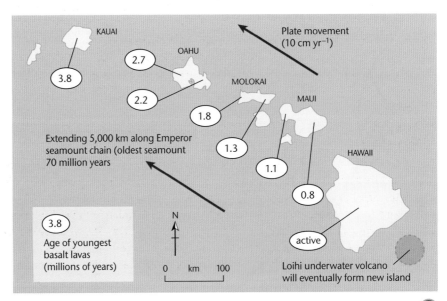

Further research

www.discoverourearth.org/student/tectonics/index.html – a wide-ranging site from Cornell University, USA.

http://pubs.usgs.gov/publications/text – an authoritative site from the US Geological Survey team.

http://earth.leeds.ac.uk/dynamicearth/index.htm – excellent visual coverage from Leeds University.

Tectonic hazard physical impacts

What impact does tectonic activity have on landscapes and why does this impact vary?

By the end of this section you should:
➤ *understand the landscape impacts of extrusive igneous activity*
➤ *have investigated the different types of volcano and eruption*
➤ *have examined the impact of intrusive igneous activity*
➤ *be aware of the effects of earthquakes on the landscape*

Extrusive igneous activity

The outpouring of material from the Earth's crust produces a variety of landforms, the most significant of which are volcanoes and lava plateaux. Their global distribution is largely determined by the pattern of tectonic plates. Their impact on the landscape depends on a number of factors, including the magnitude and scale of the event(s) causing them and the types of material being extruded.

Lava plateau

The **lava plateau** is usually an extensive area of basaltic lava, often with a layered structure. It is formed by major eruptions from vents or, more usually, from a fissure. The layered structure is caused by the accumulation of lava from a series of eruptions over a period of time. The plateau itself tends to be flat and featureless, with limited soil and vegetation cover. Eruptions from oceanic ridges produce huge **abyssal plains** on the sea floor.

Case study — The Deccan

The Deccan plateau of India is an excellent example of an extrusive landform. It is a huge expanse of lava covering 700,000 km². It consists of 29 lava flows, which have recently been dated and found to have all occurred within a time-span of less than 2 million years during the **Cretaceous period**. It is suggested that this may have been the result of a series of major eruptions from a mantle plume of rising magma. The volcanic hot spot that produced the Deccan is thought to have been under the present-day island of Réunion in the Indian Ocean. The plateau lies at about 700–900 m above sea level and has a number of major river valleys, such as the Wardha and Manjira, cutting down into it.

Volcanoes

Volcanoes occur in a series of broad bands (Figure 9.12). These tend to be either along the edge of continental land masses, for example the west coast of South America (including Cotopaxi and Nevada del Ruiz), or through the middle of oceans, such as along the mid-Atlantic (including the Icelandic volcanoes Hekla and Heimaey). There are exceptions to this pattern, for example the volcanoes of the Hawaiian Islands (such as Mauna Loa), which are more isolated. This pattern can largely be explained by the position of the various types of plate margin, as volcanoes are produced at divergent and convergent margins, as well as at hot spots.

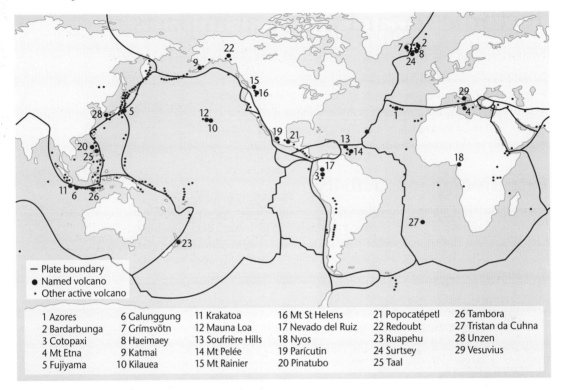

Figure 9.12 Global distribution of some active volcanoes

1 Azores	6 Galunggung	11 Krakatoa	16 Mt St Helens	21 Popocatépetl	26 Tambora
2 Bardarbunga	7 Grímsvötn	12 Mauna Loa	17 Nevado del Ruiz	22 Redoubt	27 Tristan da Cuhna
3 Cotopaxi	8 Haeimaey	13 Soufrière Hills	18 Nyos	23 Ruapehu	28 Unzen
4 Mt Etna	9 Katmai	14 Mt Pelée	19 Parícutin	24 Surtsey	29 Vesuvius
5 Fujiyama	10 Kilauea	15 Mt Rainier	20 Pinatubo	25 Taal	

— Plate boundary
● Named volcano
· Other active volcano

Types of volcano

The type of volcano produced by eruptions depends on the type of lava erupted and the nature of the eruptions themselves (Figure 9.13). These in turn are greatly influenced by the type of plate margin on which they are formed.

At divergent margins

Divergent plate margins tend to give rise to fissure eruptions and shield volcanoes (Figure 9.13). Fissure eruptions occur along fault and fracture lines, while shield volcanoes erupt from a vent. Shield volcanoes are typically low in height with long, gently sloping sides and a wide base. The lava that erupts from them is usually mafic (or basaltic), which means it has a low **viscosity** due to its low (45–52%) silica content. Being quite fluid and hot (about 1,200°C), this lava flows quite quickly and covers long distances before it cools and solidifies, which explains the shape of the cone. Eruptions are frequent but low in magnitude – magma is able to reach the surface relatively easily since the plates are diverging and the crust is fracturing. This means that there is seldom a great build-up of pressure. Such volcanoes also occur at hot spots.

At convergent margins

Volcanoes at convergent margins are different in character with contrasting cone shapes as a result (Figure 9.13). Eruptions tend to be less frequent and much more explosive. Rising magma here often has a much greater thickness of crust through

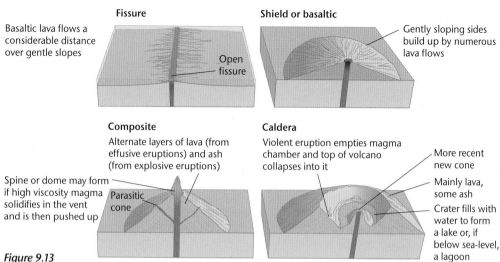

Figure 9.13
Types of volcanic cone

which to pass, and fractures providing easy routeways tend to be less common. The lava itself is typically intermediate or silicic, with more than 50% silica content. This, allied to a lower temperature of about 800°C, makes it much thicker and more viscous. It flows slowly and cools quickly, giving rise to a cone with a narrow base and a greater height.

Sometimes these have secondary or parasitic cones on their sides. These form when the passage of rising magma through the main vent is blocked, probably as a result of magma from earlier eruptions solidifying in the vent before it can escape. Pressure builds up and the magma forces its way through cracks in the sides of the vent.

These volcanoes are often composite in their structure, with alternating layers of ash and lava. The ash is produced by a highly explosive eruption, often after blocking of the vent, fragmenting parts of the cone or the plug of solidified magma.

There is no volcanic activity at conservative or collision margins, as no new crust is being created by rising magma or through the destruction of existing crust by subduction.

Intrusive igneous activity

Intrusive landforms are formed by magma rising towards the surface but cooling and solidifying before being extruded onto the surface. This is likely to be the case if the magma is rising slowly, if there is a great thickness of crust to pass through, and if there are few weaknesses in the crust through which it can flow easily. The magma cools slowly as it is not exposed to the air, and so mineral crystals, for example quartz in granite, grow to a large size.

Batholiths

Batholiths are large masses of intrusive rock that may cause a general doming-up of the surface as they are forming. However, they are only exposed after the gradual weathering and erosion of the less **resistant** overlying **country rock**. This is facilitated by the fractures and cracks formed at the surface as it is stretched during uplift. The heat transferred from the magma to the country rock causes **metamorphic rock** to be produced around the intruding magma. Examples of this include sandstone being metamorphosed into quartzite, and limestone into marble.

Sills

Sills are intrusions that are formed parallel to bedding planes in the country rock (i.e. concordant), often, but not always, lying horizontally (Figure 9.14). The bedding planes provide a line of weakness along which the magma flows before cooling and solidifying. As it cools, the magma contracts, producing cracks in the resultant rock.

Dykes

Dykes are discordant because they cut across the bedding planes of the country rock, often vertically (Figure 9.14). Magma flows through cracks and weaknesses but again cools and solidifies before reaching the surface. Contraction joints develop parallel to the surface as the magma solidifies. Once exposed, the dykes can appear as linear outcrops of resistant rock.

Figure 9.14 Dykes, sills and batholiths

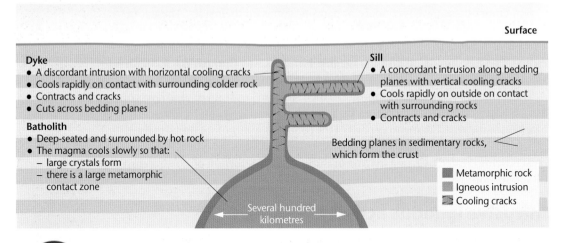

The surface landscape impacts of intrusive igneous activity

The Isle of Arran off the west coast of Scotland was created by the intrusion of a large granite batholith that domed the sandstone surface about 60 million years ago as Greenland separated from Scotland during the creation of the Atlantic Ocean. The fractured overlying sandstone and metamorphic schists have subsequently been weathered and eroded to expose the resistant granite, peaking at a height of 874 m on Goat Fell. A series of dykes, 2–3 m wide, are exposed across the beach at Kildonan, looking rather like natural rock groynes. At Drumadoon a sill has been exposed on the coast, forming a cliff 50 m high.

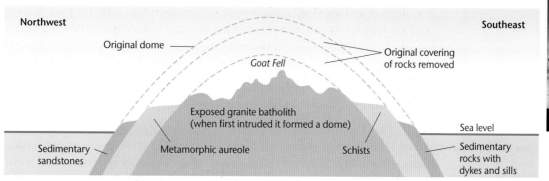

Northwest   Southeast

Figure 9.15 Idealised cross-section through the Isle of Arran

Further research

www.geology.sdsu.edu/how_volcanoes_work – a very full and detailed site from San Diego University.

www.volcano.si.edu – a Smithsonian Institute site which includes monitoring of all active volcanoes.

Effects of earthquakes on landscapes

Faults

The outer part of the Earth is relatively cold. This means that when stressed it tends to break, particularly if pushed quickly. These breaks, across which slip has occurred, are called **faults**. They tend to occur along the boundaries between plates, but faulting can also happen in the middle of the plates, particularly in the continents. In general, faulting is restricted to the top 10–15 km of the Earth's crust.

Normal faults occur when the hanging wall moves downwards (Figure 9.16). The fault plane on the normal fault is generally very steep. The two blocks involved in a normal fault are pulling away from one another, causing one to slip downwards in relation to the fault plane (in fact, it is hard to determine whether one or both blocks have moved). The exposed block forms a cliff-like feature known as a **fault scarp**. These faults are common at divergent plate margins.

Reverse faults form when the hanging wall moves upwards. The forces creating reverse faults are compressional, pushing the sides together. These tend to be found at convergent plate margins. Together, normal and reverse faults are called **dip–slip faults**, because the movement on them occurs along the dip direction – either down or up, respectively.

Rift valleys

At divergent plate margins, **rift valleys** may form. This can be where two oceanic plates are diverging, such as in the mid-Atlantic, or when an area of continental crust is being rifted by divergence, such as in east Africa. Typical rift features are a central

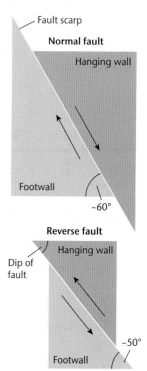

Figure 9.16 Normal and reverse faults

linear down-dropped fault segment, called a graben, with parallel normal faulting and rift-flank uplifts on either side forming a rift valley, where the rift remains above sea level (Figure 9.17). The axis of the rift area commonly contains volcanic rocks, and active volcanism is a part of many, but not all, active rift systems.

Case study: The east African rift valley

The east African rift valley is an illustration of a divergent margin in an area of continental crust. Eastern Africa is moving in a northeasterly direction, diverging from the main African plate, which is heading north. The valley, which actually consists of two broadly parallel rifts, extends for 4,000 km from Mozambique to the Red Sea. Inward-facing scarp slopes reach heights of 600 m above the valley floor. The area also experiences volcanic activity, suggesting that the crust has been weakened and thinned by tension, allowing rising magma to escape onto the surface at volcanoes such as Kilimanjaro.

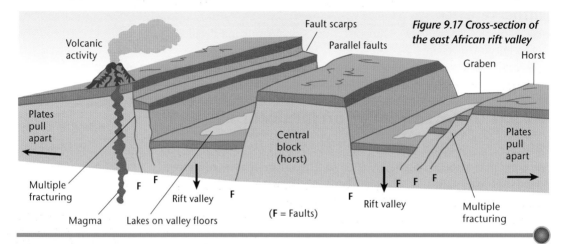

Figure 9.17 Cross-section of the east African rift valley

Microfracturing

Microfracturing, or microseismicity, is sometimes explained as a process of small-scale failures, on areas perhaps the size of a dinner plate, releasing stress under high-strain conditions. It is only when sufficient microfractures link up into a large slip surface that a significant seismic event or earthquake can occur. According to this theory, after a large earthquake most of the stress is released and the frequency of microfracturing is much lower. A related theory, accelerating moment release (AMR), suggests that the seismicity rate increases prior to large earthquakes. This could be a promising tool for earthquake prediction in the future.

Microseismicity is increasingly being used to predict rock failures in mines, and applications are being attempted for the portions of faults within brittle geological conditions. Similar behaviour is observed in the tremors preceding volcanic eruptions.

Further research

www.exploratorium.edu/faultline/index.html – Faultline, a site dealing with various aspects of the impact of earthquakes.

Tectonic hazard human impacts

What impacts do tectonic hazards have on people and how do these impacts vary?

By the end of this section you should:
➤ *understand some of the reasons why people live in tectonically active areas*
➤ *appreciate the range of hazards associated with different types of tectonic activity*
➤ *be familiar with the specific impacts of a range of tectonic hazards*
➤ *be aware of trends in the frequency and impacts of tectonic hazards*

Living in tectonically active areas

It is predicted that by 2025, 600 million people will be living in the tectonically active areas of the world. There are many reasons why people live in such locations.

Choices

In locations where the level of economic development is low, a lack of education and information may mean that residents are unaware of the **risks**, particularly if the zone is not very active.

In other cases, residents may be aware of the risks but decide to live in the area anyway – perhaps because it offers significant benefits. For some, living in southern California, with its well-paid jobs and pleasant climate, will outweigh concerns about earthquake risks.

Some people are unable to move way from hazardous areas, owing to lack of financial resources, or close links to family and tradition.

An estimated 500 million people were at risk from volcanic hazards in 2000. In the past 500 years, more than 200,000 people have lost their lives as a result of volcanic eruptions. The number of deaths in recent years runs at about 1,000 per year, which is far greater than the number of deaths for previous centuries. This rise is not due to increased volcanism but to an increase in the numbers of people populating the flanks of active volcanoes and valley areas near those volcanoes.

Benefits

Unlike earthquakes, volcanoes do have some positive impacts:
➤ *Minerals and **natural resources**.* Volcanoes bring valuable resources to the surface, such as diamonds, copper and gold. Ancient sea-floor volcanoes contributed to huge accumulations of base metals, such as lead, zinc and copper.
➤ *Fertile soils.* Volcanoes provide nutrients to the surrounding soil. Volcanic ash often contains minerals that are beneficial to plants, and if it is very fine ash it can break down quickly and get mixed into the soil (Photograph 9.2).

Photograph 9.2 Farming on the slopes of Mt Etna in Sicily

➤ *Geothermal energy.* Water running through the Earth's crust is heated by high-temperature rocks at or near active plate margins, bringing geothermal energy to the surface, where it emerges as hot springs and fumaroles.

➤ *Tourism.* Modern Western culture sees volcanoes as beautiful as well as threatening. Volcanic regions, both active and extinct, generate considerable interest from visitors, which can bring tourism employment to poor and remote regions.

The range of hazards

The range of tectonic hazards was described in some detail at the beginning of this chapter and it is important that you now refer back to that section. Tectonic hazards can have a wide range of impacts – physical (damage and destruction of homes and infrastructure), economic (factories damaged and transport networks disrupted) and social (trauma, disruption of everyday life and communities). The severity of those impacts depends on physical factors, such as the magnitude of the event, and human factors, such as population density. In the case of volcanic hazards the impacts can be positive as well as negative, but with earthquakes the outcomes are unfailingly negative.

Specific hazard impacts

The costs of tectonic hazards may be broadly classified as either human or economic.

Human costs

The human costs may be subdivided into the following:

➤ *Primary casualties.* People killed or injured by an earthquake or volcanic eruption. This might be through buildings collapsing, through being trapped in fast-moving lava, by poisonous gas or by fire. Casualties tend to be much higher in less developed countries, because of poor construction methods, limited preparedness and less effective warning systems and search and rescue services.

➤ *Secondary casualties.* People who survive the initial incident but are either injured or die because of insufficient resources and lack of emergency medical care. These again tend to be higher in less developed countries.

➤ *Tertiary casualties.* People who suffer from pre-existing medical conditions aggravated by the hazard event. This group also includes those who become ill, and even die, as a result of the post-disaster environment, largely through infectious diseases or profound trauma. In less developed countries this is often the largest group of casualties.

Economic costs

The economic costs generated by hazards are of two types. The *direct costs* include the immediate costs of repairing damage caused by the event itself. In the case of earthquakes, this will often include demolishing buildings fractured by the shock waves and rebuilding from scratch.

The *indirect costs* include the loss of earnings caused by disruption to working life. If the disruption is prolonged, these can become substantial. Increasingly, major natural hazards are causing secondary technological and industrial accidents and emergencies.

Finally, it is worth noting that in developed countries, major tectonic events tend to cause high economic costs, mainly due to the large investment in buildings and infrastructure. In developing countries they tend to cause a high loss of life.

 Case study Montserrat (1995–97)

The Soufrière Hills volcano is in the south of the island of Montserrat in the Caribbean. It is a complex composite volcano reaching just over 990 m above sea level, with many lava domes around its summit. It is an andesitic magma volcano formed by the subduction of part of the Atlantic sea floor under the Caribbean plate. After a long period of dormancy since the seventeenth century, it started erupting on 18 July 1995 with a VEI score of 3. The initial activity consisted of vigorous venting of steam and gas and a series of small steam explosions that formed ash-laden plumes less than 100 m tall. Rock debris ejected by these small eruptions killed vegetation around the vent and formed a crater that contained a pond of hot muddy water. Magma reached the surface about 4 months later.

When pyroclastic flows and mudflows began occurring regularly, the capital city Plymouth was evacuated, and a few weeks later a pyroclastic flow covered it in several metres of debris. On 3 August the first significant pyroclastic flow and associated noxious gases swept through the evacuated city. The flow triggered fires and caused extensive damage to buildings and community facilities by direct impact and burial.

On 25 June 1997 a very large pyroclastic flow came down from Soufrière Hills. In a matter of minutes it dumped 4 to 5 million m^3 of lava and covered 4 km^2 on the eastern side of the island. It also

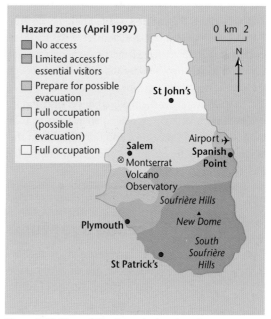

Figure 9.18 Map of Montserrat, showing danger zones

killed at least nine people, and destroyed the island's airport and more than 100 homes. A series of hazard zones was defined (Figure 9.18).

Further research

www.geo.mtu.edu/volcanoes/west.indies/soufrier e/govt/miscdocs/chronology.html – a complete chronology of all 11 stages of the Montserrat eruptions.

Case study **The Asian tsunami, 26 December 2004**

At 07:58 local time on 26 December 2004 a magnitude 9.4 earthquake occurred off the northwest coast of Sumatra, Indonesia. The earthquake had a relatively shallow focus 18 km below the surface in the subduction zone between the Indo-Australian plate and the Burma microplate. The Burma plate was raised by around 5 m, displacing huge amounts of water, which created a tsunami. The wave progressed at speeds of up to 1,000 km h^{-1}, towards Indonesia and Thailand to the east and, at right angles to the fault line at the plate margin, towards Sri Lanka, India and beyond.

The height of the tsunami was estimated to be only 1 to 1.15 m initially, but it increased to 10 to 15 m in only about 15 minutes as it neared the coast of Sumatra, forced upwards by the frictional effects of the increasingly shallow seabed. To the west the wave had to travel much further before hitting land and its height was much lower, reaching an average of 1.25 m on the coast of Sri Lanka and only 0.75 m in the Maldives, partly thanks to the protection offered by their fringing coral reefs.

The tsunami caused more than 180,000 deaths, and over 40,000 people are still unaccounted for. More than 130,000 of the deaths happened in Indonesia, with Sri Lanka, India and Thailand also suffering significant fatalities. In Indonesia, more than 500,000 people were displaced and 316 km of major roads were destroyed. More than 500 bridges and around 20 ports were destroyed or damaged in northern Sumatra alone. The World Bank estimates that $4.5 billion worth of damage and economic losses occurred in Indonesia, with a total cost of over $14 billion, only about $3.5 billion of which was covered by insurance.

Further research

news.bbc.co.uk/1/hi/in_depth/4136289.stm – BBC news site covering the causes of the 2004 Asian tsunami.

www.geographyinthenews.rgs.org/news/article/default.aspx?id=326 – 'Shock Wave', a report on the tsunami.

Trends over time

The landscape gives visible evidence of where volcanic activity is likely to take place, but not of earthquakes. This is perhaps why there has been more research into earthquakes, not just their potential locations but also their overall frequency and their frequency in particular locations.

Frequency

The number of earthquakes per year varies, but there has been a general increase in the number of recorded earthquakes over time (Figure 9.19). The increase in the number of seismograph stations across the world over the last 25 years, along with improved global communications, means more lower-intensity earthquakes have been detected than in the past. By limiting the range to earthquakes of more than magnitude 7.0, which would have been detected in earlier years, we can eliminate this distortion.

Between 1986 and 1996, the US Geological Survey listed 15 earthquakes of magnitude 7.0 or greater. This is not markedly different from earlier periods of the twentieth century, which had an average of about 18. But between 1997 and 2007 there were 99 earthquakes of this magnitude: a more than six-fold increase on

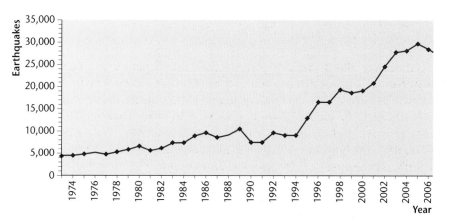

Figure 9.19 Number of recorded earthquakes per year, 1973–2006

the previous period and a significant rise compared with any earlier decade in the twentieth century.

The number of volcanic eruptions, however, does not seem to be increasing over time. Comprehensive reporting and recording has been in place since 1960. Figure 9.20 shows that the trend has been very flat during this period, with a range of between 50 and 70 volcanic eruptions per year and a mean of 58.

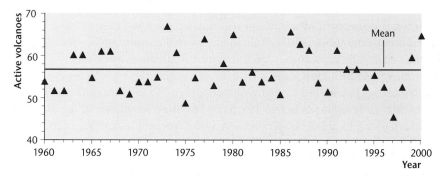

Figure 9.20 Number of active volcanoes per year, 1960–2000

Figure 9.21 Earthquake fatalities over time

Impacts

There has also been a noticeable trend in the impact of earthquakes over time. The number of fatalities has been increasing since the 1500s. This can be attributed to the increasing global population. When taken as a percentage of the population, the proportion of fatalities has decreased since 1955 (Figure 9.21) and is predicted to continue declining in the future. This is largely due to improvements in preparedness.

The impact of a tectonic hazard can also be seen to vary over time in the short term. When a hazard event strikes, it disrupts economic and social life, often immediately and totally. The Park model describes a sequence of three phases following such an event (Figure 9.22).

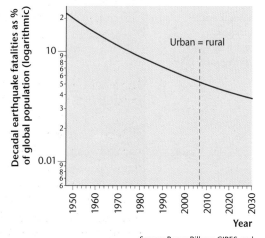

Source: Roger Bilham CIRES and University of Colorado at Boulder

*Figure 9.22 The
Park model*

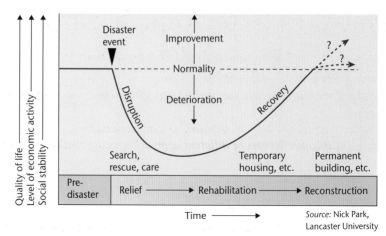

Source: Nick Park,
Lancaster University

> During the *relief phase* teams from outside the immediate area arrive to help with search, rescue and care operations (Photograph 9.3). Urgent medical supplies, rescue equipment, clothing and food may be flown in.

> After relief comes the *rehabilitation period*. This might last for several weeks or months. Actions are designed to restore physical and community structures at least temporarily. Rehabilitation is more complex than relief, and requires accurate assessment of needs and coordinated planning of responses. This is normally carried out locally. Only in exceptional circumstances – for example the Asian tsunami of 2004 – are international initiatives involved.

> In time, rehabilitation gives way to *reconstruction*, during which permanent changes are introduced to restore the quality of life and economic stability to its original level, if not better. The nature of these activities and the speed at which they are carried out are dictated by the type and magnitude of the event and the availability of contingency planning for disasters.

*Photograph 9.3
Fire engines
brought water from
other areas to
survivors
of the Sichuan
earthquake, 2008*

Responses to tectonic hazards

How do people cope with tectonic hazards and what are the issues for the future?

By the end of this section you should:

➤ *understand the various ways that people and governments cope with tectonic hazards*

➤ *be familiar with specific ways of adjusting to tectonic hazards*

➤ *be aware of the effectiveness of different approaches to the challenge of coping with tectonic hazards*

Coping with hazards

A wide range of approaches can be used to cope with tectonic hazards, but there are essentially three options: do nothing, adjust, or leave.

Which option is chosen depends on a number of factors. These include the nature of the hazard, its frequency, its magnitude, population pressure in the location and the level of economic development. Volcanoes are easier to deal with, as there is usually some prior indication of an eruption. They also originate at a known, visible point that can be monitored. Earthquakes typically occur without warning and may have their focus anywhere on a long fault line. The level of development is significant, as it will influence the extent of capital investment (a deterrent to leaving) and the level of available technology (an encouragement to adjust).

Strategies for coping

Strategies employed to adjust to hazard threat tend to concentrate on modifying the loss burden, modifying the event and modifying human vulnerability.

Earthquake risk assessment

One reason for the increased destructiveness of earthquakes is that human populations have expanded into earthquake risk zones – especially those where earthquakes are infrequent but also violent – and that buildings and infrastructure are increasingly expensive and vulnerable.

Where written records of earthquakes do not exist, geological and soil maps can be used to identify past earthquake activity. Once the geological record is understood, areas of special risk can be mapped. Areas of high risk include steep slopes, sensitive soils and low-lying coastal areas.

Risk assessment also has to take into account the nature of the settlement and its infrastructure. Medium-height buildings are more vulnerable than either tall or single-storey buildings. Masonry buildings are more vulnerable than wooden or steel-framed buildings, but wooden buildings are more prone to fire risk. The location of mains services (electricity, gas and water) may have an impact on potential damage. The size and design of roads, bridges etc. will have a considerable impact on evacuation, emergency access and potential loss of life.

Earthquake prediction

There are many possible indicators of imminent earthquake activity, but none has proved reliable. There are a number of key areas of research and monitoring:

➤ The *P wave/S wave ratio* drops prior to a large earthquake.
➤ *Warning activity.* The number of small earth tremors increases before a major shock. These are known as foreshocks and can be of different types.
➤ *Water levels in wells* rise or fall as the rocks are squeezed by the increasing strain before an earthquake.
➤ *Radon levels in wells.* This radioactive gas is squeezed out from rock pores by the build-up of strain.
➤ Swedish geologists in northern Iceland found that *levels of manganese, zinc and copper* in basaltic rocks at a depth of 1,000 m increased by over 1,000% before an earthquake and fell rapidly afterwards.
➤ *Changes in the electrical properties of rock* occur as increasing strain causes the crystals to rearrange their structures. In extreme cases this produces light displays (the so-called 'earthquake lights' phenomenon).
➤ *Ground deformation* occurs as rocks are strained. This can be surveyed on the ground with laser ranging techniques or measured by accurate radar imagery from satellites. This method is still being developed and global positioning systems (GPS) are increasingly being used.
➤ *Unusual animal behaviour* is often reported before earthquakes. It would be possible to monitor animal behaviour or identify the sensory cues they use (subsonic vibrations, magnetism, electrical sensitivity?) and monitor these.

Despite the research described above earthquakes cannot currently be predicted in any reliable way.

Volcano risk assessment

Assessing the risk of volcanic eruption includes monitoring current levels of activity and mapping the evidence of destruction caused by previous eruptions. It is possible to modify lava flows by damming, cooling (with water) and bombing, but the only realistic approach to living with volcanoes is to avoid high-risk sites (for example lava and mudflow tracks) and to evacuate as necessary.

Planning for earthquakes

The most logical assumption to make when planning for an earthquake is that everything will be destroyed. In short, we should assume that an earthquake of magnitude 8.0 or above striking San Francisco will flatten everything. It is best to plan for the situation where there are no resources available at the site of the earthquake. Even a 'moderate' earthquake of magnitude 6.0 is enough to severely damage many structures.

Regardless of the magnitude of the event, several things are true about damaging earthquakes:

➤ They occur without warning, and pre-event response activity is not possible.
➤ The probability of the event occurring during non-working hours is more than 3:1.

➤ Damage to sensitive communications systems will interfere with response management.

➤ Aftershocks are likely and will cause additional damage, interfere with response efforts, and cause unease among the population.

The key strategies to reduce the impact of earthquakes lie in the hands of governments, for example:

➤ land-use zoning
➤ building regulations (Figure 9.23)
➤ evacuation drills
➤ emergency service provision

Government bodies such as the Federal Emergency Management Agency in the USA publish advice on how to prepare for and cope with events such as earthquakes. (See www.fema.gov.)

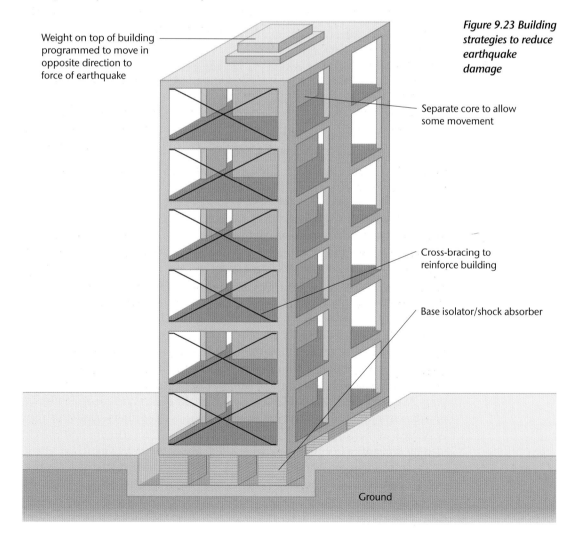

Figure 9.23 Building strategies to reduce earthquake damage

Weight on top of building programmed to move in opposite direction to force of earthquake

Separate core to allow some movement

Cross-bracing to reinforce building

Base isolator/shock absorber

Ground

Evaluating approaches

One way to evaluate different approaches to dealing with tectonic hazards is to subject them to cost–benefit analysis, a technique widely used in business and resource management (Figure 9.24). The marginal benefit of increasing investment in a given adjustment represents demand or the willingness to pay. This decreases with increasing effort or expenditure on hazard prevention. Marginal cost represents supply. The optimum exists when marginal costs and marginal benefits are equal.

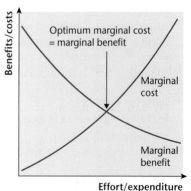

Figure 9.24 Cost–benefit analysis

Value

Such economic evaluations are useful, but the real impact of hazard events cannot be expressed in simple monetary terms. What is the 'value' of human life, for example? The Warsaw Convention places a value of $360,000 on each death, but how meaningful is this? It is also difficult to place monetary values on long-term or widespread reductions in environmental quality. How much is an attractive view worth, for instance? Because of environmental variability, different perceptions and imperfect knowledge about hazard potential, maximising the gain from investment in hazard strategies is rather optimistic.

New approaches

Much scientific research is being done to improve the accuracy and reliability of the methods used to forecast tectonic hazards. New approaches are beginning to emerge that may offer a more secure future.

A new idea in earthquake prediction is to monitor how fast strain accumulates. Scientists measure the accumulation of strain along a fault segment each year, the time that has passed since the last earthquake along the segment, and how much strain was released in the last earthquake. Another new approach is to monitor electrical charges with satellites. As pressure builds before an earthquake, the oxygen molecules inside the rocks undergo chemical reactions, creating a positive electrical charge that radiates towards the Earth's surface.

New research to improve the prediction of volcanic eruptions is also underway. In Japan, attention is focused on the temperature of escaping gases from volcanic vents. A research project on Mt Etna in Sicily digitally collects geophysical information on seismic movements and transforms it into audible sound waves, which can be 'scored' as melodies. The resulting 'music' is analysed for patterns and used to identify similarities in eruption dynamics and predict future activity.

It is hoped that this and other research will make the prediction of tectonic events, particularly earthquakes, more reliable. It is also hoped that new technology and materials can be used to improve the shock-proofing of built structures of all kinds. The need for advances of these kinds increases as the global population continues to grow. More people means more pressure to remain in high-risk areas.

Further research

www.lafd.org/eqindex.htm – advice from the Los Angeles Fire Department on how to prepare for an earthquake.

www.dis-inc.com – site of a company specialising in the design of earthquake-resistant buildings and structures.

http://vulcan.wr.usgs.gov/Monitoring/Descriptions/description_monitoring_overvi ew.html – volcano monitoring on Mt St Helens and in Hawaii.

www.eri.u-tokyo.ac.jp/VRC/index_E.html – Tokyo's Volcano Research Centre.

Suggested fieldwork opportunities

Local fieldwork

➤ Field visits to examine small-scale igneous structures (dykes, sills and tors) and their impact on the landscape.

➤ Faulting and rifting and their impact on the landscape could be illustrated by field visits.

Residential and long-haul

➤ There are many opportunities to study the nature of, and response to, hazardous events in Iceland and the volcanic fields of Italy.

➤ The impact of igneous activity on landforms and landscapes can be seen in the Western Isles of Scotland, Northern Ireland, the Lake District, north Wales and Northumberland.

Review questions

1 Compare and contrast the typical tectonic hazards experienced at one convergent and one divergent plate margin.

2 Construct annotated diagrams to show the shape, structure and other features of two contrasting volcanic cones.

3 Compare the socioeconomic characteristics of two countries affected by tectonic hazards and examine how the impacts of the hazards are influenced by these characteristics.

4 Use a news website to draw a mind map of organisations and groups involved in the response to a recent tectonic hazard.

5 Research other ways in which it may be possible to predict tectonic hazards in the future.

Chapter 10

Cold environments: landscapes and change

Cold environments include both glacial and periglacial areas. In response to climate change, their distribution has changed significantly in recent geological time and continues to do so. Much of the landscape variety of the British Isles and other countries has been created by past and present cold environment processes. Study of the British landscape can help our understanding of processes that continue in the world's high-latitude and high-altitude areas. Today's cold environments face considerable challenges, yet offer valuable economic opportunities.

Defining and locating cold environments

What are cold environments and where are they found?

By the end of this section you should:
➤ *be aware that not all cold environments are the same*
➤ *have investigated the difference between glacial and periglacial environments and between high-latitude and high-altitude glacial environments*
➤ *have studied how the distribution of cold environments has changed and continues to change*
➤ *have gained an understanding of Britain's heritage of glaciated and periglaciated areas*

Types of cold environment

Cold environments are found on much of the Earth's surface. They vary in their characteristics and locations and are broadly categorised as either glacial or periglacial. Many other locations, including the British Isles, show evidence of having been cold environments in the past, under the different climatic conditions that have existed through geological time, particularly during the **Quaternary period**. Cold environments possess a wide variety of distinctive landforms, reflecting the diversity of past or present geomorphological processes. Some of these processes are unique to cold environments, while others are found elsewhere. These processes are greatly influenced by climatic conditions, especially temperature.

The icy landscapes that occur in high-latitude (or polar) and mountainous regions of the world are characterised by severely cold temperatures, abundant snow and ice, sparse vegetation and few animal species. They have experienced relatively little commercial exploitation and therefore have low human populations. Cold environments include parts of the world currently experiencing a tundra climate, which are part of the transition from polar to temperate. Because there are significant differences between the high-latitude and high-altitude glacial areas, three types of cold environment are recognised in this chapter: glacial (polar), glacial (alpine) and periglacial.

Photograph 10.1
Gornergott glacier
in Switzerland: an
alpine glacier

Glacial (polar)

Glacial (polar) environments are landscapes of glaciers and ice sheets. The largest single glacial environment is the Antarctic ice sheet and surrounding ice shelves, which cover an area of over 13 million km^2. Other extensive glacial environments include the Greenland ice sheet and glaciated regions of the high Arctic, Alaska, and Patagonia in South America (Figure 10.1). The extremely cold climatic conditions and barren icy land surface in these environments mean that life is restricted to simple microorganisms.

Figure 10.1 Cold environments of the world

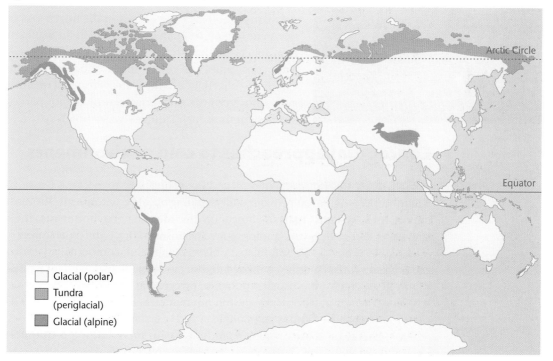

Glacial (polar)

Tundra (periglacial)

Glacial (alpine)

Glacial (alpine)

Glacial (alpine) environments are found in many mountain ranges and cover some 5% of the Earth's land surface. The principal ranges are the Himalayas, Karakoram, Tibetan Plateau, European Alps, Rocky Mountains and Andes (Figure 10.1), with summits reaching more than 5,000 m above sea level. Since alpine areas experience severely cold climates, they have both glaciers and areas of mountain permafrost.

Periglacial (tundra)

Periglacial (tundra) environments are traditionally defined as being 'at or near glacial' areas. An alternative definition is environments with a mean annual temperature below 3°C, although this includes glacial areas as well. Another categorisation of periglacial areas is those where:

➤ **permafrost** (perennially frozen ground) prevails
➤ seasonal temperatures vary above and below freezing point
➤ geomorphological processes are dominated by freeze–thaw cycles

These three criteria do not always coincide. Periglacial environments can be found in high-latitude or high-altitude areas, continental interiors, and locations with a low temperature range either side of zero. The major locations with these characteristics are tundra and alpine areas.

*Photograph 10.2
Tundra in the
Canadian Arctic*

The periglacial landscape is cold and treeless and occurs in dry high-latitude areas not covered by glacial ice (Photograph 10.2). In the northern hemisphere, such regions occur in Alaska, northern Canada, Siberia, northern Scandinavia and islands in the frozen seas of the Arctic (Figure 10.1). In comparison, in the southern hemisphere, tundra is restricted to the coastal fringes of Antarctica and the high Andes mountains. The extremely cold climate in these areas creates permafrost and, with very little solar energy available for photosynthesis at these high latitudes, vegetation is sparse.

Conceptual approaches to cold environments

Systems analysis

A number of concepts can help our understanding of cold environment. The most important is systems analysis, based on the idea that environments, their landscapes and component landforms are systems working at different scales.

A **system** is any set of interrelated objects comprising components (stores) and processes (links) that are connected together to form a working unit or unified whole. In geography, it is usual to recognise two general types of system:

➤ *Closed*. There is transfer of energy, but not matter, between the system and its surroundings. The Earth is an example of such a system.
➤ *Open*. Energy or matter is transferred from (as **inputs**) and to (as **outputs**) neighbouring systems. Most natural systems are open ones.

The cold environment and its component landscapes may be seen as systems involving inputs and outputs of energy and matter passing between climatic, geological, geomorphological and biotic systems.

Open systems

An open system displays two important attributes (Figure 10.2a):

➤ It contains energy and matter of two types: that which is simply passing through the system (**throughputs**) and that which is being held within the system (**stores**). The work that throughputs do as they pass through the system generates the **processes** of the system.

➤ When a system's inputs and outputs are equal, there is a condition of balance known as **dynamic equilibrium**. When the equilibrium is disturbed (say, by an increase in inputs), the system undergoes self-regulation and changes its form to restore the equilibrium. This is usually achieved by negative feedback, whereby the system adapts itself to counter the effects of the initial change.

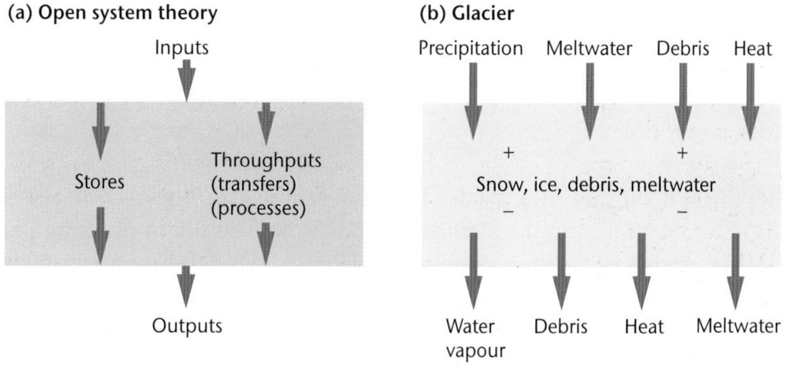

Figure 10.2
An open system

Glaciers illustrate the systems concept particularly well. In systems terms, a glacier comprises (Figure 10.2b):

➤ *inputs* including the accumulation of precipitation, debris falling onto or picked up by the glacier, heat and meltwater
➤ *outputs* including the sublimation of ice into water vapour, ablation (melting), deposition of debris and loss of meltwater and heat
➤ *stores* – mainly snow, ice, meltwater and debris in, on and under the ice
➤ *transfers* – the movement of snow, ice and debris through the glacier

Glaciers

Glaciers form when temperatures are low enough for snow that falls in one year to remain frozen throughout the year. The following year, a fresh layer of snow falls, consisting of flakes with an open, feathery structure and a low density. Each new fall of snow compresses and compacts the layer beneath, causing the air to be expelled and converting low-density snow into higher-density ice. Snow that survives one summer is known as **firn** (or **nevé**) and has a density of 0.4 g cm^{-3}.

Further compaction by subsequent years of snowfall converts it to glacier ice with a density of between 0.83 and 0.91 g cm^{-3}. This process is known as **diagenesis** and may take between 30–40 and 1,000 years to occur. True glacier ice is not encountered until a depth of about 100 m and is characterised by a bluish colour rather than the white of fresher snow, which is due to the presence of air.

Inputs and outputs

The majority of inputs occur towards the top of the glacier. This area, where accumulation exceeds ablation, is called the **accumulation** zone (Figure 10.3). Most of the outputs occur lower down, in the **ablation** zone, where ablation exceeds accumulation. The two zones are notionally divided by the firn or equilibrium line, where there is a balance between accumulation and ablation.

Figure 10.3
The glacier system

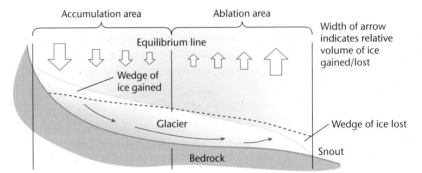

The **annual budget** of a glacier can be calculated by subtracting the total ablation for the year from the total accumulation. If the amount of accumulation equals the amount of ablation, the glacier is in dynamic equilibrium and therefore remains stable in its position. A positive figure indicates a net gain of ice through the year, i.e. net accumulation, and so the glacier will advance or grow. The firn line will, in effect, move down the valley. A negative figure indicates a net loss of ice through the year, i.e. net ablation, so the glacier will retreat or contract and the firn line will move up-valley.

There will often be seasonal variations in the budget, with accumulation exceeding ablation in the winter and vice versa in the summer (Figure 10.4). These seasonal shifts in the balance temporarily upset the dynamic equilibrium of the glacier and require some form of adjustment. However, adjustment takes time. It is also important to remember that regardless of whether the glacier snout is advancing or retreating, the ice and debris within the glacier continue to move forwards and downslope.

Figure 10.4
The net budget
in a northern
hemisphere glacier

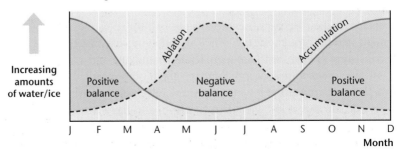

Frequency and magnitude

Landscape-shaping events can be analysed in terms of how often they occur (frequency) and their power (magnitude). In glacial systems, high-frequency/low-magnitude events include the daily abrasion taking place beneath a glacier. The abrasion rates are slow, perhaps 1 mm per year, but the process occurs regularly and the cumulative effect on the landscape is significant over long timescales. In contrast, a glacier burst or jökulhlaup is a rare event, but when it does occur it can cause major, sudden changes to the landscape. The outwash plain in front of the Solheimajökull glacier (Iceland) is 30 m thick and is thought to have been formed by four of these great events.

Equifinality

The principle of **equifinality** states that in an open system, the same end result can be reached by different means or pathways. In other words, different processes may produce the same landform or landscape feature. This concept can be linked to the concept of frequency and magnitude, in that the same type of landscape may have been produced by either high-frequency/low-magnitude events or low-frequency/high-magnitude events. Outwash plains may be produced not only by a small number of major glacial bursts, as suggested above, but also by small amounts of fluvioglacial deposition over very long timescales.

The changing distribution of cold environments

The distribution of cold environments is not constant over time. Changes in both global and local climatic conditions can lead to an expansion or contraction of the area covered by cold environments. It is calculated that today approximately 25% of the Earth's surface can be classed as periglacial; another 20–25% shows evidence of having been periglacial in the past. The increase in global temperature, particularly over the last 20,000 years, has been primarily responsible for this change. Southern England, for example, contains relict landforms produced in colder periods, such as the dry valleys on Salisbury Plain and the Marlborough Downs.

The same is true of glacial environments. Many mid-latitude, temperate locations show evidence of having been covered by glacial ice in the past.

Figure 10.5 Gondwanaland

Although landforms degrade over time, major and minor landscape features produced by glacial erosion provide evidence of the existence of glaciers. In Central Park, New York, for example, exposed rock shows striations that could only have been scratched by a glacier passing over the outcrop.

Changes also occur as a result of the changing positions of the continental land masses. Evidence of glacial processes affecting the landscape in India, Africa and Australia are thought to date from the time, 300 million years ago, when all these areas were part of the ancient continent of **Gondwana** and located near the south pole (Figure 10.5).

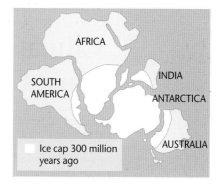

AFRICA

SOUTH AMERICA

INDIA

ANTARCTICA

AUSTRALIA

Ice cap 300 million years ago

Figure 10.6 Glacial and interglacial periods of the last 0.5 million years

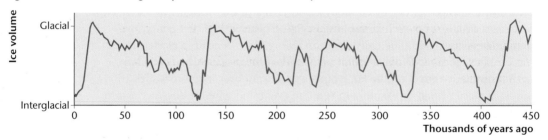

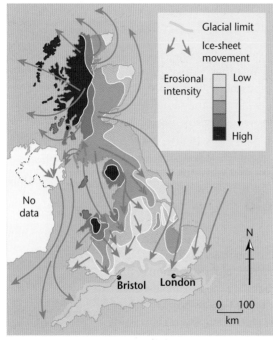

Figure 10.7 Ice sheet movement and erosional intensity in Britain during the last glacial advance

Glaciers in Britain

In the past, when our climate was much colder, glacial environments existed in Britain, mainly in Scotland, the Lake District and north Wales. They also occurred in Ireland, Scandinavia and much of northern Europe, although cover in the Alps was relatively limited in comparison. Britain has experienced several glacial periods during the last 0.5 million years, each separated by an interglacial (Figure 10.6). The main glacial advances have been:

➤ the Anglian, between 425,000 and 380,000 years ago
➤ the Wolstonian, between 175,000 and 128,000 years ago
➤ the Devensian, between 26,000 and 15,000 years ago, with a maximum advance 18,000 years ago
➤ the most recent, between 12,000 and 10,000 years ago

Figure 10.7 shows the maximum extent of glacial ice in Britain. Over the succession of glacial and interglacial periods, the extent of ice has increased and decreased. The locations of periglacial environments have shifted in harmony with these movements of the glacial front. Close to the ice margins, the movements have caused glacial and periglacial environments to become superimposed.

Climatic processes and their causes

What are the climatic processes that cause cold environments and what environmental conditions result from these?

By the end of this section you should:
➤ *be aware of the climatic causes of cold environments*

> *understand that long-term climate change leads to changes in the distribution of cold environments*
> *have investigated the meteorological processes associated with different types of cold environment*
> *have explored the spatial and temporal relationships between glacial and periglacial environments*

Climatic causes

The low temperatures that characterise cold climate environments are the result of four factors: latitude, altitude, continentality and the temperatures of ocean currents.

Latitude

In high-latitude areas (i.e. 60°–90° north and south of the equator) the sun's angle in the sky is low. This means that incoming solar energy passes through a greater thickness of atmosphere than in lower latitudes and, as a result, a relatively large proportion of solar energy is lost through:
> absorption by gases
> scattering by particles
> reflection by light-coloured surfaces such as cloud tops

In addition, the low angle of incidence means that the remaining solar energy is spread over a wide area, and much of this **incident energy** is immediately reflected back into the atmosphere from the surface of snow and ice. As a result, polar areas experience relatively little surface heating and the climate is particularly cold during midwinter, when the Earth's tilt leaves these regions in continual darkness.

The other impact of latitude is on pressure systems. Air tends to sink at or near the poles as it is cold and dense, producing areas of high pressure called polar anti-cyclones. Air spreads slowly from here into the high mid-latitude areas, causing low temperatures. High pressure areas also tend to form over continental interior locations such as Siberia. This is because their extremely low temperatures in winter lead to dense, sinking air which then spreads at ground level across surrounding areas.

Altitude

Temperatures decline with altitude because air becomes thinner and so is less able to absorb heat from outgoing long-wave terrestrial radiation. Furthermore, there is less land to absorb and reradiate heat from the sun. The decrease in temperature with altitude is known as the environmental lapse rate and on average is 6.4°C per 1,000 m. This dramatic fall in temperature explains why glaciers can exist high in the Andes mountains at places such as Huascaran, over 6,700 m above sea level but only 9° south of the equator.

Continentality

Land and sea absorb heat and radiate it back into the air at varying rates. In general, land (soil and rock) warms up, and releases the stored heat, more quickly

than water. This is mainly because water is able to transfer the heat received at the surface to greater depths than land can. Continental interiors are warmer than coastal areas during the summer because heating is more intense and the land quickly releases its stored energy. In contrast, continental interiors are much colder than coastal areas during winter because the land has lost its stored heat, whereas the sea is still radiating heat that it absorbed during the previous summer.

The effect of continentality partly explains why central Asia is very much colder in winter than places on the same line of latitude on the west coast of Europe. For example, in Omsk (Russia) the mean January temperature is –22°C, whereas in Shannon (Ireland) it is 5°C, even though they both lie at about 53° north.

Ocean currents

Oceanic currents, in combination with the pattern of wind flow, have a major effect on the distribution of cold environments. For example, the climate of Canada's eastern seaboard is chilled by the cold Labrador current, which flows southwards from the Arctic. In contrast, northwest Europe is warmed by heat released from the North Atlantic Drift, which explains why Arctic tundra in Canada extends southwards to 54° north, whereas in Britain, at the same latitude, tundra is absent and the winter climate is relatively mild.

Changing distributions

We have discussed past changes in the global distribution of cold environments and their present distribution (Figure 10.1). It is also worth considering the likely future impact of global warming on this.

It is natural to think that global warming will cause the world's ice sheets to shrink polewards and its glaciers to retreat to higher altitudes. The periglacial environments are likely to follow in the same general directions.

So what might we imagine the endgame to be? Will all the ice melt, raising sea levels, drowning vast areas and redrawing the coastlines of shrunken continents? Certainly there is much evidence of ice sheet and glacier retreat, from Antarctic and Greenland ice sheets to glaciers in the Andes and Himalayas. If you believe these are the early warning signs of the outcome of continuing global warming, the scenario will certainly be gloom and doom.

A very different view of is taken by Robert Johnson, a university professor, who has written a book entitled *Secrets of the Ice Ages*. He writes: 'Global warming may actually assist new ice sheet growth because growth depends less on cold temperatures than on a strong supply of moisture and very heavy snowfall over northern land masses.'

The ice age of 150,000 years ago was an anomaly because it occurred when maximum amounts of summer sunlight were striking temperate and tropical latitudes – a phenomenon that the most prominent theory of glaciation, Milankovitch's, cannot explain. At this time of high insolation, glaciers grew and combined across northern Eurasia from Ireland to eastern Siberia. According to Johnson, the key factor, strangely enough, was the discharge of increasingly salty water into the Atlantic. He notes that the salinity of the Mediterranean is again on the increase, so much so that he anticipates a new ice age in Canada, if not elsewhere in the high latitudes of the northern hemisphere.

Further research

To find out more about Johnson's study, visit:
www.scienceagogo.com/news/20020927213400data_trunc_sys.shtml

Meteorological processes in cold environments

Glacial environments

The climate of glacial environments is extremely variable, and glacial ice can form under varying conditions of temperature and precipitation. In maritime areas, such as the Norwegian Alps, glaciers can survive in a relatively mild climate (mean annual temperatures may be no lower than $-2\,°C$) because the growth of glacial ice is sustained by heavy winter snowfall. By contrast, in dry continental interiors such as central Antarctica, where annual snowfall is usually less than 200 mm per year, glacial ice is able to form because the extremely cold climate conditions (mean annual temperatures of -30 to $-40\,°C$) limit the amount of ice ablation. Antarctica, being predominantly flat, is the windiest continent, with the highest wind speed measured at d'Urville (327 km h^{-1}).

Alpine

The climate in high alpine areas is characterised by very low temperatures, high precipitation and wind speeds that frequently exceed hurricane force. Precipitation is high as a result of forced uplift of air over mountains (orographic precipitation) and is particularly heavy in maritime regions. The very low temperatures cause much of the precipitation in mountainous regions to fall as snow. Mountain climates in low and mid-latitude areas ($0–60°$ north and south) are also characterised by a very high daily temperature range and frequent freeze–thaw cycles, in some cases more than 300 daily cycles per year.

Recent changes in global climates are having a significant impact on the distribution of cold environments. Research in Greenland suggests that winter temperatures have increased by $5\,°C$ and summer temperatures by $3\,°C$. This has resulted in up to 20 more melting days and the ice sheet losing approximately 125 km^3 of ice per year. The ice sheet receded 7.5 km between 2001 and 2005.

Further research

www3.uakron.edu/geology/friberg/escience/lecnotes/eslec7_notes.htm – lecture notes by Dr L. Friberg at the University of Akron giving a good introduction to the topic.

www.glacier.rice.edu – from one of the specialist university departments, Rice in Canada.

Periglacial environments

The high latitude of tundra regions ensures that the climate is very cold. Average temperatures range between $-5\,°C$ and $-10\,°C$. During the long, dark, winter months temperatures regularly fall below −20°C, and in central Siberia they can drop to −80°C. Daylight hours during the summer are very long: in June and July the sun never sets. However, the angle of the sun is so low that temperatures rarely rise above 10°C. The climate of these areas is also very dry (mean annual precipitation is usually below 150 mm) since they tend to occur in regions dominated by high pressure and sinking air. These areas are technically cold deserts (Table 10.1).

Table 10.1 Climate data for Tomsk, Russia

	Jan	Feb	Mar	Apr	May	Jun	Jul	Aug	Sep	Oct	Nov	Dec
Rainfall (mm)	26.9	17.9	21.9	25.6	44.8	61.1	73.6	67.9	44.2	47.7	46	34
Temperature (°C)	−18.8	−16.5	−9.9	−0.2	8.4	15.3	18.2	15.2	9.1	0.7	−10.5	−17

Relationships between glacial and periglacial environments

As the name suggests, periglacial environments are always located peripheral to (fringing) glacial environments. They represent the transition from the ice-covered glacial environment to the temperate tree-covered environment of the taiga.

Over the long history of climate change the locations of glacial and periglacial environments have constantly fluctuated. They have alternated, shifting towards the equator and the poles. The outcome has been that glacial and periglacial environments have been superimposed, one on top of the other, at particular locations. As an ice sheet retreats, the space it leaves becomes exposed to periglacial conditions and processes. At the next advance of the ice sheet, those periglacial landforms become covered and modified (perhaps obliterated) by moving ice and meltwater. At the next retreat, the newly created glacial or fluvioglacial features, in turn, become exposed to another period of periglacial conditions. Evidence of this sequential relationship can be seen in parts of northern Britain.

Distinctive landforms and landscapes

How do geomorphological processes produce distinctive landscapes and landforms in cold environments?

By the end of this section you should:
➤ *have examined the role of geomorphological processes in glacial environments*
➤ *be aware of the distinctive landforms produced by these processes*
➤ *have investigated the role of geomorphological processes in periglacial environments*
➤ *understand the distinctive landforms produced by these processes*

Glacial processes

Glacial landforms are visible today in places that were glaciated in the past, such as the Lake District. To see how glacial processes have produced these landforms, it can be helpful to study locations that are currently being glaciated and to make linkages between the active processes and the relict landforms.

Weathering processes produce some of the glacial debris used in abrasion and enlarge joints in the rock, which assists in plucking. Two main processes are involved:

➤ *Freeze–thaw.* When water freezes it expands by 9–10% of its volume. In glacial environments this may happen as temperatures fluctuate between day and night. In areas where temperatures are generally below freezing during both day and night, it may happen seasonally. As freezing water expands, the pressure this creates breaks down jointed rocks, particularly those exposed above the level of ice.

➤ *Dilatation.* Rocks fracture when overlying pressure is eased. When a glacier is melting, losing weight and exerting less downward pressure, the rocks of the valley floor, and to a lesser extent the sides, expand and fracture. They tend to fracture parallel to the surface.

Nivation

Nivation, a complex process not readily classified as either erosion or weathering, is thought to include a combination of freeze–thaw action, solifluction, transport by running water and, possibly, chemical weathering. This is believed to be responsible for the initial enlargement of hillside hollows as part of the formation of corries (cirques).

Erosional processes

Glacial erosion occurs as glaciers move forward, mainly in upland areas. There are two main processes:

➤ *Plucking.* This mainly happens when meltwater seeps into joints in the rocks of the valley floor/sides, then freezes and becomes attached to the glacier. As the glacier advances it pulls pieces of rock away. A similar mechanism takes place when ice refreezes on the down-valley side of rock obstructions that the ice is moving over by the process of creep. Plucking is particularly effective at the base of the glacier, as the weight of the ice mass above may produce meltwater through pressure melting. It will also be significant when the bedrock is highly jointed, as this allows meltwater to penetrate. Plucking is also known as quarrying.

➤ *Abrasion.* As a glacier moves, the debris embedded in its base/sides rubs against surface rocks, wearing them away by a process like sandpapering. The coarse material scrapes, scratches and grooves the rock, while the finer material tends to smooth and polish it. The glacial debris itself is also worn down by this process, forming a fine rock flour that is responsible for the milky-white appearance of glacial meltwater streams and rivers.

Rates of glacial erosion

Figure 10.8 shows a number of factors influencing the rate of **glacial erosion**. Rates vary enormously, in both time and location.

Researchers working on rates of erosion have produced the following findings:

➤ Embleton and King (1968) suggest that mean annual erosion for active glaciers is between 1,000 and 5,000 m³.

➤ Boulton (1974) measured erosion on rock plates placed beneath the Breidamerjökull glacier in Iceland and found that under ice 40 m thick, basalt eroded at 1 mm per year and marble at 3 mm per year. The ice had a velocity of 9.6 m per year. However, if the velocity increased to 15.4 m per year, the rate of erosion of marble increased to 3.75 mm, even though the ice was 8 m thinner. This suggests that velocity is more important than ice thickness in abrasion.

➤ In comparison, ice 100 m thick flowing at 250 m per year in the Glacier d'Argentière eroded a marble plate at up to 36 mm per year.

Figure 10.8 Factors affecting the rate of glacial abrasion

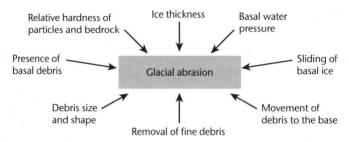

Transportation processes

Moving ice is capable of carrying huge amounts of debris. The material transported by ice sheets and glaciers comes from a wide range of sources:

➤ rockfalls
➤ avalanches
➤ debris flows
➤ aeolian deposits
➤ volcanic eruptions
➤ plucking
➤ abrasion

Figure 10.9 Location of debris during transportation

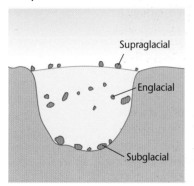

The material being transported may be classified according to its position in the glacier:

➤ *Supraglacial.* Material carried on top of the glacier. This will most often come from weathering and rockfall.

➤ *Englacial.* Material within the ice. This may be supraglacial material that has either been covered by further snowfall, fallen into crevasses or sunk into the ice as a result of localised pressure melting beneath larger stones and rocks.

➤ *Subglacial.* Material embedded in the base of the glacier which has been derived from plucking and abrasion or has continued to move down through the ice as former englacial debris.

Depositional processes

Glaciers deposit their load when they become less able to transport material. This usually occurs as a direct result of ablation (melting, sublimation etc.) during periods of retreat or deglaciation. However, material can also be deposited during advance or when the glacier becomes overloaded with debris.

All material deposited during glaciation is known as **drift**. This can be subdivided into till, which is deposited directly by the ice, and outwash, deposited by meltwater. Outwash is also known as fluvioglacial material and is dealt with later in this chapter.

Fluvioglacial processes

The meltwater produced by glaciers can carry out erosion, transportation and deposition leading to the formation of many distinctive landforms. These are described below.

Glacial landforms

There are three types of glacial landform: those resulting from the erosional work of glaciers (Photograph 10.3), those formed by deposition processes and those resulting from fluvioglacial processes.

Corel

Photograph 10.3 Alaska. A fjord is an erosional landform – a U-shaped valley which has been partly flooded by the sea

Erosional landforms

Table 10.2 summarises the most common landforms resulting from glacial erosion and Figure 10.10 illustrates the formation of some of them. Many erosional landforms, particularly in lowland areas, become hidden by later glacial and fluvioglacial deposits laid down on top of them. Others may have been modified by postglacial processes of weathering and erosion. However, those that are etched

Table 10.2 Landforms of glacial erosion

Landform	Appearance	Formation
Cirque (or corrie)	An armchair-shaped hollow on a hillside above a glacial valley	A pre-glacial hollow is enlarged by plucking and abrasion as ice moves in a rotational manner under gravity
Arête	A narrow ridge between two cirques	As two cirques are enlarged back-to-back the ridge between them becomes increasingly narrowed
Pyramidal peak	A sharp, pointed hilltop	As three or more cirques are enlarged the hilltop between becomes increasingly sharp and pointed
Trough (or U-shaped valley)	A steep-sided, flat-floored, straight valley	A pre-glacial river valley is widened and deepened by erosion from an advancing glacier
Truncated spur	A steep and possibly rocky section of the side of a trough	The pre-glacial interlocking spurs of the river valley are eroded by the much more powerful glacier
Hanging valley	A small tributary valley high above the floor of the trough, often with a waterfall	Tributary glaciers with small amounts of ice did not erode their valley floor as deeply as the main glacier and so are left at a higher altitude
Striations	Grooves on exposed rocks	Abrasion by debris embedded in the base of the glacier as it passed over bare rock. They can indicate the direction of ice movement
Roche moutonnée	Asymmetrical, bare rock outcrop with a gently sloping side facing up-valley	As ice crosses a resistant rock outcrop, the increased pressure causes melting and basal sliding and the up-valley side is smoothed by abrasion. On the leeward side pressure is reduced, refreezing occurs and plucking takes place, causing a steep, jagged slope

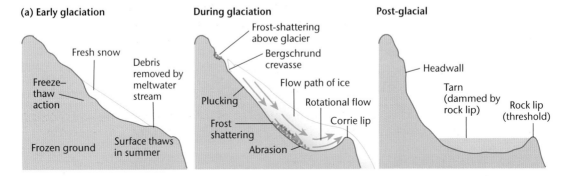

(a) Early glaciation

Fresh snow
Freeze–thaw action
Frozen ground
Debris removed by meltwater stream
Surface thaws in summer

During glaciation

Frost-shattering above glacier
Bergschrund crevasse
Flow path of ice
Plucking
Rotational flow
Frost shattering
Corrie lip
Abrasion

Post-glacial

Headwall
Tarn (dammed by rock lip)
Rock lip (threshold)

(b)

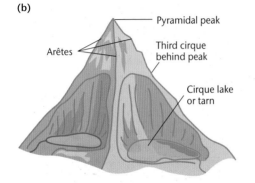

Pyramidal peak
Arêtes
Third cirque behind peak
Cirque lake or tarn

Figure 10.10 The formation of three erosional landforms. (a) Cirque, (b) arête and pyramidal peak

into the solid rock of upland areas may remain distinctive long after the end of the glacial period.

There are relatively few examples of erosional landforms resulting from fluvioglaciation, although they can be distinctive and assist in tracing the activity of a glacial period (Table 10.3).

Table 10.3 Landforms of fluvioglacial erosion

Landform	Appearance	Formation
Meltwater channels	River channels occupied by meltwater streams, perhaps with variable discharge	Channel bed and banks eroded by meltwater, possibly very abrasive due to high sediment load
Sichelwannen	Crescent-shaped marks on exposed rocks, often in dry channels	Scoured by abrasive meltwater streams and then abandoned in the postglacial period
Tunnel valleys	Large channels or small valley features now infilled with sediment	Sub-glacial meltwater streams erode channels and then deposit sediment in them at the end of the glacial period

Further research

http://uregina.ca/~sauchyn/geog323/glacial2.html – a comprehensive explanation of the formation of all the major landforms from University of Regina, California.

www.uwsp.edu/geo/faculty/lemke/alpine_glacial_glossary/glossary.html – less detailed explanations, but each landform is illustrated with a photograph.

Depositional landforms

The material deposited by a glacier or ice sheet on a land surface is referred to as **till**. There are two types:

➤ *Lodgement till.* Material deposited by advancing ice. The downward pressure exerted by thick ice causes subglacial debris to be pressed into existing valley floor material and left behind as the ice moves forward. This may be enhanced by localised pressure melting around individual particles under significant weight and pressure. Drumlins are the main example of landforms of this type.

➤ *Ablation till.* Material deposited by melting ice from stagnant or retreating glaciers, either temporarily during a warm period or at the end of the glacial event. Most other depositional landforms are made of this.

Whichever type it is, till can be recognised by three distinctive characteristics:

➤ *Jagged, angular in shape* because it has been embedded in the ice and not subjected to further erosion processes, particularly by meltwater which would make it smooth and rounded.

➤ *Unsorted.* When glaciers deposit material, all sizes are deposited together. Water deposits material in a size-based sequence.

➤ *Unstratified.* Glacial till is dropped in mounds and ridges rather than in the layers typical of water-borne deposits.

The terms till and **moraine** are sometimes regarded as meaning the same. Strictly speaking, however, till refers to the deposit itself and moraine to the surface landforms of the till.

Table 10.4 summarises the main landforms created by glacial deposition, while Figure 10.11

Figure 10.11 Glacial transportation

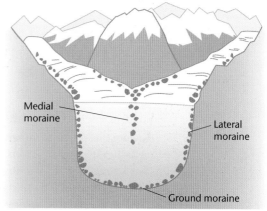

Medial moraine

Lateral moraine

Ground moraine

Table 10.4 Landforms of glacial deposition

Landform	Appearance	Formation
Ground moraine	Debris found all over the valley floor	Debris from weathering and erosion carried by the ice and deposited irregularly during melting
Lateral moraine	A ridge of moraine along the edge of the valley floor	Exposed rock on the valley side is weathered and fragments fall down onto the edge of the glacier. This is then carried along the valley and deposited when the ice melts
Medial moraine	A ridge of moraine down the middle of the valley floor	When two valley glaciers converge, two lateral moraines combine to form a medial. Material is carried and deposited when melting occurs
Terminal moraine	A ridge of moraine extending across the valley at the furthest point the glacier reached	Advancing ice carries moraine forward and deposits it at the point of maximum advance when it retreats. The up-valley (ice contact) side is generally steeper than the other side as the advancing ice rose over the debris
Recessional moraine	A series of ridges running across the valley behind the terminal moraine	Each recessional moraine, and there may be many, represents a still-stand during ice retreat. They are good indicators of the cycle of advance and retreat that many glaciers experience
Push moraine	A ridge of moraine with stones tilted upwards	Any morainic material at the glacier snout will be pushed forward during advance. The faster the velocity of advance, the steeper the angle of tilt of stones
Drumlins	Small elongated mounds, often found together in swarms	There are numerous theories but it is generally accepted that ground moraine is streamlined by advancing ice as localised pressure increases lead to basal melting and further additions of debris
Erratics	Large boulders foreign to the geology on which they sit	Boulders weathered or eroded by plucking are carried great distances and deposited when ice melts in areas of different geology. They are good indicators of the direction of ice movement

illustrates the different types of moraine. Many of these landforms are difficult to recognise in the field, as each successive advance and retreat alters the appearance of features such as morainic ridges. A single valley will have experienced several such advances and retreats in a glacial period, and may have suffered several glacial periods over the last 2 million years.

Further research

www.virtualfieldwork.com/thursaston.htm – a photographic record of the landforms left in eastern England by retreating ice.

http://uregina.ca/~sauchyn/geog323/glacial2.html – depositional landforms with photographs.

Fluvioglacial deposits

Fluvioglacial deposits are very different from glacial deposits. They are deposited by meltwater streams and rivers, which flow under, and beyond the snout of, glaciers. The material deposited, known as **outwash** or **fluvioglacial deposits**, tends to be:

➤ smaller than glacial till, as meltwater streams typically have less energy than valley glaciers and so only carry finer material

Photograph 10.4
Varves (layers of sediment in a lake bottom) in north Wales

Helen Morton

> smooth and rounded by contact with water and by attrition
> sorted horizontally, with the largest material found furthest up the valley and progressively finer material with distance down the valley, due to the sequential nature of deposition
> stratified vertically, with distinctive seasonal and annual layers of sediment accumulation in many of the landforms (Photograph 10.4)

A further division may be made between **outwash material** and **ice-contact drift**. The former is carried relatively long distances, possibly well beyond the snout and any terminal moraine, and so becomes very smooth and rounded and highly sorted. In contrast, the latter is deposited under or against the ice, and tends to be less rounded and less well sorted.

Like glacial deposits, fluvioglacial deposits are often difficult to identify in the field. Again, repeated advance and retreat alter the appearance of landforms and

Figure 10.12
Fluvioglacial features

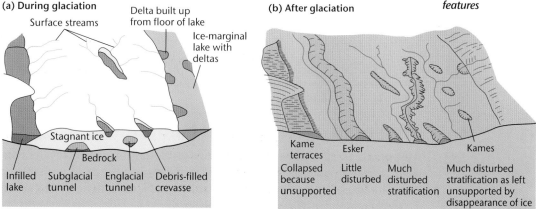

(a) During glaciation

Surface streams
Delta built up from floor of lake
Ice-marginal lake with deltas
Stagnant ice
Bedrock

Infilled lake · Subglacial tunnel · Englacial tunnel · Debris-filled crevasse

(b) After glaciation

Kame terraces
Esker
Kames

Collapsed because unsupported
Little disturbed
Much disturbed stratification
Much disturbed stratification as left unsupported by disappearance of ice

Table 10.5 Landforms of fluvioglacial deposition

Landform	Appearance	Formation
Varves	Layers of sediment found at the bottom of lakes	Sediment carried by meltwater streams is deposited on entering a lake as energy is lost. In summer, when large amounts of meltwater are available, the sediment is coarse and plentiful, leading to a wide band of sediment of relatively large material. In winter, with little meltwater present, sediment is limited in amount and size and so bands are thin and fine
Outwash (sandur)	A flat expanse of sediment in the pro-glacial area	As meltwater streams gradually lose energy on entering lowland areas, they deposit their material. The largest material is deposited nearest the snout and the finest further away
Kettle holes	Small circular lakes in outwash plains	During ice retreat blocks of dead ice become detached. Sediment builds up around them and when they eventually melt a small hollow is formed in which water accumulates to form a lake
Eskers	Long, sinuous ridges on the valley floor	Material is deposited in subglacial tunnels as the supply of meltwater decreases at the end of the glacial period. Sub-glacial streams may carry huge amounts of debris under pressure in the confined tunnel in the base of the ice
Delta kames	Small mounds on the valley floor	Englacial streams emerging at the snout of the glacier fall to the valley floor, lose energy and deposit their load, OR supraglacial streams deposit material on entering ice marginal lakes
Kame terraces	Ridges of material running along the edge of the valley floor	Supraglacial streams on the edge of the glacier pick up and carry lateral moraine which is then deposited on the valley floor as the glacier retreats
Braided stream	A river channel subdivided by numerous islets and channels	Debris-laden streams lose water at the end of the melting period. The material they can no longer carry is deposited in the channel, causing it to divide and possibly rejoin

they are also subject to weathering, erosion and colonisation by vegetation in the period since the end of the last glacial episode. The pro-glacial area, where most of the landforms are to be found, is often **chaotic** in appearance.

Meltwater deposition is particularly significant where there is variable **discharge**. During times of high flow, streams and rivers have enough energy to carry large amounts of load. As the discharge decreases, energy is gradually lost, so sequential deposition takes place and numerous landforms emerge (Table 10.5 and Figure 10.12).

Further research

http://userweb.port.ac.uk/~gilesd/pdf/2GS107%20Terrain%20Studies%20Glacial. pdf – lecture notes from the University of Portsmouth with a good section on fluvioglacial landforms.

Periglacial processes and landforms

In the periglacial environment frost processes are dominant, particularly the alternation of freezing and thawing caused by temperature fluctuations around freezing point. Frost heave can produce quite spectacular results. But water and wind action and sometimes chemical weathering are also active in periglacial areas.

Permafrost is a diagnostic feature of periglacial environments. It is perennially frozen ground, i.e. it remains frozen for at least two consecutive summers. It is estimated that for permafrost to develop, the mean annual temperature needs to be at least −4°C. There are three types of permafrost (Figure 10.13):

➤ *Continuous*. The upper limit of the permafrost effectively remains at the ground surface throughout the year with little, if any, surface melting during the summer. All the ground is frozen. This is found only within the Arctic circle and in continental areas of Eurasia and North America. It is commonly over 300 m in depth in these areas, although it may be much deeper in Siberia.

➤ *Discontinuous*. This includes noticeable areas of unfrozen ground or talik. It tends to be shallower than continuous permafrost, typically 10–50 m deep. The surface shows a significant depth of melting in the summer, forming an active layer.

➤ *Sporadic*. There is more talik than permafrost. The mean annual temperature may be around zero.

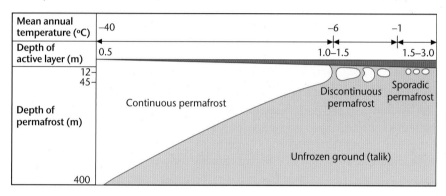

Figure 10.13 Types of permafrost

The depth and continuity of the permafrost layer decreases with decreasing latitude and altitude. Its maximum depth is limited by geothermal heat in the ground.

The **active layer** is the upper part of the ground that thaws during the summer. It is a significant feature of the landscape and is critical in the formation of landforms. As it thaws it produces meltwater which saturates the upper layer, partly because of the impermeable nature of the permafrost beneath. By contrast, the permafrost is inert and plays only a limited part in landscape shaping.

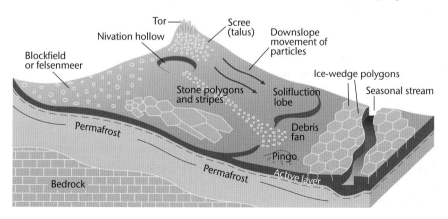

Figure 10.14 The periglacial landscape

(a) Pingo

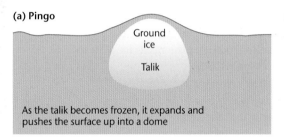

As the talik becomes frozen, it expands and pushes the surface up into a dome

(b) Stone polygons and stripes

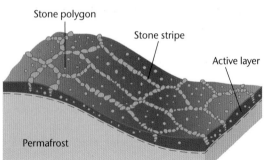

(c) Patterned ground

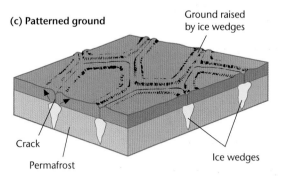

Figure 10.15 Some periglacial landforms

Periglacial landforms

The landforms of periglacial areas are varied (Figure 10.14). Some, such as pingos, patterned ground and ice-wedge polygons, are distinctive and unique to periglacial areas (Table 10.6 and Figure 10.15). Others, such as braided streams, scree and loess, are found in different climatic regions.

Table 10.6 Periglacial landforms

Landform	Appearance	Formation
Pingo	A rounded, ice-cored hill	Decreasing temperatures lead to the development of ground ice which domes the surface
Stone polygons	Small-scale polygonal arrangements of stones on the ground surface, elongated on slopes	Sorting of large stones by frost heave (push and pull)
Ice wedge polygons or patterned ground	Large-scale polygonal patterns of depressions surrounded by raised, ice-filled wedges	Ground contraction and subsequent enlargement by freeze–thaw. May become in-filled with sediment
Solifluction lobes	Tongue-like accumulations of sediment at the base of slopes	Thawed active layer moves downslope under gravity during warmer periods (gelifluction)
Scree	Angular fragments of rock, often accumulating at the base of a slope below bare rock exposures	Freeze–thaw weathering causes rock fragments to break off. These fall under gravity and build up at the base of the exposed rock
Braided stream	Stream or river with islands (eyots) of coarse sediment in the channel	During low-discharge flows coarse sediment is deposited in the channel and the flow diverges around the material
Loess	Extensive accumulations of fine material, often around the edge of periglacial areas	Fine material is carried by wind and deposited in surrounding areas

Further research

Knight, J. (2007) *Glaciation and Periglaciation*, Philip Allan Updates Advanced
TopicMasters series.

http://uregina.ca/~sauchyn/geog323/periglacial.html – a good summary from
University of Regina, California.

http://arctic.fws.gov/permcycl.htm – slides and animations of the major
landforms.

Challenges and opportunities

*What challenges and opportunities exist in cold environments and what management
issues might result from their use?*

By the end of this section you should:
➤ *understand the challenges and opportunities provided by cold environments of the
past and present*
➤ *have investigated how some of the challenges of cold environments might be
overcome by demand and technology*
➤ *have evaluated the effectiveness of different approaches to using and managing cold
environments*

Basic terms

Cold environments offer a range of challenges and opportunities. **Opportunities**
are possibilities or potentially advantageous conditions. **Challenges** are difficulties that need to be overcome before opportunities can be exploited — they are
preconditions. The challenges are greater if the opportunities are to be exploited
in a sustainable way. Modern technology often has the potential to neutralise, if
not overcome, the challenges of cold environments and so open the door to
realising opportunities. Another way of seeing the link between challenges and
opportunities is that the greater the need to exploit an opportunity (for example,
Alaskan oil), the greater the investment that will be made in order to overcome
the challenges.

Challenges and opportunities

Challenges

The challenges confronting cold environments are both physical and human.
The main physical challenges are:
➤ *Relief.* Mountainous and rugged terrain which greatly hinders accessibility.
➤ *Climate.* The extreme cold of winter and the long hours of darkness.
➤ *Unstable ground* due to processes such as solifluction and features such as the
active layer.
➤ *Natural hazards.* Largely of a seasonal nature, including avalanches, glacier
surges and meltwater floods

➤ *Fragile ecosystems*. Highly sensitive to human activity and easily damaged and disturbed.

The human challenges include:

➤ *Peripherality*. They are remote from core regions in terms of distance and accessibility, thinly populated and underdeveloped.

➤ *Low electoral importance to politicians* due to sparse population and limited economic development.

➤ *Poverty*. Endemic among indigenous people.

➤ *Vulnerability* to economic change.

Opportunities

Cold environments can offer various opportunities for exploitation of resources and economic development. They include:

➤ *minerals and energy* – particularly oil (e.g. Alaska)

➤ *wilderness and wildlife* – a prized resource

➤ *natural pasture* – traditionally grazed by herds of reindeer

➤ *water* – hanging valleys and fast-flowing rivers offer considerable hydroelectric power potential, but it is seasonal, and freezing is a problem.

➤ *fish* – the coastal waters of cold environments have good stocks

Growing global demand for such resources encourages use of modern technology to overcome the physical challenges of the environment. Increasing exploitation of these opportunities, however, is raising concern about the environmental impacts. Cold environments are fragile.

Overcoming the challenges and reaping the opportunities

Table 10.7 and the case studies that follow illustrate how some of the opportunities in cold environments can be exploited in response to demand and through use of modern technology.

Table 10.7 Some resources of cold environments: their use, impact of their exploitation and challenges

	Resources (opportunities)				
	Natural pasture	**Wildlife**	**Wilderness**	**Fish**	**Minerals and energy**
Exploiting activities	Nomadic herding of reindeer	Hunting and tourism	Tourism	Commercial fishing and whaling	Mining, smelting, oil and hydroelectric power
Environmental impact	Little or none	Disturbance and ecosystem damage	Litter, garbage, visual and noise pollution	Overfishing	Air, water, noise and visual pollution
Challenge	To preserve the traditional way of life in a modern context	To maintain biodiversity and ecosystem stability	To minimise the tourist footprint	To conserve fish and whale stocks	To reduce all forms of pollution to acceptable levels

Reindeer (also know as caribou) herding by nomadic people such as the Inuit in North America and Greenland and the Sami in Lapland is, along with hunting and fishing, the oldest means of survival in cold environments. The resource underlying this way of life was the grazing provided by the tundra or periglacial areas during the short summer and the taiga (coniferous forest) during the long winter. This pattern of food availability prompted the seasonal migrations of reindeer that continue to this day. The Inuit and Sami developed a survival strategy that involved following this mobile food supply. This traditional way of life is fairly well in tune with the natural environment: it is sustainable.

It has, however, undergone some updating. Animal-drawn sledges have been replaced by motorised skidoos. The herders now occupy seasonal cabins rather than igloos and hide tents. More recently, they have been selling skins, furs and traditional artefacts to tourists. But the lifestyles of these indigenous people are being threatened in various ways:

- Their freedom to roam is impeded by national boundaries.
- The enclosure of huge areas of taiga forest is causing a serious loss of winter grazing.
- Conservation legislation prevents them from hunting and selling the fur of some species.
- Atmospheric pollution is absorbed by mosses and lichens and enters the human food chain via the grazing livestock.
- There is government pressure in the form of money and other incentives to make the herders more sedentary. But why should they abandon such a sustainable way of life?

Case study: Avalanches: a tourist hazard

Avalanches are a form of snow slope failure. There are two basic types of avalanche: loose-snow and slab. The type of failure depends on the characteristics of the snow in the zone where they start.

Loose-snow avalanches occur when weak surface snow is on a slope that is steeper than its critical angle of rest. Typically the snow is either dry, fresh snow (powder) or wet snow resulting from melting. When the snow is disturbed, the loose snow undergoes a localised rotational slip and moves downslope in an inverted V-shape pattern. The initial slip involves very small masses of snow ranging in size from one grain to a large snowball. Typically they contain less than 1 m^3 of snow. As the avalanche moves downslope it can set other loose snow in motion. The avalanche comes to rest once the snow reaches its stable angle of rest.

Slab avalanches involve very large amounts of snow and can be hazardous. In this case, a slab of snow breaks loose from the slope and moves downslope by gravity. The slab itself is formed as snow is packed down and redistributed by wind. In the starting zones of slab avalanches there is typically a cohesive dense snow layer overlying less cohesive weak snow. When extra weight is added, perhaps by further fresh snow, the forces exceed the strength of the weak snow beneath, a fracture occurs and the resulting slab slides. The slabs can be several hundred metres wide and many metres thick and move at speeds of up to 75 m s^{-1}.

The Galtür avalanche

The worst Alpine avalanche in 40 years killed 31 people in the small village of Galtür, Austria, on 23 February 1999. Large snowfalls totalling around 4 m occurred in the preceding days. Freeze–thaw conditions created a weak layer on top of an existing snow pack, and more snow was then deposited on top.

When the frozen layer of snow failed, it sent a huge powder avalanche down the mountainside at around 290 km h^{-1}. As it travelled, the avalanche picked up additional snow and doubled in size. It took only 50 seconds to reach the village, by which time it was about 100 m high at its leading edge. It caused extensive damage and killed 31 people.

Not only do avalanches cause loss of life and damage to property, they are also very disruptive to the tourism industry that is economically vital to many alpine regions.

Further research

http://library.thinkquest.org/03oct/01886/index.
html – a wide-ranging site dealing with causes and impacts.

Case study: Oil extraction in Alaska

Alaska has huge oilfields, including those around Prudhoe Bay on the north coast. The permafrost of this region is susceptible to melting caused by the heat produced by terminal buildings, workers' housing and the transport of warm oil through pipelines such as the 800-km Alyeska pipeline from Prudhoe Bay to the ice-free port of Valdez on the south coast (Figure 10.16). Melting of permafrost can lead to frost heave in the active layer and damage to plant cover which has very slow recovery rates in these cold temperatures.

To tackle this environmental challenge:

- buildings are raised off the ground on telescopic piles to prevent melting
- the oil pipeline is raised on vertical supports 11 m deep – these cost over $3,000 each when the pipeline was built in the 1970s (Photograph 10.5)
- air cushion vehicles are used by companies such as Exxon to avoid damaging plant cover
- domestic water and sewage pipes are raised off the ground and heavily insulated with liquid ammonia and fibreglass in utilidors – insulated boxes elevated above the ground
- pipeline suspension bridges are used to cross rivers with highly seasonal discharge such as the 700-m-wide Yukon

There is increasing concern that global warming will lead to thawing of vast areas of permafrost. If this does occur, it will have serious implications for human settlement. Stable soils may become more prone to subsidence. Increase in solifluction and landslides may be seen as well. In several communities in the interior of Alaska, general thawing of the permafrost has been blamed for widespread under-

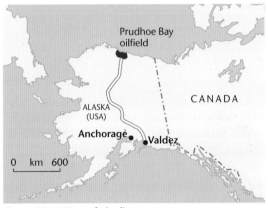

Figure 10.16 Map of pipeline route

Photograph 10.5 The trans-Alaska oil pipeline

mining of buildings and roads. A larger issue related to the thawing of permafrost is the potential release of methane from the decomposition of organic matter in the soil. Methane is a powerful greenhouse gas and could add to global warming.

There are conflicts between the local Inuit population, conservationists and the oil companies. Migrant US workers take the majority of jobs created by the oil industry but contribute relatively little to the local economy as they are on short-term contracts and spend little money. Locals fill only about 20% of the 2,200 full-time jobs. This has led to resentment and disputes.

Environmental groups such as the Alaska Wilderness League and the Alaska Forum for Environmental Responsibility have campaigned for improvements to the pipeline, which is suffering corrosion and leaks as well as disrupting the migration routes of caribou, despite crossing points being installed. In 2006, over 1 million litres of oil leaked from a corroded pipe at Prudhoe Bay. An earlier warning of the environmental risks of oil exploitation came in 1989 when the *Exxon Valdez*, a supertanker laden with 1.2 million barrels of crude oil, ran aground and spewed its contents over some 25,000 km^2 of coastal and offshore waters. The damage to wildlife was horrendous.

Further research

www.solcomhouse.com/pipeline.htm – good details of the pipeline from Solcom House.

www.alyeska-pipe.com – the official website of the pipeline.

Case study — Tourism and research in Antarctica

The largest wilderness area on Earth, largely unaffected by human activity, is a great natural attraction. In 2007/08, over 46,000 tourists visited Antarctica, a 14% increase on the previous year. Tourists visit Antarctica on cruise ships and spend a relatively small time on land, but this is 'high-impact' time compared to a scientist living in a permanent or semi-permanent research base on the continent. Tourists also want to visit the most spectacular and wildlife-rich areas that are accessible by ship during the short summer season.

The challenges associated with both tourism and research in Antarctica are immense:

■ The environment is highly sensitive to human trampling. This is a particular problem at locations where cruise ships are permitted to land passengers for short shore-based excursions.

■ The huge breeding colonies of penguins, sea birds and seals are easily disturbed by people.

■ People produce refuse. This threat is associated mainly with the scientific communities that are on the continent all year. In the past rubbish has been dropped down crevasses or abandoned where it fell. Even large items such as empty oil drums can be blown by the wind for miles from where they were originally dumped, so spreading the problem.

Antarctica needs careful and sympathetic management at an international level if its pristine wilderness is to remain intact. So far there have been three milestone agreements.

➤ The Antarctic Treaty was signed by 12 nations in 1959 and came into force in 1961. There are now 43 signatories. This established some key principles in the use of the territory, including complete freedom for scientific investigation and a ban on military use and nuclear testing.

➤ The Protocol on Environmental Protection to the Antarctic Treaty, usually known as the Madrid Protocol, came into force in 1998. This addressed some key environmental principles, stipulating:

> The protection of the Antarctic environment
> and dependent and associated ecosystems and
> the intrinsic value of Antarctica, including its
> wilderness and aesthetic values and its value
> as an area for the conduct of scientific research,
> in particular research essential to understanding
> the global environment, shall be fundamental

considerations in the planning and conduct of all activities in the Antarctic Treaty area.

- In 1991 the International Association of Antarctic Tour Operators was created, now consisting of over 100 companies from around the world. One of its objectives is 'to advocate, promote and practise safe and environmentally responsible travel to the Antarctic'.

Further research

www.antarctica.ac.uk/about_antarctica/tourism/index.php – British Antarctic Survey site dealing with tourism.

www.coolantarctica.com/Antarctica%20fact%20file/science/threats_tourism.htm – a wide-ranging site including a section on the impact of tourism.

Management

There are a number of possible approaches to the management of cold environments.

Comprehensive conservation

The aim would be to protect and conserve as wilderness all remaining cold environment areas still in a pristine condition. The only 'exploitation' might be in the form of a carefully regulated tourism like that permitted in Antarctica. This option is likely to be favoured by conservation organisations and the tourist industry (Photograph 10.6), but not by local people and industrialists in search of oil and other minerals. Governments might not be too enthusiastic either, since such areas would yield little revenue.

Photograph 10.6 Tourists walking on Walker Glacier in Alaska

Corel

Do nothing

This lies at the opposite end of the spectrum. The ethos would be to allow the cold environments to be exploited for whatever resources are in demand and profitable. This approach would be supported by industrialists, and perhaps governments (more revenue) and local people (more jobs). Conservationists, on the other hand, would condemn the irreversible damage done to the environment.

Sustainable exploitation

This represents a middle course between the two extremes above. In theory it could take into account the vested interests of all players in an even-handed manner. However, the snag is that this strategy relies on compromise for its success. Sadly, history tells us that compromise can be difficult to achieve. Perhaps the best way forward is to distinguish between those areas that should be protected at all costs and those that might be worked for their resources.

Agreeing and implementing a sustainable strategy is probably the greatest challenge facing many of the world's cold environments. But it promises a great opportunity – a sustainable future in which the resources of cold environments are enjoyed by generations to come. The resource might be their beauty and wilderness, or the material resources needed for economic development. In both instances, cold environments have a contribution to make to human wellbeing and quality of life.

Finally, there is one great challenge that threatens cold environments with disaster: global warming. Unless the global community curbs this menace, cold environments will be greatly reduced in extent and some of their precious opportunities will be lost for ever.

Suggested fieldwork opportunities

Local fieldwork

➤ Upland fieldwork to investigate the landscape impacts of past glacial and periglacial processes.
➤ The past distribution of glacial and periglacial landscapes.
➤ Investigating past cold environments in terms of fragility and threats.

Residential and long-haul fieldwork

➤ The Alps and Pyrenees afford good opportunities for first-hand study of the full range of processes, landforms, challenges and opportunities of alpine environments.
➤ Norway and Iceland are excellent locations for equivalent fieldwork in glacial and periglacial environments.

Review questions

1 Distinguish between the three main types of cold environment.
2 Explain how a systems approach helps the study of cold environments.
3 How do you expect the global distribution of cold environments to change in the future?
4 To what extent may ice sheets and glaciers be distinguished by the landforms they produce?
5 How important do you think freeze–thaw cycles are in the formation of periglacial landforms?
6 Research a specific cold environment location and draw up a table to show the challenges and opportunities that it presents to people.

Chapter 11

Life on the margins: the food supply problem

A significant number of people in the world suffer from food insecurity. The causes are complex, ranging from physical processes of land degradation and desertification to population pressure. For these people, food is scarce and malnutrition an ever-present threat. At the same time, there are others in the world who consume more than their fair share of global resources. Increasing the world's food supply represents a key challenge. Options range from reforming trade systems to the application of intermediate technology and organic farming.

Global and local feast or famine

What are the characteristics of food supply and insecurity?

By the end of this section you should:
> *have explored current issues associated with food supply and insecurity*
> *have developed an awareness of inappropriate farming techniques and their impact on the environment*
> *understand why food supply varies spatially*
> *know what living on the margins means to differing people*

Current issues

Feeding ourselves is a basic challenge. Under-nourishment is a serious global concern.

Figure 11.1 shows that under-nourishment is worst in sub-Saharan Africa. Food security refers to the availability of food and a person's access to it. A household is considered food secure when its occupants do not live in hunger or fear of starvation. Worldwide around 850 million people are chronically hungry, while up to 2 billion people lack food security intermittently. Other food supply issues include:
> the growing problem of obesity (over-nutrition)
> the distance food travels to reach the consumer – food miles
> the relationship between food production and the environment
> the impact of globalisation on diets and tastes

Obesity

The condition of obesity occurs when fat accumulates in the body to such a degree that it increases the risk of health problems such as heart disease and diabetes.

Edexcel A2 Geography

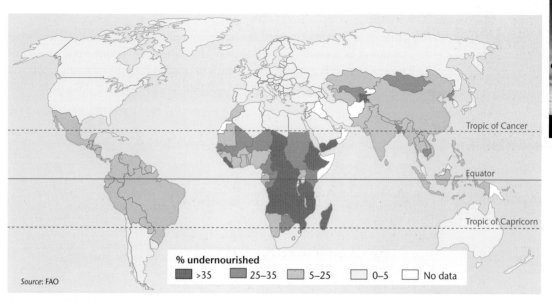

Figure 11.1 Global distribution of under-nourishment, 2003–2005

Obesity has reached epidemic proportions in the UK and the USA. It is now beginning to emerge as an issue in the developing world.

Case study — Obesity in China

Land reform in the 1950s and the development of a market economy since the 1980s have allowed China to escape major **famines** and to begin eliminating the hunger that was once widespread in its vast rural population. However, as the country urbanises and many of its people become more affluent, one set of health problems is being replaced by another.

About 20% of the 1 billion overweight or obese people in the world are Chinese. China was once considered to have one of the world's leanest populations, but it is fast catching up with the West in terms of obesity. What worries observers most is the speed of the nutrition transition from a low- to a high-fat diet.

According to recent statistics, the biggest health crisis is in China's cities, with 12% of adults and 8% of children now classified as obese. Over the past 10 years, China's overall obesity rate has virtually doubled.

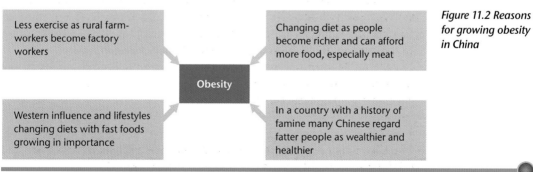

Less exercise as rural farm-workers become factory workers

Changing diet as people become richer and can afford more food, especially meat

Western influence and lifestyles changing diets with fast foods growing in importance

In a country with a history of famine many Chinese regard fatter people as wealthier and healthier

Obesity

Figure 11.2 Reasons for growing obesity in China

Food miles

The distance food is transported from the time of its production until it reaches the consumer is known as 'food miles'. This is one environmental impact of food production. It is estimated that much of our food travels between 2,500 and 4,000 km from farm to plate. The mean distance has increased by 25% since 1980.

Figure 11.3 Two ecological footprint conundrums

In the UK apples are harvested in September and October. They are then chill-stored which is energy-intensive. By May or June is it better for the environment to buy New Zealand and South African apples with many food miles, or local apples which have been chilled for months, using elecricity?

Most commercial lettuces are grown in winter in the UK in greenhouses or poly-tunnels requiring heating. So in winter is it better for the environment to buy lettuces grown in Spanish or Egyptian fields, which carry food miles but have nor required heat to grow?

Consumers can reduce their food miles by buying food grown closer to home. However, the situation is not simple (see Figure 11.3).

➤ On the one hand growing fruit and vegetables in poorer countries for export reduces the amount of land available to feed local people. In the West, buying locally grown food and eating only food that is in season reduces food miles.

➤ On the other hand the World Trade Organization and the World Bank are encouraging governments of less developed countries to produce export crops. If we stop buying imported food, we could be denying these countries a possible path to economic development.

Further research

Investigate the issues surrounding the global and local supply of food:
www.practicalaction.org/?id=food_production

Environmental issues in food production

Global food production has increased as a result of an increase in the amount of land being farmed and technological developments in farming (Figure 11.4).

In industrialised countries, the most important advance has been mechanisation. This has led to increases in yield (output per unit area). However, advances in farming have brought costs and benefits that have not been spread evenly. Costs have been mainly in the form of adverse impacts on the environment.

The **Green Revolution**, which involved the introduction of new species of cereal crops, notably rice and wheat, increased yields but has had negative environmental impacts, including:

➤ monocultures leading to a loss of biodiversity and indigenous crop types
➤ increased plant vulnerability to stress because of lack of genetic diversity
➤ clearance of large areas of land for cultivation, resulting in deforestation and loss of species and wetland ecosystems

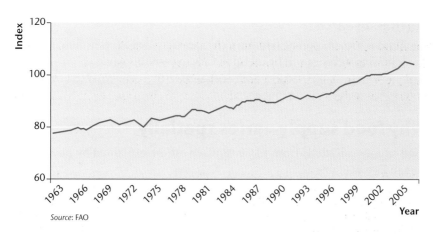

Figure 11.4
Per capita global
food production,
1961–2005

Source: FAO

➤ increased soil erosion and land degradation
➤ impacts of irrigation such as increased salinisation, overpumping of aquifers, land subsidence due to groundwater abstraction and eutrophication

Further research

Follow up these costs by visiting:

www.nature.com/nature/journal/v396/n6708/full/396211a0.html
www.ifpri.org/divs/eptd/dp/papers/eptdp02.pdf

 Case study   **Cattle ranching on the High Plains, USA**

Cattle ranching has a poor reputation with environmentalists. Beef cattle are able to consume and digest plant materials that other animals cannot. They can also find their own food and are not labour-intensive. However, a growth in meat-based diets has had two main impacts:

■ the spread of pastoral agriculture to regions that are not well suited to it

■ the intensification of animal husbandry, which means fencing off former grazing land to create feedlots and converting pasture land to arable to grow crops to feed cattle

The American love of large steaks has led to a growth in 'cornfed' beef raised in these intensive feedlots. Cattle are kept in fenced areas and fed on locally grown maize and soya rather than grazing freely on the range. This has brought problems. Tall-grass prairie has been replaced by corn and soybeans for animal feed. Short-grass prairie is now in wheat.

Photograph 11.1 A cattle feedlot in Idaho, USA

Biodiversity is lower, soil erosion has increased, and nutrient runoff is a problem, with higher levels of nitrates and heavy metals in water supplies. However, profits are greater as intensively raised cattle are ready for slaughter at 14–16 months instead of 4–5 years.

Unit 4 Geographical research

Further research

Examine how inappropriate farming techniques have led to environmental issues. The following websites will be useful in carrying out this work:

http://news.bbc.co.uk/1/talking_point/debates/earth_summit/2176313.stm

www.gwll.org.uk/index.asp?page=115

Why food supply varies spatially

Food supply variations from place to place can be explained by physical and human factors (Table 11.1).

Table 11.1 Human and physical factors in food supply variations

Human factors	Physical factors
Accessibility of markets	Climate
Land ownership systems	Precipitation
Inheritance laws	Length of thermal growing season
Markets	Relief
Competition	Aspect
Government action and support	Soil

Physical factors set natural limits to production. This means that some regions are able to produce greater quantities of food. Physical restrictions on food production can be overcome by using technology such as irrigation, fertilisers and greenhouses. However, this technology is costly and eventually the costs outweigh the benefits of the food produced.

Variations in food security are not the same thing as variations in food supply. There have been many cases in which regions suffering from famine had plenty of available food. In the 1974 Bangladesh famine, food was available to buy, but price rises put it beyond the means of poor people, increasing food insecurity and contributing to hunger. In areas where export crops are produced by commercial farmers and foreign-owned 'agribusinesses', food production can be high, but supply of food for local consumption may be low. The issue of food security is dominated by price and local availability of food rather than the amount produced.

Figure 11.5 shows that after years of falling food prices, costs started to rise in 2007 and 2008:

➤ The price of wheat rose by 130% in 2008.

➤ Rice doubled in price in Asia in the first 3 months of 2008.

From Haiti to Cameroon to Bangladesh, people took to the streets to protest because they were unable to afford staple foods. Rising food prices from 2007 were caused by a number of factors:

➤ Soaring demand in China and India, especially for meat, raising the price of feed grains such as maize and soya.

➤ Rising oil prices, increasing the cost of farm inputs such as diesel and fertilisers.

➤ Conversion of food-producing areas to biofuel production, reducing food supply.

➤ Market imbalances, which mean that in some areas locally produced food is undercut by cheap imported food.

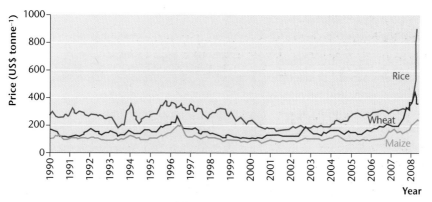

Figure 11.5 Global food prices, 1990–2008

A few decades ago Haiti was self-sufficient in rice. As a condition of receiving foreign loans, it was made to 'liberalise' its market, allowing unrestricted imports. Cheap rice from the USA put an end to local production. This left Haiti exposed to price rises (50% in less than a year in 2007) and the average Haitian could not afford to eat. Estimates suggest that the 2007–08 food price rises may have pushed 200 million people back into poverty and food insecurity.

Life on the margins

Food security depends on a number of interlinked factors (Figure 11.6), including:
➤ access to capital, human assets (farming skills, community cohesion) and physical assets (soil and climate)
➤ the 'mediating' factors (such as land ownership) that affect how people can use those assets
➤ the strategies and techniques employed by people to survive: how they work, how they divide activities in a household and how they cope in times of stress

The outcomes of these processes determine household access to food, which in turn, and depending on the structure of the household, determines individual access. These processes can be disturbed by forces of change, either natural (seasonal changes), or human – shocks such as war and civic unrest or trends such as rises in food prices.

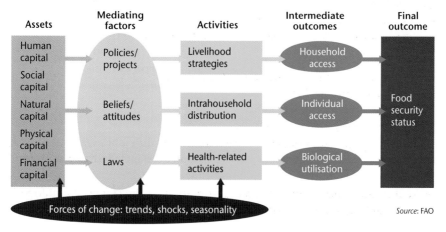

Figure 11.6 Factors affecting food security

Source: FAO

Bangladesh is the last south Asian country to have suffered famine. In 1974 an estimated 1.5 million people died – 2% of the population. It is the most densely populated non-industrialised country in the world, and it has a high risk of hydro-meteorological hazards.

Since the last famine governments in Bangladesh have pursued a policy of 'cereal self-sufficiency', achieving that goal in 2000. However, the major problem is the ability of the urban and rural poor to afford to buy food.

Urban insecurity

Dhaka, the capital of Bangladesh, is the fastest-growing megacity in the world. An estimated 300,000–400,000 rural–urban migrants arrive in the city every year. Its population of 12 million is projected to grow to 20 million by 2020.

Migration strains an already overcrowded city. The poor mainly live in slum housing. The average monthly household expenditure in the poorest households is the equivalent of US$70. The poorest people in Dhaka:

- are dependent on others for food, obtaining it through begging or charity (Photograph 11.2)
- have no secure income, depending on erratic employment, day labour or begging
- are often in female-headed households with small children and no male support
- have little education and cannot afford to send their children to school

Of all the pressures on Dhaka's poor, the greatest is managing to survive from one day to the next. Food is basic to that survival.

Photograph 11.2 A woman begging in Dhaka

Rural insecurity

As in many other countries dominated by subsistence agriculture, lack of food security in rural Bangladesh is due to lack of access to land. Poor farmers who have some land generally have a food source, although it is frequently threatened by natural disasters. It is the landless poor who are most exposed. These people (some 15% of the rural population) depend on foraging for uncultivated food. In communities where local biodiversity has been conserved, uncultivated foods such as leafy greens, tubers, small fish and small animals collected from agricultural fields, water bodies and forested areas make up nearly 40% of the diet. Other food essentials are obtained by exchange with farmers.

Where farming systems have been 'modernised' through the use of herbicides, pesticides and fertilisers, biodiversity is threatened, and so is the survival of the communities. The landless members of very poor communities depend on uncultivated sources for almost 100% of their food.

Further research

Investigate how Figure 11.6 can be used to explain different examples of food insecurity, including both urban (such as Dhaka in the Bangladesh case study) and rural (such as Darfur – see the web links below).

www.unicef.org/infobycountry/sudan_darfuroverview.html (follow the links)

www.un.org/ecosocdev/geninfo/afrec/vol16no4/164food1.htm

The complex causes of food supply inequalities

What has caused global inequalities in food supply and security?

By the end of this section you should:
- ➤ *understand how and why areas of food surplus and famine have emerged*
- ➤ *be aware of the role of population pressure in creating food insecurity*
- ➤ *have investigated attempts to increase global food supply*
- ➤ *understand who has been most affected by food insecurity, and why*

The causes of food surplus and famine

The amount of food consumed each day (calorie intake per head) varies widely across the world. In Europe and North America diet is often in excess of daily needs, whereas much of Africa experiences under-nutrition. Globally there is a **nutrition spectrum** (Figure 11.8).

Excess calorie intake leads to obesity and related illnesses such as diabetes. These are long-term problems related to a plentiful supply of cheap, high-fat foods. Obesity is also linked to a Western, urban lifestyle with high work stress levels and little exercise. Where daily calorie intake is lower than required malnutrition sets in. Some people lack key nutrients such as vitamins C or D in

Figure 11.7 Daily calorie intake per day, 1991–2001

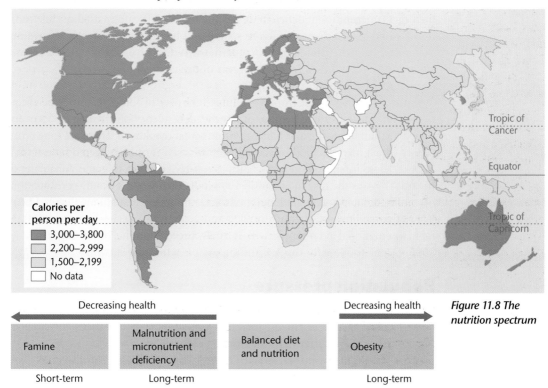

Calories per person per day
- 3,000–3,800
- 2,200–2,999
- 1,500–2,199
- No data

Tropic of Cancer

Equator

Tropic of Capricorn

Decreasing health ←

Decreasing health ←

Famine	Malnutrition and micronutrient deficiency	Balanced diet and nutrition	Obesity
Short-term	Long-term		Long-term

Figure 11.8 The nutrition spectrum

Long-term factors leading to food insecurity			
Physical	**Social**	**Agricultural**	**Economic/political**
• Long-term decline in rainfall in southern Sudan • Increased rainfall variability • Increased use of marginal land leading to degradation • Flooding	• High population growth (3%) linked to use of marginal land (overgrazing, erosion) • High female illiteracy rates (65%) • Poor infant health • Increased threat of HIV/AIDS	• Highly variable per capita food production • Static or falling crop yields • Low and falling fertiliser use • No food surplus for use in crisis	• High dependency on farming (70% of labour force; 37% of GDP) • Dependency on food imports • Limited access to markets to buy food or infrastructure to distribute it • Debt and debt repayments limit social and economic spending • High military spending

Short-term factors leading to famine

Drought in southern Sudan. Any surpluses quickly used up

Both reduce food availability in Sudan and inflate food prices

Migration from Darfur towards areas already under food stress

Situation compounded by:
• Lack of political will by government
• Slow donor response
• Limited access to famine areas
• Regional food shortages

Figure 11.9 The causes of famine in Sudan

their diet (micronutrient deficiency), despite reasonable calorie intake. This leads to increased risk of diseases such as scurvy and tuberculosis. Famine is extreme under-nourishment, caused by a short-term worsening of an already food-insecure situation. Famine differs from long-term under-nourishment in that the risk of death rises significantly.

Modern famines result from a complex interplay of forces. Famines occur in regions already vulnerable because of poverty, dependency on farming for income, poor agricultural practice and harsh environmental conditions. These are long-term factors which increase food insecurity. Famine itself is often triggered by external 'shocks'. These are short-term factors such as war, civil conflict, migration or a natural hazard. This was the case in Sudan in 1998 and 2002, when a deadly combination of conflict, drought and migration tipped the Darfur region into famine (Figure 11.9).

As Niger slid towards famine in 2004 and 2005, warning signs were ignored. A rapid international aid response will normally prevent famine, but in Niger in May 2005 it came too late for the 3.6 million people who were starving.

Population pressure

Many argue that there are sufficient resources in the world to support a population of 10–12 billion. However, inequalities in distribution mean that about 850 million people continually suffer malnutrition. The question of whether there are too many people in the world seems simple, but in fact it is highly controversial. Two contrasting viewpoints are described below.

Malthus

Thomas Malthus wrote his essay on population at the end of the eighteenth century, which was a time of great change, both economically and politically. Malthus believed that rapidly rising population could not be matched by growth in food supply. A gap between food demand and supply would lead to famine or perhaps civil war. Since the time of Malthus, world population has grown from 1 billion to 6.6 billion, accompanied by rising food production and living standards. This might suggest Malthus's ideas were incorrect. ——⟩ evaluation point

In the past 40 years **neo-Malthusians** (represented by Professor Paul Ehrlich) have updated the original Malthusian idea. They argue that the increased agricultural and industrial activity needed to feed and maintain the population will eventually lead to environmental and economic disaster. Neo-Malthusians foresee a crisis of food, energy, water and land resources rather than just food supply.

Ester Boserup

The Danish economist Ester Boserup took a different view of the relationship between population and food supply. In the 1960s she suggested that population growth has a positive impact on people, so that when food begins to run out we 'invent' or innovate our way out of the problem.

Her view can be summarised as 'population growth causes agricultural growth'. Population growth thus becomes something positive and central to our development as a species. This optimistic view has not gone unchallenged. The neo-Malthusians argue that 'more people, more wealth' may have worked for the past 200 years, but ignores the environmental impact of population growth.

The impacts of increasing global food supply

Attempts to increase agricultural output have in some cases led to significant environmental damage. The most common approach to increasing food production is to increase inputs. This has led to increasingly intensive farming (Table 11.2).

Table 11.2 Environmental impacts of intensive farming

Input	Purpose	Environmental impact
Machines such as tractors and combine harvesters	To replace human or animal labour, and increase efficiency	Increased fossil-fuel use and air pollution
Fertilisers	To increase yield, by providing high levels of plant nutrients	Eutrophication of water courses by agricultural runoff
Pesticides	To kill insects, fungi and other pests which could reduce yields	Chemicals entering the food chain and causing damage to other organisms. DDT is an insecticide linked to harmful impacts in humans
Herbicides	To kill weeds which take up space and use up nutrients	Chemicals entering the food chain and causing damage to other organisms
Antibiotics	To increase meat yield and livestock resistance to disease	Increased resistance among animals and the danger of epidemic outbreaks; fears for human health through consumption of treated meat
Animal feed	To increase the number of animals kept on a given area of land	Increased demand for food crops to feed livestock, and therefore pressure to clear areas (e.g. forests) to grow more crops

The Green Revolution, which began in the 1960s, promoted the use of high-yielding varieties (HYVs) of wheat and rice. HYVs successfully increased food production but also relied on higher quantities of inputs such as fertilisers, pesticides and irrigation. More recent attempts to increase food production through genetically modified (GM) crops have had questionable results, particularly for poorer farmers. In addition, GM crops rely on agricultural chemicals, so the dangers of environmental degradation are still present.

Most large-scale industrial farming relies heavily on chemical inputs and is a 'one size fits all' solution. In the developing world solutions to food shortage need to be based on local production systems adapted to local needs, such as:

➤ encouraging growing of legumes, which contain bacteria in their roots that fix nitrogen in the soil
➤ using plant cover and terracing to prevent soil erosion
➤ improving the soil by using organic matter such as compost and manure instead of artificial fertilisers
➤ reducing pests and crop diseases by natural means such as intercropping and agroforestry

Hardy crop varieties that can survive in marginal conditions limit the risk of a bad harvest. Most Green Revolution and GM crops require careful maintenance, a lot of inputs and ideal growing conditions. This is hard for small-scale farmers. It is possible to breed such crops without the use of GM technology. One example is the recent success of the rice Nerica (**New Ric**e for Af**ric**a) in west Africa. This cross between African and Asian varieties is rich in proteins and resistant to drought.

When agriculture and animal-rearing are carried out side by side, crop residues can be fed to livestock, and animal droppings turned into manure without being moved over distances. But farmers need access to the necessary means of production: draft animals, carts, sufficient land. This is more a question of resource allocation than of genetic manipulation.

Among the farming communities in the least developed countries there is an underexploited wealth of natural knowledge. This is demonstrated by groups that, for example:

➤ cultivate the creole gardens of Haiti and many other Caribbean islands
➤ in the Sahel region of Africa sow their cereals in parklands beneath *Acacia albida*, a leguminous tree that helps fertilise the soil

Techniques like these could be improved by agricultural researchers working with complex ecosystems.

Environment-friendly schemes

In developed countries concern about the impact of intensive farming has stimulated a growth in organic farming and other intermediate solutions such as LEAF (Linking Environment and Farming). Organic agriculture has developed rapidly in the EU. An excess of food production and greater wealth allows less productive forms of agriculture like this. Organic farming also has vociferous and politically influential supporters in the West who are not farmers. The three main claims are:

> Organic food is healthier because it does not contain synthetic pesticide traces.
> The soil structure on organic farms is better, maintaining a crucial resource for the future and leading to less erosion.
> Organic farming is more friendly to the environment and to wildlife than intensive farming.

Further research

Research the costs and benefits of different farming methods:

www.leafuk.org/leafuk

www.defra.gov.uk/farm/organic/index.htm

Who is most affected by food insecurity?

Vulnerability to food insecurity tends to be a result of a range of factors that compound each other (Figure 11.10) and lead to a situation where health, and even life, is at risk. Food insecurity is likely to affect people who:

> lack a political 'voice', such as women, children, the elderly and ethnic minorities
> have no 'safety net' (either personal or governmental) to fall back on if things go wrong
> live in areas lacking political and economic stability, as a result of conflict
> live in areas prone to natural hazards and climate change

The complexity of food insecurity and famine means that long-term sustainable solutions need to address social systems, political issues, environmental issues and economics. This of course makes improving the position of people on the margins a difficult challenge.

Food insecurity is not restricted to the 800 million inhabitants of the planet who are counted as 'hungry'. It is possible to find food insecurity in what claims to be the world's most prosperous nation. There are considerable numbers of people in the USA who depend on food aid. A great deal of research suggests that food insecurity affects some groups more than others.

Further research

Investigate the relationship between food insecurity and the political and social structures that dominate societies. Visit:

www.prb.org/Articles/2004/DarfurHighlightstheImpactofFoodInsecurityonWomen.
    aspx?p=1

www.countercurrents.org/deen300408.htm

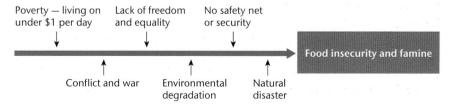

Figure 11.10
Vulnerability to food insecurity and famine

Desertification and life at the margin of survival

What is the role of desertification in threatening life at the margins?

By the end of this section you should:
➤ *be aware of the scale and impacts of desertification*
➤ *have investigated the characteristics of dryland ecosystems*
➤ *understand why dryland ecosystems are so vulnerable*
➤ *appreciate the relationship between food production and supply in desertified regions*

Scale and impact of desertification

Dryland or arid regions are defined as areas in which rainfall amounts are low and evapotranspiration potential is high. This restricts water availability and plant growth (Table 11.3). Drylands cover around 41% of the global land area (Figure 11.11) and include deserts, semi-deserts and some grasslands. They are home to around 37% of the world's population.

Hyper-arid areas have very little human habitation: they are simply too extreme an environment.

It is misleading to consider average rainfall alone, because in arid zones there may be many years when rainfall is zero. Precipitation can vary greatly both from year to year and during the year. It can also be patchy, with heavy rain in one localised area but nothing a few hundred metres away. These are **fragile** environments because the conditions for plant and animal survival are challenging.

Figure 11.11 Global distribution of drylands

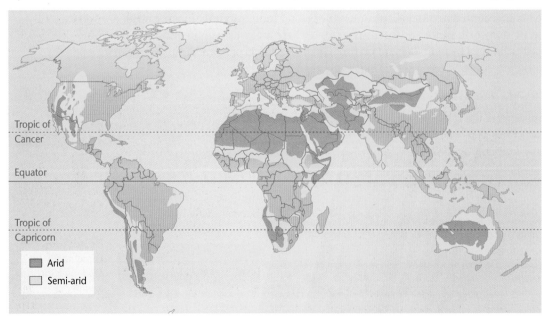

Classification	Rainfall (mm)	Area (% of land area)	Area (billion hectares)
Hyper-arid (desert)	<200	7.5	1.0
Arid (grass and shrub desert)	<200 (winter) or <400 (summer)	12.1	1.6
Semi-arid (steppes and grasslands)	200–500 (winter) or 400–600 (summer)	17.7	2.4
Dry sub-humid (seasonal forests)	500–700 (winter) or 600–800 (summer)	9.9	1.3
Total		47.2	6.3

Table 11.3
Arid areas

Seventy per cent of the world's drylands (excluding hyper-arid deserts) are degraded and many are experiencing desertification. The OECD defines **desertification** as 'the process of land degradation in arid, semi-arid and dry sub-humid areas resulting from various factors, including climatic variations (drought) and human activities, for example the overexploitation of dry lands'.

Many dryland areas in Africa are suffering from desertification (Figure 11.12). In the Sahel region of Africa desertification is a major problem. The physical causes of this process include:

➤ a significant decline in precipitation between 1960 and 1990 (Figure 11.13), i.e. increased periodic drought
➤ possible changes in rainfall patterns (amount, distribution, seasonal timing) that some scientists have linked to global warming

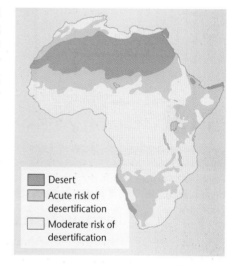

Desert
Acute risk of desertification
Moderate risk of desertification

Figure 11.12
Spreading deserts in Africa

In an increasingly arid and more variable climate, human activity has been critical in pushing some areas towards desertification:

➤ Population growth increases pressure on fuelwood resources and deforestation to obtain fuelwood then exposes soil to erosion.

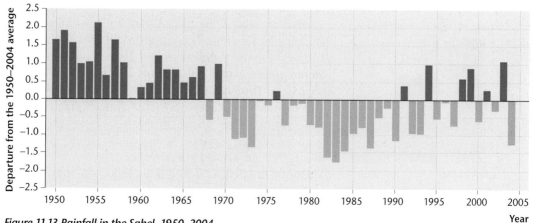

Figure 11.13 Rainfall in the Sahel, 1950–2004

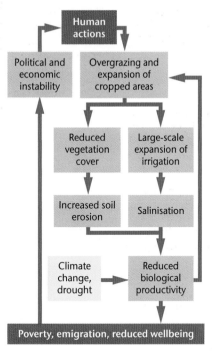

Figure 11.14 Causes of desertification

> Farmers are forced to farm marginal land such as steep slopes.
> Traditional crop rotation and fallow periods are abandoned for more intensive farming methods.
> Male out-migration leads to labour shortages, forcing women to undertake intensive farming of areas close to the home.
> Nomadic pastoralists are driven off their semi-desert grazing lands and forced into arable farming, increasing the pressure on available land.

In the Sahel, increasing physical vulnerability has been compounded by inappropriate human actions, spreading the desertification problem (Figure 11.14).

The combined effects of removal of vegetation cover, which exposes soil on steep slopes to erosion, and deteriorating soil structure as a result of over-intensive farming, are to expose the dryland soil surface to intense heat, desiccating winds and occasional intensive rainstorms. This leads to rapid erosion and a land surface so loose and mobile that vegetation cannot grow – desertification.

The characteristics and vulnerability of dryland ecosystems

There are four global-scale ecosystems (**biomes**) found in the drylands (Figure 11.15). Hyper-arid and arid drylands are dominated by deserts. Deserts have very little available moisture, low productivity and low biodiversity. They are of limited use to humans. Arid areas are used for nomadic pastoralism but conditions are often so extreme that human settlement is limited. Semi-arid areas are dominated by grassland. This is either temperate prairie or steppe, or tropical savanna. The continual vegetation cover and wet season in these areas means they often have dense human settlement and farming.

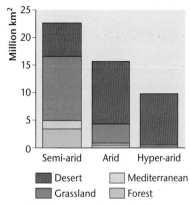

Figure 11.15 Ecosystems in drylands

Dryland ecosystems are adapted to low and seasonal rainfall. If water suddenly becomes available both plants and animals respond rapidly through growth – the 'desert in bloom' phenomenon which occurs after rainfall. In savanna ecosystems (tropical grasslands) plants have adapted to be able to survive in a seasonally arid climate (Figure 11.16). Many plants are xerophytes, meaning they can survive long periods with little moisture. Many are also pyrophytes, which means they are adapted to survive fire.

During dry periods drylands are especially vulnerable to human intervention:

> Lack of vegetation cover increases the risk of soil erosion, which may be irreversible if severe.

	Dry season				Wet season				Dry season		
	Jan	Feb	Mar	Apr	May	Jun	Jul	Aug	Sep	Oct	Nov	Dec
Temperature (°C)	21	24	28	31	30	28	27	26	27	28	26	24
Rainfall (mm)	0	0	0	8	60	120	215	310	130	18	10	0

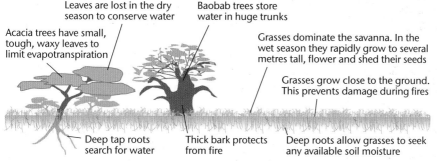

Figure 11.16 Climate and plant adaptation in the savanna ecosystem

Leaves are lost in the dry season to conserve water

Baobab trees store water in huge trunks

Acacia trees have small, tough, waxy leaves to limit evapotranspiration

Grasses dominate the savanna. In the wet season they rapidly grow to several metres tall, flower and shed their seeds

Grasses grow close to the ground. This prevents damage during fires

Deep tap roots search for water

Thick bark protects from fire

Deep roots allow grasses to seek any available soil moisture

➤ Increased human use raises the risk of fire, which can permanently damage vegetation if it is too intense or too frequent.
➤ Small areas of erosion can quickly spread and lead to full-scale desertification.

In the future, growing human populations and climate changes are likely to increase the risk that the vulnerable drylands will be misused and degraded.

Food production, supply and desertification

The most obvious problem in desertified regions is shortage of water. Many of these regions are hot and sunny and could be productive if they had available water. The Nile valley is an example of an arid region that produces very high crop yields because the river provides water.

Irrigation is a human response to water shortages and unreliability. However, it can cause problems such as salinisation (Figure 11.17) and damage to **aquifers** (see chapter 2).

Salinisation

The salinisation of soil poses a serious threat because few plants are salt-tolerant. It is caused by a combination of natural and human processes. This can be seen, for example, in Australia:

➤ Irrigation raises the water table, and if groundwater contains dissolved salts, plants will tap into the contaminated water.
➤ Groundwater is often quite salty because of millions of years of accumulation of salts dissolved from rocks and, in coastal areas, salt blown in off the ocean.
➤ High evaporation rates in arid areas draw salty water to the surface by capillary action, whereupon it evaporates, leaving behind a salt crust.

Dryland salinity currently affects more than 5 million hectares of land, mostly in southern Australia, and causes damage totalling US$270 million each year. Drylands are fragile ecosystems, and attempts to increase food production using artificial inputs such as irrigation require very careful management if they are not to lead to long-term degradation.

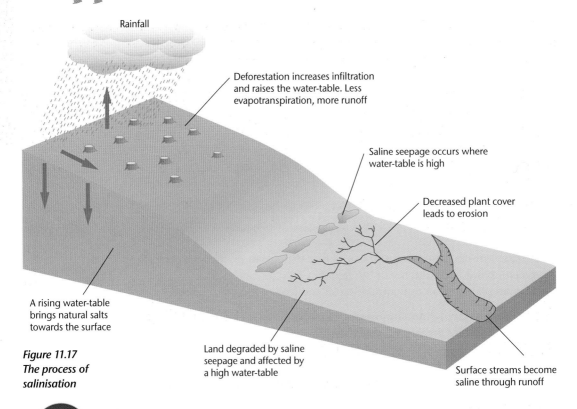

Rainfall

Deforestation increases infiltration and raises the water-table. Less evapotranspiration, more runoff

Saline seepage occurs where water-table is high

Decreased plant cover leads to erosion

A rising water-table brings natural salts towards the surface

Land degraded by saline seepage and affected by a high water-table

Surface streams become saline through runoff

Figure 11.17
The process of salinisation

Case study Lake Chad

In less than 30 years, Lake Chad, on the border of Chad, Niger, Nigeria and Cameroon has shrunk in extent from 25,000 km² to 2,000 km². Some 25 million people still live around the lake's basin, many now looking out on grounded boats and barren land which was once under water. The lake is less than 7 metres deep. Its size has always fluctuated throughout the seasons, but over the past four decades it has become progressively smaller (Figure 11.18).

Lake Chad is important as a source of water for irrigation and fish production. Many people depend on the lake, so its disappearance represents a human as well as an environmental disaster. The causes of the lake's disappearance are complex:

- Climate change (global warming) appears to be reducing rainfall in the area by 5–10 mm per year.
- A drier climate has reduced grassland vegetation around the lake, leading to overgrazing and the eventual collapse of the pastoral system. Displaced people have moved towards the lake as their only supply of water to grow food.
- The demand for lake water for irrigation has meant that demand exceeds supply.
- The damming of rivers feeding the lake for hydro-electric schemes has reduced discharge into the lake.
- Desertification of surrounding land has intensified climate change, as lower evapotranspiration enhances aridity and further reduces rainfall.
- Huge, top-down programmes such as the South Chad irrigation project in the 1970s diverted water from the lake to now failed irrigation schemes.

Lake Chad has rapidly entered a vicious circle in which reduced water availability has led to increased demands on the lake's supply, which in turn have reduced the lake water store.

This shows how important it is to understand the physical geography of dryland areas and to appreciate their vulnerability. Seemingly minor climate shifts combined with human mismanagement have led to the virtual disappearance of a critical water resource.

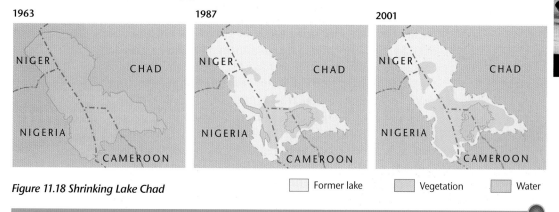

1963   1987   2001

NIGER   CHAD   NIGERIA   CAMEROON

Figure 11.18 Shrinking Lake Chad

☐ Former lake   ☐ Vegetation   ☐ Water

The role of management in food supply and security

How effective can management strategies be in sustaining life at the margins?

By the end of this section you should:
➤ *have investigated some techniques and strategies that have aimed to increase global food supply and security*
➤ *be aware that there are several alternative strategies*
➤ *be aware of the organisations involved in marginal food supply areas*
➤ *have evaluated the role of sustainable strategies*

Strategies to increase global food supply

Techniques to increase food supply have focused on farm technology. It would seem obvious that increasing food supply would make more food available to everyone. From the 1960s the **Green Revolution**, and since the 1990s the Gene Revolution (**GM**), have both attempted to increase food production, with varying degrees of success (see Chapter 6).

Simply producing more food does not necessarily mean it becomes more available to those who need it – poor people and those suffering from undernourishment. Much of the increase in global cereal production since 1990 has been absorbed by the cattle feed needed to support increasing consumption of meat in China and India. As calorie intake has risen in Asia, little progress has been made in feeding Africans effectively:
➤ Of Africa's 53 countries, 43 have low income and food shortages.
➤ Africa is the only continent where agricultural production per inhabitant has fallen over the past 25 years.

> Irrigated farming yields three times more produce than rain-based farming, yet Africa uses only 4% of its available water reserves, irrigating just 7% of its arable land. In sub-Saharan Africa, the figure is only 1.6%.

For some policy makers, the key to solving these problems is to pursue 'fair trade' in which growers are given a fair price for their crops by the companies that export them. In addition, farmers are paid a social premium on top of the price, and this extra money is invested in community development projects. The system of labelling products with the Fairtrade mark was first developed in the Netherlands in the late 1980s. For a product to display this mark it must meet international fair trade standards which have been agreed by participants in the Fairtrade scheme, including the growers themselves, traders, NGOs, academic institutions and labelling organisations. The international Fairtrade labelling scheme is run by the Fairtrade Labelling Organisation (FLO) and each country has its own organisation within this scheme. In the UK this is the Fairtrade Foundation.

Case study Kuapa Kokoo Fairtrade cooperative

In 1993 a group of farmers in Ghana formed a cooperative to sell their own cocoa. It was supported by SNV, a Dutch NGO, and the UK Department for International Development. The cooperative ensures farmers are paid for what they produce and are not cheated by middlemen. It includes:

■ *Kuapa Kokoo Farmers' Union*. This is a national body made up of 45,000 cocoa farmers who elect representatives.
■ *Kuapa Kokoo Farmers' Trust*. This is responsible for distributing money for community projects, generated from the Fairtrade income. Projects include providing clean water supplies and mobile health clinics, building schools and improving sanitation.

In 2008 Kuapa Kokoo sold 4,250 tonnes of cocoa to the Fairtrade market. This means that the farmers receive a guaranteed price. For example, even if the world price of cocoa falls to US$1,000 per tonne, the Fairtrade price remains at US$1,600 per tonne. The minimum Fairtrade price is $1,600 – if the world price goes higher farmers will receive the higher price, plus the social premium of $150 per tonne

Photograph 11.3 Kuapa Kokoo farmers spread cocoa beans out to dry

In 1998 Kuapa Kokoo came together with the NGO Twin, supported by The Body Shop, Christian Aid and Comic Relief, to found the Divine Chocolate company. As Kuapa Kokoo is part owner of Divine it not only gets a fair price for its cocoa but also has an influence on how the organisation is run and a share in the profits it has helped to create. Divine Fairtrade chocolate is sold in the UK, the Netherlands, Scandinavia and the USA.

Like all food production, fair trade will only work as a solution if it is sustainable in the long term. Income, and therefore food security, depends on maintaining soil health and water supply through good agricultural management. In Africa, a continent riven by war, conflict and corruption, political stability is equally important. Fair trade can contribute to this stability by reducing poverty.

Further research

Research the range of strategies and techniques available to solve the problems faced not just in Africa but elsewhere.

Useful links include:

www.fairtrade.org.uk/includes/documents/cm_docs/2008/m/mph.pdf (see especially the case study on Ethiopian coffee)

www.agra-alliance.org

www.ifpri.org/pubs/books/ar2002/ar02e.pdf

www.globalpolicy.org/socecon/trade/2005/0228freetrade.htm

The need for greater international efforts

The need to improve food security for the world's 800 million undernourished people is clear. Equally, better land, water and farming management strategies are needed to halt and reverse the degradation of marginal drylands. Who should take the lead in efforts to tackle these twin problems? There are many players involved, all with different roles (Table 11.4).

In recent years NGOs and international agencies, from the UN to the World Bank, have embarked upon a raft of policies to address food insecurity. Many of these support the aims of the Millennium Development Goals (see Chapter 5). Transnational corporations (TNCs) have invested in research to promote new methods of farming, especially GM crops.

Green Revolution for Africa

The Green Revolution that raised yields in Asia largely passed Africa by. Yields in Africa are typically 1 tonne of grain per hectare, around 30% of typical yields in the rest of the world. Some 95% of Africa's farming relies on direct rainfall, and up to 40% of yield is lost because of poor storage and the impact of vermin after harvesting.

Africa's food insecurity could be tackled by seeking a new Green Revolution for that continent. The Alliance for a Green Revolution for Africa (AGRA) is a partnership organisation which provides grants to scientists, NGOs and farming organisations to achieve this. AGRA is headed by former UN secretary-general Kofi Annan and funded by the Bill & Melinda Gates and Rockefeller Foundations. AGRA's research focuses not just on increasing yields but on other issues, including:

➤ developing seeds to cope with drought and localised pests
➤ improving soils by selectively using fertilisers and improving soil management
➤ improving access to water and irrigation
➤ improving access to markets

Player	Role in sustaining life on the margins	Examples
Individuals, e.g. farmers	Direct producers of food Communities harbour stores of valuable local knowledge, coping strategies and innovation Their cooperation is critical to ensuring environmental sustainability	Women's role in rice crop choice Kuapa Kokoo Fairtrade cooperative
Government	Provides funding for agricultural research and development Important in creating political and economic conditions to ensure stability of food supply Response during times of crisis	Large-scale rehabilitation projects, e.g. China's Great Green Wall Legal and conservation frameworks
Business	Research and investment into new farming methods and technologies Resource exploitation and trade in cash crops, fertilisers and farm machinery Profit motive	Development of GM crop varieties such as Golden Rice
NGOs	Community-level support for farmers in the developing world Education, training and skills providers Many promote social equity, e.g. female empowerment	Implementation of sustainable dryland farming in Sudan by Practical Action
Research organisations	Conducting scientific research on new crop varieties and farm systems Not-for-profit motives Education and skills training of farmers	The development of HYVs by the International Rice Research Institute AGRA's work on a 'Green Revolution' for Africa
International governmental organisations, e.g. UNEP, FAO	Implementation of global actions such as the MDGs Monitoring and research to identify problems and seek solutions Development assistance to the developing world	World Bank's Global Response Food Programme

Table 11.4 Life at the margins: players and roles

➤ developing local networks for agricultural education
➤ understanding and sharing the wealth of African farmer knowledge

This type of approach is only likely to succeed if the solutions AGRA implements are tailored to local needs and involve local decision making. A Green Revolution without the social polarisation and environmental damage that accompanied the Green Revolution in Asia might be judged a success. Even with the best of intentions, initiatives to increase food supply and security may fail if local sensibilities and knowledge are not taken into account, as the case study of women and HYVs in India shows.

GM controversies

High-tech strategies for increasing food security can be highly controversial. Golden Rice is a GM variety of rice (it is yellow in colour, rather than white) designed to be rich in vitamin A. According to the World Health Organization, vitamin A deficiency causes 250,000 to 500,000 children to go blind each year. A

Case study — Women and HYVs in India

Subsistence households in eastern India survive on a diet dominated by rain-fed irrigated rice. This rice-growing is not easy, but despite the long-term efforts to introduce HYVs, some farmers continue to grow traditional rice varieties. This may be due to lack of access to new seeds and to their cost.

It also results from a lack of understanding of how farmers choose rice varieties and the role of women in making that choice. In the past scientists researching farmers' views have tended to talk to men, despite the key role of women in rice production. For example, one variety, Pant-4, an HYV ideally suited to the local physical conditions of the region, has been rejected by the women who grow the rice because:

- it is difficult to thresh by hand
- it has poor cooking qualities
- it has a poor flavour

rice variety with extra vitamin A would seem to be a perfect solution to a common micronutrient deficiency (Figure 11.19).

Golden Rice is not yet grown for human consumption, despite being first 'invented' in 1999–2000. Why is this?

➤ Critics have argued that Golden Rice will not increase food production or supply other vitamins that are also deficient in people's diet.

➤ Environmental organisations such as Greenpeace are opposed to any GM crop, citing environmental and biodiversity concerns.

➤ TNCs such as Monsanto and Syngenta own patents on genes used in Golden Rice. These are 'humanitarian patents' that restrict growers to making a profit of no more than US$10,000 per year. If this is exceeded, royalties have to be paid.

➤ There are concerns that Golden Rice will not contain enough vitamin A to have an impact on deficiency.

Figure 11.19 Vitamin A deficiency around the world

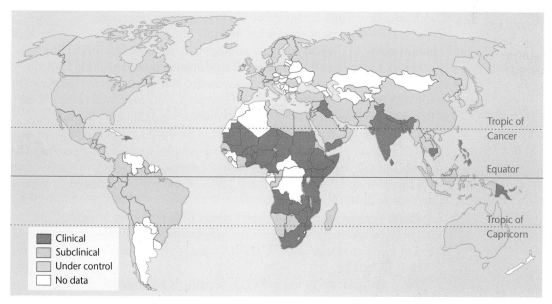

Legend:
- Clinical
- Subclinical
- Under control
- No data

Critics of the high-tech approach to agriculture argue that Golden Rice is a case of Western-style development which fails to understand the problems and needs of the developing world. Proponents of GM crops argue that the technology is young and yet to be fully developed.

Sustainable strategies in food supply

Overcoming deficiencies in food supply and security requires a range of different strategies. People sometimes need simply to be kept alive. In 2008 the World Bank launched its Global Food Response Programme (GFRP) in response to worldwide food price rises: US$1.2 billion was made available over 3 years. Early users of the money included Bangladesh, which received a US$130 million World Bank credit to allow its government to continue subsidising food so poor people could afford to buy it. World Bank research in 2008 found that:

➤ Bangladesh's poverty rate had risen by 3%, pushing 4 million people back into poverty.
➤ 8% of households had removed children from schools to get jobs and raise family incomes in order to cope with the crisis.
➤ Many poor households had cut their food intake.

Critics point out that the GFRP 'credit' is actually a loan, and as such increases Bangladesh's debt.

Combating desertification

Problems arising from land degradation affect around 500 million people in Africa. Up to two-thirds of Africa's productive land area is subject to degradation due to factors such as soil erosion, and the economic cost of this has been estimated at US$9 billion per year. Worst-case scenarios suggest that two-thirds of Africa's arable land could be non-productive by 2025 (UN 2004) as climate change, combined with poor land management, continues to degrade soil resources.

The UN convention to combat desertification (UNCCD) has encouraged governments to prepare national strategies to manage desertification. Some countries have adopted technocentric, top-down approaches. Since 1978 China has been attempting to hold back the expanding Gobi desert, which has grown by 400,000 km^2 since the 1950s, with a 4,500 km Great Green Wall (Figure 11.20). Desertification threatens more than 300 million rural Chinese people.

China's battle is backed up by legislation – the 2001 Law on Desert Prevention and Transformation and the 2002 Grassland Law both restrict grazing. The number of grazing animals on the Xilingol steppe increased from 2 million in 1980 to 18 million by 2000. By 2050, US$8 billion will be spent and 35 million hectares of trees will be planted.

Projects of this scale do not come without their problems, however:

➤ Local corruption means laws are not fully enforced and funds may be misused.
➤ Some estimates suggest that 75% of planted trees die because of drought and lack of aftercare.
➤ Relocation of farmers and herders is not strictly enforced.

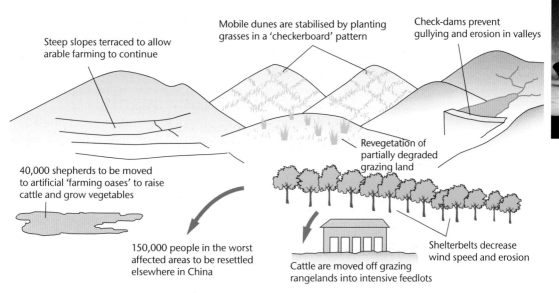

Steep slopes terraced to allow arable farming to continue

Mobile dunes are stabilised by planting grasses in a 'checkerboard' pattern

Check-dams prevent gullying and erosion in valleys

Revegetation of partially degraded grazing land

40,000 shepherds to be moved to artificial 'farming oases' to raise cattle and grow vegetables

150,000 people in the worst affected areas to be resettled elsewhere in China

Cattle are moved off grazing rangelands into intensive feedlots

Shelterbelts decrease wind speed and erosion

Figure 11.20 China's Great Green Wall

Intermediate technology

An alternative to large-scale schemes such as the Great Green Wall is the smaller-scale, bottom-up approach taken by NGOs such as Practical Action. Working in Sudan, Practical Action focused on tackling a number of problems simultaneously:

➤ soil erosion and low soil fertility
➤ low water availability and periodic drought
➤ food wastage leading to food shortages and malnutrition

Three intermediate technology solutions adopted in north Darfur are shown in Table 11.5. Together they have improved food supply and security at very low cost.

Table 11.5 Practical Action's intermediate technology in Sudan

	Zeers	Crescent terraces	Earth dams
What are they?	Locally made clay pots with a lidded inner pot. The gap between the pots is filled with damp insulating sand which cools the contents	Small earth/stone mounds about 50 cm high built along the contour lines of slopes. They are also known as bunds and 'magic stones'	Small dams taking about 3 months to build. Much of the work is done by women
How do they help?	They improve the storage life of vegetables such as tomatoes and carrots from 4 days to up to 20 days	They prevent rainwater runoff and slope erosion, and encourage infiltration, all increasing soil fertility and improving yields of crops such as millet	They store water from the short rainy season, providing year-round irrigation for crops. This reduces the risk of drought and increases yields
Are they sustainable?	Local resources Local labour Cheap to produce Less wastage means more food and improved health	Local labour No chemical or energy inputs needed to improve soil fertility Long-term solution to soil erosion	Small footprint in the landscape No imported resources Skills can be picked up quickly by local people and passed on to others They reduce vulnerability to drought hazard

Most labour is done by women, who are often members of women's development groups. As women take a leading role in improving the lives of the whole community, they are empowered, social equity is increased, and their role in community decision making is strengthened.

Small-scale NGO schemes such as those of Practical Action may be able to improve food security, but they do have limits:

➤ They are designed to meet basic needs, but not to increase incomes drastically.
➤ As they are small scale, they need to be repeated thousands of times in village after village.
➤ In areas such as Darfur, which has suffered years of conflict, continued political instability could easily reverse the small gains made.

Further research

The following sites are useful:

www.fairtraderesource.org/2008/08/14/feeling-the-heat-of-food-security
www.sustainablefood.com
www.aquamedia.org/Environment/Sustainability/default_en.asp
www.organicconsumers.org/organic/soul041604.cfm

Suggested fieldwork opportunities

Local fieldwork

➤ Investigating issues of sourcing of food, including local sourcing, for example for supermarkets, farm shops and catering establishments.
➤ Visits to contrasting local farms, including organic and LEAF schemes.
➤ Fair trade surveys within school or college, or in the wider public.

Residential and long-haul fieldwork

➤ African countries such as Morocco and The Gambia can provide the opportunity to study life at the margins and desertification.
➤ The American west could provide materials for the study of dryland management.

Review questions

1 Define 'food security' and examine what threatens it.
2 With the aid of examples, explain what 'life on the margins' really means.
3 Evaluate the different viewpoints on population pressure.
4 Distinguish between desertification and salinisation.
5 Why are drylands so vulnerable?
6 Assess the part that fair trade might play in increasing global food supply.

The world of cultural diversity

Culture is complex and has many meanings. People and culture are inseparable, as the former create the latter. Culture evolves over time and varies over space. This produces an intricate mosaic of distinct cultural landscapes. Nations vary in terms of their cultural diversity. Some are relatively homogeneous, while others embrace a mix of contrasting cultures. Cultural diversity is a marked characteristic of many cities. Such diversity can all too easily create conflict. Some groups are protective towards their culture, others see their culture as being in some way superior, while still others wish to impose their culture on the rest of society.

Defining culture and identifying its value

What is the nature and value of culture in terms of people and places?

By the end of this section you should:
➤ *have learnt the meaning of 'culture'*
➤ *be aware of the range of human cultures and cultural landscapes*
➤ *understand that some cultures and landscapes are more vulnerable than others*
➤ *have examined the value placed on cultural diversity by different players*

Defining culture

Culture is a system of shared meaning. Such systems are based on religion, ethnicity, language and tradition. Culture is collective – it is shared by a group of people and it influences their 'way of life' (Figure 12.1). Cultural values provide boundaries for behaviour. These can be as simple as acceptable ways to dress or to say hello, but may also include complex rules on relationships and marriage. Culture is dynamic:
➤ it is passed on from generation to generation
➤ it evolves over time
➤ it is open to external influences, for example from another culture

Figure 12.1 Components of culture

The word 'culture' has other meanings. It can refer to art and music. A liking for certain types of art and music may make you 'cultured'. This suggests some people believe certain cultural behaviours and attitudes are better than others. We commonly use the word to describe 'growing' activities, as in 'agriculture'. The idea that culture itself grows and develops is important because 'cultural development' can mean growth and improvement, often towards some cultural ideal.

Assimilation

In the UK there are cultural values held by the majority of people. When other cultural groups come to the UK, they are exposed to this 'core' culture and in most cases adapt to it. Recently arrived migrants may have little understanding of the core culture (Figure 12.2) and find UK life baffling and 'foreign'. Over time, immigrant groups are assimilated and assume many of the core cultural values and behaviours. However, even second and third generation immigrants hold on to some aspects of their own culture, for example their religion and traditional foods.

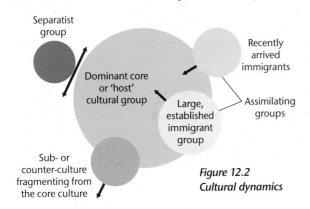

Figure 12.2
Cultural dynamics

Because culture is dynamic, cultural assimilation works both ways. The core culture assumes some aspects of immigrant culture – the British love of curry demonstrates this cross-cultural exchange.

Rejection

Groups may reject the values and beliefs of the core culture. Such groups fall into two categories:

➤ separatists, who often choose to live in their own enclaves and minimise contact with others
➤ sub-cultures which seek to challenge or undermine the core culture

The Amish in the USA are an example of separatists, as are British expatriate villa enclaves in Spain. Punk rock and even direct action environmentalists are examples of sub-cultures. Sub-cultures are often initially seen as shocking and dangerous, but watered-down versions of their 'culture' may eventually enter the mainstream.

Cultural groups express themselves by constructing a built environment which reflects their values, beliefs and traditions. This is a cultural landscape. It transforms cultural ideas in the mind into distinct geographical spaces. These cultural spaces are all around us:

➤ Detached suburban housing with its gardens and garages reflects the cultural importance of home ownership, the nuclear family and visible economic wealth.
➤ Urban subways and underpasses may be 'claimed' by people using the tag symbols of the graffiti sub-culture.
➤ Mosques, Hindu temples, restaurants, shops and festivals in cities ensure ethnic minority spaces reflect the culture of their inhabitants.

Further research

www.everyculture.com – an online encyclopedia of cultures.

www.britishmuseum.org/explore/world_cultures.aspx – the British Museum world cultures website allows you to explore ancient cultures.

Cultural landscapes

The importance of place, in both the development and growth of cultural values and the reinforcement of those values, is a significant part of our lives. It leads to wide variations in values, beliefs and symbols. Alongside this variation is a diversity of cultural landscapes. Landscapes can be:

➤ *historic* – the remains of an ancient culture's landscapes

➤ *modern* – a 'new' landscape reflecting the culture of today

➤ *mixed* – a fusion of ancient and modern

Photograph 12.1 Cardiff's Brewery Quarter

Most cultural landscapes today are complex, mixed and multi-layered, with traces of past cultures intermingled with those of today. Photograph 12.1 shows this layering in the Brewery Quarter of Cardiff. This is a landscape of an Industrial Revolution brewery transformed after deindustrialisation into a 'trendy' bar and café location by regeneration and gentrification.

Reading landscapes

Landscapes can be 'read' – we can deduce their meaning by interpreting the symbols used to create them. These symbols might include:

➤ the placement of monuments and religious structures

➤ the relationships between buildings

➤ the architecture, symbols and art of buildings

➤ the relationships between natural features (rivers, lakes, mountains) and the human built environment

Historic landscapes have a particular significance. They are often preserved and visited. The number of preserved sites is remarkable: in England alone there are:

➤ 372,000 listed buildings

➤ 19,500 scheduled ancient monuments (Photograph 12.2)

➤ 1,560 registered historic parks and gardens

➤ 43 registered historic battlefields

This might suggest that historical geography and past cultural landscapes are seen as an integral part of modern UK culture. Table 12.1 illustrates the different types of historic landscape found in Wiltshire.

Unit 4 *Geographical research*

*Photograph 12.2
Stonehenge:
Britain's best-
known
ethnographic
landscape*

Ingram

Table 12.1 Types of historic cultural landscape in Wiltshire

Type of cultural landscape	Description	Cultural signals and modern transformations
Historic designed landscapes	Landscapes that were consciously designed, e.g. country houses and parks or 'model' towns	Country houses such as Longleat were built as symbols of wealth and power. Longleat's park, designed by 'Capability' Brown in the eighteenth century, reflected an idealised, romantic view of what an English landscape should look like. Today Longleat receives 700,000 visitors a year and cashes in on the heritage industry. Its landscaped park has been transformed into the renowned Safari Park
Historical landscapes and sites	Landscapes that evolved to reflect economic and social conditions, e.g. a 'village' community or an industrial landscape	The village of Lacock has medieval roots and its wealth originally derived from the woollen industry. Largely untouched by the Industrial Revolution, it retained its medieval character. Lacock's classic English village landscapes and prettiness attract visitors but also numerous film crews seeking to recreate landscapes, especially for costume dramas. The village was given to the National Trust in 1944
Ethnographic landscapes	A landscape with special religious or social significance to a group of people	Stonehenge in Wiltshire is probably Britain's best known ethno-graphic landscape. The huge megalithic construction and earthworks show it had special significance to Neolithic and Bronze Age people, although its exact function and meaning are debated. In modern times the site has been appropriated by druids and neo-pagans, especially at the summer solstice

The cultural landscapes in Table 12.1 are all built landscapes. However, landscapes can have cultural significance simply by being there. The landscape of the American West, with its mountains, deserts, vast spaces and skies, is part of American shared culture (Photograph 12.3).

The West represents pioneering spirit, new lands, opportunity and the American Dream. In reality, of course, it is a harsh landscape that many pioneers failed to conquer – for every migrant who got to California there were others who gave up or died on the way. Hollywood movies and books such as John Steinbeck's *The Grapes of Wrath* have ensured that the landscape of the West has a special cultural significance.

Ethnoscapes	Created ethnic landscapes such as London's Chinatown or rows of British pubs on the Spanish Costas
Financescapes	Gleaming landscapes of corporate tower blocks and offices such as Canary Wharf in London and the Pudong financial district in Shanghai
Technoscapes	Centres of high-tech industry, often with high-tech architecture to match, such as Cambridge Science Park or Grenoble, France
Commodityscapes	Sites of consumption, such as Knightsbridge in London or the Mall of the Emirates in Dubai

Table 12.2 Types of cultural landscape

Globalisation

It is widely recognised that **globalisation** has affected our view of the importance of traditional cultural landscapes. Equally, it is clear that cultural landscapes have been affected by globalisation. This is especially true in world cities where new urban landscapes have emerged. These reflect the **globalisation of culture**. They cut across national and cultural boundaries (Table 12.2).

The cultural ideas of the USA dominate many of these global landscapes, especially 'mediascapes'. American music, movies, television, computer games and software are so dominant and sought after that they have 'gone global'. They are visible almost everywhere. They influence the tastes, lives and aspirations of virtually every nation.

Further research

Research how different groups of people can vary in their views about such landscapes (Table 12.1) and value them differently.

www.intcul.tohoku.ac.jp/~holden/MediatedSociety/Readings/2003_04/Appadurai. html

Vulnerable cultures and landscapes

Cultural landscapes are threatened by changing values and attitudes. Tibet is an example of a culture under threat. Many argue that since invading it in 1950, China has set about dismantling Tibetan culture to quell a troublesome region.

➤ The Chinese language (Mandarin) is used in primary schools.
➤ Primary school enrolment stands at only 67%.
➤ There is low enrolment (12.5%) among secondary school age children.
➤ A declining proportion of Tibetans enter higher education.
➤ There is around 60% illiteracy and semi-illiteracy.

Education policies imposed by Beijing are in danger of turning Tibetans into a poorly educated underclass, with the administrative and skilled jobs taken by the Chinese. The thorn in the Chinese side is the exiled Tibetan leader, the Dalai Lama, who works to keep the plight of the Tibetans in the public eye. The Chinese–Tibetan culture clash erupted into violence in the runup to the 2008 Beijing Olympics.

Case study Clearing up the cultural landscape of Beijing

In Beijing the urban landscape is changing rapidly. For centuries the *hutongs* (narrow lanes) were the basis of urban building in Beijing, providing a framework for vibrant local communities as knife sharpeners, coal merchants and fruit sellers plied their wares. They evolved along the lanes leading to and from community wells (Photograph 12.4).

By the 1980s, when China began opening up, there were 3,679 such *hutongs* in Beijing, but the fast pace of development has now destroyed many of them. They have been cleared to make way for roads and gleaming office blocks. Some of the more recent demolition was linked to projects for the 2008 Olympic Games and the desire of the Chinese

Photograph 12.4 A nineteenth century photograph (hand coloured) of a Beijing **hutong**

leadership to make Beijing a world city, complete with world-scale financescapes and a global mediascape Olympic park. Beijing is becoming increasingly like other cities around the world, with a 'globalised' structure dominated by office space and modern accommodation.

Tourism

For many isolated and poorly connected regions and countries, tourism provides a tempting route to economic development. However, it challenges cultural values and landscapes. Tourism can be an economic lifeline, but even in the UK it has meant huge cultural upheaval for rural communities. As farming has declined, a post-productive landscape of campsites, B&Bs and farm shops has emerged in its place. Rural communities have seen farming reduced from a key industry to a minority pursuit in a generation (Photograph 12.5). At the same time socioeconomic change has brought mass counter-urbanisation to accessible parts of the countryside. Urban dwellers have moved out to rural areas, pitching rural and urban values against each other.

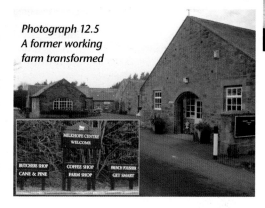

Photograph 12.5
A former working farm transformed

Case study   Bhutan: trouble in paradise

There are many case studies of the negative impacts of tourism. At first sight, it would appear that the remote and beautiful mountain kingdom of Bhutan has learnt from those mistakes. Squeezed between China and India, this very new democracy is trying to limit the impact of tourism, although tourism is the largest earner of foreign currency (Figure 12.3).

According to the national tourism board:

> Tourism in Bhutan is seen not only as a revenue and employment generator but also as a means of strengthening the country's cultural and natural heritage. Therefore, from the time that Bhutan was opened for tourism in the mid-1970s we have followed a cautious path of tourism development.

Figure 12.3
Bhutan's tourism earnings, 1995–2005

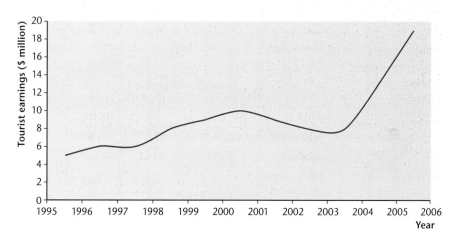

This sales pitch is both sustainable and sensitive, and a number of strategies have been adopted by the government to ensure that what the board calls the country's 'unique culture and pristine environment' is not eroded by tourism. For example:

■ Tours have to be booked through a Bhutanese tour operator and led by a trained Bhutanese guide.
■ The number of tourist visas issued each year is strictly limited.
■ Not all parts of the country, nor all its temples and monasteries, are open to tourists.

The image of Bhutan as an expensive destination adds to its exclusivity and appeals to a certain group of people, usually older and wealthier than the average international tourist. The revenue from tourism is used for improving education and health programmes. This knowledge appeals to tourists who feel that they have contributed to the social and economic development of the country.

There is a darker side to Bhutan which casts doubt upon claims that it is seeking to preserve its 'unique culture'. Bhutan is made up of two major ethnic groups, the majority Drukpa people and the minority Nepalese. The traditions and culture sold to tourists are those of the Buddhist Drukpa majority, who until recently were obliged to wear national costume. The Nepalese resent this cultural dominance and the lack of any political representation. Violence erupted in the early 1990s and tens of thousands of Nepali-speakers fled to refugee camps in Nepal. Today nearly 100,000 refugees live in UN camps in Nepal. The carefully preserved culture loved by tourists has a human cost.

Protection and players

One of UNESCO's aims is 'the preservation and promotion of the common heritage of humanity'. This raises interesting questions about:
➤ which cultures and cultural landscapes should be preserved
➤ who should decide how and where cultures are to be preserved and promoted

UNESCO World Heritage sites represent that organisation's view of the world's 'best' cultural sites and landscapes. Some, such as Machu Picchu in Peru, are ancient sites, while others are natural wonders, such as Australia's Great Barrier Reef. Others are modern developments, such as Brasilia.

The distribution of sites (Table 12.3) is interesting. The majority are in Europe and North America. Asia, the world's most populous region, only manages 21% of the sites. The site list is skewed towards the developed world because of economics. The richer countries have the money to finance preservation, but there is also the global dominance of 'Western' culture. Preserving the past may be given a greater priority in some cultures than in others (Table 12.4).

Table 12.3 UNESCO World Heritage sites, 2008

	Natural sites	Cultural and mixed sites	Total	% of all World Heritage sites	% of world population in that region
Africa	33	43	76	9	13
Arab world	4	61	65	7	3
Asia-Pacific	48	134	182	21	60
Europe and North America	54	381	435	50	16
Latin America and Caribbean	35	85	120	14	8

Table 12.4 Three different attitudes to cultural landscapes

Types of cultural landscape	Explanation	Example
Landscape as a commodity	Landscapes, whether real or imagined, can be 'sold' to the public as worthy destinations for spending time and money	Many 'countries' in the UK (e.g. Herriott country, Thomas Hardy country) are real landscapes which have been popularised by writers or television programmes and are visited because of this
Landscape as a national symbol	Landscapes can be used to promote a particular identity and culture, and even to reinforce political messages	The Highlands of Scotland are used as a symbol of Scottish nationalism and identity, and feature heavily in 'Visit Scotland' television adverts. The thistle is used as a universal symbol of Scotland, even by the Scottish National Party
Landscape as the enemy	Landscapes can be seen as a danger, if they are culturally symbolic	The Buddhas of Bamyan were two huge fourth-century sandstone Buddhist statues in Afghanistan. In 2001 the Islamic Taliban destroyed them with dynamite

Case study: The Basque country: defined by language

The Basque country of southwest France and northern Spain is defined by its mountainous and coastal landscape, together with its distinctive architecture, sports, festivals and language (Euskara).

The Basque part of Spain is an autonomous region (Euskadi, Figure 12.4). Of the 2,800,000 Basques, some 632,000 are Basque language speakers and about 566,000 live in Euskadi, with the rest in the French Basque area. Less than 25% of the population is fluent in the cultural language Euskara, although after centuries of repression this figure is quite impressive.

Basque nationalism is a relatively new phenomenon: its founder was Sabino Arana i Goiri (1865–1903). More recently, the call for Basque independence has been promoted by public protests and acts of terrorism by the separatist organisation Euskadi Ta Azkatasuna (Eta).

Today Basque culture is an important part of the region's attraction to tourists and is marketed

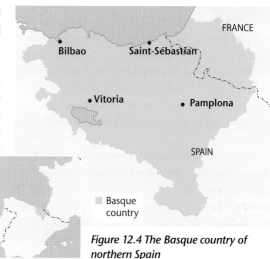

Figure 12.4 The Basque country of northern Spain

strongly. Basque flags fly on both sides of the border and the traditional farmhouses reflect the national colours. Many incomers adopt and modify these cultural elements with enthusiasm.

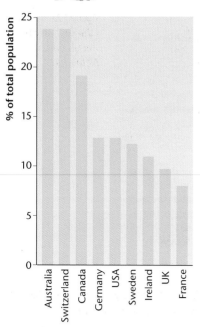

Figure 12.5 Foreign-born citizens in selected countries, 2005

The geography of culture

How and why does culture vary spatially?

By the end of this section you should:
➤ *realise that some countries are more culturally homogeneous than others*
➤ *understand that cultural diversity is greatest in cities*
➤ *be aware that there are conflicting views about the value of cultural diversity*
➤ *have examined the mechanisms of cultural imperialism*

Diversity and homogeneity

Migration creates ethnic and cultural mixing. Few countries remain untouched by this mixing (Figure 12.5). Japan is said to be one of the most uniform (homogeneous) cultures of all. It is struggling to maintain international competitiveness because of its rapidly ageing population, a problem 'solved' in other developed countries by encouraging in-migration (see case study).

 Case study **Japan: isolation and cultural identity**

In Japan fertility rates are low and the population is rapidly ageing. In the past Japan met its labour requirements by mechanising and rationalising production. It made greater use of previously untapped female and elderly workers. As a result, it created a highly efficient and competitive industrial system.

By the mid-1980s Japan gave in to the pressures of global migration. Because of demographic changes and the refusal of increasingly affluent Japanese to perform '3D' (dirty, dangerous and difficult) jobs, the workforce could not meet the rising demand for unskilled labour. As a result, the country began to accept migrant workers from Pacific rim developing countries.

The Japanese describe their culture as being founded on a homogeneous, united and stable society. To some extent, no matter how nice you are, or how good your Japanese becomes, you will always be treated as an outsider. In fact, the Japanese

refer to all foreigners as *gaijin* (outsiders). Foreigners are warmly welcomed, provided they do not stay. This is deeply embedded in the current form of nationalism known as *Nihonjinron*.

Figure 12.6 shows that in the UK and Netherlands cultural diversity is much greater than in Japan. There are many reasons for this, including:
■ the colonial past of the UK and the Netherlands
■ the host population's attitude to newcomers and immigrants
■ government policies on immigration, border control and citizenship
■ the longstanding maritime and trading history of the UK and the Netherlands

The strength of *Nihonjinron* is being tested in a Japan which may have reached critical mass in terms of growing numbers of international migrant settlers. In-migrants find it hard to tolerate a culture of ethnic homogeneity that excludes other ethnic groups from

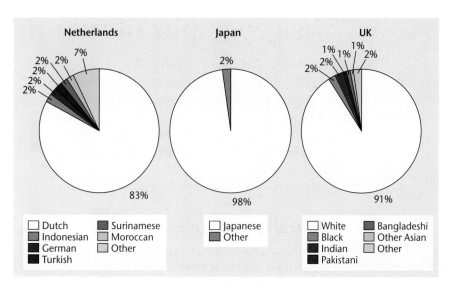

Figure 12.6
Ethnicity: Japan, the UK and the Netherlands

Netherlands

- 83%
- 7%
- 2%
- 2%
- 2%
- 2%
- 2%

Legend:
- Dutch
- Indonesian
- German
- Turkish
- Surinamese
- Moroccan
- Other

Japan

- 98%
- 2%

Legend:
- Japanese
- Other

UK

- 91%
- 2%
- 2%
- 1%
- 1%
- 1%
- 2%

Legend:
- White
- Black
- Indian
- Pakistani
- Bangladeshi
- Other Asian
- Other

citizenship. There are other issues too, including the absence of a women's perspective in the dominant *Nihonjinron*. This may stimulate in-migrants to challenge this aspect of Japanese identity.

Further research

The UK's cultural landscape has become increasingly diverse. Research can focus on how immigrant groups have asserted their differences and how the issue of assimilation fits uneasily with that of cultural diversity.

A good source of documents for research is: **www.jrf.org.uk/knowledge/findings/housing/1950.asp**

Cultural diversity in cities

Successful cities, particularly world cities, attract immigrants because of the number and variety of jobs they offer. This increases cultural diversity, which in turn can be attractive to employers seeking new ideas and skills. Remote rural areas tend to be unattractive to migrants. Such areas are also more likely to suffer out-migration, often of young and ambitious people.

Jane Buekett

Photograph 12.6
New York is a highly diverse city

London and New York are among the most diverse cities in the world (Photograph 12.6). Tokyo is different, for reasons outlined in the case study on Japan. Just over one-third of London's working-age population was born outside the UK. There are many reasons for this:

➤ *Transport*. Stansted, Gatwick and Heathrow international airports, international rail services.

Figure 12.7 Ethnic diversity: London Borough of Brent, 2005

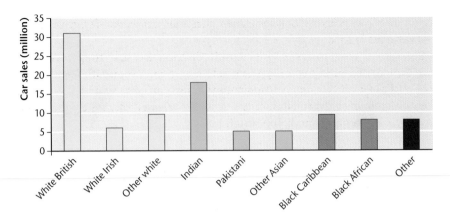

➤ *Prestige*. London is a global financial centre, attracting skilled migrants and international companies.
➤ *Language*. Many immigrants already have some English, as it is an international language.
➤ *Ties*. Former colonial links, family and friendship ties.
➤ *Reputation*. London is seen as a relatively open, tolerant city and society.
➤ *Politics*. Links with the EU and reasonably open borders.

London might be described as a global gateway or hub, a city with a huge cross-section of the world's population living, working and passing through. The London Borough of Brent illustrates this diversity (Figure 12.7).

Inner areas of the city, particularly those close to the old docks, have long been centres of immigration. Many early migrants have made good and moved out to the suburbs. They have been replaced by immigrants from countries such as Bangladesh (Figure 12.8). Ethnic diversity is usually seen as a sign of success in a city. The very fact that Bangladeshi immigrants and other cultural groups are not

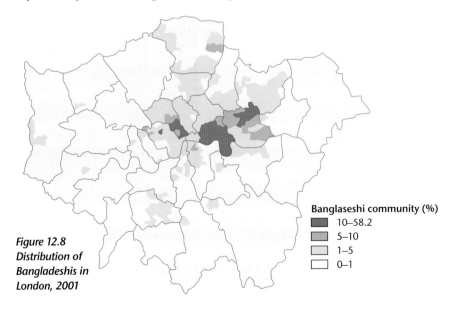

Banglaseshi community (%)
■ 10–58.2
■ 5–10
□ 1–5
□ 0–1

Figure 12.8 Distribution of Bangladeshis in London, 2001

evenly distributed across London raises questions about the degree to which cultures actually mix.

Rural areas tend to have lower ethnic diversity because they have fewer employment opportunities and greater isolation. Rural communities may be less open to different cultures, and immigrants may feel conspicuous and out of place. There is a tendency for immigrant groups to be less well off and rural living is costly, with few employment opportunities.

Further research

Cultural diversity is most obvious in cities, especially large cities. Material on diversity in European cities can be found at:

www.london.gov.uk/mayor/economy/docs/london_divided_summary.pdf
www.guardian.co.uk/graphic/0,5812,1395103,00.html
www.nyidanmark.dk/bibliotek/publikationer/rapporter/uk/cultural_diversity/index.htm

This material can be used to show that larger cities have greater ethnic diversity than smaller cities, and that coastal and gateway cities have greater diversity than inland cities.

Attitudes towards cultural diversity

Not all cultural and political groups agree that cultural diversity is positive. Tolerance of 'others' is not universal. In the UK, immigration and increasing diversity have generally been accepted. However, a tipping point may be reached when the scale of immigration becomes a general concern. Recent immigration changes might suggest this point has been approached in the UK:

➤ A tougher government line has been taken on asylum seekers since 2001.
➤ In 2008 a new points-based system for immigrants was introduced to further control immigration.

There are few countries in the world with truly open borders, and most countries seek to manage cultural change. Some, like the UK and USA, attempt to assimilate diverse cultures by making immigrants take citizenship tests.

Equality

Cultural diversity can be promoted by ensuring equality between different cultures. This can be done through the legal system, but there is no guarantee people's attitudes will follow the law. Diversity and tolerance can also be promoted through education and the workplace. Some examples of UK measures are:

➤ the 1976 Race Relations Act, which created the Commission for Racial Equality and made discrimination on the grounds of race illegal
➤ the 1998 Human Rights Act
➤ the inclusion of citizenship and identity and cultural diversity in the school curriculum
➤ the Equality and Human Rights Commission, which advises and campaigns on equality and diversity issues

Figure 12.9 World Heritage sites in Israel

Other countries

Diversity can be perceived as a threat. Spain under the fascist dictator Franco banned the use of the Catalan, Basque and Galego languages. Regionalism was discouraged in favour of centralised power and the Castilian language. Regional languages have tended to flourish in more recent times as diversity has been promoted. Revivals of Breton, Welsh, Gaelic and Catalan have occurred in the last few decades in Europe.

Israel joined the UNESCO World Heritage convention in 1999. It currently has six World Heritage sites and has requested that 20 more be considered (Figure 12.9). This includes east Jerusalem, which will not be considered until the Israel–Palestine conflict has been settled. Israel's interest in preserving heritage sites could be seen as having a political motive, as UNESCO status confers global importance on cultural symbols.

A resolution of the Palestinian claim to an independent state has been made more complex by Israel's settlement policy. Since the Six-Day War of 1967, when Israel occupied Palestinian Gaza and the West Bank, around 260,000 Israelis have settled in the West Bank. Palestinians argue the settlement is an illegal occupation of their land.

Further research

Tibet, which was the centre of global attention before and during the 2008 Olympics, provides an interesting lesson in how cultural landscapes can be viewed very differently by different groups:

www.international.ucla.edu/article.asp?parentid=2732
http://mondediplo.com/2008/05/09tibet

Cultural imperialism

Cultural imperialism means the imposition of one culture on another. The term appeared after the Second World War as the colonial system broke down and new mechanisms of power emerged. The global export of the 'Western' culture of Europe and North America is referred to as 'westernisation', 'americanisation' or 'McDonaldisation'. The characteristics of Western culture include:

➤ an emphasis on consumerism and consumption
➤ a specific view of what democracy is
➤ a reliance on and belief in technology

Those promoting Western culture believe it to be superior to other cultures, and that adopting it represents progress. Western culture is supported by global media corporations (e.g. BBC, CNN), television from the USA, Hollywood films and global brands such as Coca-Cola and McDonald's (Figure 12.10). Supporters of the Western cultural model would speak of modernisation or development rather than cultural imperialism.

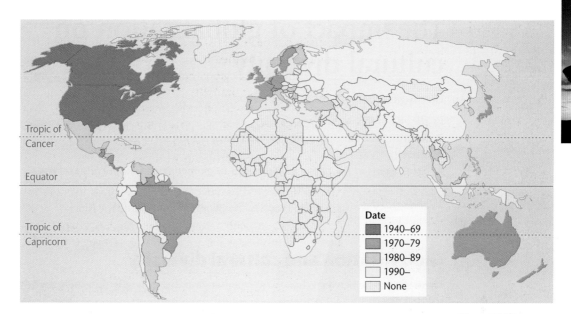

Figure 12.10
Global spread of
McDonald's since
1940

Opposition

There are many groups of people who do not view Western culture as superior and are concerned by cultural globalisation. In the 1960s, hippy counter-culture rejected Western middle-class values and consumerism and set out to create a culture based on community living, sexual liberation and alternative music. Hippies were usually anti-war (in particular opposed to the Vietnam War) and many were vegetarian and eco-aware — radical ideas in the late 1960s but now accepted as mainstream.

Other groups are more vocal, and even violent, in their rejection of Western culture. The anti-globalisation movement focuses on the perceived exploitative nature of capitalism, the unfairness of free trade and the power of TNCs. The meetings and summits of global organisations such as the WTO, IMF and G8 have become the focus for anti-globalisation protests. Violent clashes erupted at the G8 meeting in Genoa, Italy, in 2001 and again at the Gleneagles G8 summit in 2005.

It is possible for whole nations to be sceptical about the merits of a global culture. France is protective of its national identity, traditions, language and art. In 1993 it negotiated the *exception culturelle* as part of a world trade agreement. In effect this allows France to support its own French-language film industry and limit the number of US films imported into France. Only about 65% of films shown in France originate in the USA, compared to at least 90% in the UK.

Further research

You might examine the mechanisms of this process, which has become stereotyped as 'McDonaldisation', and the counter-cultural movements that it has given rise to. See:

www.thehumanist.org/humanist/articles/essay3mayjune04.pdf
www.wsu.edu/~amerstu/pop/cultimp.html

The impact of globalisation on cultural diversity

How is globalisation impacting on culture?

By the end of this section you should:
- ➤ *be aware that there are different views about the impact of globalisation on cultural diversity*
- ➤ *have examined the role of global media in promoting dominant cultural values*
- ➤ *have investigated the variety of localised forms of culture*
- ➤ *understand that there is a divergence of opinion about the impact of global consumerism*

Globalisation and cultural diversity

There is a debate between those who feel that **globalisation** will ultimately destroy cultural diversity and those who are sceptical about its power to do so (Table 12.5).

Table 12.5 Contrasting views of cultural globalisation

Group	Hyperglobalisers	Transformationalists	Sceptics
View	Globalisation will reduce the relevance and power of countries as the world becomes ever more integrated. This will reduce cultural diversity	Globalisation is a process that constantly forces countries and governments to adapt and change in uncomfortable ways	Globalisation is not really global: it simply maintains existing global economic power centres (Europe, North America and Japan) and excludes developing regions such as Africa
Evidence?	Increasing power of TNCs The rise of a global consumer culture and loss of local and national identity	Formation of the EU to maintain Europe's power USA and UK reaction to the 2008 global financial crisis	85% of world trade is still between developed countries Increasing divide between rich and poor

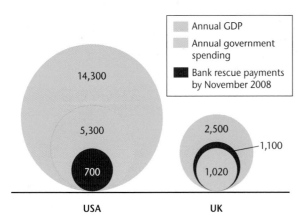

Figure 12.11 The credit crunch – a transformationalist's moment

Hyperglobalisers are pessimistic about the future of culture. They foresee a world where everyone wears NY Yankee baseball caps and drinks Coca-Cola. The sceptics see globalisation as nothing new. It continues to funnel wealth towards those who are already rich. The transformationalist middle ground sees globalisation as a difficult force that challenges nations and forces them to react in new ways. The 2008 global financial crisis (the 'credit crunch') can be used to illustrate this (Figure 12.11).

Starting in September 2008, the UK, US and European governments were forced to rescue their banking systems in various ways:

- nationalisation of some banks and other financial institutions, such as Northern Rock (UK) and Freddie Mac (USA)
- government bailouts to keep banks afloat, such as RBS in the UK
- government-sponsored sales of a collapsing bank to a stronger one, such as Merrill Lynch (USA), sold to Bank of America, and Bradford and Bingley (UK), taken over by Santander

This reversed decades of policy in which many Western governments have adhered to the maxim that 'the market knows best'. It has proved a severe test for the Western culture of globalised capitalism.

Global media corporations

Media corporations play a significant role in spreading cultural values. They may point out that people are not forced to consume their television programmes, films and magazines, but against this argument is the view that people lack alternative sources for news and entertainment. Big global media corporations are so dominant that there is little competition (Figure 12.12).

Mergers and takeovers have left much of the global media in the hands of a few companies. News Corporation, for example, owns the publisher HarperCollins, over a dozen newspapers in Australia, the *Sun* and *The Times* in the UK, the *New York Post* and the *Wall Street Journal*, Fox film and television, parts of ITV and Sky, and much more. Critics argue that media conglomerates have stifled diversity by transmitting the same product

Table 12.6 The top ten global languages

Language	% of world speakers
Mandarin	16
English	8
Spanish	5
Arabic	4
Hindi	3
Portuguese	3
Bengali	3
Russian	3
Japanese	2
French	2
Total	49

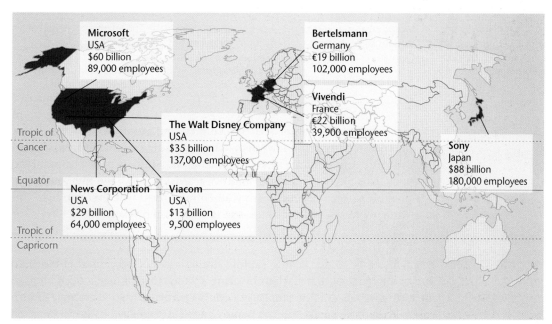

Figure 12.12 Global media and entertainment TNCs

worldwide. The dominance of Western media corporations may be one reason why languages are under threat worldwide. It is estimated that just 10% of the 6,800 languages spoken today will survive at the current rate of decline. Of these 6,800 languages,

➤ 1,700 (27%) are under threat
➤ 357 have fewer than 50 speakers each
➤ 83% are restricted to single countries

Localised culture

Despite the powerful forces of globalisation, or perhaps because of them, new cultural forms and even new languages have emerged – a process described by some as 'the periphery talks back'. This suggests that wherever cultural traditions mix and interconnect, they create new practices and worldviews. Perhaps the idea that globalisation will produce one global culture is too simple (Table 12.7).

In the well-known *Gastarbeiter* (guest worker) generation of Germany, new communities such as Latinos or Afro-Germans have emerged. There are an estimated 400,000 Germans with mixed black and white ancestry, who identify themselves as Afro-Germans. Residents born in Latin America marry, work and mix with Germans. Germans change their lifestyle as a consequence: they get inspired by writer Eduardo Galliano, learn salsa dancing and study Spanish. The Latino community has, as yet, very little political impact, but it is changing German society in a fundamental way.

Table 12.7 Possible cultural outcomes of an interconnected world

Westernisation	Global mixing	Cultural layers	Glocalisation
One global culture	Hybrid cultures	Global + national + local	Globalised local cultures
Globalisation destroys local cultures and leads to increased cultural homogeneity	Mixing creates new hybrid cultures such as Afro-Germans or British Bhangra music	A people share a global cultural worldview but maintain their national and local cultural identities (three cultural layers)	The adaptation of global products to suit local markets, and the use of technologies such as the internet to maintain long-distance cultural contacts

Modern technology can be seen as a cultural opportunity as well as a threat. The internet in particular allows people from a culture who are spread around the world to communicate over long distances. Sites such as MySpace and Facebook, plus blogs and the availability of television, news and film, mean that it is possible to keep in touch with your cultural roots wherever you live. This may work to preserve at least some aspects of cultural diversity.

Further research

Research can be undertaken to explore similar cases of hybridised or creolised music, film and social behaviour by using a wide range of media from blogs to interactive web media. The film *Paper Dolls* is a particularly good example of such cultural complexity and, closer to home *East is East* and *Bend it like Beckham* are well known.

The impact of global consumerist culture

Increasing wealth and globalisation might be expected to make people happier. More than ever, we can choose where to go on holiday and from a seemingly endless range of food, possessions, music and arts. Some researchers have begun to question the benefits of consumerism. Figure 12.13 shows that increasing choice is initially positive – it makes people happier. However, too much choice increases negative emotions. This idea lay behind a 2006 *Daily Mail* headline – 'Do we really need 38 types of milk?' – making the point that choice in the supermarket aisle may lead to irritation and confusion.

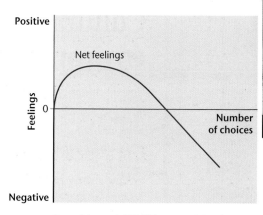

Source: Schwartz, B. (2004) 'The tyranny of choice', *Scientific American*

Figure 12.13 Choice and emotion

Too much choice irritating shoppers is not really a big issue, but a consumer society can create more fundamental cultural changes. Since 1990, China has increasingly embraced Western consumer culture (Table 12.8).

The Chinese landscape has been a victim of globalisation. The Communist Party has taken the view that parts of the landscape have to be sacrificed to fuel the consumerist boom. The Three Gorges dam has flooded iconic Chinese landscapes, as well as more than 1,300 archaeological sites and key cultural features such as the hanging coffins in Qutang gorge.

Some cultures resist the consumerist society, perhaps sensing that it would threaten key aspects of their culture. In 2004, Starbucks opened its first café in France. Starbucks is competing with more than 55,000 traditional, locally owned cafés. So far, this particular standard-bearer of US capitalism has been unsuccessful. It has opened around 40 outlets in France compared to over 600 in the UK, and three directors have come and gone as Starbucks France has struggled to make a profit. It seems the French prefer their café landscape local and home-grown.

Table 12.8 The outcomes of economic growth and consumerism in China

Positive impacts of cultural change	Negative impacts of cultural change
200 million fewer people in poverty compared to 1990	Clearance of ancient *hutongs* to make way for skyscrapers in Beijing; loss of community cohesion
Increased access to labour-saving consumer goods	Increased work stress linked to the need to maintain incomes
Increased numbers of women (called '*fumchis*') in high status jobs	Extended family breakdown as the rural young migrate to coastal cities
Increased access to global information and different cultures (although internet content is controlled by the state)	Rising levels of obesity and diabetes linked to the spread of Western diets
Increased range of opportunities, especially for the young	Increased potential for political instability as 'Western' ideas of 'freedom' become widely understood
	Growing inequality between a wealthy middle class, low-income migrant factory workers and the rural poor
	A gradual erosion of important cultural concepts such as humility and respect for elders

Cultural attitudes to the environment

How do cultural values impact on our relationship with the environment?

By the end of this section you should:
- ➤ *be aware that cultures have different attitudes to the environment*
- ➤ *understand that these different attitudes affect the way in which the environment is valued*
- ➤ *have examined how growing consumption requires people to see themselves as commanding the physical environment*
- ➤ *have investigated the conflict between environmentalism and consumer capitalism*

Different cultural attitudes

There is no single view of what 'the **environment**' means. Different groups have different perceptions and place varying degrees of importance on the environment (Table 12.9). Even supposedly universal concerns such as climate change have wide variations.

Table 12.9 shows that 'landscape' is linked to environment for Poles and Finns, but less so for French and British people. For over one-third of Italians environment means urban pollution, an issue hardly on the radar in Slovenia, where climate change and environment are perceived to be strongly linked. The results in Table 12.9 may be clouded by language and translation but they may also reflect wider cultural concerns and traditions.

Western capitalism carries with it distinctive ideas about the natural environment. These emerged as the feudal system broke down and private ownership of land grew rapidly. In recent years enhanced awareness of environmental issues has

Table 12.9
Responses to the question: 'When people talk about the environment, which of the following issues do you think of first?'

Country	Urban pollution	Climate change	Landscapes	Protecting nature	The environment our children will inherit	Man-made disasters	Local quality of life	Natural disasters	Using up natural resources
EU-27	22	19	13	12	12	8	5	4	3
Italy	36	9	15	11	7	7	6	3	3
UK	28	26	8	5	15	4	5	3	3
Poland	20	10	26	17	8	8	4	4	2
France	19	18	6	13	20	12	4	2	5
Denmark	12	32	7	15	15	12	1	2	2
Slovenia	7	39	13	4	20	10	1	3	3
Finland	4	23	21	9	18	11	7	2	4

Source: Eurobarometer survey, 2008

increased landscape protection. Cynics might argue that protected landscapes make more money from leisure and tourism than degraded ones.

Pre-industrial

In agricultural and hunting societies there was often no concept of land ownership. A lot of land was held in common. The belief that the landscape belonged to everyone and no-one tended to lead to its collective protection.

Capitalist

Industry depends on its control of natural resources – land, trees, coal, water etc. Each resource has a value, but only if it is removed from the landscape and used. During the colonial period Western power frequently came into conflict with indigenous people over resources, and indigenous people almost always lost.

Socialist

The socialist model of development pursued in both the Soviet Union and China was no kinder to the environment. Mega-projects, from the rice fields of Uzbekistan to the Three Gorges dam, suggest that nature was seen as a force to be harnessed.

Post-industrial

In a world dominated by service industries, 'nature' has been established as something to be preserved in special reserves, wildernesses such as the North American National Parks (Photograph 12.7).

Further research

Many websites can be explored to establish the history of the changing attitude towards nature and the cultural landscape. A well-known one is: www.greenpeace.org/international

Photograph 12.7 Zion National Park: a protected landscape in the USA

Valuing landscapes

The environment and landscape are valued in different ways by different cultures (Table 12.10). People's cultural perceptions of landscape value determine how land and resources are exploited or protected.

Two-thirds of Japan is covered by forest. This is a surprising figure for a developed country (although much of this land is steeply mountainous).

➤ Forests have traditionally been preserved to protect steep slopes from landslides and flooding.
➤ The Shinto religion has a deep reverence for nature.
➤ Forests are seen as sacred and are worshipped.
➤ Trees such as the cherry have strong religious symbolism.

Table 12.10
Different ways of
valuing the
landscape

Landscape as sacred	Landscapes are considered to have religious significance. Deities may be linked to landscape features such as rivers and mountains, or plants and animals	Landscapes are preserved
Landscape as pleasure	Landscapes are places to be used for recreation. They may have heritage value. They are consumed for enjoyment, often by visitors. Judgements are made about which landscapes are most valued	Landscapes are conserved, but may become degraded and polluted
Landscape as life	Landscapes are considered valuable in their own right, because of the essential goods and services they provide to humans, e.g. biodiversity	Landscapes are protected
Landscape as profit	Landscapes are seen as a bank of resources to be exploited, and little thought is given to landscape futures	Landscapes become degraded and even destroyed

Villagers in Japan carefully manage the forest resources close to villages called *satoyama*. Japan has many forest protection laws, and the Shirakami-Sanchi area of virgin forest on Honshu is a 10,000-hectare UNESCO World Heritage site. It is ironic that Japan is the world's largest importer of tropical timber.

In Finland the ancient 'everyman's right' means that everyone has the right to access and use forests. This right entitles anybody to move about on foot, skis, bicycle or horseback on somebody else's property, provided they cause no damage. This gives forests in Finland a special, collective significance.

The dominant cultural paradigm in the developed world is that the landscape needs to be protected and that policies developed in order to allow us to do so more effectively. This was not always the case. As Figure 12.14 shows, there is a relationship between development and protecting the landscape and environment.

Figure 12.14
The development–
environment
relationship

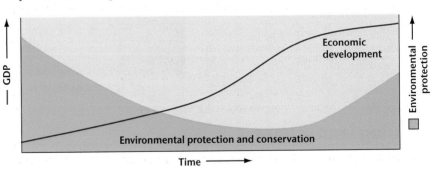

Pre-industrial	Industrial	Post-industrial
Landscape and resources conserved due to necessity; most income is from farming, fishing and forestry	Landscape and resources used for raw materials leading to degradation and pollution. Most jobs in industry. Conservation given low priority	Landscape and resources conserved, rising environmental concern, desire for an attractive environment for leisure and funds available for conservation

Edexcel A2 Geography

Sustainability

Sustainability has many meanings. The concept emerged in the 1980s as an idea closely linked to development and defined as 'development which meets the needs of the present without compromising the ability of future generations to enjoy the same quality of life'. Sustainable development sought to generate economic progress that was equitable, would last, involved ordinary people in decision making and did not needlessly damage the environment.

Today sustainability is most commonly a 'green' concept which focuses on environmental issues rather than social equity and public participation. This may be more accurately described as 'environmental sustainability'. For local councils the emphasis is on recycling, reducing car pollution and planting trees. For others, sustainability is a useful, perhaps essential, part of any institution's public profile, showing its concern about the environment. The Shell company, for example, says, 'Shell is a worldwide group of oil, gas and petrochemical companies with interests in biofuels, wind and solar power and hydrogen. We help meet global energy demand in economically, environmentally and socially responsible ways.'

Critics believe that TNCs use the term 'sustainable' to mean only lasting for a long time. They would argue that it is difficult to see how an oil and gas company could be environmentally sustainable without huge changes to its corporate structure and aims.

Further research

Research should be carried out to evaluate these attitudes and to debate the cultural positions which they occupy with respect to nature.

Consumer culture

The core assumption of Western culture is that greater material wealth means happier people. The richer we get and the more 'stuff' we have, the happier we will be. Some counter-cultures and environmental movements believe this idea is at the root of the environmental challenges facing the planet.

Some environmentalists argue that we are anthropocentric – we believe humans should dominate the planet because we are more important than anything else on it. Only when we recognise that the natural world around us has equal value to ourselves will we begin to solve environmental challenges.

There is a range of public attitudes towards the environment. A recent US survey showed how members of the public assessed the quality of the environment (Table 12.11). Marked differences were uncovered between people of different political persuasions. While left-wing people were quite keen for more government intervention to help the environment, very few right-wing people saw this as acceptable. Most seemed to think that less government regulation was the action that would most help the environment. These views can be contrasted with European attitudes, which tend to be much more concerned about environmental protection. For example, 90% of Europeans believed that large corporations should be made responsible for cleaning up the environment (EU Eurobarometer report 2008).

Table 12.11 Quality of the environment: a public survey

	Very good (%)	Fairly good (%)	Fairly bad (%)	Very bad (%)
Global environment	5.3	38.2	43.4	13.1
National environment	11.1	41.9	37.1	9.9
Local environment	16.8	56.0	22.8	4.4

Environmentalism vs consumer capitalism

The question about the compatibility of environmentalism and consumer capitalism is at the core of many of the most critical debates in the world today. For some, capitalism is an economic and political system that inevitably leads to destruction of the environment. This is because:

➤ the drive for short-term profits disregards concern for the environment
➤ businesses are accountable only to their shareholders, not the wider public
➤ businesses produce what they can sell at a profit, which is not necessarily what would be good for the wider population
➤ the system leaves some people poor, and they turn to practices such as deforestation as the only way to survive

The world is dominated by capitalism. Those who spend thousands of pounds on consumer goods are the same people who express concerns about global warming, tropical forest destruction and the plight of the polar bear.

The spread of consumption to China, India and the Gulf states (Photograph 12.8) presents some frightening prospects. If Chinese consumption and economic growth continue, they will reach levels per person similar to those of the USA by 2031. The Chinese would then be consuming:

➤ 1,350 million tonnes of grain per year (66% of current world production)
➤ 180 million tonnes of meat per year (80% of current world production)
➤ 2.8 billion tonnes of coal per year (current global production 2.6 billion)
➤ 1.1 billion cars (current global total 800 million)

Photograph 12.8 A temple to consumption: the Mall of the Emirates, Dubai

Cameron Dunn

It is debatable whether it is even possible to provide these resources, and the environmental damage of doing so would be severe. At the same time people living in poverty clearly need greater access to resources:

➤ 800 million people lack enough food
➤ 1 billion lack clean water
➤ 2 billion lack adequate sanitation
➤ 950 million adults are illiterate

Contraction

How can the need for development and environmental protection be resolved? One suggestion is to allocate an equitable share of resources to each human. Using the ecological footprint concept, the contraction and convergence model would:

➤ allow developing nations to increase their resource use
➤ force developed nations to reduce theirs (contraction)
➤ aim for an average human footprint of just under 2.0 global hectares

Achieving contraction would involve major changes in resource consumption:
➤ eliminating inefficiency and waste
➤ restricting fossil-fuel use and moving towards a renewable energy economy
➤ emphasising local production for local consumption
➤ curbing the rising consumption of meat
➤ reducing reliance on energy-intensive technology
➤ refocusing human concepts of happiness and success towards quality and harmony and away from consumption
➤ providing what people need, not what they want

These moves towards a 'green economy' are seen by many people and organisations as radical and even anti-globalisation in nature. It is probably fair to say that proponents of a green economy are mainly anti-global. They see a green economic future as a fundamentally local one, which would protect diverse cultures from the march of cultural globalisation.

Suggested fieldwork opportunities

Local fieldwork

➤ Fieldwork in a major city exploring the cultural characteristics of areas with distinct ethnicities.
➤ Cultural landscapes in the UK could be compared, for instance, those of Cornwall, Wales and the Western Isles..
➤ Cultural globalisation may be investigated in world cities and megacities.

Residential and long-haul fieldwork

➤ Some relatively close areas have distinct cultural landscapes, such as Catalonia and the Basque country, Brittany and the border zones of Wales and Ireland.
➤ There may be opportunities for exchange visits to places further afield, such as China or countries in Africa and these are to be encouraged.

Review questions

1 Explain what you understand by the term 'culture'.
2 Examine the arguments for and against protecting cultural diversity.
3 Why are some cultures more vulnerable to pressures than others?
4 Explain what is meant by 'cultural imperialism' and 'cultural globalisation'.
5 Why is cultural diversity usually greatest in cities?
6 Discuss the conflict that exists between environmentalism and consumer capitalism.

Chapter
13

Pollution and human health at risk

Health is a concern for all of us, no matter where in the world we live, and it can have a significant effect on our quality of life. Our health is put at risk by a number of factors, including the national level of economic development, our exposure to transmissible diseases and the quality of our living environment. Environmental pollution is a key risk, especially in countries where rapid economic development may take precedence over concerns about the environment and human health.

Defining the risks to human health

What are the health risks?

By the end of this section you should:
➤ *have explored the range of health risks*
➤ *be aware of the patterns of health risk at different spatial scales*
➤ *understand how health risk patterns can change over time*
➤ *appreciate how health affects both quality of life and economic development*

The range of health risks

The most significant risks to human health are related to disease, lifestyles and the environment. Of these, disease is the greatest potential killer. The medical profession recognises three main categories of disease.

➤ *Genetic or inherited diseases*, for example haemophilia, are carried in people's genes.
➤ *Infectious diseases* are caused by bacteria and viruses which multiply in the body (Photograph 13.1). They are broken into two groups: vectored (e.g. malaria, which is borne by a mosquito) and non-vectored (e.g. influenza) diseases. The ease of international travel today means that new and re-emerging diseases can spread fast. The two most lethal infectious diseases today are malaria and HIV/AIDS. Some infectious diseases are classified as *acute*, which means they last only a short time but have a rapid onset and/or intense symptoms.
➤ *Chronic or degenerative diseases* result mainly from longevity. They do not kill instantly but cause long-term deterioration of the body. They include heart disease, stroke, cancer, diabetes and dementia. They were once common only in countries with high longevity, such as the USA, Japan and Europe, but are

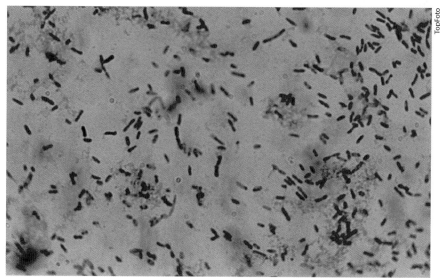

TopFoto

Photograph 13.1
Bacteria that cause diarrhoea – a major cause of death in developing countries – seen under a microscope

now a feature of newly emerging countries such as Brazil, India and China. In 2005, the World Health Organization (WHO) estimated that chronic diseases accounted for 60% of all global deaths, double the percentage for infectious diseases.

Rich and poor

The impact of lifestyles on health risks is greatest at the ends of the poor–rich continuum. The poor are likely to experience malnutrition, poor water and sanitation and substandard housing, which lead to chronic and infectious diseases. Some wealthy people put their health at risk through obesity and high alcohol consumption. Smoking is a habit of rich and poor, and increases the risk of heart and respiratory diseases, as well as lung cancer. Pollution of the environment, particularly of the air and water, affects everyone, increasing the risk of diseases like typhoid and asthma.

Time and space

When a disease persists over a long time in a particular area, it is called **endemic.** The prevalence of some diseases, however, fluctuates over time: a period of high prevalence is called an **epidemic**. When an epidemic affects a wide geographical area, as is the case with HIV/AIDS, it is called a **pandemic.**

In 2007 a ground-breaking WHO report, *A safer future: global public health security in the 21st century*, showed that health risks have increased and will continue to do so globally. Public health security is threatened not just by disease and epidemics but also by industrial accidents and natural disasters. The scale and **transboundary** nature of today's health risks mean that a more globalised approach is needed if they are to be contained. Table 13.1 shows anticipated changes in the morbidity of individual diseases by 2030: these will have a direct impact on health risks.

Table 13.1 Leading causes of death, 2004 and 2030

2004			2030		
Disease or injury	Deaths (%)	Rank	Disease or injury	Deaths (%)	Rank
Ischaemic heart disease	12.2	1	Ischaemic heart disease	14.2	1
Cerebrovascular disease	9.7	2	Cerebrovascular disease	12.1	2
Lower respiratory infections	7.0	3	Chronic obstructive pulmonary disease	8.6	3
Chronic obstructive pulmonary disease	5.1	4	Lower respiratory infections	3.8	4
Diarrhoeal diseases	3.6	5	Road traffic accidents	3.6	5
HIV/AIDS	3.5	6	Trachea, bronchus, lung cancers	3.4	6
Tuberculosis	2.5	7	Diabetes mellitus	3.3	7
Trachea, bronchus, lung cancers	2.3	8	Hypertensive heart disease	2.1	8
Road traffic accidents	2.2	9	Stomach cancer	1.9	9
Prematurity and low birth weight	2.0	10	HIV/AIDS	1.8	10
Neonatal infections and other	1.9	11	Nephritis and nephrosis	1.6	11
Diabetes mellitus	1.9	12	Self-inflicted injuries	1.5	12
Malaria	1.7	13	Liver cancer	1.4	13
Hypertensive heart disease	1.7	14	Colon and rectum cancers	1.4	14
Birth asphyxia and birth trauma	1.5	15	Oesophagus cancer	1.3	15
Self-inflicted injuries	1.4	16	Violence	1.2	16
Stomach cancer	1.4	17	Alzheimer and other dementias	1.2	17
Cirrhosis of the liver	1.3	18	Cirrhosis of the liver	1.2	18
Nephritis and nephrosis	1.3	19	Breast cancer	1.1	19
Colon and rectum cancers	1.1	20/21	Tuberculosis	1.0	20
Violence	1.0	22	Neonatal infections	1.0	21
Breast cancer	0.9	23	Prematurity and low birth weight	0.9	22
Oesophagus cancer	0.9	24	Diarrhoeal diseases	0.9	23
Alzheimer and other dementias	0.8	25	Birth asphyxia and birth trauma	0.7	29
			Malaria	0.4	41

Source: World Health Statistics 2008, WHO

Patterns of health risk

Patterns of health risk may be investigated at a range of spatial scales.

Global

The Worldmapper representation of the patterns of unhealthy life (Figure 13.1) is a stark illustration of the global disparities in health risk and security. It shows the time spent in poor health in a person's life. The global average is 10 years, but there is a large range. In Swaziland (Africa) the average is 1 year of unhealthy life, but life expectancy is less than 36 years, while in the Asian state of Azerbaijan

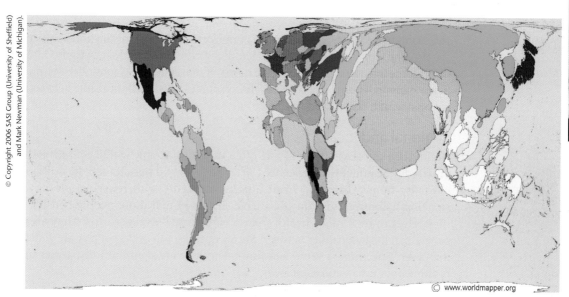

© www.worldmapper.org

Figure 13.1 Global distribution of unhealthy life

people may expect more than 20 years of poor health in an average life expectancy of 70 years.

In Figure 13.1 countries are drawn in a size proportional to their share of the global total of unhealthy life years. China and India show that the map as a whole is distorted by population size. Figure 13.2 reveals significant differences in deaths according to income level in the country.

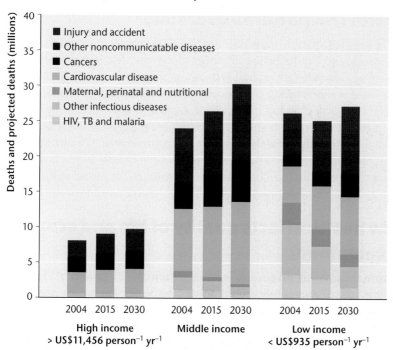

Figure 13.2 Deaths by cause for economic global regions

National

The health risk equation is much more complex than a simple distinction between countries on either side of the North–South divide. Careful analysis of Figure 13.2 shows some interesting patterns in the causes of mortality. The Gapminder website (www.gapminder.org) has some useful resources on the relationship between national wealth (GDP) and health.

Regional and local

Health risks and levels of healthcare often vary considerably within countries. In the UK, the National Health Service (NHS) has achieved significant reductions in mortality from cancer and heart attacks, especially with fewer people now smoking. However, opinion polls have suggested that more people consider themselves to be in poor health than was the case 10 years earlier. They also believe that the inequalities between the north and south of the country are wider than ever. Government surveys indicate that there are significant disparities in health within urban and rural areas.

Further research

www.worldmapper.org/display.php?selected=244#

http://go.worldbank.org/E0CMVLHFU0

http://ucatlas.ucsc.edu/blog/?p=39

www.gapminder.org/

www.communities.gov.uk/communities/neighbourhoodrenewal/deprivation/
    deprivation07/

Health risk patterns over time

Just as the demographic transition model (DTM) shows stages in the evolution of a country's population as it moves along the development pathway, so Omram's epidemiological model defines four stages or 'ages'. Table 13.2 provides an updated version of the 1971 model. It clearly shows how the pattern of health risks changes over time and essentially in tandem with economic development.

Remember that models such as Omram's are generalisations. Countries will not all follow exactly the same sequence at the same speed. It is already apparent that some of the countries that began developing rapidly in the late twentieth century, such as India and China, are passing through the model at an accelerated rate. They face a double burden of health risk: infections and chronic disease.

How health affects quality of life and economic development

We have already seen that health is adversely affected by poverty, and the impact that has on quality of housing, food and water supply. With economic development comes the expectation of a larger personal income. This, in turn, promises better housing, better education and better healthcare. In short, quality of life improves and so does personal health.

Table 13.2 Simplified version of Omram's epidemiological transition

	Age of pestilence and famine	Age of receding pandemics: early phase	Age of receding pandemic: late phases	Age of degenerative and human-made disease
Population characteristics	Stage 1 DTM Mortality dominates, with crude death rates of 30/1,000 and above Population is young, with very large young dependency ratio	Stage 2 DTM Population is still young, but proportion of elderly begins to increase as mortality rate falls Low rate of population growth Rural–urban migration becomes more evident	Stage 3 DTM Mortality rate continues to fall, but a significant fall in fertility rate begins Population growth explosive High levels of rural–urban migration	Stage 4 DTM Mortality and fertility rates fall to below 20/1,000 Population growth stagnant to small Progressive ageing of whole population
Economic development	Traditional society. Low income	Pre-conditions for 'take off' improve. Low income	'Take off'. Sustained economic growth. Middle income	High mass consumption. Shift from producer to consumer goods and services
Living standards	Very poor; unsanitary conditions prevail	Standards are still quite low, but there is some improvement	Hygiene and sanitation improve, except in urban slums, where conditions grow worse	Progressive improvement enjoyed by large segments of the population
Health risks	Leading causes of death: epidemics; endemic, parasitic and deficiency diseases	Leading causes of death much the same, except for the appearance of industrial diseases	Pandemics of infection, malnutrition and childhood disease recede. Infection remains the leading cause of death, but non-infectious diseases become more significant	Heart disease, cancer and stroke replace infection as prime killers. HIV/AIDS pandemic
Disease examples	TB Smallpox Rheumatism Malnutrition	As in previous age	Heart disease Respiratory disease Cholera Malaria	Heart disease Cancer HIV/AIDS Malaria
Pollution	Localised pollution, especially of water	Rise in air and water pollution as industrialisation begins	High levels of air, land and water pollution	Concerted efforts to reduce all forms of pollution

It is claimed that poor levels of health can seriously retard a country's economic development. How might this be? One obvious link is that a sick labour force is unlikely to be as productive as a healthy one:

➤ Productivity will be reduced by people having time off work and underperforming while at work.

➤ Coping with poor health can consume financial resources that might be reinvested to support further economic growth.

➤ Short life expectancy deprives a country of the benefits of worker experience and honed skills.

The HIV/AIDS pandemic in southern Africa has led to the death and illness of a large proportion of the population of working age, and this is having a serious impact on the economic status of the region.

Spirals

There is something of the 'chicken and the egg' riddle in the relationship between health and economic development. While it may be helpful to think of the relationship as circular in nature, we need to understand that it can spiral in two different directions:

➤ *Upwards*, as economic development supports better healthcare, and this in turn leads to higher labour productivity and further economic growth.
➤ *Downwards*, as poor health retards economic development, which means either there is less money to spend on healthcare or money is diverted that should be spent sustaining economic development already achieved. The net outcome is that the economy either stagnates or regresses.

In Europe there is a proven statistical correlation between rising life expectancy (a health indicator) and improved economic wealth. For example, a survey of regions in 26 of the most affluent countries found that a 10% reduction in cardio-vascular disease was associated with a 1% increase in annual per capita growth of income. In the Russian Federation, good health was found to increase wages by 22% for women and 18% for men (1960–2000).

The complex causes of health risk

What are the causes of health risk?

By the end of this section you should:
➤ *be aware of the different causes of health risk, including pollution*
➤ *appreciate the relationship between socioeconomic status and health*
➤ *understand the links between some diseases and geographical features*
➤ *be familiar with models that help in the understanding of health risks*

The complex causes of health risks

Overall, people today, especially those in the West, are living longer than two centuries ago. This increase in life expectancy is closely related to a decrease in infectious diseases such as cholera, measles and influenza. The downside of longevity is a rise in degenerative diseases, such as cancer and dementia, in older people.

The so-called 'health map' (Figure 13.3) identifies the main factors affecting human health, and from this we can extrapolate those that contribute to health

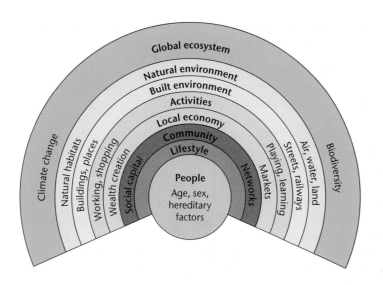

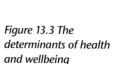

Figure 13.3 The determinants of health and wellbeing

risks. The causes of health risks are essentially physical and socioeconomic, with personal wealth being one of the most fundamental factors. Globally, 15% of the population live in high-income countries, but they account for only 7% of annual deaths.

Physical causes

The physical causes of health risks are diverse and exist at a range of scales. They include:

➤ poor sanitation and water supply, which increase the risk of infectious diseases, especially cholera and diarrhoea
➤ stagnant and polluted water that encourages vector insects such as malarial mosquitoes
➤ changing global conditions, such as ozone depletion, which leads to skin cancer; global warming, which increases the spatial incidence of malaria; more climate shocks of extreme heat or cold; more lethal natural hazards such as tsunamis and floods

Human causes

The human causes of health risks are even more varied. The more migratory and mobile nature of today's population is resulting in a more rapid spread of infectious diseases.

The spread of industrialisation and its pollution of air and water are boosting the incidence of a range of diseases (Table 13.3). Infectious diseases are now spreading geographically faster than at any time in the past. It is estimated that 2.1 billion airline passengers travelled in 2006; air travel allows diseases to spread across the world. The overuse of antibiotics is creating resistant bacteria, and an obsession with sterility (e.g. 'antimicrobial' products for the kitchen) is reducing the efficiency of human immune systems. The nature of our diverse lifestyles creates all manner of health risks:

Table 13.3 Potential relationships between forms of pollution and health risks: pink cells show links

Health risk	Polluted air	Excreta and household waste	Polluted water	Polluted food	Insanitary housing	Climate change
Respiratory infections						
Diarrhoeal diseases						
Malaria						
Cancer						
Typhoid						
Cholera						
Cardiovascular disorders						
Mental disorders						
Respiratory diseases						
Poisonings						

➤ *Poverty* leads to malnutrition, which is an underlying factor in infectious diseases such as pneumonia, diarrhoea, malaria, measles and HIV/AIDS. Poverty is also associated with pregnancy and childbirth problems.

➤ *Affluence* can lead to over-nutrition, obesity and the abuse of tobacco and alcohol. Diabetes, heart disease, strokes, and lung and gastro-intestinal cancer are the health risks. Once considered a problem only in high-income countries, obesity is now dramatically on the rise in low- and middle-income countries, particularly in urban areas. 'Globalisation' of food tends to lead to increased consumption of fats and sugars, and this excess of calories is exacerbated by increasingly sedentary lives. Latest figures indicate that in 2005 at least 400 million adults globally and 20 million children under the age of 5 years were obese.

➤ *Poor education* and the low status accorded to women in some parts of the world heighten health risks. Children who complete primary school are more likely to know about diseases and how to protect themselves and, in due course, their children. The UN has estimated that for each year of education a girl receives, the risk of her own children dying before the age of 5 years is reduced by 10%. Little wonder that education has been described as the 'social vaccine' against many health risks, including HIV/AIDS.

➤ *Accidents* (traffic and industrial) and food poisoning are now accepted as part of everyday life, but clearly are inherently health risks.

New diseases

New infectious diseases continue to emerge. Since the 1970s, they have been identified at the unprecedented rate of one or more per year. There are now nearly 40 diseases that were unknown a generation ago. They include variant CJD and SARS.

Socioeconomic status and health

Socioeconomic status (SES) is an individual's ranking in relationship to others in their society. The most common indicators are income, educational attainment, type of occupation and social standing in the community. Table 13.4 shows the social classifications used in the UK census until 2000, and Table 13.5 the socioeconomic classifications used in the 2001 census. The latter is less overtly about social class and status.

Table 13.4 Social class based on occupation (OPCS, 2000)

Social grade	Social status	Occupation
A	Upper middle class	Higher managerial, administrative or professional
B	Middle class	Intermediate managerial, administrative or professional
C1	Lower middle class	Supervisory or clerical, junior managerial, administrative or professional
C2	Skilled working class	Skilled manual workers
D	Working class	Semi-skilled and unskilled manual workers
E	Those at lowest level of subsistence	State pensioners or widows (no other earner), casual or lowest-grade workers

Status	Operational classes
1	Higher managerial and professional occupations
2	Lower managerial and professional occupations
3	Intermediate occupations
4	Small employers and own-account workers
5	Lower supervisory and technical occupations
6	Semi-routine occupations
7	Routine occupations
8	Never worked and long-term unemployed

Table 13.5 Socioeconomic status (OPCS, 2001)

There is a large body of evidence indicating that SES is a strong predictor of health. Better health is associated with having more income, more years of education and a more prestigious job, as well as living in neighbourhoods where a higher percentage of residents have higher incomes and more education. More specifically, research has indicated the following:

➤ The effects of poverty and extreme adversity alone do not explain the association of SES and health. Health improves with each step up the SES ladder.
➤ With a few exceptions, disease is more prevalent and life expectancy shorter the lower one is down the SES hierarchy.

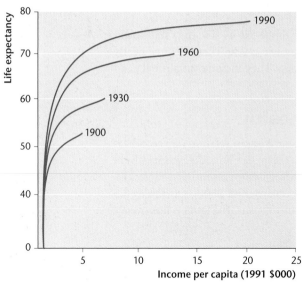

Figure 13.4 Per capita income and life expectancy, 1900–90

➤ There are multiple pathways by which SES may affect health, including access to and quality of healthcare, health-related behaviour, and physical and social environments.

➤ The association of SES and health begins at birth and extends throughout life, but the strength and nature of the relationship can vary at different stages of life.

Figure 13.4 demonstrates the impact of increasing income (an important component of SES) on life expectancy. Small increases are shown as bringing about significant gains in life expectancy. This suggests that, in general, health risks are inversely proportional to income.

Links between disease and geographical features

The development and spread of diseases, particularly those of an infectious nature, can be linked to a range of **geographical features**, such as transport routes, water bodies and climate. For example, humid tropical and equatorial climates produce optimal conditions for many infectious diseases. But it is not only physical geographical features that are associated with particular diseases. The urban or built environment, for example, has characteristics such as dense population, poor housing and high levels of pollution that contribute to disease.

Some diseases flourish in particular environmental circumstances, but others appear to be associated with specific geographical or environmental changes (Table 13.6). The case studies on HIV, tuberculosis and malaria illustrate a few of these links between disease and geographical features.

Table 13.6 Environmental changes and related diseases

Environmental change	Related diseases	Pathway of effects
Dams, canals and irrigation	Malaria	Breeding sites for mosquitoes
	River blindness	Blackfly breeding
Urbanisation	Cholera	Poor sanitation and hygiene; water contamination
	Dengue fever	Water collecting rubbish
Deforestation	Malaria	Immigration of susceptible people
	Oropouche	Contact with breeding vectors
Reforestation	Lyme disease	Tick hosts; outdoor exposure

Case study **The road to death in China**

Figure 13.5 China's 'road to death'

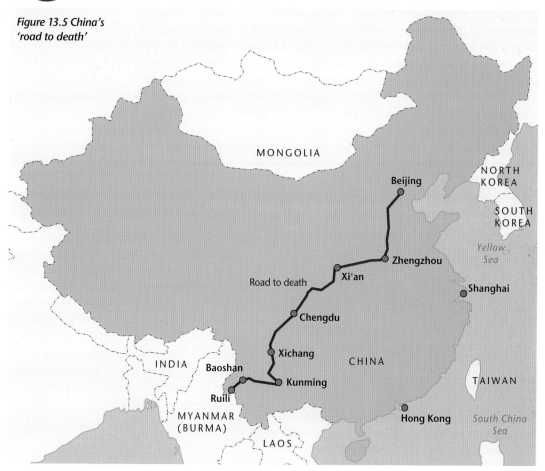

China is facing an HIV/AIDS epidemic that in some areas has already left 80% of the population infected. The spread of the infection has been particularly aggressive along a main road that runs across almost the whole country (Figure 13.5). What is now known as the 'road to death' starts in the heroin fields on the border with Myanmar and ends in Beijing. Along the route of the road live thousands of drug dealers and hundreds of thousands of addicts, most of whom are taking heroin intravenously. Needle-sharing plays a major role in the transmission of HIV.

But two other factors are playing their part. Each year, millions of migrant workers (the 'foot soldiers' of China's emerging economy) pass along the road. Away from home for months or years, many of them have sex with prostitutes in roadside hostels and workers' camps. Condom use is minimal. In addition, in order to supplement meagre wages, workers sell their blood to blood banks. Without proper screening of donors, HIV-contaminated blood is spreading the disease even further through the population. The situation is made worse by the fact that until recently the Chinese authorities denied the existence of HIV/AIDS in the country.

Unit 4 Geographical research

Case study Tuberculosis

Tuberculosis (TB) is an infectious disease, the symptoms of which are fever, weight loss, persistent coughing and spitting blood. Very much a disease of urban areas, it is closely associated with bad housing, poor diet and a generally unhealthy environment. It is estimated that a third of the world's population is infected with TB bacteria. Each year about 8 million people develop the disease and up to 2.5 million people worldwide are killed by it.

Vaccination programmes successfully eliminated TB in many countries in the second half of the twentieth century. This was the case in the UK, but recently migrants from the Indian subcontinent have reintroduced the disease. If people have not been vaccinated and become infected, it is possible to treat the infection with a combination of antibiotics. However, there is growing evidence that a drug-resistant form of the disease is emerging.

Case study Malaria: once contracted, never cured

Photograph 13.2 A malaria education programme run by pharmaceutical TNC GlaxoSmithKline in Burkina Faso

Malaria is an infectious disease caused by the presence of protozoa in the red blood cells. It is a vector-borne disease transmitted by the blood-sucking female *Anopheles* mosquito. The mosquito is only found in regions with a tropical or subtropical climate, and it requires water to breed, so thrives in

poorly-drained areas. When the mosquito bites, malarial parasites picked up from someone who had malaria are injected into the bloodstream of the person being bitten and migrate to the liver and other vital organs, where they multiply. The parasites later return to the bloodstream, invade the red blood cells and cause fever, shivering and sweating. These symptoms will recur at fairly regular intervals for the remainder of the victim's life. In due course, malaria can cause both liver and kidney failure, as well as damage to the brain and lungs.

About 270 million people are believed to be infected with malaria. Most of them are in Africa. More than 2.4 billion people, over a third of the world's population, are at risk of contracting the disease. Up to 2 million people each year die from it and its complications. The best way of tackling the disease is prevention – using mosquito nets, draining marshes, taking drugs that prevent the disease – but all of these cost money.

Models of health risk

Geographers have long been involved with epidemiologists in studying outbreaks of cholera, yellow fever and influenza. There are many models of the development and spread of particular health risks which can be used to manage outbreaks. Some models (known as chronological models) focus on how diseases spread over time. Examples include Kilbourne's model of influenza in 1999 and Bartlett's model of the minimum number of people needed in any population to support

Figure 13.6 Types of spatial diffusion

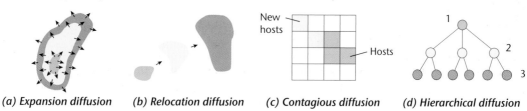

(a) Expansion diffusion   *(b) Relocation diffusion*   *(c) Contagious diffusion*   *(d) Hierarchical diffusion*

an endemic disease. Others concentrate on the spatial patterns of diseases. Some of the most useful are those that deal with **diffusion**, namely the ways in which infection spreads out from a central point. Such models take into account the two dimensions of space and time.

There are four types of spatial diffusion (Figure 13.6):

➤ With **expansion diffusion**, the infection simply spreads out in all directions from the point of origin.

➤ With **contagious diffusion**, infection is spread by direct contact, so the risk of being infected lessens with distance from the point of outbreak. Measles epidemics usually spread by this type of diffusion unless there are significant amounts of migration.

➤ With **hierarchical diffusion**, infection is spread through a particular class or group. For example, the disease might break out in a large settlement and gradually spread to progressively smaller ones. An example can be seen in the spread of HIV/AIDS from the major cities of the USA to the nation's small towns.

➤ With **relocation diffusion**, an infection spreads into a new area but leaves its source behind, as is seen in some influenza epidemics. Migration plays a key role here: a disease may 'jump' to a distant country simply as a result of an infected person taking a long-haul flight.

Pollution and health risk

What is the link between health risk and pollution?

By the end of this section you should:

➤ *understand the link between different types of pollution and health*

➤ *be aware of the distinction between one-off and sustained pollution in terms of their health risks*

➤ *recognise the link between economic development, pollution and changing health risks*

➤ *appreciate how pollution fatigue can lead to the effective management of pollution*

Pollution and health

Pollution is defined by the medical profession as 'the presence of substances, usually toxic chemicals, and conditions in the environment, especially in the air and in water supplies, that create a risk to the health and wellbeing of people within a community.' There are three realms of environmental pollution:

➤ *hydrospheric*, e.g. pollution of water by household and industrial effluent or by seepage of agrochemicals
➤ *atmospheric*, e.g. pollution of the air by the burning of fossil fuels
➤ *terrestrial*, e.g. pollution associated with landfill sites

We should not forget noise and light pollution, but into which of the three categories do these fall? Pollution has two types of source:
➤ *point based* – from a specific source, such as a factory or power station
➤ *diffuse* – involving a number of sources, e.g. nitrate leaching from agricultural use, causing eutrophication in water bodies, or cars emitting carbon dioxide

Pollution begins at a **source**, follows a **pathway** and then reaches an end point, referred to as its **sink**.

Global issue

History shows that pollution has changed from a relatively localised problem to a globalised issue. The environmental risk transition model (Figure 13.7) divides this change into three successive stages:
➤ *Household-scale* pollution is associated with poor water and sanitation, inadequate dwelling ventilation and poor-quality food. These problems begin to decline with economic development and higher incomes.
➤ *Community-scale* pollution grows as development and wealth increase. Particularly associated with emerging urban areas, its features include poor air quality, occupational hazards, use of toxic chemicals, abuse of rivers and streams, and traffic pollution. Eventually these forms of pollution are reduced by community management of aspects of everyday life such as sewerage, refuse, public transport and the location of economic activities.
➤ *Global-scale* pollution is the outcome of global population growth and economic development. The scale of atmospheric pollution reaches a threshold

Figure 13.7 The environmental risk transitional model

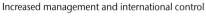

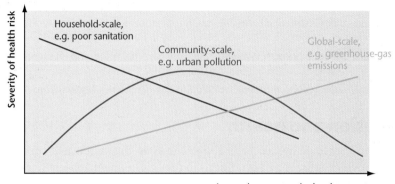

at which it begins to disturb the basic natural systems of the Earth. Atmospheric movements, for example, are inherently **transboundary** and can affect the whole globe. Global warming and related sea-level rises are a warning that we must take action to curb this diffuse form of pollution.

Precautionary principle

The last few decades have seen a move towards adopting the **precautionary principle** with regard to pollution control. This involves erring on the side of caution if the environmental impacts of any new development or emission into the environment are not fully understood. However, it is hard to change existing polluting practices. Just think how long it is taking to reduce plastic bag use or to increase the use of public transport in the UK. Many pollutants are persistent – they take long periods to decay, and some can accumulate in organisms. Relatively few pollutants are biodegradable.

Distribution

The distribution of pollution and its associated health risks varies not only over time but also from place to place. There are pollution **hotspots** or **clusters**, such as air pollution concentrations over large cities, areas polluted with radioactive waste, and water contaminated by mining processes. Figure 13.8 shows the distribution of the world's top pollution hotspots, while Table 13.7 gives some detail of the 30 worst locations. One country stands out as having the most serious pollution problems – China.

It is important to remember that the distribution of pollution, and therefore its health risks, changes over time. In the nineteenth and twentieth centuries, much of Europe was polluted by industrialisation, but with the global shift in manufacturing, pollution is now greater in the emerging economies of China, India and

Figure 13.8 The world's most polluted places

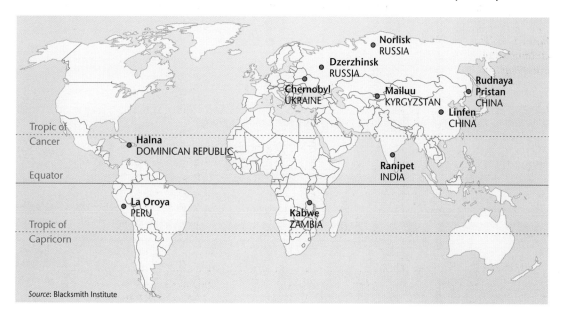

Source: Blacksmith Institute

Table 13.7 The 'dirty thirty': the world's most polluted places, 2007

World region	Type of pollutant/source									
	Mining	Metals	Petro-chemicals	Nuclear	Weapons	Industrial complex	Multiple pollutants	Urban waste	Air pollution	Other
Africa	Kabwe, Zambia							Dandora dumpsite, Kenya		
China	Wanshan	Tyanying				Huaxi			Lanzhou, Linfen, Urumqi	
Eastern Europe and central Asia	Chita, Russia	Norilsk, Russia; Rudnaya Pristan, Dalnegorsk, Russia	Bratsk, Russia	Chernobyl, Ukraine; Mailuu-Suu, Kyrgyzstan	Dzerzhinsk, Russia	Sumgayit, Azerbaijan; Ust-Kamenogorsk, Kazakhstan			Magnitogorsk, Russia	
Latin America and the Caribbean	Huancav' Ica, Peru; La Oroya, Peru	Haina, Dominican Republic	Oriente, Ecuador							Matanza-Riachuelo river basin, Argentina
South Asia	Sukinda, India	Hazaribagh, Bangladesh; Ranipet, India				Mahad industrial estate, India; Vapi, Gujarat, India				
Southeast Asia							Meycauayan City and Marilao, Philippines			

Source: Blacksmith Institute

Russia. Another significant factor helping to change the distribution of pollution is government action. Many countries have legislation to restrict pollution, for example, clean air legislation, controls on effluent emissions, pressing for the use of renewable energy, or requiring catalytic converters to be fitted to motor vehicles.

Further research

Visit http://news.bbc.co.uk/1/hi/sci/tech/ for snapshots of the sustained pollution problems of the Arctic (notorious for its concentration of persistent chemicals), the 'dead zone' of the Gulf of Mexico and the long-running saga of Bhopal (India), perhaps the best-known major pollution incident after Chernobyl.

For developing countries, see the Blacksmith Institute (www.blacksmithinstitute.org), which publishes an annual pollution hotspot list to shame offenders and improve pollution management.

Look up the pollution and potential health issues in your own home area by using the UK Environment Agency's 'What's in your backyard?' postcode check at www.environment-agency.gov.uk/maps/info/epopra/?version=1&lang=_e

Links

The link between pollution and health risk is illustrated in Table 13.8 by means of three examples involving different types of pollution at different spatial scales. The example of DDT shows not only the complexity of using a product that can be both harmful and helpful to people, but also the importance of public intervention. The health threat of indoor air pollution is widespread, but undervalued as a problem, mainly because of its 'hidden' nature. Lastly, there are the more publicised health impacts of recent climate change.

One of the challenges to proving that a link exists between a particular form of pollution and a specific health risk is the difficulty of obtaining reliable statistical information. By the time the link is confirmed, there may be many victims. In the case of DDT, it was extensively used to kill mosquitoes and prevent malaria. When the health risks were discovered, effective action was taken to ban it, although farmers in some parts of Africa still use it as an agricultural pesticide.

Table 13.8 Three examples of pollution and their health risks

Persistent organic pollutants: DDT	Indoor air pollution	Climate change linked to air pollution
Dichloro-diphenyl-trichloroethane (DDT) was used for over 50 years as an insecticide, particularly by farmers and in malarial areas against mosquitoes. It was banned in 2001 because of its toxic bio-magnification effects, which pose a serious threat to people and wildlife	The WHO estimates that about 2,500 million people in the world are exposed to excessive levels of indoor air pollution. Most comes from burning biomass and coal indoors in ovens that lack a proper chimney. Using aerosols and smoking tobacco increases the risks of respiratory infections, including TB and pneumonia, as well as cataracts	The WHO estimates that there are over 150,000 deaths each year and a global loss of 5.5 million 'disability adjusted life years' due to the health risks of climate change. These include skin cancer, heat-related diseases and a faster and wider spread of infectious diseases such as malaria and diarrhoea. The prognosis is for much worse to come

Relative risks of incidental and sustained pollution

The level of health risk associated with any form of pollution depends on:

➤ the type of pollutant – some substances are more toxic than others
➤ the amount and intensity of the pollutant
➤ the duration of a person's exposure

Some substances are acutely toxic and exposure can quickly lead to death. Others act over a long time and slowly weaken the human body, so that it becomes vulnerable to other diseases and possibly other forms of pollution.

Incidental pollution

Incidental pollution can range enormously in scale. Some incidents have disastrous impacts on human health. The classic examples are Chernobyl and Bhopal (see the case studies).

Case study   Chernobyl

In April 1986, Chernobyl was an obscure city on the Pripiat River in north-central Ukraine, then part of the Soviet Union. It shared its name with the nuclear power station located about 25 km upstream. During a test at 01:21 on 26 April, the Number 4 reactor exploded and released 30–40 times the radioactivity of the atomic bombs dropped on Hiroshima and Nagasaki.

Ranking as one of the greatest industrial accidents of all time, the Chernobyl disaster and its impact can scarcely be exaggerated. No one can predict what the exact number of human victims will ultimately prove to be. Thirty-one lives were lost immediately. Hundreds of thousands of Ukrainians, Russians and Belorussians had to abandon entire settlements within the 30-km zone of extreme contamination. Estimates vary, but it is likely that some 3 million people, more than 2 million in Belarus alone, are still living in contaminated areas and may be suffering from radiation sickness and cancers caused by radiation. The city of Chernobyl is still inhabited by almost 10,000 people. Billions of rubles have been spent, and billions more will be needed to relocate communities and decontaminate the rich farmland.

Case study   Bhopal

On 3 December 1984, toxic gas leaked from a Union Carbide factory in Bhopal, Madya Pradesh, India, killing thousands of people. Union Carbide estimates that 3,800 were killed, but workers who took bodies for burial believe there were at least 15,000. Decades on, people are still dying from the after effects.

The Bhopal factory was built in the 1970s to make pesticides for the Indian market. Sales were not good and the plant ceased production in the early 1980s. However, vast quantities of chemicals remained at the plant, including three tanks of methyl isocyanate (MIC), a reactive and deadly gas. At the same time the plant fell into disrepair.

On the night of 2 December a failure of stopcocks allowed water to flow into the largest tank of MIC. The tank exploded and a deadly cloud of MIC, hydrogen cyanide and other chemicals was released. It settled over much of Bhopal. The gas burned peoples' lungs and eyes, attacked their nervous systems and led them to lose control of their bodies.

Some people choked to death in their own body fluids, others had convulsions, some were crushed in the stampede to escape the gas.

Since the disaster survivors have suffered an epidemic of cancers and children in the area have been born with disabilities. Both Union Carbide and the new owner of the company, Dow Chemical, have refused to release information about the effects of MIC, and the site has never been cleaned up. Some compensation was paid 5 years after the incident but many people felt this was inadequate. 50,000 Bhopalis are unable to work due to their injuries and many survivors have no family left to take care of them.

At the other end of the spectrum is a small incident such as an accidental spillage of chemicals into a river or an oil spill in coastal waters. If such incidents are small-scale and of short duration, they might pass almost unnoticed except for dead fish floating on the water. With luck, the pollutant will be rapidly diluted and dissipated, with no obvious impact on human health. The challenge in dealing with incidental pollution is to be prepared, with contingency or emergency plans in place.

Sustained pollution

It could be argued that sustained pollution is more worrying than acute incidents, because it has a cumulative and debilitating effect on the health of people living in the affected area. Such pollution operates over months, years and even decades and health risks may be only slowly recognised. It seems likely that sustained pollution affects more people globally than incidental pollution, but it tends not to hit the headlines so quickly. Nevertheless, once a link has been established between a form of sustained pollution and a specific health risk, remedial actions may be taken.

For example, motor vehicle exhaust fumes have been shown to contain substances such as lead, sulphur dioxide, oxides of nitrogen and particulates that are injurious to human health (Figure 13.9). Removing lead from petrol and fitting vehicles with catalytic converters has reduced health risks in many parts of the world.

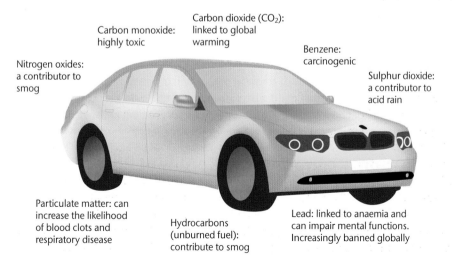

Carbon monoxide: highly toxic

Carbon dioxide (CO_2): linked to global warming

Benzene: carcinogenic

Nitrogen oxides: a contributor to smog

Sulphur dioxide: a contributor to acid rain

Particulate matter: can increase the likelihood of blood clots and respiratory disease

Hydrocarbons (unburned fuel): contribute to smog

Lead: linked to anaemia and can impair mental functions. Increasingly banned globally

Figure 13.9 Toxic content of motor vehicle exhaust fumes

Other examples of links between pollution and health are:

➤ depletion of the stratospheric ozone layer (the 'ozone holes') by the use of CFCs in aerosols and refrigerants, which allows more ultraviolet light to penetrate the atmosphere and leads to increases in skin cancer and cataracts

➤ global warming, boosted by pollutants such as carbon dioxide and methane in the atmosphere, which is allowing diseases such as malaria to spread to new areas

Further research

www.greenfacts.org/air-pollution/ozone-o3/

Case study: Water pollution in China

In 2007 the OECD found that 300 million people in China were using contaminated water and that 190 million of them suffered from water-related illnesses. Riverside power plants and factories producing chemicals, paper, textiles and food are a big source of pollution of China's rivers and lakes. A spillage of benzene into the River Songhau near the city of Harbin in November 2005 (see www.worldwatch.org/node/3884) is an example of a typical event. Water supplies are also being contaminated by arsenic and sewage. One-third of China's rivers, three-quarters of its major lakes and a quarter of its coastal estuaries are now classed as 'highly polluted'. In rural areas, hotspots or 'cancer villages' are being identified. The likely cause is the contamination of water supplies by the mining of heavy metals and by chemical factories.

The country's rapid economic growth is contributing to the deterioration in its water system. Central government investment in environmental protection remains well below the 2.2% of GDP that Chinese scientists claim is the minimum necessary to prevent further degradation of the environment. Pollution fines have traditionally been so low that it has been cheaper to pollute and pay up. There is little

Photograph 13.3 Industrial pollution of the Suzhou River, China

tradition of recycling or conservation, while administrative bureaucracy and inaction seriously undermine the possibility of improvement in water quality.

Pollution, economic development and changing health risks

Pollution is often regarded as 'the price of progress'. Economic development creates new threats to health, and brings about change in the nature and the pattern of health risks.

- Economic development involves greater use of resources, from minerals and energy to climate and soils. This tends to generate environmental pollution, for example the pollution of land and water by mining and the use of modern agricultural fertilisers.
- Industrialisation leads to increases in air pollution and discharges of untreated effluent.
- Greater affluence means increased car ownership and more exhaust gases polluting the air. It may bring a better diet, but it also increases obesity.

Economic development of a region or nation deepens its ecological footprint, with a corresponding impact on health risks. It does so mainly through environmental pollution (Figure 13.10). You should already be familiar with the types of disease that come into greater prominence as a result of pollution.

Changing patterns

One hundred years ago, the pollution hotspots were in the advanced economies of the USA and western Europe. Today, the main polluters are the newly emerging economies of Brazil, Russia, India and China. The global pattern of economic development is constantly changing, and therefore so is the global pattern, and scale, of pollution and related health risks.

Not all is gloom and doom, however. While Figure 13.10 shows a rising limb of environmental degradation, the curve eventually takes a downward turn. This change coincides with the onset of deindustrialisation, as manufacturers move to more profitable locations and the industry that remains becomes of a lighter and less polluting kind. Post-industrial society has a greater desire to reduce pollution and to find more environmentally friendly solutions, such as cleaner generation of electricity and more efficient handling of waste. One obvious benefit of the plunging degradation curve is the reduction of many health risks – and so the pattern of health risks continues to change.

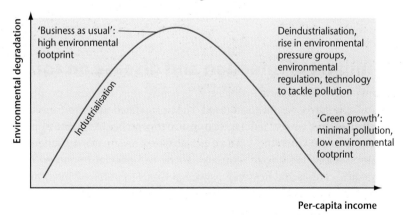

Figure 13.10
The environmental degradation curve

Pollution fatigue

Pollution fatigue comes in two forms. The first is found in individuals and communities that are not immediately affected by pollution. In these circumstances,

pollution is perceived as someone else's problem, with frequent media reporting of pollution incidents creating a sense of boredom and complacency. A 'topic fatigue' occurs – a turning-off of interest and concern. The danger of this type of fatigue is that it dilutes the general will to take action to curb pollution and reduce its health risks. It can also create difficulties for charitable organisations trying to raise public support for the victims of a pollution incident in a distant country.

The second form of pollution fatigue is a kind of resignation experienced by people who suffer sustained pollution as part of their everyday lives. To them, the problems seem so immense that nothing can be done. Repeated protests may have failed to lead to remedial action.

Pollution fatigue in both its forms can become a polluter's charter and lead to further health risks. Some would argue that in this situation, traditional forms of public outcry such as the protest march, the pressure group and the consumer boycott need new energy.

Today's communications technology has created a new medium of protest: **cyber-activism**. This has taken a variety of forms, including the mass sending of e-mails to relevant government departments and campaigns of coordinated 'hits' on a company's website to generate adverse publicity and force changes. It seems that the power of the internet has considerable potential to further the cause of pollution control and reduce associated health risks.

Managing the health risk

How can the impacts of health risks be managed?

By the end of this section you should:
➤ *appreciate the socioeconomic and environmental impacts of health risks*
➤ *understand how these health risk impacts lead to differing management strategies*
➤ *be aware of the agencies involved in managing health risks at an international level*
➤ *recognise the difference between health risks that can be managed effectively and those that cannot*

The impact of infection and disease on society

The first impact of infection and disease is, of course, that individual people become ill and incapacitated. At the social level, sickness-related absence from work and reduced output per worker reduce economic performance. A further impact is the social requirement for some form of healthcare. This creates a challenge and a burden on society. Healthcare requires the use of financial resources (capital to build medical centres and hospitals as well as funds to purchase medications and equipment) and human resources (doctors, nurses and other staff).

A healthcare system is essentially an integrated system of facilities and personnel, ranging from people in the community providing primary care, to universities carrying out research and producing qualified staff, to tertiary care in hospitals and clinics. Over the past century, health services have evolved from informal, small-scale, often family-based systems into large, often state-run systems, sometimes paralleled by private organisations catering for the more affluent and charitable organisations filling some of the 'gaps'.

The costs of healthcare are escalating, as population numbers increase, and people demand higher standards of health provision. This is all part of the globalised culture of consumerism and social equity. The bottom line is that since high health risks tend to debilitate society, it is in every nation's interests to achieve the best healthcare possible. This is what ignites the virtuous upward spiral to better health and improved quality of life. There is a huge 'health divide' in the world separating those who have access to appropriate healthcare from those who do not.

Prevention

Short-term healthcare has to be both curative and palliative (alleviating the symptoms of the illness). Longer-term healthcare should aim to prevent disease, for example by immunisation. A second aim is to eliminate the cause of much disease: poverty. A third aim should be to anticipate the changing needs of a population as it passes through the demographic and epidemiological transitions – shifting the balance of provision from the young (maternity units, paediatric care) to the elderly (nursing homes and geriatric care).

How do societies implement this need to confront disease and reduce health risks?

Management strategies and policies

There has been a long history of intervention in health risk, from the UK's Public Health Acts of the nineteenth century, through the formation of the World Health Organization (WHO) in 1948 to the UN Millennium Development Goals of 2000 and the current involvement of charities such as the Gates Foundation in reducing levels of malaria. Management and intervention can take many forms (Table 13.9).

Table 13.9 Coping with health risks: management types, interventions and players

Direct management (curative, palliative and preventative)		Indirect management (reducing exposure to risks that lead to poor health)	Methods of intervention	The players
The whole public. For example: vaccination and immunisation school food campaigns legislation to ban smoking in public places	Targeted individuals, especially if they combine risk factors and occur in sizeable numbers. For example: males who are obese, smokers and take little exercise infants vulnerable to sunburn	Reduce poverty Improve housing Improve water supply and sanitation Improve access to education	Legislation Taxation Financial incentives Education Campaigns Technology, from safety belts and efficient boilers to syringes and medicines	Governments NGOs TNCs Private organisations Local people

Management policy increasingly emphasises prevention rather than treating symptoms. In the issue of pollution, preference is given to treating the problem at its source, by applying the precautionary principle, rather than treating the sink where the pollution is manifested. In health, simple strategies involving education and propaganda targeted, for example, on changing lifestyle habits (particularly diet) can be highly effective.

It is generally more cost-effective in terms of money and lives to control health risks at source. For this reason, primary healthcare is seen as a vital underpinning of any management strategy. However, significant variations can be observed at the global scale. It might be said that the inverse law of care applies, namely that those in most need of prevention and care receive the least.

Challenges

There is increasing debate in the health community over the pros and cons of eradication strategies: are they less costly and more effective than primary health and prevention policies? The WHO programme which resulted in the global eradication of smallpox between 1967 and 1979 raised hopes, but it has not proved possible to eradicate any other human infectious disease.

Today, ageing and mental disorders (sometimes related, but not always) present a particular challenge to health managers. In the extended family that prevails in the developing word, looking after the elderly is seen as a family responsibility. But in the developed world, where the nuclear family is more common, care of the elderly is being transferred from the family to professional providers. The immediate issues here are the costs of care, and who pays. Should care be provided by the state at little or no cost, or should the elderly and their families pay the full price?

According to the WHO, mental disorders are an increasing feature of all societies. Depression is particularly common, affecting about 121 million people, and is among the leading forms of disability globally. It can be reliably diagnosed and treated by primary care, yet fewer than 25% of those affected have access to effective treatments. Constraints on its prevention and treatment centre on the lack of resources and trained providers, and the social stigma associated with it. In many countries this stigma is a major cause of ineffective response to mental health problems.

In some areas of health, risk can be reduced by strategies aimed at modifying lifestyles and behaviour. But much depends on how individuals perceive their own health risks. It is perhaps a human tendency to believe in one's own indestructibility and to think that HIV/AIDS, heart disease and lung cancer only happen to other people. Statistics and advice about unsafe sex, smoking-related diseases, eating disorders and road accidents may not lead to a change in behaviour, even when backed by government. But when governments resort to legislation they risk being accused of creating a 'nanny state'.

The strategies and policies considered so far are mainly to do with long-term health risks. Also required, however, are strategies to deal with short-term health risks such as epidemics and hazards: what might be termed 'emergency' situations.

Responsible national governments have strategies in place to deal with regularly experienced hazards, such as minor earthquakes or outbreaks of influenza. But sometimes the scale of an emergency can be more than even the best laid plans can cope with, in which case a large-scale international response may be required. The 2004 Asian tsunami is an example of this (see case study).

Case study | The health risks of the Asian tsunami

The Asian tsunami of 2004 killed more than 280,000 people and displaced 1 million. The top health priorities immediately following the disaster were to rescue and treat the injured, bury the dead, restore the supply of safe water, ensure adequate sanitation and maintain basic standards of hygiene. This was followed by the mass immunisation of 1.2 million children against measles, a major potential killer that flourishes in the aftermath of such emergencies. Undernourished refugees and displaced people are particularly vulnerable. Essential drugs and vitamin A were supplied to more than 3 million people. Thanks to an effective and coordinated short-term response to the disaster by governments and non-government bodies from around the world, there were no large-scale outbreaks of infectious diseases.

The provision of primary health centres in many of the affected areas of Indonesia, Sri Lanka, India, Thailand, Malaysia, the Maldives and Somalia has already done much to minimise the longer-term

Photograph 13.4 Packaged meals at a US Air Force base in Japan en route to southeast Asia as aid to tsunami victims

health risks following the disaster. There is, however, one persistent medical need, namely counselling for the hundreds of thousands traumatised by the loss of family, friends, homes and material possessions.

Further research

www.who.int/hac/crises/international/asia_tsunami/en/

Agencies involved in health risk

A range of governmental bodies, transnational corporations and non-governmental organisations are involved in trying to reduce health risks. These operate at different levels: global, national and local.

Global

International organisations, TNCs and NGOs are all involved in managing health risk. An example of each is given below.

World Health Organization (WHO)

The WHO was set up in 1948 by the UN and now numbers 191 states as its members. Currently, it main objectives are:

➤ to help strengthen national health services around the globe, particularly in low-income countries

➤ to promote and protect health
➤ to prevent and control specific health problems
➤ to support medical and health research

AstraZeneca

This is one of the world's top five pharmaceutical TNCs, active in more than 100 countries, with a workforce of more than 65,000 people engaged in the **research and development** (R&D), manufacture and marketing of drugs and the supply of healthcare services. It has 17 major R&D centres in 8 countries and manufactures in 29 countries, with products focused on a number of medical conditions, including cancer, gastro-intestinal infections, cardiovascular and respiratory diseases. In 2007 sales totalled $29.6 billion and operating profit was $9 billion. More than $5 billion was spent on R&D.

Médecins Sans Frontières

Médecins Sans Frontières (MSF) is an independent international medical human-itarian organisation founded in 1971 by doctors and journalists. It is now a worldwide movement with regional offices in 19 countries, delivering emergency aid in more than 60 countries to people affected by armed conflict, epidemics, natural or human-made disasters or exclusion from healthcare.

In emergencies and their aftermath, MSF rehabilitates and runs hospitals and clinics, performs surgery, treats disease, carries out vaccination campaigns, operates feeding centres for malnourished children and offers mental healthcare.

Through longer-term programmes, MSF treats patients with infectious diseases such as tuberculosis, sleeping sickness and HIV/AIDS and provides medical and psychological care to marginalised groups such as street children.

National

Most countries today have some form of national health scheme. Their quality and achievements vary enormously. Cuba offers an interesting example.

Cuba's consultorios

Since 1958 the Caribbean island of Cuba has been ruled by a Communist regime. One of the major achievements of that regime has been healthcare which is free to every citizen. The basic health indicators for Cuba are far above low-income country norms – and in some cases ahead of high-income countries. This is all the more remarkable in view of the fact that Cuba has a lower per capita GDP than any other country in Latin America. Life expectancy is the same as in the UK.

As in many countries, healthcare is delivered by a three-tiered system:
➤ *Primary*. Provided in the home, in a clinic or at a health centre. Services include prescribing medication, immunising children and screening for diseases.
➤ *Secondary*. Essentially care that is provided in hospitals. The access route for such care is normally via the primary care system.
➤ *Tertiary*. Specialist investigation and treatment, such as hospitals specialising in the diagnosis and treatment of cancer or undertaking heart and transplant surgery.

A crucial role is played at the primary level by the *consultorios*. These are three-storey buildings where the ground floor is a clinic, the first floor a doctor's flat and the third floor a nurse's flat. They provide a 24/7 medical service.

Local

Many agencies operate at the local level. One example originated in China.

Barefoot doctors

The term 'barefoot doctor' was first used to describe a system of local medical care established in China during the 1960s. Men and women with a little formal training provided basic medical services and helped to educate rural communities in preventative healthcare matters, such as healthy diet, good hygiene and family planning. The system proved a huge success in China and has since been widely imitated in many low-income countries.

Further research

www.who.int – World Health Organization.
www.astrazeneca.com – AstraZeneca:
www.msf.org.uk – Médecins Sans Frontières
www.guardian.co.uk/world/2007/sep/12/film.health – Cuba's health service
www.npr.org/templates/story/story.php?storyId=4990242 – barefoot doctors.

Which health risks can be managed?

It is tempting to think that it should be possible to manage all health risks. We have seen in this chapter that many of today's high-profile diseases are related to forms of pollution. The responsibility for causing most pollution rests broadly with the business community. The responsibility for ensuring that pollution is reduced rests with government. There are encouraging signs that some countries, particularly high-income ones, are capable of gaining the upper hand in the fight against pollution and its health risks. Pollution still exists, but levels have been significantly reduced in post-industrial countries.

However, countries which are just beginning to enjoy some of the fruits of economic development are understandably reluctant to impose controls that might damage industrialisation.

The need to curb the burning of fossil fuels in order to tackle global warming is well known, but the world faces other pollution-related challenges. There are particular problems connected with the disposal of waste, for example the highly toxic components found in many redundant electronic goods. In countries such as India and China, industrial and domestic waste is subject to unregulated scavenging and recycling by the very poor, including children. Meanwhile, as some countries move from fossil fuels to nuclear power, safe disposal of nuclear waste poses a huge challenge. All these types of waste represent considerable health hazards.

It is possible that many, but not all of the health risks associated with pollution can be managed in the sense of reducing the causal factors. But what about diseases that are largely to do with lifestyle? Again, in theory it should be possible

to achieve much by way of management through health education. But this can be a slow process, and it may require some reinforcement by legislation.

Finally, there are the degenerative and chronic diseases, physical and mental, associated with ageing and with genetic disorders. Such health risks are unavoidable. The best hope in terms of management is the delivery of good-quality and appropriate palliative healthcare.

Suggested fieldwork opportunities

Local fieldwork

➤ Use GIS and primary surveys to investigate patterns of mortality and disease.
➤ Use surveys of selected diseases and problems such as drug addiction, obesity and cancer to study patterns of occurrence. This can serve as an introduction to epidemiology.
➤ Study surveys of particular types of pollution using primary and secondary data to identify spatial patterns and areas of risk.

Residential and long-haul

➤ 'Virtual' fieldwork might include surveys of health issues and healthcare access in a low-income country.
➤ Undertake a similar type of fieldwork to assess levels of pollution within a large urban area, a river catchment or a stretch of coast.

Review questions

1 Suggest and justify a classification of health risks.
2 Explain and illustrate the link between health and quality of life.
3 To what extent do you agree with the view that pollution is the greatest source of health risks?
4 Explain and illustrate why some diseases are associated with geographical features.
5 Assess the relative health risks of incidental and sustained pollution.
6 Why and how does pollution change with economic development?
7 'Reducing health risks is best tackled by local rather than international agencies.' Discuss.
8 Select one health risk not related to pollution that you think is difficult to manage. Give your reasons.

Consuming the rural landscape: leisure and tourism

Rural areas are undergoing a structural shift from production to consumption as less land is used for agriculture and more for leisure and tourism. This shift is most marked in accessible rural–urban fringe areas, but it is also occurring even in the most remote rural regions. The consumption of rural space for leisure and tourism is putting pressure on fragile rural landscapes. Such a threat requires careful management.

The growth of leisure and tourism landscapes

What is the relationship between the growth of leisure and tourism and rural landscape use?

By the end of this section you should:
➤ *understand the reasons for the global growth in leisure and tourism*
➤ *be aware of the range of rural landscapes, from the urban fringe to wilderness, and the recreational activities they provide*
➤ *be familiar with the values and attitudes of different groups using rural landscapes*
➤ *realise that different activities in the same rural area may lead to conflicts*

The rise of leisure and tourism

In recent decades farmland and under-utilised green spaces in higher-income countries have often become commercialised spaces for leisure and tourism (Figure 14.1). Several factors explain this. Economic changes such as falling farm incomes mean that new uses must sometimes be found for rural land if local communities are to gain sustainable incomes. Social forces mean that

Figure 14.1
Tourism, leisure and recreation

Non-local recreation

Local recreation

Business and recreational travel

Leisure

Business and personal travel

Recreation

Tourism

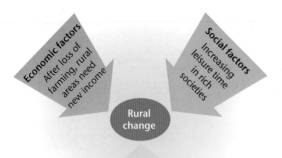

Figure 14.2
The context for a changing countryside

people have more time to devote to leisure and tourism activities. A cultural shift, involving a view of the natural world as something to revere and protect, also helps explain the rise of a more diverse set of uses for the countryside (Figure 14.2).

In the twenty-first century, many low- and middle-income nations have started to experience a similar shift in rural function, driven by:

➤ *local economic need* for sufficient food and stable employment
➤ *globalisation* – the opportunity to benefit from involvement in the global economy

Leisure and tourism, two terms with different meanings, both increased greatly in importance during the twentieth century (Figure 14.1). In the nineteenth century, holidays were still the preserve of the well-to-do. Working people were allowed little time off work. Since then, social and economic changes have brought leisure and tourism into the lives of ordinary people in the world's richer nations:

➤ *Longer annual holiday leave*. At the start of the Industrial Revolution there was no legal requirement for employers to give paid leave to their employees. The UK legal minimum is now 24 days, including bank holidays.
➤ *More free time*. A reduction in the length of the working week has been achieved over time, mainly through trade union lobbying. Many employees can work extra 'flexitime' hours between Monday and Thursday, and take Friday off. Self-employed and home-working people arrange their working weeks to suit themselves. Many people now regularly take short-break (3-day) holidays throughout the year.
➤ *Rising incomes*. The tertiarisation of society (upwardly mobile families shifting from industrial work to office employment) has brought wage rises for many, allowing more people to afford expensive holidays at home and overseas.
➤ *Retirement*. With rising life expectancy in richer nations, millions of active pensioners are looking for new ways to spend their leisure time.

These factors have encouraged rapid expansion across the tourism and leisure sector. Additional influences have helped make rural landscapes an attractive destination for visitors:

➤ *Car ownership*. After the 1920s, rising wages and cheaper cars meant more British families could visit the countryside at weekends.
➤ *Cheap flights*. Falling costs and online booking have made air travel more affordable and accessible.
➤ *Books and magazines*. In 1952, Alfred Wainwright began to publish UK Lake District walking guides; these have brought as many as 2 million visitors to the region. Today, *Rough Guide* publications introduce people to new international

rural destinations. Magazines such as *Country Living* continue to market rural living as an idyllic choice.

➤ *Television and film.* Popular films and nature documentaries attract millions of viewers, many of whom want to visit the places they see.

➤ *Government subsidies for rural areas.* During the 1990s, the UK government encouraged farmers to diversify land use. The Environmental Stewardship initiative pays farmers to maintain their land and buildings in attractive ways that walkers will appreciate. Government agencies, most recently the Countryside Agency, have been created to help manage the countryside.

➤ *Extreme sports.* White-water rafting, paintballing and mountain running are among the outdoor activities that rural landscapes offer to fitness enthusiasts and adrenaline junkies.

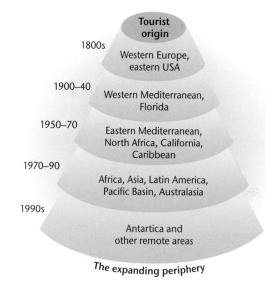

Figure 14.3 The pleasure periphery

➤ *Hippies, artists and artisans.* The 1960s hippies were idealists whose motto was 'Turn on, tune in and drop out.' In the UK, many moved to rural areas such as Cornwall or the Scottish Highlands to follow a 'self-sufficient' lifestyle. Today, artists and artisans still migrate from cities to rural settlements such as Glastonbury, where they aim to make a living producing crafts, organic food or herbal remedies for sale to tourists.

While the masses in high-income nations have new rural tourism and leisure opportunities, billions of people still lack the luxury of leisure time or the resources for tourism. However, that is beginning to change in the emerging economies (Brazil, Russia, India and China) as the rich seek leisure pursuits and begin to travel at home and abroad.

Geographers describe this phenomenon as the growth of the **pleasure periphery** (Figure 14.3). Areas previously viewed as peripheral to the world's economy, some categorised as 'Third World', are now experiencing rising wealth, with increasing numbers of their populations beginning to pursue pleasure. For instance, South Africa now has a large internal rural tourism market. KwaZulu National Park has 8.8 million visitor-days per year; nearly 150,000 people find employment here and it contributes around 10% of the region's GDP.

The range and variety of rural landscapes

While there is no universally agreed definition of 'rural', population statistics often form the basis for measurement. For example, in the UK, a settlement of less than 10,000 people is *not* classified as an urban area. Most attempts to define 'rural' also make a useful contrast between rural 'types' based on levels of remoteness or land use. The UK possesses a highly differentiated rural landscape, with a complex evolution. Distance from major conurbations clearly impacts on the characteris-

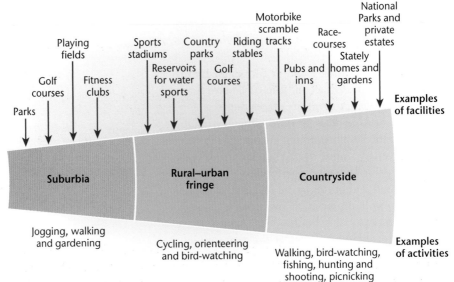

Figure 14.4 Leisure activities along the rural continuum

tics of rural areas. Higher-threshold activities such as golfing are likely to be found in the accessible rural–urban fringes, while more specialised activities such as game hunting may be found in remoter places (Figure 14.4).

Wherever they are in the world, rural areas are diverse – physically, economically and socially. Some areas are well integrated into global networks, linked with other places by varied commercial flows and population movements, both permanent and touristic. Many rural tourist initiatives, especially **rebranding** exercises, aim to give places a heightened profile within a globalised tourist industry. This helps them to become more 'powerful' localities, as measured in terms of their ability to attract people over long distances. Some rural places have become significant tourist hubs through intelligent management of their physical resources for tourism. However, there is also an argument for protecting some rural landscapes from excessively commercialised tourist flows and retaining them as wilderness areas.

Wilderness

Wilderness areas are remote parts of the world whose unspoilt characteristics have ecological, scientific and/or cultural and aesthetic value. Their scale can vary. Large continental areas of the Americas are defined as wilderness, but so too are small corners of rural Britain, such as the granite tors of Dartmoor or remoter parts of the Pennines. A wilderness continuum can be recognised, ranging from truly isolated regions such as Antarctica and Amazonia to tiny pockets of land exhibiting some wilderness characteristics (Figure 14.5).

Wilderness landscapes are commonly seen as those unmodified by any significant human impact. However, some commentators maintain that very few natural environments are truly 'untouched' (Photograph 14.1). Much tropical rainforest is actually secondary growth, thanks to the age-old practices of shifting cultivation. Tropical and temperate grasslands, such as New Zealand's Canterbury

Low wilderness quality			Moderate wilderness quality		High wilderness quality
Urban industrial environment	Rural environment intensive farming: cattle farming market gardening	Rural environment: extensive farming	Natural environments used for leisure and farming	Conserved natural environments	Pristine wilderness

Examples

Urban parks	Small nature reserves, large parks	National Parks and marine parks, e.g. English Lake District	UN World Heritage sites e.g. Iguazu National Park, Argentina	Antarctica, Alaska, Gobi Desert

Figure 14.5 The wilderness continuum

Plains, may owe much to ancient human practices of burning forest to flush out game. The UK's wilderness moors have usually been exposed to sheep farming.

However, the world's wildernesses are now under pressure as a result of what the geographer Janelle called 'time–space compression'. Tourists and venture capitalists pay greater attention to previously isolated regions such as Antarctica, as distance is 'eradicated' by transport and communications technologies such as air travel and the internet. In this 'shrinking world', wilderness regions are opened up to the flows of globalisation.

Photograph 14.1 A road and vapour trails in the 'wilderness' of Utah, USA

Simon Oakes

Further research

www.wild.org – the Wild Foundation, dedicated to wilderness protection.
www.discoveringantarctica.org.uk – an education site about Antarctica.

Migration

Recent migration trends also influence the rural patterns that have emerged in more affluent nations. In Europe and North America, counter-urbanisation has affected not only fringe regions but increasingly the more remote or 'deep' countryside. In some remote parts of the British Isles, such as the Scottish islands of Arran, Islay and Mull, incomers have established innovative tourist ventures. But this has sometimes sparked conflict with other migrants, attracted to these same places by their commercially 'unspoiled' wilderness characteristics.

Contested space

European Union concerns about food security mean that agriculture is supported and often subsidised under Common Agricultural Policy regulations, adding weight to farmers' influence over the use of rural space. Another influence is the need to protect areas of unique biological or geological interest. In the UK, these are known as Sites of Special Scientific Interest (SSSIs). There are over 4,000 of them in England.

The range of powerful forces brought to bear on the UK countryside leads human geographers to describe it as a **contested space**, meaning that its use is often disputed, which results in diverse characteristics.

Attitudes towards the use of rural space

Rural geographers use the word **rurality** to describe a particular perception of rural space. For example, some people see rural areas purely in terms of their natural resources, such as their suitability for agriculture. Others enjoy rural landscapes for aesthetic reasons, such as beauty or cultural heritage. Still others see rural areas principally as places where low-income indigenous people live and thus as a problem to be managed. The key groups of players with varying and often conflicting 'ruralities' include:

➤ *Government.* The primary concern of local government is to ensure local people have good quality of life and opportunities to earn a living. It could be keen to promote a 'whatever works' model of economic development, even if the environmental impact is relatively high.
➤ *Governmental agencies.* Some UK agencies, such as Natural England, have a duty to preserve protected areas and the species that live in them.
➤ *Farmers and businesses.* Farmers and other commercial land users may wish to restrict the number of people walking on their land, which is why 'right to roam' proposals are often controversial. Natural England wants to see the entire UK coastline opened up to walkers. This would require many landowners to grant public access.
➤ *Environmental pressure groups.* Friends of the Earth, Greenpeace and other lobbying and campaigning groups may attempt to block the commercial development of ecologically sensitive rural areas.
➤ *Communities and individuals.* Many rural communities and individuals mobilise opposition to planning permissions for new tourist, agricultural or industrial ventures in their area. Counter-urbanisation incomers are often professional people able to articulate NIMBY ('not in my back yard') and other objections.

Case study

Rural landscapes of the UK

During the 1990s a team of rural geographers identified four 'typical' rural landscapes in the UK and analysed who holds power over these places.

Preserved countryside

Typical of the English lowlands (including large areas of Surrey and Kent) and more accessible upland areas such as the Lake District, this type of rural landscape is characterised by 'preservationist' attitudes. Middle-class incomers now dominate areas perceived to be rich in natural and/or cultural heritage. New development plans that threaten the 'chocolate box' image of the area are likely to be challenged by these migrant home-owners who use the local planning system to preserve the rural landscape.

Contested countryside

In areas just out of reach of the metropolitan commuting zone, farmers and industrial development interests may still exercise power, especially if the landscape lacks special environmental quality. However, these remoter rural areas are also starting to receive larger numbers of in-migrants, thanks in part to the availability of work-from-home broadband internet access. Conflicts arise because incomers want to see the countryside preserved as a wilderness, while farmers instead want a productive working landscape. Parts of Yorkshire fit this profile, notably areas where villages were abandoned to make way for reservoirs.

Paternalistic countryside

This term describes rural landscapes where the 'paternal' power of old (perhaps aristocratic) estate owners and large farms has gone almost entirely unchallenged. However, in the face of falling estate incomes, some major landowners are now actively seeking to diversify, introducing new ventures such as hunting trips, with a view to achieving economically sustainable long-term estate management. Because such areas often have not experienced large-scale in-migration, it may be possible to maintain a sense of wilderness. Scotland's Isle of Jura (Photograph 14.2) fits this profile well: here the Ruantallain estate offers rich tourists a deer-stalking opportunity at '£371 per stag'.

Clientelistic countryside

In some of the UK's most remote rural areas, economic activity is not viable without state support. Counter-urbanisation has brought few incomers here. The remoteness, inaccessibility and poor climate in these areas mean tourism revenues are limited. Local politics are dominated by concerns about employment and the sustainability of the community. People here have become highly dependent on government grants and subsidies. These are features of life for many fringe areas of the Highlands and Islands of Scotland and parts of mid-Wales.

www.islayinfo.com

Photograph 14.2 The 'paternalistic' Jura landscape

Leisure and tourism activities and their conflicts

The contested nature of the countryside makes conflict a recurring feature in studies of rural tourism. Increasingly, such conflicts have spread from high-income countries to rural regions of lower-income nations situated on the pleasure periphery.

One example of this is Machu Picchu, an Inca city lying 2,430 m above sea level in Peru's upper Amazon basin. In 1981 the Peruvian government established a rural land reserve in this area to protect its diverse and fragile ecosystems, but it is now suffering from 'loved to death' syndrome, and the Inca Trail is threatened with erosion by growing numbers of walkers. Tourism is encouraged in Peru, where over 50% of the population live below the poverty line. A doubling of the nation's tourist industry between 1990 and 2000 should therefore have been a cause for celebration. But an increase in visitor numbers from 200,000 to over 500,000 per year has resulted in Machu Picchu being placed on the World Heritage 'endangered list'.

More on the subject of conflict is to be found later in this chapter in the section on impacts on rural landscapes and management issues.

The significance and fragility of rural landscapes

What is the significance of some rural landscapes used for leisure and tourism?

By the end of this section you should:
➤ *understand the physical significance and ecological value of some rural landscapes*
➤ *be aware of the complex links between people and ecosystems*
➤ *understand the value of carrying capacity and resilience models*
➤ *be familiar with a range of qualitative and quantitative criteria used to measure the quality of rural environments*

Ecological value and fragility

The ecological value of many rural landscapes invests them with special significance. Rural areas also include historical and cultural resources for tourism, of course: for example the site near Hastings where Norman invaders defeated the English in 1066. But in this section we focus on the unique status rural areas derive from their physical and ecological attributes, and at how they may be protected if they are also to be enjoyed by people.

Plant succession

Rural landscapes such as woodlands have developed over centuries through a sequence of changes known as plant succession (Figure 14.6). Initially, only very simple organisms such as lichens, mosses and grass can survive on an unvegetated site. Over time, these pioneer species modify their environment by increasing the depth of soil and its nutrient content and allowing more complex, deeper-rooting species to invade and colonise. In the UK, in the absence of any local arresting factors woodland is usually the final stage of plant succession – known as climatic climax vegetation.

Windsor Forest is one of the last small areas of the UK's ancient and natural climatic climax woodland to survive into the modern era. Once a vast royal hunting estate, the 3,100 hectares of woodland hold more than 900 oak and beech trees that are over 500 years old. More than 2,000 species of invertebrate and 1,000 species of fungi have been found here, testimony to the rich **biodiversity** of Britain's native deciduous forest. Natural England now manages Windsor Forest as a 'post-industrial forest' dedicated to recreational uses and conservation.

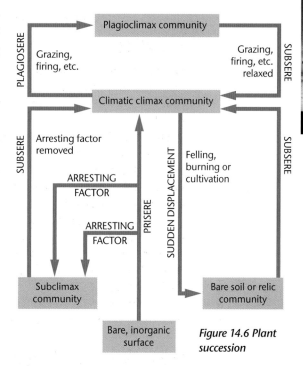

Figure 14.6 Plant succession

Fragility

Fragility is an inherent property of all ecosystems. It is their vulnerability to disturbance, particularly by human activity. Identifying individual species and whole ecosystems that are likely to be seriously damaged by human activities is an important part of nature conservation. Measuring fragility is an essential part of environmental impact assessment. Clearly, the degree of fragility will vary according to the nature and pressure of particular human activities.

Natural world–human world linkages

Much of our seemingly 'natural' countryside is actually the result of thousands of years of intervention and modification of ecological processes by people working the land for food, fuel and timber. Large areas of the UK are covered with heather moorland which in many cases is a **plagioclimax** community. This landscape has been shaped by land-use factors such as repeated burning and sheep grazing. Such practices have prevented tree seedlings from recolonising, ruling out any secondary succession towards woodland.

Non-biological physical systems also influence landscapes in rural areas. Hillside erosion and mass movement processes give the land its relief, assisted by fluvial downcutting and the lateral erosion that rivers bring to floodplains. The hydrological process of runoff also shapes the land, especially in arid regions, where the absence of vegetation allows surface wash and gullying to act unimpeded during extreme rainfall events. The contours of dry rural landscapes are consequently both smoothed and rounded yet also deeply dissected by channels known as wadis that are only filled with water during brief intermittent periods of rain.

Non-biological processes also aid the creation of ecological habitats. For instance, an appreciation of the interconnectedness of different biological and non-biological physical systems has been the key to successful river restoration aiming to replenish fish stocks for the leisure pursuit of angling (see case study).

River restoration is the process of reintroducing important physical and biological characteristics to a stretch of water that has previously suffered from overexploitation. It can include efforts to reconstruct meanders along an artificially straightened river, or the reintroduction of key species that have been lost to pollution, fishing and hunting.

Case study   River restoration for leisure and trout fishing

River restoration is an important tool for both rural and urban tourism. Simple passive enjoyment of the beauty of riversides attracts visitors in large numbers, making such sites popular locations for new restaurants and bars (flood risks notwithstanding). Clean water also provides opportunities for more active pursuits such as angling, boating and water sports.

River restoration schemes are now found throughout the UK, Europe and North America. In south London, both the ecology and morphology of the River Wandle have been restored to a high level. Riverside walks and new visitor shopping sites such as Merton Abbey Mills bring greatly enhanced opportunities for leisure in an urban area previously associated with low environmental quality.

Rural river restoration often aims to restore biodiversity so that anglers are provided with good stocks

of fish. In such cases, geomorphological restoration is also necessary, because physical and biological elements are intimately connected via habitats. For example, the continued residence of trout in a stream depends on there being a wide variety of river channel features for their use and enjoyment. Adult fish prefer deep meander pools to lounge around in, while riffles and gravels are an essential habitat for spawning. Oxbow lakes that connect with the main river channel provide an important refuge from predators. They also offer relatively warm water temperatures to young fish during their crucial first winter.

If any one of these vital habitat components is missing, so too are the trout. Where rivers have been 'canalised', it becomes necessary to restore a range of landscape features. Meanders, pools, riffles and gravels are all needed if the full range of trout

Figure 14.7 River landforms that serve as favoured trout habitats

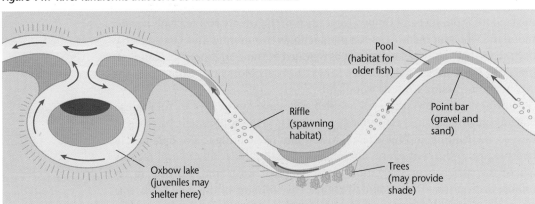

habitats is to be replicated (Figure 14.7). If one important landform element is not restored, the life cycle of the adult fish cannot be completed. Attempts to repopulate the river with trout are likely to fail and anglers will seek leisure opportunities elsewhere.

Further research
www.wildtrout.org
www.monnow.org.uk/project.html
http://waterworlds.wordpress.com/2008/03/29/26
    -river-restoration-%E2%99%A5-meanders

Case study: The significance and fragility of four ecosystems

Heather moors

Large areas of Britain's heather moors are actually plagioclimax (partly manmade), often underlain by a thick blanket of peat. Their aesthetic appeal merited poetry from Wordsworth, while the works of Beatrix Potter and the Brontë sisters also feature a backdrop of upland moors. The Highland Clearances left Scotland's moors with a dark and bloody history. Today, tourists from all over the world enjoy visiting Britain's moors, regardless of whether or not they are a truly 'natural' wilderness (Photograph 14.3).

Did you know...?
- During the foot-and-mouth outbreak of 2001, widespread culling of sheep led to the re-invasion of woodland in parts of the Lake District.
- Peat is a significant carbon store.

Further research
www.heathertrust.co.uk

Alaska

Covering nearly 2 million km², Alaska borders the Arctic Ocean and is home to species such as caribou, wolverine and brown bear. Glacial retreat is closely monitored here, as well as tectonic activity along the western seaboard. Oil extraction from Prudhoe Bay remains controversial. When the *Exxon Valdez* oil tanker ran aground in 1988, Alaska's fragile food web disintegrated along its polluted coastline. With great reserves of oil untapped, will Alaska remain strictly protected if US fears over energy security grow?

Did you know...?
Much of Alaska is underlain by permafrost. If climate change causes this to melt, vast amounts of methane (a potent greenhouse gas) will be released, contributing to even more global warming.

Further research
http://home.nps.gov/applications/parksearch/state.cfm?st=ak

Photograph 14.3 Heather moorland on the Kintyre peninsula

Simon Oakes

Formby sand dunes

North of Liverpool, a remarkable little UK nature reserve clings to the shoreline. The Formby sand dunes are actively conserved by the National Trust, meaning that they are no longer 'natural' in the strictest sense. The hollows between dune ridges are home to small ponds that have become an important ecological habitat for rare species. Most famous of these is the natterjack toad. The National Trust manages these ponds, preventing them from in-filling with sand. If the area is to remain popular with nature lovers, continued survival of this species is important.

Did you know…?

Formby is also one of the few remaining strongholds of English red squirrels, whose numbers have been reduced by competition and disease from American grey squirrels. The red squirrel is also a key species for tourism – children love to feed them.

Further research

www.bbc.co.uk/naturescalendar/spring/sandy_coast/formby/formby.shtml

Bryce Canyon

Bryce Canyon National Park, in the High Plateaus region of the Colorado Plateau in Utah, was established in 1928. The canyon includes striking rock spires called 'hoodoos'. The four rock types found here, limestone, siltstone, dolomite and mudstone, erode at different rates, which is what causes the undulating shapes of the hoodoos (Photograph 14.4). Bryce is a true wilderness destination, with minimal visitor facilities.

Did you know…?

Although much of southern Utah is semi-arid, ice is the dominant weathering agent at Bryce Canyon. The region experiences about 200 daily freeze–thaw cycles each year.

Further research

www.brycecanyon.com

Photograph 14.4
Bryce Canyon
National Park

Cameron Dunn

Carrying capacity and resilience

Protecting fragile rural environments requires that we develop tools:

➤ to decide whether a place deserves the financial investment needed to deliver special protection, such as National Park status
➤ to monitor the impacts that visitors bring
➤ to investigate whether a rural area has experienced too much stress

One of the hardest tasks facing environmental agencies wishing to designate areas in need of special protection is to identify and establish a clear spatial boundary. Unfortunately, ecosystem boundaries rarely coincide with government boundaries.

Resilience

The **resilience** of environments and their organisms to visitor or use impacts can be analysed (Figure 14.8). In this context, resilience is the ability of an ecosystem or other physical system to recover and return to a normal state of equilibrium after a disturbance or disruption caused by its **recreational carrying capacity** being exceeded (Figure 14.9). The carrying capacity concept has its origins in studies of ecology, animal grazing and agriculture. It describes an important aspect of the relationship between grazing animals and their food – namely the limit or threshold of the system. When applied to studies of tourism and leisure, it is called recreational carrying capacity, and includes:

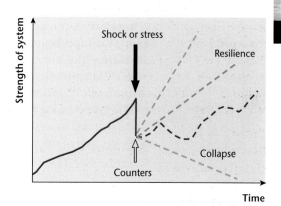

Figure 14.8 The concept of resilience: a resilient system recovers after a shock or stress; it does not collapse

➤ psychological capacity (when a sense of overcrowding begins to occur)
➤ environmental capacity (unacceptable change to flora, fauna and habitat)

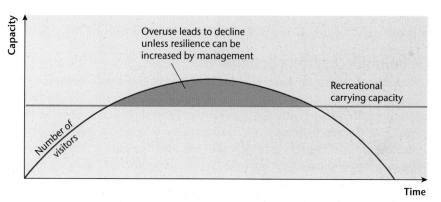

Figure 14.9 Recreational carrying capacity.

In order to use this concept effectively as a management tool, stakeholders need to reach consensus concerning a *measurable* threshold of *acceptable* environmental quality that should not be crossed. Various quality standards and sustainability indicators can be chosen to assist with this process, including:

➤ agreeing maximum acceptable numbers at a peak moment – although it is sometimes argued that numbers of *activities* should be limited rather than numbers of *people*
➤ regular monitoring of sites, with special attention to desire lines or 'social trails' where visitors stray from established routes

> giving wardens, local guides, site staff and volunteers a checklist of items to monitor in their daily routines, e.g. looking at damage to important monuments, trail erosion, pollution, ecosystem status and visitor numbers

Managing carrying capacity

What management responses can be put in place if carrying capacity thresholds are breached? Common mitigation measures include reducing promotional activity, issuing advance bookings only, closing some car parks and paths and introducing price increases at peak times.

It is also important to recognise that the 'recreational capacity' of a site or area is never fixed. It can always be changed through management intervention, for example by increasing the size of buildings or walkways.

Applying the concept of recreational carrying capacity is sometimes difficult, mainly because of the subjective and potentially conflicting views of stakeholders on what constitutes an 'acceptable' appearance and level of stress, both aesthetically and in terms of protection. Any site is also unlikely to be uniform in character, and a 'one size fits all' approach may not be the best way to run a visitor site.

Measuring environmental quality

If uncontroversial boundaries are to be set for protected areas, environmental quality measurements must be made. You will already be familiar with the maps geographers routinely use to show distribution patterns for the soils, vegetation and geology of a region. Of these, geological maps are least likely to be controversial, because abrupt changes in rock type occur all the time in nature as a result of faulting and folding. Geological margins can be identified and mapped.

Delimiting ecosystem boundaries

Unless it is an island, however, establishing boundaries for an ecosystem can be far more problematic. For example, one does not directly exit a canopy of lush equatorial rainforest to enter the grassy plains of western Africa, as some world biome maps seem to suggest. In reality, there is a broad transitional area to explore. Rainforest trees gradually thin out and diminish in height across a 500-km-wide zone called the **ecotone**. Yet for the purpose of drawing maps, a definitive boundary is often required, rather than a 'grey area'.

How do we establish where the line should be drawn? A range of quantitative and qualitative data is required to support the judgement. Quantitative data are 'hard' numerical facts, such as the frequency of occurrence of key indicator species recorded along a transect through the imagined boundary. A threshold level may be applied which then allows the boundary to be formally established. Similar tests can be applied to local soils, perhaps investigating changes in soil pH or horizonal development.

There are also qualitative measures to consider, such as the overall 'look' or 'feel' of the landscape. These might perhaps be assessed using an environmental quality index. However, such techniques rely on subjective interpretations made by researchers as they explore their environment. Inevitably, personal aesthetics will

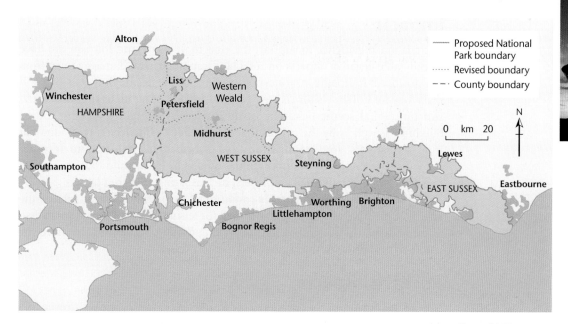

Figure 14.10
Proposed
boundaries for
South Downs
National Park, 2008

intrude on each researcher's observations. For this reason, qualitative judgements may be deemed unreliable.

A good example of this kind of work in practice is efforts made in the UK since 2002 to set a boundary for the proposed South Downs National Park. Originally it was suggested that this include a region called the Western Weald (Figure 14.10). However, a more recent official recommendation now excludes this region on the basis of differences in geology: the Western Weald lacks chalk parent rock. Many local people disagree with this ruling, arguing that it still shares a 'general character' with the rest of this rural region.

Further research

For information about the South Downs National Park:

www.countryside.gov.uk/LAR/Landscape/DL/new_designations/SouthDowns/index
   .asp www.planning-inspectorate.gov.uk/southdowns
www.countryside.gov.uk/LAR/Landscape/DL/new_designations/SouthDowns/whole
   _boundary.asp

Impact on rural landscapes

What impact does leisure and tourism have on rural landscapes?

By the end of this section you should:
➤ *be aware of the negative and positive impacts of leisure and tourism on rural landscapes*
➤ *appreciate that these impacts change over time*
➤ *realise that the level of economic development affects the opportunities and threats associated with tourism*

Impacts

There is much evidence to support the view that leisure and tourism can have considerable negative impacts on rural landscapes. Physical damage ranges from the erosion of footpaths in honeypot locations to the destruction of habitats to make way for hotels, visitor centres, golf courses and other items of tourist infrastructure. Rural scenic beauty is easily marred by unsightly modern tourist buildings as well as by the pylons that supply them with electricity. Traditional rural settlements and communities are disturbed by visitors and incomer residents. The employment opportunities offered by leisure and tourism make it more difficult for traditional employers, such as farms, to recruit labour.

The severity of these impacts is conditioned by broader factors, such as the appeal of the rural area, whether it is used for leisure or tourism, and its accessibility, particularly from large, leisure-seeking urban populations. In short, the nature of the leisure or tourist demand has an impact.

Positive impacts

Not all human impacts on rural landscapes are catastrophic or irreversibly destructive. There are many positive interventions, such as wildlife protection and nature conservation. Over the last 200 years, laws have been passed to protect animals, plants, ancient monuments and landscape elements from harm or exploitation. Important benchmarks include:

➤ *The foundation of the RSPCA (1824) and the RSPB (1889)*. These are two of the UK's largest charities and have pursued private prosecution of people found to be causing suffering to animals or birds. This would have seemed an absurd idea to people alive in Britain 200 years ago, when attitudes towards wildlife were very different.

➤ *The US Endangered Species Act (1973) and the foundation of IUCN (International Union for Conservation of Nature and Natural Resources) (1948)*. Throughout the world, harsh penalties now exist for poachers caught shooting rare species such as the rhino and tiger. In the UK, it has even become an offence to pick endangered flowering plants or to disturb nesting wild birds.

➤ *World Heritage sites*. Since 1972, over 800 sites have been awarded official recognition by the UN, many of them in rural areas.

However, World Heritage site status or SSSI designation cannot always guarantee environmental protection. Pollution of air, land and water blights even wilderness regions. The beaches of Antarctica and Alaska are strewn with the plastic flotsam of global consumerism, while the foothills of Mt Everest now look like a municipal dump.

Changing impacts over time

The uses of rural landscapes have changed significantly over time. From Mediterranean coastal resorts to true wilderness regions, visitor numbers have risen and impacts have intensified. Even Antarctica is now a commercialised continent – the British Antarctic Survey has opened a gift shop (in Port Lockroy) that now receives 7,000 visitors each year. On a smaller scale, the long-deserted Scottish island of St Kilda, one of only 24 global locations awarded World Heritage site status for both natural and cultural heritage, has begun to attract day visitors for the first time, since a speedboat service has been introduced.

The media play a major role in unleashing tourist impacts on distant places. Remote rural locations used in films can often experience a sudden wave of tourism. For example, Alnwick in Northumberland has become a popular destination for fans of Harry Potter films. Thailand's Phi Phi islands, once the exclusive preserve of a handful of privileged visitors, have become a playground for the masses since *The Beach* was filmed there. Television also creates magnets for rural tourism. Filming of the BBC children's television show *Balamory* on the Scottish island of Mull (Photograph 14.5) triggered an influx of tiny tourists (accompanied by their parents).

Photograph 14.5
Tobermory on Mull has had an influx of tourism owing to the children's television programme **Balamory**

In such media hotspots a period of high popularity can lead to market saturation, after which visitor numbers and impacts fall. Equally, after an initial time lag, visitor facilities may catch up with the rise in demand, but by this time damage has been done. Improved sewerage treatment was only introduced to many Mediterranean resorts long after the early boom decades had heavily polluted inshore waters.

Further research

The following websites give details of film and television locations:
www.imdb.com/Sections/Locations
www.scotlandthemovie.com
www.visitbuckinghamshire.org/site/midsomer-murders

Different economic development contexts

Much of this chapter is about the impact of leisure and tourism on the landscapes of high-income countries. But as the pleasure periphery expands and disposable income and leisure time increase, tourism hotspots are beginning to emerge in lower-income countries. Table 14.1 looks at two countries at different stages of development.

Table 14.1 Rural tourism in Ethiopia and China: opportunities and threats

	Ethiopia	China
Opportunities	Ethiopia is more often associated with famine than tourism. Now, the government wants to see the country rebranded as a tourism hotspot. Ethiopia's landscapes include highlands, the Great Rift Valley, white-water rivers, waterfalls, rainforest and the source of the Nile	China's emerging middle class is looking for tourist and leisure opportunities close to home. Greater numbers of international tourists are also arriving
	In recent years, several National Parks have been designated, e.g. Nechisar. As Ethiopia lacks the resources to promote its National Parks, a non-profit organisation has been called in to help. In 2 years, visitor numbers have almost quadrupled	The Great Wall of China (a World Cultural Heritage site) is a popular visitor attraction. But in the desert of Xinjiang and the plains of Shanxi, where few people visit, thousands of kilometres of the wall are disappearing
	Ethiopia is the birthplace of humankind. The skeleton of *Australopithecus afarensis*, a human ancestor who lived 3.5 million years ago, was unearthed in 1974. Hadar, in the Afar region, where the discovery was made, has become a World Heritage site	China's rich dinosaur fossil beds make 'dino-tourism' a potential growth pole for rural areas such as Liaoning province in the northeast
		The 2,000-km^2 Wolong nature reserve in the mountains of Sichuan province is one of the last protected homes of the giant panda. It is a UNESCO 'Man and Biosphere' protected area; 1,000 local jobs have been created in tourism and forest protection
Threats	Afar is a haven for bandits, thanks to its remoteness. In 2007, 12 European tourists were kidnapped here. Conflict with neighbouring Somalia also poses dangers. Areas near the Eritrean border, in the Gambela region to the west and in Afar are now off limits to tourists	In Wolong, restrictions on logging and collection of firewood and medicinal plants have caused hardship to local people. Some 176 mine sites and 25 micro-hydro projects have been closed down, causing more job losses; 5,000 indigenous people have been resettled
	As the local population increases, so do pressures to graze cattle in Nechisar National Park, to fish and to collect wood. The government has decreed that recent migrants to the park must leave. The Guji tribe have had their homes burnt by government officials. The conservation organisation managing the park has left in protest	NASA satellite images suggest that habitat loss has increased since the reserve was created, as a result of tourist impacts and growth in numbers of indigenous people. The Great Wall is under considerable visitor pressure and suffering erosion
Further research	http://tourismethiopia.org/	www.unep-wcmc.org/sites/wh/sichuan.html

Photograph 14.6 Tourists in Ethiopia

Trevor Cole

Rural landscape management issues

How can rural landscapes used for leisure and tourism be managed?

By the end of this section you should:
➤ *be familiar with the arguments for and against the management of rural landscapes*
➤ *be aware of the range of possible management strategies*
➤ *understand the conflict that arises between users and managers of the rural landscape*
➤ *appreciate the effectiveness of different management strategies*

To manage or not to manage?

Many groups and organisations help shape the relationship between rural landscapes and the varying forms of tourism and leisure.

In high-income nations, **governance** becomes especially complicated. The term describes a more diffuse power structure than 'government' and includes the actions of many organisations. Some of these hold direct power because they have unrestricted access to funding, while others exercise a broader influencing or advisory role. Rural areas that politicians regard as 'problem regions', such as the rural coast and islands of Strathclyde in Scotland, tend to generate exceptionally complex governance actor-networks (Figure 14.11).

Where a rural community's continued social and economic cohesion are in doubt, tourism can become a vital tool for regional development. Both **top-down** and **bottom-up** efforts are likely to focus on driving visitor numbers as high as possible – which may bring conflict if other organisations (such as nature agencies) wish instead to preserve the landscape and protect it from tourist pressures.

There is also a newly revived conflict between productive activities

Figure 14.11
Governance of the rural coast and islands of Strathclyde: the actor-network of stakeholders

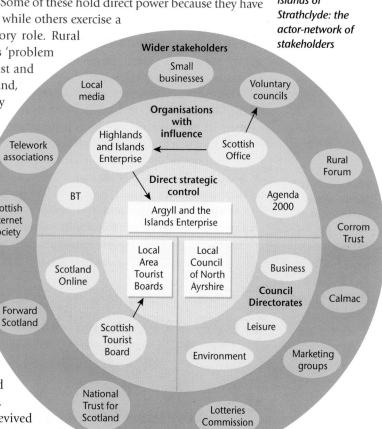

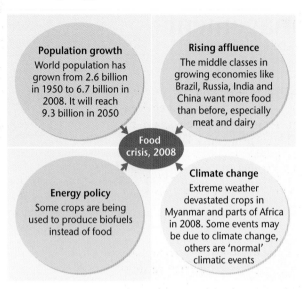

Population growth
World population has grown from 2.6 billion in 1950 to 6.7 billion in 2008. It will reach 9.3 billion in 2050

Rising affluence
The middle classes in growing economies like Brazil, Russia, India and China want more food than before, especially meat and dairy

Food crisis, 2008

Energy policy
Some crops are being used to produce biofuels instead of food

Climate change
Extreme weather devastated crops in Myanmar and parts of Africa in 2008. Some events may be due to climate change, others are 'normal' climatic events

Figure 14.12 The global food crisis, 2008

(farming) and consumption interests (leisure and tourism) to consider. Since 2008, global concerns over escalating food prices have brought nations fresh worries about **food security** (Figure 14.12). In 2008, for example, European ministers announced that the farming set-aside scheme, which funded farmers to leave land uncultivated, would be phased out. This decision was prompted by worries about food shortages, but set-aside land is valuable for wildlife.

Meanwhile, the growth of affluent populations in China and India has sent global demand for dairy and meat products soaring. Enormous amounts of grain are needed to feed cattle on the scale required. As the world's population continues to grow not just in numbers but also in wealth, will some rural landscapes currently used for leisure purposes need to be returned to agriculture? The move towards greater adoption of **biofuels** is also certain to make some rural recreational areas revert to crop growing, notably in the USA.

Perhaps the new global food crisis makes talk of a 'post-productive' countryside appear premature. Questions are increasingly being asked about existing rural land management strategies, including:

➤ *What rights should indigenous people hold over their land and its ecology?* In 2008, the US Supreme Court made polar bears an endangered species (20,000 remain). Native American Inuit people gain part of their living by acting as guides for rich tourists who wish to 'bag a bear'. They believe the ban will slow their economic development. Can a compromise be found?

➤ *Should rural landscapes be restored, wherever possible, to an 'authentic' state?* Many rural landscapes are not 'natural' at all. In the UK, 85% of forest had been converted to grazing land and heather moor by the time of the Norman Conquest. Should more forest in Britain be restored?

➤ *Should dangerous species be returned to rural landscapes?* The EU has paid for the restoration of habitats in Scotland's Caledonian forest reserve – including the reintroduction of wild boar. As part of the quest for greater authenticity, campaigners now want bears and wolves reintroduced (Photograph 14.7). Can this really be justified?

Photograph 14.7 Should wolves be reintroduced to Scottish forests?

Ingram

Rural management strategies

A range of strategies is available for managing rural landscapes.

Conservation

The strategy of **conservation** involves the efficient and non-wasteful use of natural resources, including landscapes, for tourism, as well as more general environmental protection. It is an important concept on which to base **sustainable management** (or **sustainable development**). It acknowledges that humanity has an obligation when consuming resources not to deprive its descendants of what they will need to survive. Some commercially orientated management approaches, such as Alpine ski resorts or Iceland's thermally heated outdoor spas, are compatible with attempts at nature conservation.

Preservation

While conservationists view rural landscapes as a natural resource that can be made available for sustainable commercial exploitation, a **preservation** management approach views nature, and especially wilderness, as something best left untouched by human commerce. The UK's National Parks strategy has its roots here. Criticism of preservationist attitudes has often focused on where the power lies to decide which areas should be preserved. Decision making will most likely be rooted in the understanding of ecosystems or geology. However, there is strong potential for adverse economic effects on *people* already living in areas earmarked for preservation.

Responsible ecotourism

One model for addressing the problems of sustainable exploitation is responsible **ecotourism**. This approach attempts to enhance rather than diminish the prospects of local people. For example, in South Africa's KwaZulu National Park, local people have become stakeholders in ecotourism. Earnings from tourism are taxed and the money used to build schools, clinics and housing – as well as to establish of community-run ecotourism businesses (one local group now takes tourists to view the sea turtle beaches during the nesting season).

Environmental stewardship

Closely associated with ecotourism is the strategy of **environmental stewardship**, whereby people become 'caretakers' of rural landscapes. This links with sustainability approaches as it suggests that the natural world is entrusted to our care before being passed on to successive generations, thereby delivering intergenerational equity.

In the UK, environmental stewardship rules encourage farmers to make land management improvements that will bring benefits for the environment, people and wildlife. The scheme's primary objectives are to:
- conserve wildlife (biodiversity)
- maintain and enhance landscape quality and character
- protect the historic environment and natural resources
- promote public access and understanding of the countryside
- protect natural resources

Further research

www.defra.gov.uk/erdp/pdfs/es/es-promotional-booklet.pdf
www.qca.org.uk/geography/innovating/examples/ecotourism_safrica.rtf
www.iucn.org/what/issues/protected/index.cfm?uNewsID=1719

Conflicts between users and managers

This chapter has explored ways in which tourism and leisure activities reveal the contested character of rural environments in countries at all income levels. Indeed, conflicts do seem more or less inevitable, given the range of demands placed on rural space and the wide variety of user groups found there. These include tourists, nature lovers, established residents, recent incomers, established and new start-up businesses, major landowners and government agencies (Figure 14.13).

Figure 14.13 A conflict matrix for rural areas

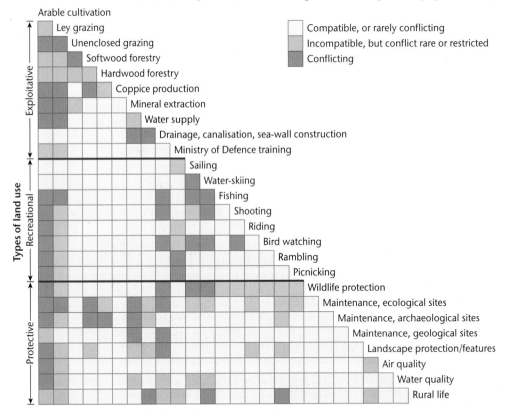

Case study — Managing tourism in Arran

During the twentieth century the island of Arran became a popular summer destination for hill walkers and campers. It was believed that the island's beauty should be preserved, as this was the way visitors wanted it. However, while employment in farming and fishing declined, tourism failed to provide replacement full-time work for local people. The problem was that the visitors only came in summer, and spent little money.

Local government and development agencies

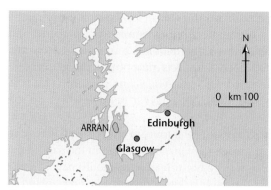

Figure 14.14 Map showing the location of Arran

in the hope that they will spend more and help to generate jobs. However, Arran is now home to many people who originally discovered it through hill-walking holidays. They have become residents precisely because they thought the island would be preserved as a wild and unspoiled place. These are the people who now object to the commercial model of tourism being pursued by local government and businesses.

have recently tried to steer leisure use of the island away from backpacking nature tourism. Instead, they have granted planning permission for a number of large new visitor attractions, including an all-weather sports complex and a whisky distillery visitor centre. The aim is to attract weekend visitors all year round,

The Tourist Board's response is that left to itself, a wild rural landscape cannot deliver social and economic sustainability for the island community as a whole. Highlands and Islands Enterprise (HIE) and other agencies believe that while the natural environment must be safeguarded, the island needs to be managed commercially, not exclusively preserved as a walkers' wilderness, so that its economic potential can be maximised.

The UK's outdoor music festival industry shows how rural management choices can polarise communities. In addition to 20 major festivals, such as Glastonbury and Leeds, around 50 smaller weekend events with a capacity of around 10,000 people are staged each year. Several hundred one-day and small-scale musical outdoor events annually staged in scenic rural settings also attract visitors.

The land used to stage an outdoor festival cannot have special ecological significance – it will most likely be pasture for cattle at other times of the year. Pasture has remarkable resilience and can recover from the 'scorched earth' trampling effect that tens of thousands of feet bring over a festival weekend. Carrying capacities are carefully worked out by concert promoters to ensure that festival-goers do not feel psychologically stressed and ecosystems will recover. However, the noise and other stresses on local residents during the festival can bring opposition. The Glastonbury promoter has fought numerous legal battles with his neighbours since the festival was first held in 1970.

Evaluating different management strategies

What constitutes a successful strategy for the management of rural tourism? As the case studies have shown, the answer very much depends upon the viewpoint of the person asking the question. From a socioeconomic point of view, visitor numbers and capital raised locally are key indicators of success. For many of the world's rural landscapes, the primary issue of concern remains their level of integration into global networks in ways that ensure beneficial flows of commerce and investment can take place. Models of tourism that generate a successful **multiplier effect** for local areas are viewed as the most economically successful (see *Edexcel AS Geography*, Figure 10.6, p. 116).

Managers of rural areas who focus on the interests of local people are primarily concerned to attract money to a region, developing its honeypot potential and making it a hub for national, and perhaps international, tourist flows. However, for incomes to be sustained, environmental impacts must be minimised to ensure that what attracted visitors is preserved. Far too often, economic success leads to the building of visitor centres and hotels that have a negative effect on the landscape or environment.

In the near future, successful strategies for rural tourism and leisure will require a far more adaptive and flexible approach to management than in the past. In the UK, for example, climate change poses a major threat to the biodiversity of some coastal SSSIs. Rare species such as the natterjack toad may try to move inland as sea levels rise or rates of coastal erosion accelerate, but they will be unable to migrate if their nature reserve is surrounded by urban settlement or agricultural monoculture. In the long term, Natural England believes that some SSSIs will need to be enlarged and ultimately linked together to form one long biodiversity corridor as part of a sustainability strategy that will leave coastal ecosystems better placed to adapt to climate change. In practice, this could be very difficult to achieve.

Further reading

For impacts of climate change on tourism: www.yourclimateyourlife.org.uk/a_tourism.html

Suggested fieldwork opportunities

Local fieldwork

The UK is home to a rural continuum, ranging from its 'rurban' fringes to the wilderness of the Scottish Highlands. Possible destinations for the study of themes followed in this chapter are:

➤ Dartmoor, the Lake District, the Peak District (among others), to investigate the physical significance of the moors landscape, the extent to which it is actually 'natural', and visitor pressures
➤ Western Weald (South Downs), to investigate the delimitation of the South Downs National Park
➤ the Isle of Arran, to investigate the move away from preservationist management towards a consumption-led rural strategy
➤ Formby (Sefton) coastline, to examine the National Trust's response to trampling and other visitor pressures

Residential and long-haul

Relatively accessible (and safe) overseas locations include:

➤ Ireland (the Aran islands could make an interesting study)
➤ the Mediterranean coastline or Alpine ski resorts, to investigate visitor pressures and carrying capacities
➤ southern Tunisia, to investigate the growth of the 'pleasure periphery'

Further afield, studies of the rapid expansion of tourism could be conducted in southeast Asia, the middle east (golf courses outside Dubai) or South America. The midwest of the USA is home to spectacular National Parks, such as Grand Canyon and Joshua Tree, the management strategies of which could be critically examined through fieldwork.

Review questions

1 Outline the factors that have contributed to the boom in rural leisure and tourism.
2 Illustrate some of the conflicts that exist between different users of rural landscapes.
3 Explain and illustrate what is meant by 'ecological value' and 'ecosystem fragility'.
4 Why are the concepts of 'carrying capacity' and 'resilience' relevant to the study of rural landscapes?
5 To what extent do you agree that the impacts of leisure and tourism on rural landscapes are overwhelmingly negative?
6 Explain and illustrate the conflicts that arise between the users and managers of rural landscapes.

Glossary

Abyssal plain The deep ocean floor at a depth of 4,000–6,000 metres. It is relatively flat and featureless.

Actions Strategies, management methods and technologies that could be applied to global issues by different players.

Aid Help and assistance given by one group to another. Often aid refers to financial and technical help given by developed world governments and NGOs to the developing world.

Alien or invasive species An introduced, non-native species present in an ecosystem.

Alternative technology Technology designed to be environmentally sustainable and to minimise resource consumption.

Appropriate technology Technology that is adapted to suit local conditions: it can be high- or low-tech.

Aquifer Underground porous rock layers which store groundwater. This is extracted using wells and boreholes.

Artificial scarcity A shortage resulting from the high price of something which is cheap to produce, such as software CDs.

Asthenosphere The upper part of Earth's mantle. It is partially molten, which allows the lithosphere to move over it.

Attitudinal fix A solution involving a change in people's attitudes, leading to a change in behaviour.

Biodiversity The range of genetic, species or ecosystem diversity in a given area.

Biofuels Substitutes for petrol or diesel, produced by processing biomass, usually crops, e.g. sugar cane.

Biomagnification The progressive concentration of pollutants up the food web, towards top predators.

Biome A global-scale ecosystem, such as tropical forest or tundra.

Bottom-up Management and problem-solving which comes from within a community, often using local skills and resources.

BRICs Brazil, Russia, India and China: often seen as the emerging superpowers.

Carrying capacity The population size that an area's resources can support without long-term degradation. It is related to technology as well as resource quantity.

CCS (carbon capture and storage) Extracting carbon dioxide from exhaust gases before it is released into the environment, and storing it, usually underground.

Chaotic Random, having no structure.

Conservation The active management of areas, ecosystems and landscape. It seeks to balance the need to protect and conserve with the demands of human activity.

Consumption The use by humans of resources such as food, fuel, land and water.

Contested space A location which is the subject of conflict over how it should be used.

Convection cell The flow of heat upwards in the Earth's mantle, which provides the driving force for tectonic plate motion.

Country rock The rock of the crust, into which magma is injected.

Cretaceous period The geological period between 145 and 65 million years ago. Many dinosaurs became extinct at the end of the Cretaceous.

Culture A set of shared beliefs, symbols, values, social norms and traditions within a cohesive society.

Cyber-activism The use of electronic media and communication to protest against local or global issues.

Debris The remains of a geological process, such as the broken rock and soil left after a landslide.

Desalination The removal of salt from seawater to make it fit for humans to drink. It is very energy-intensive.

Desertification Land turning to desert, often involving increased aridity and vegetation loss, usually as a result of human mismanagement.

Developed world The wealthy countries of the OECD and G8, including some first-generation NICs such as Singapore and South Korea.

Developing world Countries which are industrialising, such as the RICs and most NICs, plus the less and least developed countries.

Development The process of improving the human condition. Often it describes economic growth and industrialisation, but it should also include improvement of human health and wellbeing.

Development gap The widening income and prosperity gap between the global 'haves' of the developed world and the 'have-nots' of the developing world, especially the least developed countries.

Diffusion The ways in which disease spreads in space and time.

Digital divide The gap between those in the developed world who have access to digital communications (mobile phones, internet etc.) and those in the developing world who do not.

Discharge The rate of water flow in a river, measured in cubic metres per second (cumecs).

Drainage density The density of rivers and streams in a given area, such as a river catchment.

Earthquake A sudden release of energy in the Earth's crust, leading to ground shaking at the surface as energy spreads out from the origin (focus).

Ecosystem services The benefits ecosystems provide to humans in the form of provisioning services (goods) and regulating services such as flood control.

Ecotourism Tourism which attempts to minimise environmental impacts and promote cultural and ecological understanding.

Emerging economy A developing country which is industrialising and gaining economic wealth and power. These are the **NIC** and **RIC** countries.

Endemic disease A disease which is always present in a population. An **epidemic** disease is one which is significantly present for a short period. A **pandemic** is an epidemic covering a large area (possibly global).

Endemism Being unique in ecological terms, e.g. species which are found nowhere else.

Energy gap The difference between secured energy supply and projected future energy needs.

Energy pathway The routes along which energy sources move from producer to consumer, e.g. gas pipelines or oil tanker routes.

Energy security The extent to which an affordable, reliable and stable energy supply can be achieved.

Energy transition Moving from 'traditional' energy sources (such as fuel wood and dung) to 'modern' sources, usually fossils fuels, as a result of development.

Environment The natural world within which humans live, consisting of the atmosphere, hydrosphere, biosphere and geosphere.

Environmental degradation The steady decline in the quality and health of the natural environment as a result of human activities such as air and water pollution, soil erosion and ecosystem destruction.

Environmental determinism The view that as a result of lack of technology, some people's lives are shaped by physical forces such as the weather and hazards.

Environmental stewardship The idea that humans are 'caretakers' of the natural environment and should seek to pass it on undamaged to the next generation.

Eutrophication The pollution of ecosystems with excessive nitrate and phosphate from human activity.

Explosivity The eruptive force of a volcano, measured using the volcanic explosivity index (VEI).

Externality An impact, either a cost or benefit, which is not accounted for in the economic cost of a product or process.

Famine A short-term, severe and widespread shortage of food (dramatic increase in food insecurity) which endangers the lives of vulnerable groups and leads to increased mortality.

Fault A crack or fissure in the Earth's crust. Major faults occur at plate boundaries. Earthquakes occur as a result of fault movements.

Food security The availability of food in a given area and the extent to which individuals can access food supplies.

Fossil fuels Hydrocarbons (coal, oil, gas, oil shale, tar sands, peat) in the Earth's crust, usually millions of years old, which when burnt (oxidised) release heat energy. Burning them also releases carbon dioxide. Fossil fuels are a non-renewable energy source because of their finite supply.

Fragile (fragility) Describes ecosystems and landforms which are easily damaged or destroyed and vulnerable to change.

Frequency How often an event of a particular magnitude occurs.

Gene pool A measure of biodiversity based on the number of unique genes in an ecosystem.

Geoengineering Planetary-scale technologies designed to alter the properties of Earth to make it more habitable.

Geopolitics Global-scale political systems, allegiances and negotiations, including global governance and agreements.

Geosequestration Burying captured carbon dioxide underground in rocks, spent oil wells or aquifers.

Globalisation The economic process of increased global connectedness and inter-dependence resulting from rapid increases in trade, financial flows, global communication and migration.

Global warming The increase in Earth's average temperature since around 1900 as a result of anthropogenic amplification of the greenhouse effect.

GM Genetically modified, as in organisms whose characteristics are altered by bioengineering of their DNA.

Gondwana A supercontinent that existed around 500 million years ago in the southern hemisphere.

Green Revolution Farming technology introduced in the 1960s which increased yields by using high-yielding varieties of crops such as maize and rice, as well as fertilisers, irrigation and mechanisation.

Green taxation Use of taxes to influence consumer behaviour, in order to encourage more environmentally friendly consumption.

Habitat The ecological and environmental area a species lives in.

Helsinki Rules A 1966 international legal agreement on the fair use of international waterways, such as a river used by two countries.

Hotspot A pivotally important location, e.g. for biodiversity value, energy supply or political instability.

Hydropolitics Political negotiations centred on conflicts over the shared use of water sources, especially rivers that form an international border. Sometimes called water diplomacy.

Impermeable Rock or soil which will not transmit water. Permeable rock and soil will allow water to flow through.

Incident energy Energy received at the Earth's surface from the sun (solar radiation).

Initial advantage The benefit gained by developed countries through developing first; those which developed later are always in a race to catch up.

In situ/ex situ The conservation of species in their natural habitat (in situ) or in another place (ex situ), e.g. in a zoo or game park by captive breeding.

Intergovernmental organisation (IGO) A group or organisation made up of different member states, such as the UN or the EU.

Intermediate technology Low-technology solutions which are often cheap, easy to build and maintain, adaptable to local conditions and labour-intensive. Many are environmental friendly.

Investment The allocation of money or resources into an area by a company or government in order to make a profit. Often this is in the form of commercial property or factory development. When the investment is from one country into another it is called foreign direct investment or FDI.

Jökulhlaup A subglacial flood, often caused by an eruption beneath a glacier or ice sheet.

Knowledge economy Economic growth based on information and data rather than products and services. Knowledge becomes a saleable commodity.

Koppen climate classification The most widely used way of classifying climates, using differences in temperature, precipitation and seasonality.

Lahar A volcanic mudflow caused when ash is mobilised by heavy rain or ice melt.

Lithosphere The outermost rigid rock layer of the planet. Its upper part is the crust and its lower part the upper mantle.

Lithospheric plates Earth's tectonic plates. The brittle crust forms the upper part of the lithosphere.

Luddite A person who shuns new technology, often because of its perceived negative social impact. Sometimes called a technophobe.

Magnitude The size or strength of an event, especially a tectonic hazard such as an earthquake.

Megaproject An expensive, large-scale civil engineering project, usually with major impacts.

Metamorphic rock Rock which has been altered by heat and/or pressure.

Microgeneration Small-scale renewable energy generation by individual house-holders or businesses.

Monopoly Control over a product or technology by one company or individual to the extent that there is no competition.

Multi-energy systems Use of a mix of sources (renewable, non-renewable and recyclable) to reduce dependency on one energy source.

Multiplier effect (positive) A virtuous cycle of economic growth, whereby the creation of jobs and opportunities generates further growth.

Natural resources Any physical material which is consumed by humans, such as water, crops, oil or rock.

Neo-Malthusians Modern-day followers of the ideas of Thomas Malthus. They believe population will eventually outstrip available natural resources.

NIC Newly industrialising country. This describes countries which developed manufacturing industries in the late twentieth century, including Malaysia and Taiwan.

Nuclear power Use of controlled nuclear fission of uranium in a reactor to produce heat energy, and hence generate electricity.

OPEC The 12 nations of the Organization of Petroleum Exporting Countries. They are all net oil exporters, accounting for two-thirds of world oil reserves.

Over-abstraction The consumption of groundwater and surface water resources beyond their sustainable level, so the resource is gradually depleted.

Pangea A supercontinent in existence 250 million years ago, when most of the Earth's continental crust formed one single continental plate.

Pathways The routes taken from production site to consumption location for energy and water supply.

Peak oil (and gas) The theory that oil production will peak in the near future, then gradually decline. A steep increase in cost is expected as production declines.

Peripheral On the edge, not part of the core, especially in an economic and political sense.

Permafrost Soil and rock ground which is permanently frozen for two consecutive summers.

Petrochemicals Chemical products made from hydrocarbons such as oil and gas. They include plastics, fuels, solvents and lubricants.

Phenology The study of the seasonal behaviour of plants and animals, which may indicate climate change.

Plagioclimax An ecosystem which has developed as a result of human activity. Frequently perceived as 'natural'.

Player An individual, group or organisation which has a stake in an issue.

Pleasure periphery The spread of leisure time and recreation into developing and peripheral regions.

Pollution Substances with the potential to harm people and the natural environment, released into the environment by humans.

Precautionary principle The idea that humans should not carry out an action if there is uncertainty about its outcomes.

Precursor Unusual activity that may indicate a future event, such as minor earth tremors being felt as a precursor to a volcanic eruption.

Preservation Management which seeks to maintain the status quo, often by restricting human activity to a minimum.

Primary production The conversion of energy from sunlight into chemical energy by plants through photosynthesis to produce new biomass.

Pyroclastic flows Dense, fast moving surges of hot ash, gas and tephra. They hug the ground and speed down the flanks of volcanoes at up to 700 km h^{-1}.

Quaternary period The most recent geological period, usually taken as being the last 2.6 million years.

Rebranding The regeneration and reimaging of urban and rural spaces, often linked to economic renewal based on leisure and recreation.

Relict Small, isolated, vulnerable pockets of plant or animal species which are extinct across their broader ecological range.

Renewable energy Energy sources which are effectively limitless due to natural regeneration of the resource, such as solar, wind and hydro power.

Research and development A branch of industry focused on the development of innovation and new technology.

Reserves The remaining, recoverable amount of a natural resource such as oil.

Resistant Type of rocks which are not easily weathered (chemically or mechanically) or eroded, e.g. granite or basalt.

Restoration Returning a degraded ecosystem or natural system to its former state.

RIC Recently industrialising country. The second generation of industrialising countries, following on from the NICs. Examples include Indonesia and Mexico.

Richter scale The logarithmic magnitude scale measuring earthquake energy.

Risk The probability of a negative consequences and losses. Greater potential losses and increased likelihood of losses occurring increase risk.

River regime The variation in annual river discharge. Closely related to climate and seasonality.

Salt water incursion The pollution of coastal groundwater by inflowing seawater. It happens as a result of over-abstraction.

Spectrum A range, e.g. of management approaches, attitudes or policies. The outer limits of a spectrum will be 'poles apart' but there is common ground in the centre.

Superpower A country with dominant global political and economic influence.

Supervolcano A very low-frequency, high-magnitude eruption (VEI 7 or 8) with the potential to alter climate for years or decades.

Sustainable Describes actions and processes which minimise negative consequences for the environment and ecosystems and promote human wellbeing.

Sustainable development Development that meets the environmental, economic and social needs of today's population without compromising the ability of future generations to meet their own needs.

Technocentric The view that technology will, and should, provide solutions to the problems facing humans.

Technological fix An innovation that can be used to solve a problem facing humans.

Technological leapfrogging The adoption of a new technology by a developing economy without it having to use a more basic technology first.

Technology Tools, systems, processes and structures invented by humans which allow them to control their environment and satisfy their needs.

Technology transfer The flow of technological innovations from the developed to the developing world, to assist development.

Terraforming The theoretical concept of engineering a new planet to be 'Earth-like' and habitable.

Terrestrial On the land, as opposed to 'marine', which means in the seas and oceans.

Top-down Management solutions and other measures imposed from above, e.g. by national governments.

Trade The exchange of goods and services, usually involving money.

Transboundary An issue or problem which crosses international borders.

Transfer The movement of resources, particularly energy and water, from a source region to a region of consumption. Resources move along pathways.

Trophic level The position an organism occupies in a food chain. Trophic level 1 consists of primary producers (plants), trophic level 2 primary consuming herbivores and level 3 secondary consuming carnivores.

Viscosity The stickiness of lava and magma, in other words its resistance to flow. Highly viscous lava is sticky, and produces explosive volcanoes. Viscosity is a result of temperature, silica and gas content.

Volcano A landform erupting lava, formed as magma rises through a fissure in the Earth's crust.

Water security The extent to which a community, region or country can secure sufficient, reliable water supplies.

Water stress Lack of reliable, cost effective water supplies in a community, region or country. Health and wellbeing are likely to be affected. When water supply falls below 1,000 m^3 per person per year, a region enters water scarcity.

Wellbeing The health of either humans or ecosystems. It is increasingly recognised that human wellbeing depends on healthy ecosystems and a healthy environment.

Index

Page numbers in **bold** refer to definitions in the glossary.

Index